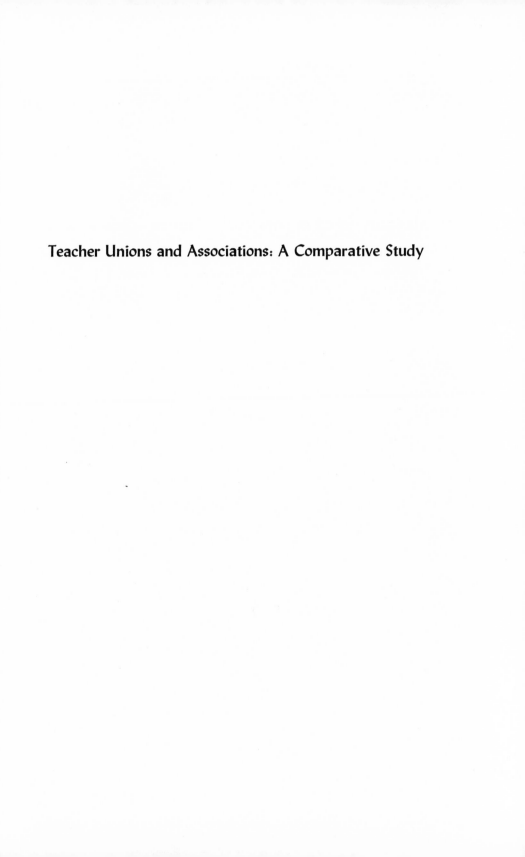

Teacher Unions and Associations: A Comparative Study

UNIVERSITY OF ILLINOIS PRESS   Urbana   Chicago   London

TEACHER UNIONS AND ASSOCIATIONS
A Comparative Study

Edited by Albert A. Blum

*To Steven and David,
and, of course,
Roslyn*

Preface

The romantic picture of the teacher quietly working with students while absentmindedly ignoring his private needs is rapidly disappearing in the face of school systems closed by striking teachers after bargaining collectively (whatever the terms used) in support of their demands for such things as better wages and a voice in educational decision-making. One can indeed say "Goodby, Mr. Chips," for he has at last put down his pipe and has instead picked up a placard and is out picketing.

This change troubles many people, for they fear what this metamorphosis will do to the educational system. To give us some insight into the problem is the purpose of this volume. We decided to ask some experts to look at teacher unions and associations in a number of countries so that we could better understand the organizations teachers are developing as they make their demands.

Not all countries are covered in this survey. The choices were not systematic; they were instead mainly pragmatic. Areas, such as Eastern Europe, were ignored not out of choice but because it was impossible at the time to secure an appropriate person to write a section. And since education is so important in developing countries, we thought that a number of studies of teacher organizations there would be useful.

Readers, of course, will differ in their reactions to the organized role teachers are playing. Those who are convinced that teacher unionization and teacher militancy are horrible will probably not be converted to a different faith by the pages that follow. The committed trade unionist will not burn his membership card as he enters the classroom. Still we can hope for one common result: namely, a better perspective concerning the nature of teacher organizations. Surely, one of the major contributions comparative studies can make is to permit us to see our own problems and our answers to these problems from a wider vantage point. If the reader recognizes that teachers in other countries have some similar questions to answer and similar difficulties to resolve, the fact that they use different answers and solutions ought to tell us something about the society itself. Moreover, the variety of reactions ought to suggest alternatives for us to consider. Thus, the American teacher who angrily organizes in defense of his economic and educational self-interest is surely not alone; he has brothers and sisters in many other countries.

Although, as one would expect, there are many differences among the countries, there are, however, a few issues concerning which there have been much conflict and some confusion in nearly all of the countries studied. These involve the goals and techniques of teacher organizations.

The first conflict has been over the goals sought by teacher organizations. When most teacher organizations first started, they had mainly professional aims. Control of entry into the profession usually through raising standards; improved job tenure; professional training; and limitations on external interferences with the educational profession were a few of the goals sought. Their concern with economic matters at this early stage was usually reflected in platitudes about the need for higher salaries rather than in any real action demanding raises. Eventually, however, a conflict developed as to whether the teacher organization should be concerned only with professional matters or should also fight for better salaries. Even more important in recent years has been the teacher organization's claim that as professionals, not only do they want a voice in seeing that they receive an adequate income, not only do they want to participate, through their organizations, in determining broad educational policies, but now they also want to have a voice in the resolution of such local matters as transfers and assignments of teachers, size of classrooms, and a host of other issues once deemed the sole domain of the local managers of the school system.

The second broad area of conflict is over the form to be used in striving to secure these goals. Should teachers form a union, frequently as part of a federation of unions, normally including only nonsupervisory teachers, or should they form an association, normally independent of any other group of employees, also usually including supervisors? (The issue of whether teaching supervisors such as principals, chairmen, and superintendents should belong to the same organizations as teachers in itself is a source of conflict whatever the type of organization.) Should the organization make use of tactics, such as collective bargaining, strikes, and sanctions, normally associated with unions in the private sector, or should the organization emphasize persuasion, through public appeals and political pressure, or should a combination of both approaches be used?

To many persons, the techniques practiced by teachers and their organizations seem more important and more disturbing than the goals sought. Many educators, frequently those who teach teachers, have become convinced that there is an unresolvable conflict between the teacher as a professional and the teacher as a unionist; and the latter means membership in any organization which uses the aggressive tactics associated with labor organizations. But as the following chapters indicate, and as the previous paragraph implied, teachers who join together in fact are demanding that they be treated as professionals and as such have a voice in educational decision-making. In a sense, the very act of joining such an organization makes this inevitable. An elementary school teacher, uncommitted to an association or a union, tends to have ties not to the profession of teaching but to the local community and the local school. Her horizons are not professional but communal. The act of joining and the act of involvement in the teacher organization, with its broader goals, help change her self-concept from that of only a local schoolteacher to that of a professional educator. She begins to compare her economic standing with that of other professionals; she begins to compare her role in decision-making in her field with the role played by other professionals in decision-making in their respective fields. Thus, by joining an organization which has been demanding many of those rights which as a professional she should have had all along, she may have indeed acted for the first time as a professional.

Still, the conflict over the various techniques teacher groups may use justifiably continues, for not all of the methods used in the private sector of an economy to resolve disputes may be applicable to public education. And the fact that education, with the exception of private schools, is a public program and essentially a public monopoly, leads us to the third broad conflict area.

Schools are frequently used by the state to foster whatever goals it wishes. This topic is discussed in the following chapters, particularly in the sections dealing with developing countries as well as in a few of the others. The issue which is raised, sometimes indirectly, concerns the appropriate role that teacher organizations should play vis-à-vis the state in such situations. In some cases, teacher organizations have acted as arms of the state, supported by it, and used by it. As such, the teacher groups are no longer independent voices but echoes of national policy.

But there is the reverse problem; namely, that teacher organizations may claim to be all-knowing in the field of education and may demand powers which society, speaking through its elected representatives, feels belong to the public. Not only is the teacher concerned that a child receive a good education, but so is society in general and his parent in particular. And members of society pay the taxes which cover the costs of education. But unlike other situations, whereby a buyer or user of a service has some free choice, in a school situation, if the parent does not like what the teacher does, he cannot go elsewhere. The child has to go to the school designated and be taught by the teacher so assigned. The only thing the dissatisfied parent can do is to demand a voice in educational decision-making, and this, at times, puts him in conflict with the teacher. And the teacher, particularly when organized, seems to the individual parent to have an unfair advantage over him in any dispute, particularly in the face of job tenure rules which actually, though not necessarily in theory, protect the incompetent teacher more than most union contracts protect the incompetent worker.

And then there is the role of society. Formal education is supposed to strive to achieve the ends sought by society. Sometimes these goals may conflict with what teachers want. Thus, public policy may demand that a teacher be transferred to a school where he may be needed, such as in a section where poor people predominate; the teacher organization may instead favor the use of seniority as the criterion for transfer. If the teacher organization wins in this dispute, experienced teachers will be able to transfer to the easier schools in middle- and upper-class neighborhoods, as they frequently have when given this right, leaving the inexperienced teachers in the schools in the poor districts, thus defeating society's desire to help the poor. Or, as another example, the public may favor comprehensive secondary schools, while the teachers may prefer specialized schools. Other cases will be discussed in the chapters that follow. But one thing is clear: this conflict between teacher and public policies may become increasingly sensitive as teacher organizations grow and make more and more demands concerning items which once were the sole prerogatives of the educational hierarchy.

Fortunately, an editor of such a book as this does not have to offer answers to such perplexing problems. He and his contributors need only point them out, note how they have been resolved at times, and hope that other, perhaps wiser men, can provide better solutions. But the editor can do one thing: he can thank all of those who helped raise these questions. The first I would like to thank is Professor Cole Brembeck, Director of the Institute of International Studies in Education at Michigan State University for providing the financial assistance, the stimulating suggestions, and the enthusiastic encouragement so helpful in an enterprise such as this one. A number of people made comments concerning the manuscripts. Subbiah Kannappan, Robert Banks, and other colleagues at the School of Labor and Industrial Relations have made appropriate suggestions and have asked "inappropriate" questions for they have resulted in further work for me and for the authors. The authors were most cooperative and patient with my editorial recommendations, and for this I am most appreciative.

Mrs. Nancy Hammond helped in the early editorial stages of the manuscript; Mrs. Alice Jackson and Mrs. Marlene Ehrlich helped handle the typing and retyping of the sections.

My wife, Roslyn, helped in many ways in editing and discussing the articles with me. But more important, she joined me in a love of education and a rigorous demand for excellent teaching. We had good teachers; we wish our children had better ones. In a sense, that is what this book is about—teachers who want to improve their standard of living while improving the standards of education. Whether they have used the right technique is for each reader to decide.

ALBERT A. BLUM
Michigan State University
October, 1968

Contents

Canada   1

J. Douglas Muir

INTRODUCTION

When examining teachers' associations in Canada one cannot help
being impressed with the magnitude of the economic and social
advances made by the teaching profession since the turn of the
century. These advances appear to parallel the growth in the size
and power of teachers' associations in Canada and can be separated
into two fairly distinct periods. To the first period, from about
1900 through to the 1930's, must be attributed not only significant
social and educational advancement but also the formation of provincial teachers' associations as we know them today. The developments during this first period elevated the teachers' position in the
community and provided the basic requirements for the establishment of a profession. While the emphasis during these earlier years
was focused primarily upon teacher organizing and upgrading, the
emphasis during the second period, the years since the late 1930's,
has been upon the improvement of the teachers' economic position.
As a result, the economic status of teachers has changed from one of
underpaid individuals to one of a highly organized professional
group, receiving a relatively appropriate level of remuneration.

An example of this latter development can be gained by examining the teachers' economic position held shortly before the turn of
the century. One of the early issues of the newspaper, *The Nova*

J. DOUGLAS MUIR is Associate Professor of Industrial Relations, Faculty of
Business Administration, The University of Alberta, Edmonton, Canada.

Scotian, stated that "a teacher is no more thought of in the country villages than a menial servant." [1] At this time teachers' salaries were said to be "equal to the wages of a driver of oxen" [2] and that "the name 'school master' is synonymous with poverty." [3] Thus, between the late 1800's and the 1960's both the economic and the social positions of the teachers have significantly changed.

Indications are that the teachers, at least in Ontario and Western Canada, are now entering a third period. In this period there appears to be a declining emphasis on the economic and an increasing emphasis upon the educational and professional aspects of teaching in that there is a more sophisticated approach to salary negotiations and a greater emphasis upon such things as teacher certification, teacher aids and assistants, and in-service training programs. We shall probably see significant activity in these areas in the coming years.

The purpose of this chapter is to examine the growth of teacher organizations in Canada to gain an understanding of the influence of teachers' organizational and collective bargaining activities upon their social and economic advancement. Before looking at the development of the various teacher organizations in Canada and their collective bargaining activities, the background must be set by commenting briefly upon Canada's governmental system and economy.

CANADA

General

Although Canada is a large and diversified country with a land area of over three and one-half million square miles, it has a population of only 20 million people—roughly the size of California. Nearly two-thirds of these people live in the provinces of Ontario and Quebec, and in addition the majority of Canadians live in the southern portions of the country (within 100 miles of the Canada/ United States border). As a result, Canada is a large geographical area with an extremely uneven population distribution. This distribution, coupled with the climatic conditions in the Northern areas,

---

[1] "In the Beginning," *The Nova Scotia Teachers' Bulletin* (December 1959), p. 9.
[2] J. M. Paton, *The Role of Teachers' Organizations in Canadian Education* (Toronto: W. J. Gage, 1962), p. 35.
[3] "In the Beginning," p. 9.

has significantly complicated the problems of teachers and teachers' organizations in all of the Canadian provinces. For example, almost one-half of the Canadian teachers are teaching and living in rural areas or small towns. This not only detracts from the attractiveness of the profession to university trained personnel but also handicaps the organizational activities of the teachers' associations.

It is convenient at this point to note that the ten provinces of Canada may be separated into four geographical regions—Pacific, Prairie, Central, and Atlantic. Beginning in the West, the Pacific region consists of British Columbia where the economy is based upon lumber, paper, fishing, and some mining industries. The Prairie region includes the provinces of Alberta, Saskatchewan, and Manitoba whose economies are based upon oil, gas, farming, ranching, and some mining. The provinces of Ontario and Quebec make up the Central region which, in addition to its mining and paper industries, is the commercial, manufacturing, and industrial center of Canada. (It should be noted that most of Quebec is French-speaking.) The Atlantic region, consisting of New Brunswick, Nova Scotia and the two island provinces of Newfoundland and Prince Edward Island, is economically the poorest region of Canada. The economy of this region is supported by the pulp and paper industry, fishing, some farming, and a faltering coal and mining industry.

These differences are important to remember. For example, the low per capita personal income in the Atlantic provinces affects their ability to pay teachers' salaries which in turn influences the comparative social position of teachers.

Government Structure

Confederation of the provinces of Canada occurred in 1867. At that time those in French-speaking Canada and the Atlantic region were reluctant to surrender legislative jurisdiction to any central authority. Therefore, the British North American Act, referred to as the Canadian Constitution, signed at that time, left considerable powers in the hands of the provinces. Under this act the provinces were given the right to legislate local matters which included property and civil rights, health, municipal regulations, and education. Matters of national concern such as defense, trade, banking, and external relations were specifically placed within the jurisdiction of the federal government.

Responsibility for Education

Under the terms of Sections 91 and 92 of the British North America Act total responsibility for education in Canada rests with the provinces. The only exception to this is the education of Indians and Eskimos which comes under federal jurisdiction. This means that in Canada there is not one but ten completely autonomous education systems—one corresponding to each of the ten provinces. In addition, all of the provinces, except Newfoundland, have delegated much of the responsibility for educational practices to the local authorities at the municipal level, in most cases to boards of school trustees. The costs of education are shared by the provincial and municipal authorities in varying proportions depending upon the grant structure existing in each province. However, in all provinces, except Newfoundland, the local boards of school trustees are completely responsible for the operation of the schools which includes recruitment of teachers, determining salaries and working conditions,[4] administration of the schools, conveyance of pupils, etc. In Newfoundland, teachers are employed and paid directly by the provincial government.

In recent years the costs of education for Canada as a whole have been shared almost equally between the provincial governments and the local municipal authorities. There is, however, a significant variation in the amount of the provincial contribution to education in some provinces. It may be as low as 40 per cent, as in Manitoba, or as high as 87 per cent as in Newfoundland, since the expenditure sharing scheme within the various provinces depends upon the ability of the local municipal authorities to raise the necessary funds. The economic base and ability to pay varies from province to province and has produced serious inequities in the educational systems. The cost sharing formulas introduced in some provinces have eased many of the intraprovincial inequities. Nevertheless, the economy, the tax base, and the philosophy of the local authorities contribute to the wide variations that exist in teachers' salaries among municipalities in Canada.

Responsibility for Labor Relations

The British North America Act was drafted at a time when the labor movement in Canada was in its infancy and therefore it did

[4] As of 1967 salaries are now determined on the provincial level in Quebec and New Brunswick.

not allocate responsibilities for matters relating to labor relations. As a result, the courts have been relied upon to distribute this responsibility. The federal government first assumed this responsibility when it passed the Industrial Disputes and Investigations Act in 1907. The constitutionality of the federal government's jurisdiction in this area was tested and upheld in 1911 but was again challenged and defeated in the courts in 1925.[5] It was this 1925 decision that gave the major responsibility for labor relations matters to the provincial governments. Initially the provinces agreed to adopt the federal legislation and thereby maintain a uniform policy on industrial disputes settlements across Canada. As might have been expected such uniformity was not maintained, since one province after another introduced modifications and altered the principles originally established by the federal legislation. By 1935 it became evident that the provinces had taken charge of their own labor relations problems and were accordingly formulating their own policies. Due to the forementioned, there is a strong similarity in the underlying philosophy of the public policy on labor relations in each province but the approach varies substantially from one province to another. For example, the provinces of New Brunswick, Prince Edward Island, Ontario, Saskatchewan, and British Columbia specifically exclude teachers from the provisions of their respective labor acts. In the provinces of Newfoundland, Nova Scotia, and Manitoba teachers are not referred to in the labor acts and by practice are excluded. Only in Quebec and Alberta are teachers specifically included under the provisions of the labor acts.

ORIGIN OF TEACHERS' ASSOCIATIONS IN CANADA

Educational Associations

Since the responsibility for education rests entirely in the hands of the provincial governments, teachers' organizations have also developed on a provincial basis. In Canada, the first organization of any type in the educational field dates back to the early 1850's when the Ontario Educational Association was formed. This association was the forerunner of others (most of which were called institutes) which subsequently developed in each province prior to the turn of the century.

5 Toronto Electric Commission v. Snider, Appeal Cases 1925.

These institutes were, for the most part, organized and sponsored by the officials of the provincial departments of education and served the purposes of (1) general in-service training (since the majority of teachers at that time had little or no professional training), (2) providing an opportunity for people from all walks of life with a general interest in education to meet annually and discuss common education problems, and (3) providing a forum for the various Ministers of Education to make public pronouncements. Membership in these institutes was open to almost anyone interested in education and generally included officials of the provincial department of education, members of boards of school trustees, representatives of home and school groups, university personnel as well as individual teachers. The teachers themselves appeared to have a relatively minor influence in these institutes, since the records show that their presidents and executives were generally department of education officials, university personnel, or distinguished laymen.

Some educational historians trace the origin of present-day teachers' associations back to these early institutes.[6] Although it is true that a few of these organizations, such as the Ontario Educational Association, still exist today they do not and never did fulfill the role of teachers' associations as we now know them. The educational institutes consisted of groups of interested people who gathered annually to discuss broad "educational" issues. One might conclude that those at the institutes were motivated by the "inspirational" aspects of education (by speeches on subjects such as "The Nobility of the Teaching Profession" [7]) rather than by the practical, occupational, and professional problems of the teachers. Teachers' associations, on the other hand, are composed of professionally orientated teachers who, throughout the year, actively pursue solutions for their economic, occupational, and educational problems. Therefore, although many of the teachers' associations developed within, and broke away from, these provincial institutes, it is not realistic to attribute the origin of today's teachers' professional associations to these institutes.

It was not until about World War I that Canadian teachers developed associations which were specifically devised to meet their

6 C. E. Phillips, *The Development of Education in Canada* (Toronto: W. W. Gage & Company, 1957).
7 A. D. Talbot, *The P.A.P.T.'s First Century* (Gardenvale, Quebec: Harpell's Press, 1963).

occupational needs and which were under their control. Up to this time teachers appeared to be content to look to department of education officials, heads of universities, and prominent laymen for organizational leadership. Needless to say, many teachers felt restricted by these early organizations because they were not designed to discuss or act upon such matters as salaries, pensions, and the low status of teachers. World War I changed all this, for it was at this time that the teachers' dissatisfaction came to a head and they began to break away from the institutes and form their own professional associations.

Teachers' Associations

Teachers, shortly after the turn of the century, became dissatisfied over the institutes' inability to represent them. The records in each province show an increase in the number of occupational items appearing on the institute agendas during this period. As the teachers found that little or no action was being taken regarding their problems they began to form separate organizations of their own (although some groups were formed within the framework of the established institutes). Most of these original groups developed either as teacher benevolent societies or as occupational organizations patterned after the British National Union of Teachers.

Although at first there were a number of separate groups of teachers formed within some of the provinces, many of them soon faded out of existence or merged to form stronger organizations. The result is that in Canada today there are 16 provincial teachers' associations, all but one of which are affiliated either directly or indirectly with the Canadian Teachers' Federation. There is one provincial teachers' association in each of the provinces except Quebec and Ontario. In Quebec there is a Protestant association, an English Catholic association, and a French Catholic association (which is not affiliated with the Canadian Teachers' Federation). In Ontario there are five separate provincial associations all affiliated with the Ontario Teachers' Federation which in turn is affiliated with the Canadian Teachers' Federation. Looking at the development of these provincial associations we find that ten were formed and two reorganized between 1914 and 1920. The remaining four Catholic teacher associations were not organized until the late 1930's and early 1940's.

Almost without exception, as soon as an occupational association was formed in each of the provinces it immediately gathered support from the teachers and sought professional and economic improvement for them. The objectives of these associations were (1) to improve teachers' salaries and working conditions; (2) to establish a code of ethics and a system of discipline as the basis for their profession; and (3) to win a place for the association in the provincial educational power structure.

One indication of the teachers' enthusiasm was the development of the Canadian Teachers' Federation. The Canadian Teachers' Federation was organized in 1920 by representatives of the associations in the Prairie and Pacific regions and in Ontario. It was established almost as soon as the provincial associations themselves and within seven years all the existing provincial associations had affiliated and were contributing to its support.

During its early years, the Canadian Teachers' Federation acted as the nationwide "voice" of the teachers advocating collective bargaining, denouncing the economic plight of the teachers and recommending substantial salary increases for teachers in all provinces. The Federation continued to perform this rather radical role for a number of years, but as it matured its role changed to one of coordinating information and promoting cooperation among its provincial affiliates. The CTF has recently concentrated its attention upon the promotion and development of research in education as well as the promotion of national workshops and seminars for the professional development of teachers in Canada.

The drive on the part of the teachers in the various provinces to form their own occupational associations can be attributed to four major factors.

1. The large number of teachers who immigrated to Canada from Great Britain at the turn of the century. These teachers were accustomed to strong occupational organizations (such as the National Union of Teachers of England and the Education Institute of Scotland) and were not afraid of collective bargaining or being associated with the labor movement.

2. The inflation which developed immediately after World War I. This inflation seriously affected the underpaid teachers and created enough stress to make even the timid and conservative teachers want to stand up and do something to improve their economic situation. An indication of the level of salaries at this time is given by J. M. Paton [8] who reports that in 1911 the average salary for

8 Paton, p. 35.

teachers in the rural counties of Quebec was $162 per year or $13.59 per month. By 1919, during the postwar inflation, rural elementary teachers in Quebec were receiving an average of $242.20 per year or about $20.00 per month. At this same time the salaries of elementary teachers in Montreal were in the range of $850.00 to $1,250.00 per year ($71.00 to $104.00 per month). These teachers' salaries may be compared to the salary range of $62.50 to $150.00 per month paid by the Canadian Pacific Railway to its female clerks at this same time.

3. The impact of the war itself. The war not only produced a social upheaval in Canada but also developed an intense awareness of the democratic process and the importance of education. These factors aggravated the impatience on the part of many teachers with the number of restraints imposed by the various departments of education.

4. The teachers were aware of the gains and advances being made by those in the labor movement. Such a comparison made them realize that their relative salary position was weakening and therefore many teachers began to demand monetary as well as inspirational rewards from the teaching profession.

It can therefore be concluded that prior to 1910 teachers in Canada were neither strongly organized in occupational groups nor appeared to possess any clear objectives regarding professional recognition. As members of education institutes they appeared to respect and follow, almost without question, their superiors in education. In addition, they appeared to know their place in the educational hierarchy and generally refrained from any kind of self-assertive action. It took the war and its impact on ideas about equality of educational opportunity, the pressures of inflation, and leadership from British and Canadian trade unionists to force the classroom teachers, almost in spite of themselves, to stand on their own feet and accept responsibility for their own economic and professional development.

ASSOCIATION MEMBERSHIP

The tendency today is to take the matter of association membership for granted without appreciating the struggle that most of the associations had in building and developing membership to its present level. Teacher support of these associations was generally low and in most cases unenthusiastic during the 1920's. Furthermore, the depression of the 1930's seemed to affect the teachers more than those in any of the other professions. During this period teachers' salaries were drastically reduced and a large number of teachers were laid off. The associations lost in the early 1930's whatever gains they had made during the 1920's, consequently they not only had trouble attracting and retaining membership but also in collecting dues.

These hardships were particularly acute in the Prairie region where the effects of the depression were aggravated by severe drought conditions. Yet in 1935, the teachers in Saskatchewan were the first to be granted, by provincial legislature, statutory membership with payroll deduction of membership fees.

When the Saskatchewan Teachers' Federation was finally organized at the beginning of 1934, one of its stated objectives was to obtain statutory compulsory membership of the teachers in the province. At that time only 45 per cent of the Saskatchewan teachers had voluntarily joined the Federation. In reply to the Federation's presentations to the provincial government, the Minister of Education indicated that such statutory membership would be granted only if the Federation was able to increase its membership on a voluntary basis from the existing 45 to 70 per cent. As a result of the ensuing organizational effort by the Federation, paid-up membership was increased to 73 per cent by the end of 1934. Thus, early in 1935, the Saskatchewan government passed An Act Respecting the Teaching Profession, the first of its kind in the English-speaking world.[9] This act established the Federation as a "body corporate and political," granted the teachers professional recognition, and made it compulsory that ". . . all persons employed as teachers in schools (which receive provincial grants) . . . shall, as a condition of employment, be members of the Federation." [10]

The associations in other Canadian provinces were also seeking statutory membership at this same time. The breakthrough in Saskatchewan gave them renewed hope and most of the associations increased their pressure upon their provincial governments. Thus, the 1935 Saskatchewan decision was one factor instrumental in forcing the other provinces to review their policies concerning teachers' organizations. Another factor was the agitation by the en-

[9] S. McDowell, *Four Issues* (Saskatoon: Saskatchewan Teachers' Federation, 1965), p. 55.
[10] *Ibid.*, p. 54.

tire labor movement to have the provincial governments review all of their labor-management policies. This agitation was due, in part, to the 1935 passing of the Wagner Act in the United States, which gave the American unions the full right to organize and bargain. As a result of this union pressure, legislation similar to the Wagner Act was enacted in six of the Canadian provinces by 1938. Therefore, the change that occurred in the governments' policy concerning statutory membership for teachers must be viewed as part of the total change in provincial public policy which took place during the late 1930's.

The next province to grant statutory membership to teachers was Alberta. The teachers in Alberta had been seeking statutory membership since 1920, but the government had been unsympathetic to their pleas. This situation was altered in 1935 when the Social Credit party came into power in Alberta—a party which was organized and led by a teacher. Hence, in 1936 a teachers' professional act was passed granting statutory membership to the Alberta Teachers' Association.

Although these two provinces established a pattern which was eventually followed by the other provinces, this pattern was not followed by most of the other provinces until the end of World War II. It was not until 1960, when the Catholic associations in Quebec received statutory recognition, that all of the teachers' associations in Canada had received statutory recognition coupled with some form of a statutory membership.

The policies of the various provincial governments differ to some extent regarding statutory membership requirements. All of the provinces require that school boards deduct association membership fees from the payroll of member teachers. Only the provinces of British Columbia, Alberta, Ontario, and New Brunswick have followed the Saskatchewan policy of requiring that *all* teachers, as a condition of employment *must* be members in good standing of the association. The provinces of Manitoba, Quebec, Nova Scotia, Prince Edward Island, and Newfoundland provide, on the other hand, automatic membership but allow teachers to opt out of the association each year during a stipulated "escape" period. Experience has shown that these escape provisions are not significant since less than five per cent of the teachers have chosen to opt out of any of the associations. Table 1 summarizes the membership provisions in the various provinces.

It is doubtful that at the time many people fully realized the significance of the breakthrough that had been made in 1935. Looking back, it is obvious that obtaining professional statutes and statutory membership has played a crucial role in providing the means for teachers to exercise a significant influence in provincial

TABLE 1. SUMMARY OF MEMBERSHIP PROVISIONS IN THE VARIOUS PROVINCES

	Year Statutory Membership Implemented	Membership		Number of Members 1966–67
		Compulsory	Automatic but with Write-Out	
British Columbia	1947	X		16,966
Alberta	1936	X		16,358
Saskatchewan	1935	X		10,923
Manitoba	1924		X	9,192
Ontario	1944	X		73,943
Quebec—Protestant	1945		X	5,192
—Catholic—French	1960		X	3,748
—Catholic—English	1960		X	50,009
New Brunswick	1942	X		6,927
Nova Scotia	1951 [a]		X	7,427
Prince Edward Island	1945		X	1,270
Newfoundland	1951		X	5,370

[a] Fully automatic provision not implemented until 1953.

SOURCE: Tom Parker, "Collective Negotiations in Canada" (paper presented to the National Institute on Collective Negotiations, Rhode Island College), July 1965.

educational power structures. Furthermore, this closed shop imposed and enforced by statute is perhaps the most powerful single influence affecting the operation and results of the collective bargaining process. Similarly, it is this provision, coupled with the statutory obligations of school trustees, that helps to distinguish the collective bargaining process in schools from that in industry.

RIGHT TO BARGAIN

The primary reason for the development and growth of teachers' organizations in Canada was to provide a vehicle through which teachers could improve their economic position. Teachers had already learned that employing school boards could not be relied upon to pay unilaterally what the teachers considered to be reasonable salaries. They also recognized that the economic improvements they sought could only be achieved through the united action of all teachers as a group and not by individual action. As the associations developed they had to choose among five alternative courses of action for obtaining their economic objectives. They could (1) seek voluntary recognition from the employing school boards, (2) in some provinces, seek certification and bargaining rights under the labor act as a trade union, (3) obtain statutory membership and unilaterally establish minimum salaries below which no teacher would agree to work (similar to the medical profession), (4) obtain statutory membership and bargain collectively, or (5) appeal to the government to establish statutory minimum or standard salaries. Most of the associations looked into the possibility of seeking certification and bargaining rights as a trade union but rejected this alternative as it conflicted with their professional objectives. In addition, the alternatives which involved statutory membership were unacceptable to the provincial governments (until after 1935). Thus, in their early years, the only alternative open to most associations was voluntary recognition which many of them sought and obtained during the 1920's and early 1930's.

Although the actual dates that such voluntary recognition was granted by school boards varied from one jurisdiction to another, the same pattern of development existed in all provinces. For example, the provincial associations built their organizational strength and initially concentrated their attention on teachers in the urban school jurisdictions. As a consequence recognition was first granted to the associations by the urban boards in all provinces. Associations focused on urban communities since rural school jurisdictions at that time were small and decentralized (for example, there were over 5,000 individual school boards in Saskatchewan prior to 1945). As a result of the large number, there were variations between those boards which granted recognition and those which did not. Thus there were substantial variations in the salaries paid to teachers with the same training and experience from one school jurisdiction to another even within the same province.

The question of bargaining rights was significantly influenced by the depression of the 1930's. The teachers found that most of the advances that they had made through voluntary negotiations during the 1920's were unilaterally removed by the trustees during the early 1930's. For example, in Alberta the average teacher's salary was $1,160 per year in 1921 and $746 per year in 1933.[11] In addition the remuneration of teachers in some of the rural areas had been reduced to only the provision of room and board. Teachers concluded, therefore, that voluntary recognition had failed and was unacceptable, and like the trade unions, they would have to obtain compulsory recognition. As a result, they concentrated their efforts upon the achievement of statutory membership as discussed earlier. The teachers felt that once statutory membership had been obtained, compulsory bargaining would come as a natural second step. Such was the general pattern in most of the provinces.

Pacific Region

The Case of British Columbia

The British Columbia Teachers' Federation (BCTF) was incorporated under the Benevolent Societies Act and there was therefore no obligation on the part of either the local school boards or the Department of Education to recognize it, let alone bargain with it. However, in 1919, almost immediately after the Federation was incorporated, the teachers in the Victoria Teachers' Association went on a strike which lasted for two days. The school board appealed to the Department of Education to take action against the teachers but the Department refused and instead mediated a settlement satisfactory to the teachers. The Department, by mediating the dispute, recognized the Federation and provided the first form of recognition by any provincial government of the teachers' right to bargain. This strike in Victoria is cited as being the first teachers' strike in the British Empire.[12] As a direct result of this strike, the government amended the Public Schools Act so that a school board "could" enter into an agreement with its teachers and the act provided a weak form of voluntary arbitration. Another strike, this time by the New Westminster Teachers' Association, in 1921, clearly pointed out the weaknesses of the voluntary arbitration procedure in the act. These weaknesses were (1) no provision for compulsory arbitration, (2) no recognition of the local teachers' association or the BCTF as the official bargaining agent for the teachers, and (3) no provision enabling or compelling a board to pay the

[11] *A.T.A. Magazine*, Vol. 13, No. 9, p. 6.
[12] F. H. Johnson, *A History of Public Education in British Columbia* (Vancouver: University of B.C. Press, 1964), p. 240.

additional salaries awarded by the arbitration board. Despite these problems it was not until 1937, after considerable lobbying by the Federation, that the government passed an act which provided compulsory arbitration in teacher salary disputes, plus an implicit recognition of their right to bargain. Thus in 1937, arbitration became a right for the teachers rather than a privilege sometimes granted by a school board. This arbitration requirement in the act was tested and upheld in the courts in 1939 when the Langley school board refused to have their salary dispute submitted to arbitration. As a result, teacher salary disputes in British Columbia have been settled since 1937 through a process which has provided compulsory arbitration as a final step. Up to 1958 teachers in British Columbia did not have the explicit "right" to bargain, although most school boards voluntarily agreed to bargain with them. In 1958 the trustees fell back on a provision of the Public Schools Act, which gave them the right to fix salaries. The B.C. Teachers' Federation reacted to this by forcing 58 school districts to arbitration under the act. This was enough to persuade the Provincial Government to amend the act and provide teachers with the full right to bargain for salaries.

Prairie Region
The Case of Alberta

The Alberta Teachers' Association was the first Canadian association to obtain the specified right to bargain collectively with school boards on behalf of its teachers. This right came with the passage of the Industrial Conciliation and Arbitration Act in 1941. As a result of considerable lobbying by the ATA this act specifically included teachers as "employees" which for the first time gave the ATA, their "bargaining agent," the specified right to bargain with school trustees matters relating to teachers' salaries and working conditions.

The Case of Saskatchewan

Unlike Alberta, there was very little voluntary bargaining in Saskatchewan prior to World War II, and the little that was done was concentrated in the large urban centers. At this time, the Saskatchewan Teachers' Federation concentrated their efforts on obtaining a statutory minimum teachers' salary through the provincial government. The Federation took this approach since bargaining with the

5,000 individual school boards in the province was virtually impossible. Although the teachers actively lobbied and solicited public support it was not until 1940, when three-quarters of the teachers signed a pledge that they would not accept a teaching contract for less than $700 per year, that The School Act was amended to provide the first minimum salary for teachers—$700 per year. When many of the school jurisdictions were consolidated into larger units in 1945, the teachers attempted to initiate voluntary negotiations with the larger boards. At this time trustees were experiencing difficulty recruiting teachers and consequently many boards were receptive to voluntary negotiations. The teachers, however, recognized the weak position they held in these voluntary situations and the Federation initiated steps to have its locals become certified bargaining units under the Labour Relations Act. The Minister of Education was reluctant to make negotiations compulsory, and in 1946 he established a series of steps which the parties could follow to voluntarily bargain. However, by 1948 it had become obvious that such voluntary machinery was inadequate and in 1949 The Teachers' Salary Negotiation Act was passed. This act required teachers and trustees to negotiate salary schedules and provided conciliation machinery to aid them in arriving at a settlement.

The Case of Manitoba

There were few voluntary negotiations conducted in Manitoba prior to the passing of The Labour Relations Act in 1948. The local associations of the Manitoba Teachers' Society qualified, applied, and received bargaining rights under this act. Thus, the teachers of Manitoba bargained along with industrial employees under this act until 1956. In 1956 the Public Schools Act was amended to transfer teachers' bargaining rights from The Labour Relations Act to the Public Schools Act with provision for compulsory, binding arbitration.

Central Region

The Case of Ontario

It is ironic that in Ontario, Canada's most industrialized province, teachers still do not have the "right" to bargain. They are specifically excluded from the jurisdiction of the Ontario Labour Relations Act and no other legislation provides collective bargaining for teachers. Ontario teachers have never felt the need to seek the right to bargain. Negotiations between teachers and trustees are conducted in Ontario under an effective voluntary system of negotiations supported by the government, the teachers, and the school boards. Teachers view this as an effective professional approach rather than a trade union approach and therefore feel that "bargaining rights" are not required.

The Case of Quebec

Teachers of Quebec could have obtained the right to bargain under the 1944 Labour Relations Act. Few teachers exercised this right until the 1950's because (1) Catholic teachers' associations were dominated by clerical teachers who opposed such procedures, (2) Protestant teachers felt such action to be "unprofessional," and (3) An Act Respecting Municipal and School Corporations gave many teachers access to compulsory arbitration. While many of the Catholic teachers' association locals became certified under the Labour Relations Act, it was not until this act was replaced by the Labour Code in 1964 that locals of the Protestant teachers' association applied for certification. Thus it was 1965 before the majority of teachers in Quebec legally obtained the right to bargain.

Atlantic Region

The Case of New Brunswick

Prior to 1968 teachers of New Brunswick did not have the right to bargain. They were excluded from the Labour Relations Act and no other statute gave them bargaining rights. Many school boards had, however, agreed to bargain informally with their teachers. In 1967 the responsibility for education was moved from the municipal to the provincial level and under the 1968 Public Service Labour Relations Act the New Brunswick Teachers' Association obtained the right to bargain with the government on behalf of the teachers in the province.

The Case of Nova Scotia

There were virtually no negotiations between teachers and trustees prior to 1953. After considerable pressure by the Union, the Nova Scotia Teachers' Union Act was amended in 1953 to incorporate permissive machinery for negotiating teachers' salaries. This act was again amended in 1956 to make conciliation mandatory if requested by either party. Thus, although negotiation machinery was included in the act in 1953, the teachers of Nova Scotia did not obtain the right to bargain until 1957.

The Case of Prince Edward Island and Newfoundland

In the remaining two provinces the teachers' associations submit salary proposals to their respective provincial governments but do not have the "right" to bargain.

SALARY DETERMINATION MACHINERY

One Influence

In Canada, except for the provinces of Newfoundland, Quebec, and New Brunswick, the local boards of school trustees have the final authority and responsibility for determining the salaries of teachers within their jurisdiction. These school trustees are responsible, not only for the administration of the schools, but also for controlling the costs of education. Hence, these trustees are subjected, on the one side, to pressures by teachers for increased salaries, while on the other, they feel the pressures from their electorate to control the sky-rocketing costs of education and its impact upon property taxes. This situation is further complicated by the constraints of inflexible school budgets since the size of the school budget is usually determined by the provincial municipal cost sharing formula (based upon the number of students and teachers) and the ability of the trustees to obtain additional supplemental requisitions from their ratepayers. These pressures upon the school boards are intensified by the shortage of teachers in all provinces.

Teachers' salaries in Canada account for 56 per cent of the school boards' total annual current expenditures. Therefore, most trustees are sensitive to both the teachers' and the ratepayers' pressures and are fully aware of their effects upon current expenditures. One way that this sensitivity is displayed is that most trustees when presented with a teachers' salary proposal will first convert it into equivalent mills to determine its effect upon the tax structure and then compare it to the salaries paid in other jurisdictions to determine its influence upon teacher recruitment.

The foregoing illustrates that, even in provinces such as British Columbia where the salary negotiation process is rigidly controlled by legislation, an examination of the legislative provisions alone can not provide a complete understanding of how teachers' salaries are established. The variations in the composition and background of the elected trustees result in a different philosophy and approach to teachers' salaries from one board to the next. Hence, the following examination of the legislation cannot be considered in isolation of these other factors.

Salary Determination Procedures

The primary method used for determining teachers' salaries in Canada is collective bargaining. In six provinces [13] this bargaining is conducted at the local level between the teachers and the school board while in two other provinces it is conducted at the provincial level (between the provincial teachers' and the trustees' associations and the government in Quebec and between the government and the teachers' Federation in New Brunswick).[14] Regardless of the parties involved, the process used in eight of the provinces *is* collective bargaining in its true sense.

This bargaining is usually conducted in a somewhat formal, businesslike manner, in which in addition to proposals and counterproposals, there are often exchanges of briefs or "position papers." This is not to infer that teacher negotiators are soft, because they are not. These negotiators, particularly those from the provincial associations, are experienced bargainers and are able to utilize union techniques and to be as shrewd in their dealings as their industrial counterparts. Furthermore, their support by the teachers enables them to enforce demands through strikes, mass resignations, or "in-dispute" designations.

The role that the provincial teachers' associations play in collective bargaining varies among provinces. Naturally in Quebec and New Brunswick the entire negotiations are conducted by the provincial associations. However, in the six provinces where bargaining is conducted at the local level, it is usually conducted directly between the school board and a committee of the teachers. The use of intermediaries, such as superintendents or school secretaries, to represent the board is almost unknown in Canada. In addition, the amount of direct assistance provided to the local parties by the provincial associations is minimal. However, if agreement cannot be reached and the issue is referred to conciliation (and, in some prov-

[13] British Columbia, Alberta, Saskatchewan, Manitoba, Ontario, and Nova Scotia.
[14] Although the teachers in Prince Edward Island and Newfoundland present salary proposals to their provincial governments it can not be considered to be negotiations, and no established procedure is followed.

inces, arbitration) then the provincial teachers' associations almost always handle the case on behalf of the local teachers.

Most provincial teachers' associations provide either direct or indirect assistance to local teachers' negotiation committees. Many associations have staff specialists who travel throughout the province conveying their knowledge and skill to local negotiators and, if requested, may assist the local bargaining committees during negotiations. In addition, these associations conduct short courses, seminars, and workshops on collective bargaining techniques for local negotiators and provide them with statistical and economic information of assistance to them during negotiations.

Bargaining procedures vary considerably from one province to another. These range from highly structured, formal procedures (in British Columbia) [15] to very informal almost casual arrangements (in Ontario). The procedures are formalized to the extent that they are contained in the legislation in seven provinces as follows:

		Legislation Provides for			
Province	Statute	Collective Bargaining	Conciliation	Binding Arbitration	Right to Strike
British Columbia	Public Schools Act	x	x	x	
Alberta	Alberta Labour Act	x	x		x
Saskatchewan	Teacher Salary Agreements Act	x	x		
Manitoba	Public Schools Act	x	x	x	
Quebec [16]	Labour Code	x	x		x
New Brunswick	Public Service Labour Relations Act	x	x		x
Nova Scotia	Nova Scotia Teachers' Union Act	x	x		

By statute in all seven of these provinces and by agreement in Ontario there is some form of compulsory conciliation if the parties

[15] British Columbia's procedure is formalized to the point that inflexible time limits are imposed for the completion of each stage of negotiations.
[16] The provisions of the Labour Code have been modified by the passing of Bill 25 in 1967 which, temporarily at least, has removed the teachers' right to strike.

themselves are unable to arrive at an agreement. In this way these eight provinces involve a third party in the dispute. Depending upon the province, this third party may be an official from either the department of labor or the department of education or he may be a distinguished layman. The parties in Ontario are strongly opposed to government involvement in the process in any way and therefore rely upon a committee from the Ontario Teachers' Federation and the Trustees' Council to conciliate all disputes. Although conciliators in Alberta, Saskatchewan, Ontario, New Brunswick, and Nova Scotia are required to make formal recommendations, their basic function is to assist the parties in arriving at an agreement.

Should conciliation fail to produce an agreement, then the dispute must be referred to binding arbitration in British Columbia and Manitoba. In Alberta and New Brunswick, if conciliation fails a conciliation board (fact finder in U.S. terminology) becomes involved. In Alberta, if the conciliation board fails teachers are free to strike. In New Brunswick, if the conciliator fails the teachers' Federation may pursue either an "arbitration" or a "strike" route. If arbitration is chosen the step after conciliation is binding arbitration, whereas if the strike is chosen the step after conciliation is a strike.

In the procedures followed in Saskatchewan, Ontario, and Nova Scotia there are no formal stages beyond conciliation. By practice, however, the teachers in Saskatchewan reserve the right to strike, while in Ontario and Nova Scotia the issue may either be referred back to the local parties for further negotiations or action such as mass resignation or an "indispute" designation may be taken.

Area Bargaining

In the six provinces where teachers and trustees negotiate salaries on a local basis there is a separate series of negotiations conducted for each school jurisdiction. The teachers claim, and with some justification, that negotiations should properly be conducted on a local basis since salaries and working conditions are items of local concern between the school board and its teachers. Many trustees, on the other hand, argue that salaries are usually comparable within particular areas and therefore separate negotiations are inefficient and an unnecessary duplication of effort. Consequently, trustees in most of these provinces have unsuccessfully attempted to have all the negotiations in a particular geographical area conducted jointly and a common salary schedule established for the entire area. These attempts failed not only because of teacher resistance (since it weakens their bargaining position) but also because of trustee resistance (some boards attract the scarce supply of teachers by paying the highest salaries in the area). Under the 1968 Saskatchewan Salary Agreements Act the province has been divided into ten "Areas" and future negotiations will be on an area-wide basis.

Teachers' Demands

Scope of Negotiations

The scope of items negotiated by teachers normally includes salaries plus terms and conditions of employment. The only province which has tried to restrict the scope of negotiable items is British Columbia. Prior to 1965 the British Columbia Public Schools Act restricted teacher negotiations to "salaries" defined as, ". . . The basic salary received from the employer, and includes the allowance paid by the employer for supervisory and administrative duties or special qualifications, but does not include any other allowance. . . ." [17] The courts narrowly interpreted this definition and excluded other conditions of employment from negotiations. After considerable pressure by the Federation, the act was amended in 1965 so that "bonuses" could also be negotiated. Bonuses are defined in the act as, ". . . an amount of money paid as a financial benefit or financial benefits provided in lieu thereof. . . ." [18] The Federation is now attempting to negotiate "bonuses" for such things as oversized classrooms, duty during lunch periods, and for working under onerous conditions. By requesting bonuses for these items they feel that they are then able to introduce these other working conditions as legal items for negotiations and, if necessary, subject to arbitration under the act.

In general, all items included as salaries and working conditions are negotiable in Alberta, Manitoba, Ontario, Quebec, and New Brunswick. In Saskatchewan and Nova Scotia the practice has been to negotiate salaries, allowances, and leaves of absence. In Prince Edward Island and Newfoundland, however, only salaries are generally discussed with the governments.

[17] Province of British Columbia Public Schools Act, Section 135.
[18] *Ibid.*, Section 135 (b).

Salaries

Throughout Canada teachers' salaries have been established on the basis of a salary grid system. The two components of this grid are years of teaching experience and the number of years of university education (or teacher training). Thus, the grid establishes minimum salaries for teachers with various levels of university education but with no teaching experience. To these minimums a salary increment is automatically added for each year of teaching experience possessed to a stipulated maximum. This system has a number of inherent disadvantages since it (1) treats all teachers as equals, (2) fails to recognize ability, (3) fails to provide an incentive to improve teaching performance, and (4) assumes a direct relationship between teaching ability and years of education and experience. The development of this grid system has been partly due to the teachers' refusal to agree to any form of merit rating or merit pay.

An examination of salary grids alone does not yield information about the actual salaries being paid to teachers because these salaries are also dependent upon the education and experience level of the teachers. Salary grids, however, do permit a comparison to be made of the salary which a teacher with specific qualifications would be paid in each of the major Canadian cities.

Table 2 reports the salary grids for the major cities in Canada for the school year 1966–67. In addition, this table also shows the average annual earnings received by industrial employees in these same cities during 1966. Industrial earnings are reported for the sole purpose of providing a relative indication of the overall level of earnings in each of these cities. This facilitates the making of not only a direct inter-city comparison of teachers' salaries, but also allows a comparison to be made of teachers' salaries relative to industrial earnings in these cities. Such a comparison can be made for any position on the salary grid. For example, it allows us to draw the following conclusions concerning the starting salaries for teachers with a bachelor's degree (that is, with five years of training beyond junior matriculation and no teaching experience).

1. Actual starting salaries for those with degrees are highest in Regina, Vancouver, and Winnipeg and are lowest in Charlottetown, Montreal (Protestant) and Newfoundland (provincial scale).
2. Starting salaries relative to industrial earnings are the highest in

TABLE 2. COMPARISON OF TEACHER SALARY SCALES IN THE MAJOR CITIES OF CANADA FOR THE SCHOOL YEAR 1966–67 [a]

| | Teachers' Years of Formal Training Beyond Junior Matriculation | | | | | | | | | | | | | | | | Average Wage and Salary Paid in Industry for Year 1966 [b] |
| | 1 | | 2 | | 3 | | 4 | | 5 | | 6 | | 7 | | 8 | | |
	Min	Max	Min	Max	Min	Max	Min	Max	Min	Max	Min	Max	Min	Max	Min	Max	
PACIFIC REGION																	
British Columbia																	
Vancouver	3325	4105	4190	6440	4640	6990	5135	8255	5600	9370	6200	10400					5382
Victoria			4000	6300	4500	6900	5000	8060	5500	9205	6000	10130					4716
PRAIRIE REGION																	
Alberta																	
Calgary			3700	6100	3950	6650	4500	7200	5650	9900	6100	10850	6550	10800			—
Edmonton			3100	5850	3650	6400	4200	6950	5450	9700	5925	10175	6400	10650			4620
Saskatchewan																	
Regina			3350	5150	4050	6120	4550	6890	5800	9650	6250	10155	6700	10660			4539
Saskatoon—elementary			3200	5480	3900	6155	4400	6820	5650	9500	6150	10000					4282
—secondary			3800	—	4400	6800	5200	7700	5900	9900	6400	10400					
Manitoba																	
Brandon—elementary			3250	4550	3800	5700	4400	6500	5000	8200	5300	8900	5600	9600	—	—	4815
—secondary			3500	5300	3400	5925	4500	6750	5300	8600	5700	9300	6100	10000	6500	10700	
Winnipeg			3650	4750	3925	5650	4600	6475	5550	8675	6000	9425	6375	10800	6900	11250	4191
CENTRAL REGION																	
Ontario																	
Ottawa—elementary			3800	5700	4100	6700	4400	7500	5100	8700	5400	9000	6100	10200	6500	10800	4637
—secondary									5400	9400	6400	11100					
Toronto—elementary			4100	5700	4400	7100	4700	7900	5400	9100	5700	9400	6400	10600	6800	11200	5210
—secondary									5400	9400	6400	11200					

	1 Min Max	2 Min Max	3 Min Max	4 Min Max	5 Min Max	6 Min Max	7 Min Max	8 Min Max	Wage and Salary for Year 1966
Quebec									
Montreal—Protestant	2800 5100	3300 5700	3600 6400	4200 8000	4500 9500	5400 10000			5005
—Catholic		3800 7000	4200 7600	4700 8000	5200 9900	6200 10400			
Quebec—Protestant	2800 5100	3300 5700	3600 6400	4200 8000	4500 9500	5400 10000			4279
—Catholic men		3800 7200	4120 7390	4900 8280	5150 9310	5680 10050	6570 10630		
women		3380 7290	3590 7390	4510 8280	4800 9310	5680 10050	6570 10630		
ATLANTIC REGION									
New Brunswick									
Provincial Scale	2800 4000	3200 4400	3600 5250	4200 6400	5200 8450	5700 9200	6300 10300		4404
Nova Scotia									
Provincial Scale	2200 3100	2700 3900	3600 5100	4200 6000	5000 7400	5600 8400			3998
Dartmouth	2250 3475	2800 4875	3700 5500	4400 6600	5200 8200	5900 9000	7600 10200		
Prince Edward Island									
Charlottetown	2400 4000	3200 4700	3500 5200	3800 6000	4250 7250	5000 8600			3376 [c]
Summerside	2400 4125	3200 4790	3500 5300	3800 6200	4250 7450	5000 8600			
Newfoundland									
Provincial Scale	2646 3530	3087 4413	3528 5296	4079 6289	4630 7061	5181 7833	5732 8605		4117

[a] Canadian Teachers' Federation, *Selected Teachers' Salary Scales 1966-67* (Ottawa: Canadian Teachers' Federation, 1966).
[b] *Employment and Average Weekly Wages and Salaries*, Dominion Bureau of Statistics, No. 72-002, January–December, 1967.
[c] Provincial average.

Winnipeg, Dartmouth, Regina and Charlottetown, and are the lowest in Montreal (both Protestant and Catholic), Toronto and Vancouver.

Thus, a teacher with these qualifications would earn more by starting teaching in Regina, but would be relatively better off if he started in Winnipeg or Dartmouth where his salary would be at least 1.3 times greater than the earnings of the average industrial employee.

An examination of the salary grids reported on Table 2 indicates that overall teachers' salaries are the highest in the cities located in Ontario, British Columbia, and Alberta, and are the lowest in the cities in Prince Edward Island and Newfoundland. In some respects these are puzzling results. One might have expected that salaries would have been highest in provinces where collective bargaining is compulsory and where teachers have the right to strike. However, this is not necessarily the case. For example, in the three provinces where salaries are the highest, bargaining is compulsory in Alberta and British Columbia but not in Ontario and teachers have the right to strike in Alberta but not in British Columbia or Ontario. However, the overall level of industrial earnings is higher in these three provinces than in the others. This suggests that there is a stronger correlation between the level of teachers' salaries and industrial earnings than there is between the level of teachers' salaries and the legislative provisions governing the process used for determining teachers' salaries.

Teachers in the various provinces have approached the problem of salary determination in a number of ways. Some have utilized a traditional trade union approach while others have developed various professional approaches. Some have employed the strike weapon, some have developed other forms of sanctions while others do not appear to utilize any pressure tactics. In all provinces the teachers' associations have been instrumental in developing the salary determination techniques employed and have the full support of their members in this respect. Teachers, trustees, and the government in each province are accustomed to determining salaries in a certain manner and have developed their relationships accordingly. Thus, the method used for determining teachers' salaries must be examined in the context of the social, political, and economic climate that exists within the province. Therefore, neither an examination of the techniques employed nor a comparison of the salary levels established can lead to the conclusion that one system or technique for determining salaries is better than another. Both the level of salaries *and* the effectiveness of the technique used will be affected by other factors. One of these other factors, the overall level of industrial salaries in the province, has already been suggested, but some other important factors are (1) the attitude of the government, trustees, and the teachers themselves, (2) the existing shortage of teachers, (3) the overall development of unionism within the province and (4) the state of economic development within the province.

THE RIGHT TO STRIKE

The teachers' right to strike is only specifically prohibited by statute in Manitoba and, temporarily at least, Quebec.[19] However, this right is curtailed to a degree in all of the other provinces (except Alberta and New Brunswick) by the individual teaching contract the teacher signs with the school board. These contracts, or the regulations relating to them, are designed to ensure continuity in teacher-student relations. They thereby specify that termination, except for cause or by mutual consent, can only occur at the end of the school year and provided that proper notice is given (from one to three months depending upon the province). Technically, therefore, a strike unless it occurs at the end of the school year and unless the proper notice is given would constitute a termination of services and a breach of the teaching contract. Such a breach of contract is ground for legal action, or as in the British Columbia school regulations, cause for the suspension of teaching certificates. These individual teaching contracts do not limit the teachers' right to strike in Alberta or New Brunswick since a teachers' strike is a legal activity under the relevant statutes. Thus in eight provinces the teachers' right to strike may be prohibited because of these teaching contracts. The term "may be prohibited" is used because this prohibition requires that school boards or the

---

[19] The teachers in Quebec were granted the right to strike when the Labour Code was amended in 1965. In February, 1967, when one out of five Catholic students in the province were out of school because of strikes, the government passed Bill 25. This bill forced the teachers back to work, removed their right to strike, and established that negotiations would be conducted at the provincial level. This bill temporarily removed the teachers' right to strike in Quebec until July 1, 1968.

Departments of Education initiate action against striking teachers. The shortage of teachers coupled with the political influence of teachers in some of the provinces may make trustees and government officials reluctant to take such action. As a result, the teachers in Saskatchewan and Nova Scotia consider that they "reserve" the right to strike.

The tendency is for teachers, trustees and the general public to compare the strike in the school system to that in the industrial sector. Such a direct comparison is not relevant because of the following basic but vital differences:

1. Teachers have used the industrial comparison to argue that they must have the right to strike to offset the trustees' right to lockout. This is an unsound comparison because locking teachers out is not a realistic alternative for school trustees. Trustees are committed by statute to operate the schools for a specified number of days each year (usually 200) and few elected trustees would risk public animosity by locking teachers out and denying children their educational rights.

2. The statutes in five provinces stipulate that membership in the teachers' association is compulsory and that only teachers who are members of the association may legally staff a classroom. Therefore, unlike the industrial situation, trustees are unable to use "strike breakers" since any member who crossed a picket line would no longer be a member in "good standing" and therefore, by legislation, could not teach in the school.

3. Unlike corporate executives, school trustees are neither profit orientated nor profit motivated. Trustees do not fear that the increase in costs due to an increase in teachers' salaries will price them out of the market (although it may price them out of an election). Similarly, trustees do not fear that a strike will result in a loss of business to competitors.

4. A strike in the private sector primarily exerts economic pressure upon the company, whereas a strike in a school system exerts political and social (but not economic) pressure upon the school board.

5. The individual teaching contracts and other tenure arrangements prevent teachers from seeking other teaching employment either prior to or during a strike. Therefore, unlike the industrial employer, the school board is protected against a loss of teachers during a strike.

6. The degree of third-party concern and involvement is much greater in teacher-trustee disputes than in industrial disputes. This third-party involvement is due, in part, to the government being the primary source of school revenue and, in part, to the sensitivity of a dispute affecting school children. The public is more sensitive to a teachers' strike than to most industrial strikes and both the teachers and the elected trustees are more concerned about public opinion than are the parties in most industrial disputes.

The school trustees feel that they have little power to compare with the teachers' right to strike. They are "trustees" and as such are bound by both legislative and moral obligations which prevent them from exercising the economic powers available to industrial employers. Furthermore, they feel that threats of strikes have the same effect, or are intended to have the same effect, as strikes themselves, namely the application of naked force, irrespective of the justice or injustice of the claims made by teachers. Trustees feel that there is little to choose between a strike and a threat of strike. Similarly they feel that the "in-dispute" declarations and mass resignations are based on a belief in the efficacy of force rather than on justice and reason. They feel it matters little whether capitulation to the application of force comes on the eve of a strike or shortly thereafter. As a result trustees in all provinces have resisted any attempts on the part of the teachers to obtain or retain the right to strike. In Alberta, where the teachers have this right, there have been attempts on the part of the trustees to both limit and remove this right.

Many teachers, on the other hand, state that they must have the right to strike in order to offset the economic powers of the trustees. They feel that the board's right to say "no" to the teachers' request is very powerful in that, ". . . a school board, simply by refusing any proposed change in the agreement, by declining to meet frequently with the teachers' committee, and by rejecting a conciliation award, can and does exert massive and effective power in the negotiation process." [20] The teachers argue that in order for effective bargaining to take place, both parties must have an equality of power at the bargaining table. Thus, teachers must have some means

[20] Saskatchewan Teachers' Federation, *Submission to the Committee of Inquiry on Teacher Salary Negotiation Proceedings* (Regina: Saskatchewan Teachers' Federation, 1966), p. 41.

of bringing pressure to bear upon the trustees so that they will seriously consider the teachers' aspirations. Teachers claim that only when they have the right to strike will there be this counterbalance of force which will then compel the parties to give their earnest consideration to all avenues of settlement. Thus, there has been an organized attempt by teachers in all provinces except Ontario, Prince Edward Island, and Newfoundland to obtain or retain the legal right to strike.

The records show that there have been 22 strikes by teachers in Canada over the past seven years.[21] All of these strikes occurred in three provinces—Quebec, Alberta, and Saskatchewan. Neither the frequency nor severity of teachers' strikes in Alberta and Saskatchewan is alarming. The one strike in Saskatchewan (1964) closed the Regina schools for three days and amounted to 1,617 lost teacher days. The three strikes in Alberta (1960, 1963, and 1969) closed Leduc schools for nine days, Strathcona schools for seven days, and Three Hills schools for four days, and amounted to a total of 3,451 lost teacher days. Since the remaining 19 strikes all occurred in Quebec, there has been considerable concern expressed over both the severity and frequency of teachers' strikes in this province.[22] Eleven of these 19 strikes closed the schools for 15 days or more with seven of them lasting for longer than one month. Teacher strikes in Quebec amounted to 444,362 lost teacher days [23] from 1963 to February, 1967, when the government removed their right to strike through the passing of Bill 25, discussed earlier. It should be noted that teacher strikes were only legal in Quebec for 15 months of this period.

Recently there has been either a special legislative committee or a Royal Commission established to investigate teachers' bargaining rights in Alberta, Saskatchewan, and New Brunswick. After a thorough investigation, the Committees in Alberta and Saskatchewan refused to make any formal recommendations regarding the

---

21 Excluding the nine recorded one- to three-day "study sessions" and the recent series of illegal one-day "rotating" strikes held in Quebec.
22 The frequency of teacher strikes in Quebec has been:
- 1963 – nine "study sessions" and three illegal strikes
- 1964 – one illegal strike
- 1965 – two illegal strikes
- 1966 – six illegal strikes
- 1967 – six legal and one illegal strikes
23 This figure includes both strikes and "study sessions" but excludes one 21-day strike because the number of teachers involved is not known.

teachers' right to strike whereas the Royal Commission in New Brunswick recommended that the teachers be granted the right to strike.

ALTERNATIVES TO THE STRIKE

Compulsory Arbitration

Canadian teachers are, in general, opposed to compulsory or imposed settlement of disputes. They believe that the existence of such machinery results in the parties giving little earnest consideration to proposals, thereby leading to abuses in the negotiation process. They feel that often parties who are oversold on their own cases, impatient with the frustrations of the negotiation process, and unskilled in the art of compromise may simply go through the motions of negotiating and instead wait for the arbitrator's decision. This is particularly pertinent in nonprofit educational systems where both the elected trustees and the teachers' committee are reluctant to assume responsibility for a settlement or its impact. Thus, compulsory arbitration can mitigate real collective bargaining.

Where the parties may voluntarily submit their disputes to arbitration, the arbitration awards have generally followed the pattern established by negotiated settlements. In areas, however, where all disputes must go to arbitration, a significant pattern of settlement may not be established through negotiated settlements and therefore the arbitrator may not have this guide to follow. This may result in inexperienced arbitrators (and the turnover of arbitrators acceptable to both parties is high) "splitting the difference" between the position of the parties. The fear that this will happen results in the parties either assuming and retaining unrealistic positions throughout negotiations or, as in Manitoba, reverting to their original positions as soon as the dispute is referred to arbitration. In either case, arbitration tends to hinder rather than aid collective bargaining.

The experience with arbitration in the two provinces where it is compulsory for teachers' disputes has been quite different. For example, in the five school years since 1963–64 there have been 28 disputes resolved by arbitration in Manitoba and 125 in British Columbia.[24] Arbitration therefore plays a much more important

24 Even though there are more than twice as many collective agreements negotiated in Manitoba each year than in British Columbia.

role in teacher-trustee negotiations in British Columbia than it does in Manitoba. The major reasons advanced for the high number of arbitration awards in British Columbia are (1) high teacher demands, (2) trustee reluctance to accept responsibility for increases in teachers' salaries, and (3) the tight, inflexible negotiation schedule whereby all settlements must be reached by November 14th or be referred to arbitration.

Canadian experience with obligatory awards among teachers has been that they do not eliminate strikes but merely make them illegal. In general, it is impossible in a free society to coerce any substantial segment of the population into freely accepting unsatisfactory conditions. The right to withhold services is considered as an inalienable right in a free society. As a result, in those provinces where obligatory awards are made, or where salaries are primarily unilaterally determined, teachers have developed techniques such as coincidental resignations, "study sessions" and in-dispute designations.

Coincidental or Mass Resignations

The coincidental resignation or simultaneous termination of individual contracts between teachers and board has been used chiefly when there are not statutory procedures for collective bargaining. This technique has been used in both Ontario and Nova Scotia.

Coincidental or mass resignation occurs when all or a majority of teachers employed by a school board individually submit their resignations in accordance with their individual contracts. This is usually done only after approval is obtained from the provincial association. For example, the practice in Nova Scotia has been that, if settlement is not reached by March 31st, the majority of the teachers will "coincidentally" submit their resignations to be effective July 31st. This pressure is usually enough to force the school board to re-appraise its salary position. The practice in Ontario has been slightly different. In Ontario, the teachers will give their resignations to their negotiator some time prior to May 31st. The negotiator may then use these resignations as a negotiation's ploy and, if necessary, he will submit all of them en masse to the school board across the bargaining table. Again these resignations are not effective until August 31st which usually provides enough time for settlement to be reached before the teachers' resignations take effect.

In either province, once these resignations have been submitted either "coincidentally" or en masse, every teacher in the province is notified by mail and may be reminded by daily notices in the press that unsatisfactory working conditions prevail in the particular school jurisdiction. As a result of the resignations and notices, the school board may be unable to recruit teachers for the start of the next school term. In the majority of cases the sanction is effective and a settlement is reached before the start of the next school term, but if such is not the case then the schools remain closed. In this sense, coincidental resignations are really delayed strikes.

The technique of coincidental resignation is not as clean as that of the strike. Often many of those who coincidentally resign do not return to that school jurisdiction because they accept positions with other school boards. This happens even if the dispute is settled before the end of the school year and before the resignations become effective. The reason for this is that when the resignations are submitted in the spring there is a degree of uncertainty as to whether or not an agreement will be reached before the end of the school year. There is the possibility that the school board may be recalcitrant and accept the resignations. This uncertainty produces anxiety because this is the same period of the year that most teacher recruitment is done. Therefore many teachers seek and accept other employment even though they are not dissatisfied with their current working conditions.

As a result of coincidental resignations a school jurisdiction may be short of teachers for the entire school year. Hence, these coincidental resignations, besides placing temporary pressures upon the board, may also have a most serious effect on the operation of the school system for a two- or three-year period. In spite of these drawbacks, the use of coincidental resignation by teachers has been accepted by the public and the press in many parts of Canada where there has been a strong reaction against the idea of teacher strikes. The effectiveness of this technique is dependent upon the support of the individual teachers frequently determined by the availability of other teaching positions. Consequently this technique may be effective only as long as the present teacher shortage exists.

Publicizing Dispute Situations

The third alternative sanction, the publicizing of dispute situations, has been used most widely in Ontario, but has also been used by teachers in Nova Scotia, Saskatchewan, and Manitoba. Under this technique the teachers' association sends letters to all teachers advising them against applying for or accepting employment with a certain school board where agreement has not been reached. This letter is usually followed with daily notices in the press. This highly effective device is a form of blacklisting of these school boards and is euphemistically referred to as "pink-listing" or "grey-listing" in Ontario, depending upon the color of paper on which the letter is printed.

A dispute designation is not a new concept in that it has been used by those in the labor movement for many years. It can be compared to both the union blacklist and to the picket line. It is simply a method of declaring that a dispute exists and appealing to others, who are not directly involved in the dispute, to support the employee group involved. In the case of the teachers, the publicizing of a dispute situation is usually coupled with a mass resignation by the local teachers. In this way the school board is unable to recruit the replacement teachers it needs. It is an effective technique in that it applies pressure to the board but does not develop public resentment, and it is considered to be a "professional" sanction.

The dispute declaration is very different from a strike or a mass resignation in that its success is entirely dependent upon the support of teachers who are not directly involved in the dispute and therefore are neither financially nor emotionally committed to it. This sanction is therefore most effective in Saskatchewan and Ontario where membership in the teachers' association is required as a condition of employment. In these, as in the other provinces, the teachers' association may discipline its members for ignoring a dispute designation. Naturally, the impact of such disciplining is much greater where suspension from the teachers' association results in the teacher being unable to continue teaching in that province.

Study Sessions

A fourth sanction used by teachers is the declared study session. Again it is not a new technique as forms of protest strikes have been used by the European trade union movement for a long time. Teachers, in provinces where the strike is illegal, may call a one- or two-day study session in order to register their dissatisfaction with either the school board or the government. These study sessions are legal in that they take the form of the principal calling an all-day meeting in order that the teachers may "study" their grievances. This technique has been most widely used by the teachers in Quebec. A most impressive study session occurred when the Quebec government removed the teachers' right to strike by passing Bill 25. When this happened, all of the teachers throughout the province registered their objection to the government's action by leaving the classrooms and holding a one-day session to "study" the bill.

Political Action

Another possibility, political action, is not really a sanction. Teachers in Canada have traditionally been active in politics and are at present the second largest professional group in politics at all levels. Undoubtedly this fact has assisted them in securing the governmental and legislative support that they have. In addition, the use of political action has been common throughout the history of teachers' associations in Canada and there is every likelihood that its use will continue in the future.

In examining the impact of sanctions, there is some evidence to suggest that the strike is a cleaner, more effective, and a less disruptive weapon than either the coincidental resignation or the dispute listing, for the latter two may be more disruptive to the school system in the long run than is the work stoppage. In a strike, the teachers stand ready to resume services as soon as a settlement is reached. Mass resignations and dispute listing, on the other hand, have more permanent effects and therefore can do much greater damage for a longer period of time because they involve a potential permanent loss of teaching staff.

TEACHERS—PROFESSIONALS OR TRADE UNIONISTS?

General

There has been much debate over the years as to whether or not teachers properly come within the definition of "professionals." Teachers, through their associations, have accepted and try to fulfill the four characteristics in a definition of a profession:

1. Teachers, as other professionals, possess a specialized body of knowledge, and the profession finds its origin at the university.
2. Teachers are given corporate form through their association by statute in all of the provinces.
3. Teachers possess special skills and techniques derived from edu-

cation and training and are prepared to exercise these skills primarily in the interest of others and in the service of the public.

4. Teachers' associations exercise considerable control and discipline over their members through powers accorded to them either through their constitution or the incorporating legislation.

The teachers' associations in most provinces have actively ensured that these criteria are met. Although their control over certification is incomplete, the associations in all provinces (1) provide teachers with a corporate voice, (2) are active in establishing and enforcing entrance standards, and (3) control and discipline their members. All of the associations have actively encouraged the upgrading of teachers and some have established professional and non-professional teacher classifications based upon the possession of a bachelor's degree.

This question of professional status is further complicated by the deemed conflict between the occupational and economic goals of the teachers and their professional and social goals. For example, teachers may bargain for salary increases and use the strike weapon while at the same time strive for professional recognition and the upgrading of teacher qualifications, curriculum, and educational standards. This mixture of activities raises the question of whether teachers in Canada are professionals or trade unionists. This point is seldom raised by teachers themselves as they appear to have rationalized their various activities. It is, however, still raised by many school trustees and by the general public. In all fairness, the only answer to this question is that teachers strive for and consider themselves as having professional status while at the same time employ whatever trade union tactics are necessary to achieve their economic objectives.

Certification of Teachers

The question of certification is of vital concern to all Canadian teachers' associations. At present there is no effective control by teachers' associations in any of the provinces over the entrance requirements and standards of interim and permanent certification of teachers. This means that the teaching profession has no control over who enters its ranks and under what conditions. It is not always clear just who actually has the final word on admission to the profession since some provinces have certification boards while others do not. In most cases, in theory, it is the Minister of Education and, in practice, his immediate or senior advisor.

In the Atlantic and Central regions, as in Manitoba, there appears to be a degree of informal consultation between the Departments of Education and the teachers' organizations concerning certification. Teachers in these provinces do not, however, have membership on certification boards or advisory committees. In Quebec, on the other hand, the Provincial Association of Protestant Teachers does have one member on a ten-member certification board. This member is appointed for life by the government from a panel of three who are named by the Association. It is generally understood that the Association avoids this life-time appointment provision by prearranging a resignation date with its member before he is appointed.

In the Prairie region the Saskatchewan Teachers' Federation names a representative to three separate committees, which are advisory to the Minister on matters allied to certification. It has, however, no say in the actual certification. Teacher certification in Alberta is done by the Department of Education. Prior to 1966, evaluation of Alberta teachers for salary purposes was determined by the University of Alberta by a twelve-member board composed of three members each from the University, the Department of Education, the Alberta School Trustees' Association and the Alberta Teachers' Association. At the end of 1966 the University refused to continue making these evaluations and therefore a new evaluation board had to be established. The ATA naturally wanted to assume these responsibilities and started issuing their own certifications which the ASTA refused to recognize. The ASTA, on the other hand, pressed to have the Department of Education make these evaluations. A long and fierce political debate between the ATA and the ASTA took place over this issue with many of the teachers' locals refusing to bargain their salary agreements until this issue was resolved. After much controversy the issue was resolved in the teachers' favor with the establishment of an ATA Teachers' Qualification Board composed of three representatives from both universities, two from the Department of Education, two from the ASTA and three from the ATA (one of whom is chairman). This gives the ATA a form of control (the extent of which has yet to be seen) over the supply of teachers entering the province from other areas.

The British Columbia Teachers' Federation does not have any responsibility for teacher certification. Certification is the total responsibility of the Department of Education. A few years ago the Federation started issuing its own teacher certifications as part of an attempt to obtain control over certification. This attempt has not been successful and the Federation is contemplating ceasing the practice. In general, however, it appears as if teachers' associations will pressure for more voice in teacher certification.

Role of the Principal

Principals are normally both members and active leaders of the teachers' association in each of the various Canadian provinces. For example, approximately one-half of the teachers' negotiating committees in Alberta are composed of principals and vice-principals. Principals in Canadian schools do not, however, fulfill supervisory or managerial roles as the terms are understood in industry. Although principals are responsible for administration of the schools and supervision of the pupils, they are not completely responsible for the supervision of the classroom teachers, since they do not appoint, dismiss, discipline, or transfer teachers, or make recommendations for permanent appointments, or for promotions to supervisory positions. The superintendent, as representative of the board, is responsible for these matters.

The school trustees in most provinces have tried unsuccessfully to have principals excluded from the bargaining unit. At present, the associations generally represent all those in the school system who possess a teacher's certificate. The trustees claim that it is entirely unreasonable to expect the superintendent to supervise effectively all the teachers in the school jurisdiction, and they feel that such supervision can only be achieved if the principals do it, and this could only be done if principals were removed from the bargaining unit.

In most cases the salaries of principals are negotiated along with those of the classroom teachers. Some principals in the larger school jurisdictions in Ontario and Quebec have formed their own local bargaining associations and negotiate separately from the other teachers. Similarly some of the principals in those provinces where teacher association membership is automatic but not compulsory have opted out of the association and bargain individually with the school board. Principals are usually paid the salary they would receive as a classroom teacher plus an administration allowance based upon the number of rooms, teachers or pupils in the school.

Trade Union Affiliation

During the post-depression period of the 1930's while the labor movement in Canada, as elsewhere, was gaining substantial membership support, a movement developed within the teachers' associations advocating that teachers affiliate with the labor movement. This movement was supported by immigrant teachers from Great Britain who were used to bargaining techniques and to being affiliated with labor. It also gained support by teachers who realized that the trade union movement was obtaining economic advances at a time when they themselves were losing many of the benefits gained during the 1920's. Hence, between 1931 and 1938 most of the teachers' associations seriously considered affiliating with the trade union movement.

Only in British Columbia did anything concrete materialize from this movement.[25] During the late 1930's, the rural teachers in British Columbia became most dissatisfied since their salary schedules were considerably lower than those for urban teachers. Consequently, they formed a Rural Teachers' Association within the British Columbia Teachers' Federation in 1935 and brought the question of unionism to each of the general meetings and conventions. Finally in 1938 a committee was established to consider the question of affiliation with the labor movement. Action was not taken until 1943 when the Federation voted (by a very slim majority) to affiliate with organized labor. Their objective accomplished, the Rural Teachers' Association voted themselves out of existence. The British Columbia Teachers' Federation affiliated with the craft unions in the Trades and Labour Congress (similar to the American Federation of Labor). This affiliation met with strong opposition from many teachers and was debated at each annual teachers' convention up to 1956. In 1955, the AFL and the CIO merged in the United States; during the following year, the Trades and Labour Congress and Canadian Congress of Labour also merged in Canada to form the Canadian Labour Congress. At that time it was necessary for all affiliated unions to reaffirm their affiliation after the

[25] Although the teachers' organization in Nova Scotia is called the Nova Scotia Teachers' Union, its activities are the same as the other teachers' associations in Canada.

merger and accept an increase in their membership dues to the CLC. As a result, once again this matter was raised at the British Columbia Teachers' Federation's annual general meeting, and it was decided (again by a slim majority) not to reaffiliate with the Canadian Labour Congress.

Since their disaffiliation in 1956 the question of professionalism versus unionism has been debated from time to time within the Federation in British Columbia. In retrospect, it appears as though the major benefit of the Federation's affiliation with labor was that it forced teachers psychologically to accept the use of such union tactics as collective bargaining. The British Columbia teachers' disaffiliation with labor was not due to a rebellion against unionism but more to a belief that they had not directly benefited from their affiliation, and that the same objectives could be accomplished without affiliation. Furthermore, as salary levels increased, teachers were inclined to devote more attention to professional improvement and development, while at the same time utilizing collective bargaining to further their economic objectives.

The teachers of Canada are not opposed to organized labor although a majority are opposed to any affiliation with labor. The teachers' associations, however, have much in common with the unions in their objectives, their organization, and their bargaining tactics. The teachers in Canada have clearly benefited, both directly and indirectly, from the trade unions' battles with management and with the government. This is evident in both the salary structures and in the legislation established in each of the provinces.

In general, the teachers in the Atlantic region and in the provinces of Ontario, Manitoba, and Saskatchewan have not been too concerned over the question of unionism. They have generally considered unionism to be unprofessional and have therefore utilized other avenues in their efforts to improve their economic position. The teachers in Quebec held this same general attitude. In the last few years, however, their attitude has changed and they now consider that union activities are necessary and are not in conflict with professionalism. The teachers in British Columbia have accepted the use of many union tactics and do not feel them to be opposed to their professional objectives, while teachers in Alberta have accepted all of the benefits of unionism and freely utilize all trade union techniques.

FUTURE TRENDS

An examination of the development and the existing structure of the teachers' associations in Canada leads to the following six general observations for the future.

1. Teachers' associations in Canada developed primarily during the period from 1900 to the 1930's and have since focused their attention upon the improvement of the teachers' economic positions. It is now evident that some associations, particularly those in Ontario, Alberta, and British Columbia, are entering a third stage of development—a stage wherein most of their energies and resources will be devoted to professional development. The case of British Columbia is an example of the transition into this third stage. Prior to 1963–64 the major concern of the British Columbia Teachers' Federation was the improvement of the economic welfare of teachers; less attention was paid to their professional development. Now the attention of the Federation is primarily focused upon professional development with economic welfare relegated to a secondary position. For example, the number of in-service educational courses, which are entirely financed and sponsored by the Federation, has increased from one in 1957 to 32 in 1966.

The transition from the second to the third stage of development is dependent upon the achievement of a relatively satisfactory level of salaries. The associations now entering this third stage are in the three provinces which have the highest level of teachers' salaries. It is expected that the associations in the Atlantic region will continue to devote their primary attention upon the economic aspects of the profession until they obtain salary levels comparable to those in other provinces. In any event, it is likely that as teachers' salary levels increase in each province, that teachers' associations will find their organizational strength in their professional development activities rather than through their economic welfare activities.

2. Educational costs in all provinces are increasing at a spectacular rate. These costs are becoming too great a burden for property holders alone to bear. Thus, both teachers and trustees recognize the need to develop new methods of financing education and as a result of their combined efforts, some provinces have partially begun to finance education out of the province's general revenues. With the provincial governments financing a larger portion of

these expenditures they are naturally becoming more concerned with teacher salary determination (teacher salaries accounted for 56 per cent of current educational expenses in 1966–67). Therefore, it is expected that there will be greater direct government involvement in teacher salary determination in the future. This trend may have already begun as seen by the changes which have occurred in New Brunswick and Quebec in 1967. In Quebec the government is now a party to the collective agreement along with the provincial trustees' associations. In New Brunswick the government has taken over full responsibility of salary determination from the trustees.

3. The future will probably see more regional and provincial bargaining of teachers' salaries than at present. This trend will arise from (1) increased government involvement, (2) more consolidation of rural school jurisdictions, (3) the narrowing of salary differentials between school boards within geographical areas of the provinces, and (4) a reduction in the number and importance of local factors affecting salary levels. It is, in the 1967 development of province-wide bargaining in Quebec and New Brunswick and the 1968 move toward regional bargaining in Saskatchewan, where this trend finds its origin.

4. The importance of collective bargaining on the part of teachers will be likely to increase rather than decrease in the future. At present there is little concern in Canada over the teachers' use of collective bargaining. Teachers in Canada have legally bargained collectively since 1941 and have not abused the right. Furthermore, it is expected that as more and more professionals and government employees examine and adopt collective bargaining as a means of establishing salaries, the little resistance that does exist will diminish. The teachers themselves believe that the essence of professionalism rests in the nature and quality of the service rendered and not in the manner used to determine salaries. Thus, collective bargaining has become, and will continue to be, the accepted method for determining teachers' salaries in Canada.

5. While the history of teacher-trustee bargaining relations has been relatively peaceful, it is expected that there will be more conflict in the future. This conflict will be caused by (1) increased trustee resistance to teacher demands as a result of taxpayers' pressure upon trustees over rapidly increasing taxes, (2) teachers' bargaining power being reduced due to a decline in the existing teachers' shortage (most forecasts predict that the teacher shortage will

be below the critical level between 1972 and 1975), (3) teachers introducing non-monetary policy and curriculum items into negotiations, and (4) an overall increase in society's acceptance of conflict as part of the compromise process.

6. While there has been general acceptance of the teachers' right to bargain there has not as yet been complete acceptance of their right to strike. It is, therefore, expected that the controversy over the teachers' right to strike will not only continue, but will increase in the future. This controversy will be nurtured by such external influences as the federal government's granting of a limited strike right to its public employees in 1967. The controversy centers not so much on the strike being unprofessional per se but on the impact of the strike upon innocent school children. Thus, it becomes a controversy over the teachers' right to withdraw their services versus the students' right to an education. Because of this, the discussion will continue to be highly emotional with the result that the public policy introduced will likely vary considerably depending upon the political situation in each of the provinces.

England 2

Norman Morris

DEFINITION

Teacher associations in England are many and varied. Some are devoted to the development of particular subjects, such as English or mathematics. Many grades of administrators, such as youth leaders, school welfare officers, and chief education officers, have their own separate organizations. The Conservative and Unionist Teachers Association feeds the educational views of conservative-minded teachers into the Conservative Party machine, while the Labour Party is served by the Socialist Educational Association. There is an organization for the advancement of public or state education, and another whose sole purpose is to promote comprehensive secondary schools. But when all these bodies have been listed, they are only a small proportion of the total. Teachers are by nature articulate; they divide and re-combine with the exuberance of chromosomes. Name an educational interest, whether it be the promotion of school libraries or the defense of privately owned schools, and you can find at least one organization (frequently more) dedicated to it.

For the purposes of this article it is clearly necessary to be restrictive and I have decided to treat only those associations which can be called trade unions in the accepted sense. Even so, selection is not easy. In the industrial field, trade unions are officially registered,

NORMAN MORRIS is Senior Lecturer in Education, University of Manchester, Manchester, England.

and a trade union is, by definition, a body which appears on the register. In education, however, organizations of teachers which perform the functions of labor unions have refused to accept the nomenclature; they have persisted in regarding themselves as professional associations and, consequently, are not officially registered. Since some additional criteria have to be adopted, I intend to limit myself to combinations of teachers which participate officially in salary negotiations with a public authority and also offer facilities for the legal protection of their members. This excludes both teachers in nonstate schools (about six per cent of the total) who do not negotiate with public bodies, and also organizations of administrators, such as chief education officers and local authority inspectors, who do negotiate but are not teachers. This still leaves seven major organizations which cover the fields of primary and secondary education, and a further three, which deal mainly with institutions beyond the secondary school stage. In the first category are the National Union of Teachers (N.U.T.), the National Association of Schoolmasters (N.A.S.), the National Association of Head Teachers (N.A.H.T.), the Incorporated Association of Head Masters (I.A.H.M.), the Association of Head Mistresses, Incorporated (A.H.M.I.), the Association of Assistant Mistresses, Incorporated (A.A.M.I.), and the Assistant Masters Association (A.M.A.). These last four, while retaining their existence as independent bodies, are also federated for certain purposes under the name of the Joint Four. The unions serving institutions beyond the secondary stage are the Association of Teachers in Technical Institutions (A.T.T.I.), the Association of Teachers in Colleges and Departments of Education (A.T.C.D.E.), and the Association of University Teachers (A.U.T.). All ten bodies claim to be concerned in a field much wider than that of labor relations, and all would stress their interest in educational development in general; they all, however, have protection of their members' interests as one of their main functions and so qualify for consideration here.

THE UNIONS

The N.U.T.

Elementary school teaching began to emerge as a profession in England in the years between 1840 and 1860. At that time, elementary schools for children of the laboring poor were provided by the various religious sects, with financial assistance from the central government toward the cost of both the school house and school equipment. In order to qualify for governmental subsidy, assisted schools had to be open to inspection by Her Majesty's Inspectors, and the master or mistress in charge had to hold a certificate granted by the central government. Teachers (certificated, uncertificated, and apprentice teachers alike) were engaged by the managers of the school in which they taught and were paid by them. Certificated and pupil teachers received an augmentation to their salary direct from the central government, which also began to work out a national pension plan for elementary school teachers of all types. In 1862, however, changes were made in the method of financing elementary schools which seriously affected existing conditions of service. Under the Revised Code issued in that year, all specific grants to schools, including teachers' augmentation payments, were abolished. Instead, school managers received a single block grant, calculated partly on the number of pupils in attendance and partly on the results of individual examination of pupils in reading, writing, and arithmetic. This annual examination was conducted by Her Majesty's Inspectors and the system, known as Payment by Results, persisted for 30 years.

Teachers were entirely dependent for their remuneration on whatever bargain they could strike with their managers. Since the income available to managers was governed by the amount of grant earned by pupils' successes in the examinations, the salary which a teacher secured depended, in effect, on the results of his own industry and his efficiency in procuring examination passes. The new system was a straightforward application of nineteenth century principles of laissez-faire and open competition, but it tended to diminish the status of teaching as a profession. Teachers no longer had independence in the classroom; they instead became technicians, rather than practitioners of an art.

They had other grounds for feeling aggrieved. The proposed governmental pension plan was abandoned. Career prospects were slight. One possible line of progression—from the classroom to the inspectorate—was closed by an insuperable social barrier: elementary schoolteachers were of working-class origin while Her Majesty's Inspectors (H.M.Is.) were recruited from the universities and the upper classes. As a result, they never taught in the schools whose standards they set. This injustice was felt all the more acutely after

1862, when H.M.Is. became inquisitors on whose judgment teachers' salaries depended. The introduction of free bargaining placed managers and teachers in a master-servant relationship. Since schools were provided by churches, teachers might also be subjected to parochial demands by local clergy. The Education Act of 1870, in addition, created an entirely new situation. This act was designed to ensure that there would be enough elementary schools to provide places for all children, except for those privately educated. The country was to be divided into school districts; the child population was to be set against available school accommodation and ad hoc school boards were to be elected in those districts which showed a deficiency of accommodation. These boards would erect and manage schools, to the amount required to eliminate the deficiency, using the proceeds of a local rate levy to do so. It was clear, therefore, that many teachers would soon serve new masters, the local school boards, composed of public functionaries with probably little knowledge of or experience in education. To the teacher, anxious to be regarded as a professional worker, the prospect in 1870 appeared bleak. Major developments were taking place; teachers were increasing in number at a rapid rate. But the ability of teachers to influence what was happening, both to education and to themselves, seemed to be decreasing.

In this atmosphere of resentment, frustration, and fear of the unknown, teachers turned seriously to combination. Previous attempts at unionization had been sporadic and uncoordinated. Some unions, such as the Nottingham Schoolmasters Association, had been centered in particular localities. Others (the General Associated Body of Church Schoolmasters is a good example) served specific denominational interests. Most of them were little more than mutual improvement societies. It was the 1870 Education Act, bringing both new hopes and new forebodings, which caused responsible teachers to think in terms of something larger than these early organizations. The National Union of Elementary Teachers was formed in September, 1870, within a month of the act being signed. From its inception, its prime object was nothing less than the creation of a teaching profession, by uniting teachers of all types in a single combination. This aim was taken a stage further in 1889, when the word "elementary" was discarded from its title and the new union became simply the National Union of Teachers.

The first policy statement of the N.U.E.T. contained ten main

points, four of them directed to the teachers' immediate employers
—the new school boards and the boards of managers of denominational schools—and the remainder dealing with matters which concerned the central government. From the employers the union
sought (1) a standard contract of service, specifying the causes for
which a teacher could be dismissed; (2) freedom from compulsory
extraneous duties, such as training a church choir or playing the
church organ; (3) freedom from "obnoxious interference" by
managers in internal school affairs; and (4) adequate salaries. It is
interesting to note that for many years the N.U.E.T. placed little
emphasis on this fourth point. From the central government the
union demanded (1) more stringent requirements for entry into the
teaching profession; (2) the official registration of teachers in order
to maintain teaching standards and to protect children from unqualified practitioners; (3) the right of teachers to promotion to the
Inspectorate; (4) the right of appeal against an Inspector's recommendation to cancel a teacher's certificate; (5) the restoration of an
adequate superannuation or pension plan; and (6) the abolition of
the system of payment by results.

Some of these points are now period-pieces, but taken together
they demonstrate the N.U.T.'s interest, from the very beginning, in
the work which teachers undertake, as well as in the conditions of
pay and service under which they carry on their employment. This
dual concern was undoubtedly farsighted and has provided the
recipe for the union's success over almost a century. Improvement in
the quality of education, and in public regard for it, leads inevitably to higher status and better conditions of work for those who
teach; conversely, the quality of education cannot improve unless
there are better teachers; but if better teachers are to be obtained,
service conditions, remuneration and the status of teachers in the
community must be made sufficiently attractive.

The ten-point declaration of 1870 also reveals the method by
which the union thought it could achieve its objectives. Teaching
should be a closed shop consisting of only those on the teacher
register; a high standard of entry should be set and only those who
achieved this standard should be admitted; those who qualified
should be registered; and the right to teach should be reserved for
those whose names appeared on the register. Registered teachers
should be permitted a large measure of freedom in practicing their
vocation.

Just how little fundamental change has taken place in the union's policies can be seen by comparing the 1870 statement with the aims set out in N.U.T. recruitment literature in 1965. These are stated as: (1) to improve the standing of teachers in the community by raising entrance qualifications and creating an all-university graduate teaching profession; (2) to obtain salaries and conditions of service which will enable teachers to enjoy a professional standard of life; (3) to secure for teachers a widows, orphans, and dependents pension plan similar to that in operation in the Civil Service; (4) to unite the teaching profession; and (5) to establish teaching as a self-governing profession. To some extent, these five points of present-day policy suggest failure over the intervening 100 years; teachers are still dissatisfied with their status, and professional unity is still a will o' the wisp. The main new point is that the desired closed shop for teachers should be operated and enforced by teachers themselves. By and large, however, the 1965 list illustrates a remarkable continuity of basic policy aims; in 1965, as in 1870, the one un-faltering desire of the N.U.T. is to see teaching established as a recognized profession.

Today, the union claims a membership of about 270,000, of whom approximately 60 per cent are women. There are two types of membership: full membership, which is open to all practicing teachers, whether heads or assistants, in any type of educational establishment; and associate membership, which is available to students preparing to become teachers. There is also a section for retired members, numbering about 28,000. Thus, about 70 per cent of all practicing teachers in primary and secondary schools, and considerably more than half of the total teaching force in England and Wales, are N.U.T. members. Since there are many teachers who join no union at all, it is clear that the vast majority of organized teachers fall within the N.U.T.'s purview.

The N.U.T. is a democratic organization, consisting of local associations, a national executive committee, and a policy-making annual conference. The annual conference is attended by at least two representatives of each local association. Motions are submitted either by the executive committee or by the local associations. Decisions of the annual conference are binding on both the executive and the local associations.

The 43-member executive committee consists of the president, the immediate past-president, a senior vice-president, a junior vice-president, a treasurer, and one representative each from the Association of Teachers in Technical Institutions (A.T.T.I.) and the Association of Teachers of Domestic Subjects (A.T.D.S.) with whom the union has a partnership agreement. The president, vice-presidents and treasurer are elected by a national postal ballot of all members of at least one year's standing in the union. The remaining 36 members are also elected by postal ballot, on a geographical basis. For this purpose the country is divided into 11 electoral regions, each returning two, three, or four members according to the size of its membership. Each local association may nominate candidates, and all members of one year's standing may vote. Elections are biannual and results are determined by a system of proportional representation. Once elected, the executive meets monthly.

The basic unit of organization is the local association; there are now 699 of these, covering the whole country. They range in size from perhaps 20 teachers in the smallest rural associations, to 4,000 or 5,000 in the larger county boroughs. Each local association is free to organize itself as it pleases, provided that its rules accord with the general rules of the union. Normally, each association elects at least a president, a secretary, a treasurer, and a local committee. Every teacher is eligible for membership and has local voting rights. In addition, local associations within a county normally join together to form a county association. There are 62 of these, each with its own officers and committees. County associations afford an opportunity for local associations to meet and talk with one another, but they have no formal place in the N.U.T. power structure.

In each of the 11 electoral areas there is a resident, regional officer, who is employed full-time by the union. This means that there is one such officer for every 24,000 members and some question has been raised whether this proportion is satisfactory. A considerable amount of work, including negotiations with local education authorities, inevitably falls on the shoulders of the honorary officers of the local associations, for whom union work is a leisure-time activity.[1]

[1] As a member of a city council, and therefore as an employer of many types of labor, I have been frequently involved in negotiations, both with teachers and with other workers. In dealing with industrial unions, many of which are far smaller than the N.U.T., I have always met a full-time officer, trained in the techniques of bargaining and compromise. In dealing with teachers, I have been invariably faced with teachers who have taken time from school to attend and

There is the same mixture of amateur and professional at the N.U.T.'s head office. Members of the national executive committee, who direct policy, devote considerable time and energy to the union, many of them traveling long distances to attend meetings. They are, however, working teachers; their professional careers are in the schools and colleges, and they conduct union business mainly in their leisure time. Full-time staff at the head office consists of the union's general secretary and some 230 others. Theoretically, this staff exists to carry out union policy, not to make it. In practice it is likely that senior permanent officials play a part in the formation of policy, as well as in executing it. The executive committee has six standing subcommittees—Finance and General Purposes, Membership and Organization, Law, Salaries and Superannuation, Education, and Public and International Relationships. Each executive committee member serves on at least two of these, but each subcommittee also has its full-time officers, who draw up agenda papers, supply information, prepare reports and working documents, and advise the members. If lack of adequate professional guidance is a weakness at local level, part of the N.U.T.'s national strength must lie in the successful marriage which it has brought about between elected representatives and highly competent, permanent, professional officers.

The scope of union activity can best be appreciated from a survey of some of the work carried out at the head office. A teacher, for example, may require union help because he has become involved with the law; he may find himself charged with assaulting a pupil, subjected to a claim for damages for alleged negligence arising from an accident to a pupil, or he may claim industrial injury to himself. The union provides free legal assistance to members in all matters affecting them in their professional capacity. Cases are normally handled by local associations, which engage solicitors (lawyers), who are in general law practice in their own area. At the head office, however, the Law and Tenure Department which has a full-time staff of two solicitors and a team of law clerks, has accumulated a store of expert knowledge on the law relating to teaching, and this knowledge is at the disposal of the local associations.

The Salaries and Superannuation Department specializes in (1)

state their case. The difference between professionalism and amateurism can be startling and I have often felt that teachers would be better served in union matters if they had more full-time officers on whom to call.

teachers' salaries; (2) teachers' superannuation (pension) contributions; (3) retired teachers' pensions; and (4) national insurance payments and benefits. It is this department which prepares the case for new salary claims, calls meetings of the teachers' representatives on official negotiating committees, and conducts the day-to-day work of applying salary agreements to individual cases. Not all teachers have salary problems; on the other hand, as he approaches retirement, almost every member consults the union about his pension rights. Legislation in the fields of superannuation and national insurance is complex, and individual cases can only receive justice if they are handled by men of experience in these fields.

Because education is a public service and teachers depend, ultimately, on the taxpayer both for their livelihood and for the conditions under which they work, public relations are probably of greater importance to a teachers' union than to most industrial unions. A climate of opinion favorable to the betterment of the teaching profession can only exist if the public has a favorable image of the teacher and accepts the importance of the work he does. Constant publicity is, therefore, an essential part of the N.U.T.'s activity, and the union's Publicity and Public Relations Department is responsible for more than 50 press releases a year. This department handles the publicity for union publications, conferences, and meetings; it is always available to answer inquiries from the press, and maintains relations with the group of educational correspondents to the press. It distributes documentary films dealing with educational topics, and since 1960 has made two television films, "I Want To Go To School," shown in 1960 to an audience of 15 million, and "Our School," which had an audience rating of 10 million from two showings in 1962. An educational exhibition at Olympia attracted 150,000 visitors; a subsequent exhibition, which toured the country in 1961 and 1962, drew a total attendance of 200,000.

The Publicity Department issues a stream of newspapers, leaflets, pamphlets, and discussion documents. "University and College Entrance," first published in 1960, is probably the best guide to Britain's complex university entrance requirements, and the "Annual Guide to Careers for Young People" provides a tabulation of qualifications and training required for entry to a wide range of occupations. It is clearly the N.U.T.'s belief that one way of arousing favorable public interest is to provide the public with a service.

Literature which is designed for the sole purpose of fostering recruitment of new members into the union is handled by a separate department.

The union has a section, the Education Department, which is entirely devoted to assisting the union to formulate its educational policy. The field which this department covers is as wide as education itself, and for this reason the standing subcommittee, which directs it, is itself assisted by a number of specially convened advisory committees. Each advisory committee deals with the work of a particular type of school or college and most of its members are directly elected, on a regional basis, by union members who teach in the particular type of establishment concerned. This enables the union to draw advice from a wider circle of competence than the executive itself, and the advisory committees have, therefore, an important place in the union's democratic structure.

The Education Department maintains close contact both with the central government and with local education authorities. It is represented on a variety of educational bodies, and serves on advisory committees set up by governmental departments and public corporations. It submits evidence to governmental commissions of inquiry and comments on drafts of governmental policy statements during their preparatory stages. In general, its speciality is the theory and practice of education, and the knowledge and experience in these fields which it has built up over the years, out of its nationwide contracts, is constantly called upon both by other departments of the union and by outside bodies.

The union conducts two separate organizations for the purpose of assisting members in need. The Teachers' Provident Society was founded by the union in 1877 and provides various forms of life insurance, a sickness benefit plan, annuities, and loans for the purchase of houses. It has 100,000 members and invested funds of more than £21,000,000. Only members of the N.U.T. can join, and the benefits offered are regarded as an important inducement to teachers to join the union. The Benevolent and Orphan Fund was also established in 1877, to assist teachers in sickness and need, and to aid widows and orphans of teachers. Today, the welfare state takes care of the basic needs for which the fund was first designed, but there are still circumstances in which additional help may be required. The fund is used to provide life annuities for incapacitated teachers or widows of teachers and to make grants to orphans of teachers and loans to teachers who are in temporary financial difficulties. It maintains a convalescent home and three homes for aged and infirm teachers. Altogether, the fund disburses £150,000 a year, which is raised by subscription, gifts, and social functions.

The N.U.T. is deeply concerned with the position of teachers overseas and maintains close relationships with teachers' organizations in other countries. It plays an important role in the work of both the Secondary Teachers International (FIPESO) and the Primary Teachers International (IFTA). The N.U.T.'s present general secretary, Sir Ronald Gould, has been president of the World Confederation of Organizations of the Teaching Profession (WCOTP) since its inception in 1952.

This sketch of the union's work has been necessarily brief; many of its activities have had to be omitted. Its story is one of general success. It has always been the largest of the teachers' unions in Great Britain, and continues to increase its membership each year. Its influence on education is considerable. It has high public standing, and the central government undoubtedly regards it as a power to be treated with respect. As mentioned earlier, there are a number of reasons for this success; the union has consistently sought to improve the condition of teachers by raising the quality and status of education; it retains the confidence of its members because it is they who control policy; at the same time, the union is large and wealthy enough to employ the professional services of able, and in many instances, outstanding officers. In addition, the union has the capacity to specialize. Many of the departments at the head office have a body of knowledge and experience in their particular fields which is unrivalled anywhere; consequently, members are offered more comprehensive services than they can obtain elsewhere. The N.U.T.'s professionalism and departmentalization are, of course, functions of its size; on the other hand, they play an important part in ensuring its continued growth.

The Joint Four

As mentioned before, the early N.U.E.T. set out to create a united profession, and in 1889 it dropped the word "elementary" from its name in order to demonstrate that it was not exclusively a combination of elementary school teachers. The move was timely because the number of grammar (i.e. middle-class) schools, both for boys and for girls, was then increasing. It is doubtful, however, if anything could have brought grammar and elementary school teachers together. During the final 30 years of the nineteenth century, each type of school had its own place in a social hierarchy. Upper- and upper-middle class pupils made use of a few well-known schools (such as Eton and Winchester). The old established grammar schools had been revived and refurbished to serve the needs of the new "middle" middle class. Elementary schools, which were used almost entirely by working-class pupils, sprouted "higher grade" schools or departments for children of upper-working class or lower-middle class origin. Elementary teachers were ex-elementary scholars, who had gained a certificate via the pupil-teacher system and the vocationally-oriented teacher training colleges; grammar school teachers were, for the most part, products of the grammar schools and the liberal universities. Elementary schools were state institutions; until 1902, grammar schools were entirely private.[2]

Grammar school teachers were just as anxious as their elementary colleagues to achieve professional status, but they also stood higher in the social order and were well aware that combination between themselves and teachers in elementary schools would diminish, not raise, their standing. Consequently, grammar school principals and assistant teachers in grammar schools formed their own combinations. The Association of Headmistresses was formed in 1874, the Assistant Mistresses followed in 1885, the Headmasters in 1890, and the Assistant Masters in 1892. These associations set up a joint committee in 1919, through which a tradition of cooperation has been created. In its statement of evidence to the Royal Commission on Trade Unions and Employers Associations in 1966, the Joint Four summarize their aims as being "to promote the cause of education generally; to protect and improve conditions of service and further the legitimate professional interests of teachers; to obtain for teachers the status and authority of a learned profession; to initiate and promote or oppose legislative or administrative mea-

---

[2] The school boards, which had been established under the 1870 Education Act for the purpose of supplementing voluntary provision of elementary schools with schools financed from a local rate, were abolished in 1902. Elementary schools, both board and voluntary, were handed over to the local councils of their area. County and county borough councils were also permitted to establish "secondary" schools, which offered a grammar school type of education. Teachers in these new schools tended to combine with teachers in private grammar schools, despite the fact that they had the same employers as their elementary colleagues.

sures in Parliament or elsewhere conducive to the attainment of these aims." All these seem to differ very little from the aims of the N.U.T. Historically, however, different status, different employers, different rates of pay, and different social aspirations have all added up to a division of interests which so far has not been bridged. Although the rules of the Joint Four associations do not prohibit members from other types of secondary schools, in practice members have been drawn predominantly from grammar schools.

Each of the four associations maintains its own separate, but parallel, organization. Local branches elect their own officers and committees. Members of each association elect their own national officers and executive council. All four headquarters, although separate, share the same building. Methods of working vary from one organization to another, but by and large all four associations do much the same things.

Because the associations restrict their recruitment (1) to secondary schools, (2) to a single sex, and (3) to heads or assistants, but not both, each tends to be small; the Headmistresses, for example, have a total active membership of only 1,000, plus 400 retired heads. Full-time staffs also tend to be small. The largest is that of the Assistant Masters, who have five officers and some additional clerical assistance; the Headmistresses have no professional aid at all. It was probably individual weakness, as well as common interest, which led the associations to form the Joint Committee of 1919, and to reconstitute it in 1946 as a Joint Executive Committee through which the four organizations could act together.

The joint committee has 28 members—seven from each association—who are appointed annually by the executive committees of the constituent associations. The Headmasters and Headmistresses hold the chairmanship and vice-chairmanship in turn; the full-time secretaries of the assistant Masters and Assistant Mistresses hold office together as permanent joint honorary secretaries. Local Joint Four committees have also been set up in almost all local education authority areas. As a general rule, casework, involving a member's salary or tenure, is handled by the association to which he belongs. Each association may also make its own pronouncements on matters of educational or professional policy. On the other hand, there are occasions when it would be a waste of time and energy for each association to act separately; thus, a model contract of service for teachers in private schools was the product of the joint committee, since it was a matter of equal concern to all. In addition, any matter referred by central government departments or local authorities, either to the joint committee or to a single association, is handled by the joint committee.

The N.A.H.T.

As the number of trained teachers increased toward the end of the nineteenth century, it became possible to divide pupils into classes, and to give each class its own separate room and its own teacher. A wedge was now driven between school heads (principals), who were endowed with a certain degree of autonomy and responsibility for running the school, and class teachers who, although not employed by the head, were nevertheless under his control. A Class Teachers Association, formed in 1890, opted to remain as a section of the N.U.T.; operating within the larger body, it did valuable work in making rank and file opinion known to the union leaders. The principals, however, formed their own association, the National Association of Head Teachers (N.A.H.T.), in 1897, and have remained separate ever since. A recent recruitment leaflet states proudly that the N.A.H.T. was founded "by Head Teachers for Head Teachers," and adds, "Head Teachers long ago realised that by forming a National Association they could ensure that their views on educational and professional matters were properly represented; and that such an Association would provide opportunity for meeting together to discuss the problems arising from their special responsibilities."

The N.A.H.T. is open to men and women heads of any type of school and therefore recruits members who are also eligible to join the N.U.T., the Headmasters, or the Headmistresses. A considerable number of its members belong, in fact, both to the N.A.H.T. and to one of these other organizations—mainly to the N.U.T. Total membership of the N.A.H.T. is 15,000—about 55 per cent of all heads.

The N.A.H.T. is organized into 260 local associations, and maintains a central office, a single full-time paid officer, and limited clerical assistance; the central office is too small to house committee meetings, which have to be held in a hotel. As with all the unions, the governing body is its annual conference, and business between conferences is carried on by a council elected by the membership. The Association is prepared to deal with matters of salary, pensions, and tenure, and claims to have built up a body of special knowledge on matters affecting heads. Personal benefits offered to members include insurance against legal liability for accidents to staff or pupils. The Association publishes a quarterly, *The Head Teachers Review,* and issues circular letters at regular intervals in order to keep members informed.

The N.A.S.

The policy of the National Association of Schoolmasters (N.A.S.) is (1) to safeguard and promote the interests of men engaged in the teaching profession, (2) to insure recognition of the social and economic responsibilities of men teachers, (3) to insure adequate representation of schoolmasters on any committees concerned with education, (4) to provide the Ministry of Education, and local education authorities, with the advice of experienced schoolmasters, and (5) to recruit every schoolmaster into the N.A.S. It is, therefore, a union with a mission.

It was formed in 1923, by men who had fought in World War I, at a time when the official national salary scales for teachers were first under consideration. It was clear that women would continue to be paid on a lower scale than men, and this led to the fear that, in a competitive market, local authorities would tend to favor the employment of women. Many schoolmasters also believed that the N.U.T., with a predominantly female membership, would be half-hearted in its promotion of the male interest. Without in any way being antifeminist or advocating that women should be relegated to the kitchen, the N.A.S. has championed the schoolmasters' cause by making two demands which are not included in the aims of any other teacher union. These are: (1) that all boys over the age of seven should be taught mainly by men, and (2) that schoolmasters should not serve under women heads.

Membership of the N.A.S. is open to heads and assistants from any type of school. Members must be qualified teachers and they must accept the doctrines of the association. The overall membership, including retired members and students who are still at college, is now about 30,000; the association is, therefore, correct in its claim that it is the largest organization of all-male teachers in the country; but, since there are more than 100,000 men teachers in primary and secondary schools, it is clearly a long way from its goal of organizing all males in the profession.

The organization and structure of the N.A.S. are very similar to those of the N.U.T. There are 400 local associations, which are left very much on their own. Policy is determined centrally by an annual conference of local association representatives. Members also elect the national officers and executive committee. There are six full-time officers and an adequate clerical staff at the central headquarters, but the Association has no paid officials in the regions. Since its aim is to enroll all men teachers, it has to offer as full a range of services and benefits as can be obtained from other unions. It offers free legal advice and defense; although it does not employ its own full-time legal staff, it has retained the same firm of private solicitors for almost 40 years. Insurance plans cover loss by fire, or by theft of personal property or cash at school, third party risk for accidents to pupils in a teacher's care, and payment for death or disability. A Benevolent Fund is operated by a central committee. The N.A.S. publishes *The New Schoolmaster* and a wide range of leaflets, pamphlets, and books.

The A.T.T.I.

Technical education has developed considerably since the beginning of the century. At that time, the main work of technical teachers was to prepare part-time students (craftsmen, technicians, and office workers) for examinations set either by the City and Guilds of London Institute, or by the Science and Art Department, a governmental agency, now defunct. Remuneration of technical teachers was low; they had no salary scales or pension plans and no voice in the examinations for which they prepared their pupils. Technical education was frowned upon by professional men who had received their own education in liberal institutions and also by industrialists who believed that it led to the indiscriminate distribution of trade secrets. Founders of the Association of Teachers in Technical Institutions, the A.T.T.I., in 1905, had, therefore, two objectives—first, to protect their members, and, second, to sell the idea of technical education to the public. These are still very much the aims of the A.T.T.I., even in the changed climate of today.

The Association recruits its members from every type of post-secondary college and institution, with the exception of teacher training colleges and universities, which are organized by the Association of Teachers in Colleges and Departments of Education, the A.T.C.D.E., and the Association of University Teachers, the

A.U.T., respectively. The A.T.T.I. has members, however, in colleges which train technical teachers and also in the technological departments of universities. Present total membership is 24,000, of whom ten per cent are women and 1,000 are part-time teachers. There are 330 local branches.

Nationally, the association has the usual honorary officers and executive council, elected by the members, and its full-time staff includes a general secretary, a deputy secretary, and three officials who deal, respectively, with finance, publicity, and information. The A.T.T.I. has also entered into a partnership agreement with the N.U.T., under which A.T.T.I. members who are full-time teachers are automatically enrolled as full members of the N.U.T. without extra charge. This means that A.T.T.I. members are entitled to the help of the N.U.T.'s legal department, and receive exactly the same protection, coverage, and indemnity as ordinary N.U.T. members. The practical gain from this partnership to a small organization is obvious. The A.T.T.I. preserves its own identity and its special function; at the same time, it offers its members services which only a much larger organization can provide. But both the A.T.T.I. and the N.U.T. see in the arrangement something more than a pragmatic solution to a small union's difficulties; they regard it as a contribution toward professional unity and an example which they hope other unions will follow.

The A.T.C.D.E.

This is a quite separate union, organizing teaching staff engaged in the training of teachers, whether in training colleges (colleges of education) or in the education departments of universities. It arose in 1943 from an amalgamation of two bodies, the Training College Association and the Association of Training College Principals. Staffs of the university departments of education (U.D.E.s) were also included in the new association in order to strengthen the links between training colleges and the universities. Today, the A.T.C.D.E. claims the membership of the principals of each of the 170 colleges of education, all heads of university institutes of education, most of the heads of the U.D.E.s, and about four-fifths of all teaching staff in the colleges of education. Membership from staffs of U.D.E.s has declined, no doubt because teachers in these departments look to the A.U.T. as their natural trade union and are unwilling to pay a separate subscription to an organization which, to them, is merely another forum for educational discussion. Total membership of the A.T.C.D.E. in 1965 was about 4,300.

The unit of administration is the college branch, which communicates directly with headquarters. Regional branches, which organize their own committees and meetings, are a means by which college groups can come together and discuss common problems, but, like the county associations of the N.U.T., they have little function in the structure of command. The association is governed by its annual conference and its elected council. National officers are a chairman, past-chairman, vice-chairman, and treasurer. The vice-chairman is elected by postal vote and becomes chairman the following year. It is traditional that this office should be held alternately by a man and a woman.

Until recently the association was served by an honorary secretary for two days a week. With the tremendous growth in the numbers now engaged in teacher training, this system has broken down, and the first full-time general secretary (a former college principal) took office in 1966. He has a staff of five. The Clearing House for student admissions to colleges of education, which was first set up by the A.T.C.D.E., is still housed in its offices. The association conducts salary negotiations, provides members with legal aid and protection, and arranges favorable terms for house, car, and personal insurance. It publishes its own quarterly, *Education for Teaching,* a yearbook, and a variety of newssheets, brochures, and memoranda.

The A.U.T.

It is so common in England to regard university teachers as members of the upper classes that it is strange to find them combining for the same ends, and in the same way, as industrial workers. That they have done so is a reflection of the changing nature of universities and university conditions. During World War I, nonprofessorial teachers, who had been growing in numbers, resented the fact that they had no voice in the government of the institutions in which they taught; corporate control was held by professors. The first moves toward unionization of university teachers were made, therefore, by lecturers, and were directed against professors; these early attempts expressed internal frustration within university staffs. But by 1919 this situation had changed and professors and lecturers found themselves united. Two things had happened to bring this about; the central government, which was giving increasing financial aid to universities, had set up the University Grants Committee (U.G.C.) as a central agency through which it could channel its subsidy; and the vice-chancellors and principals of universities had formed themselves into a committee for the purposes of formulating common policies and conducting a dialogue with the U.G.C. Thus professors and lecturers alike were now excluded from a voice in many areas of vital importance to their interests, and the Association of University Teachers, the A.U.T., came into being. The rules of the A.U.T. express its aims in a single sentence: "The objects of the Association shall be the advancement of University Education and Research and the promotion of common action by University Teachers and the safeguarding of the interests of the members."

The A.U.T. now has a membership of about 13,000. It constitutes the United Kingdom section of the International Association of University Professors and Lecturers and is the only union dealt with in this study whose members come from Scotland as well as from England and Wales. Each university forms a local branch for its own staff, and these branches have considerable autonomy in deciding their own policy on matters of local concern. As a national organization, the A.U.T. is a federation of the local associations. It is governed by a council, consisting of representatives of the local associations, which meets, normally, only twice yearly. The council itself nominates six officers (a president, four vice-presidents of whom at least two must be ex-presidents, and a treasurer) and 15 of its members who, together with the officers, two Scottish representatives, and not more than three co-opted members, make up the executive committee. This structure, which avoids direct election of officers and executive by the general membership, is the most hierarchical of all the unions. The executive, which reports to the council, has surrounded itself with about 30 subcommittees—many more than the other unions find necessary. There is a full-time staff of ten.

The union's main work is probably in connection with salaries and superannuation. It has an honorary legal advisor and legal aid (or financial assistance toward legal costs) can be given to members who are in dispute with their institution or involved in legal action arising from their professional work. A benevolent fund is being set up. Publications include *The British Universities Annual* and the quarterly *A.U.T. Bulletin* in addition to a variety of occasional reports on such subjects as university organization and pension plans. Members are given an annual handbook containing details of various trading concessions and income tax agreements which have been negotiated for them.

THE UNIONS AT WORK

Negotiation

If we compare what teachers receive today with what they were paid immediately prior to World War II, it can be shown that, in terms of real purchasing power, teachers' salaries have advanced very little. Since 1939, the wage differential between teachers and certain other classes of workers has actually altered to the disadvantage of teachers. Few teachers believe that they are paid enough. Officers and executive members of all the unions are constantly exhorted by rank and file members to be more militant than they are. Nevertheless, a century of union agitation has had its results and prizes have been won, not least in the fields of pay and pensions. As far back as 1898, the N.U.T. was successful in obtaining a governmental pension plan for elementary school teachers, which was comparable to that enjoyed by civil servants; this plan, with modifications, has since been extended to all types of teachers, except university teachers. The right of most teachers to national minimum salary scales, enforceable by law, was won in 1919, when the first Burnham committee, to be explained shortly, was set up.

About one teacher in every 15 is employed in a private school outside the state system. Some nonstate schools are run as a business, for private profit; teachers in these schools are employed by the proprietor. Other private schools are controlled by nonprofit-making trusts, and teachers in them are employed by governing bodies. During the present period of acute shortage of teachers, private, independent schools which cannot afford to pay national rates are driven to employ unqualified teachers; on the other hand, more prosperous schools frequently pay above national levels in order to attract teachers away from the state schools. This is an area of private bargaining, and the unions are not likely to intervene in it. They are, nonetheless, opposed to the employment of unqualified teachers. With the possible exception of the Joint Four, which has members in independent schools, the unions also believe that the practice of enticing staff by offers of higher pay leads to an unfair distribution of teachers throughout the nation's schools as a whole.

Most teachers have their contracts of service with one or other of the 162 local education authorities, and are paid in accordance with the national scales applicable to the type of work which they do. Scales are arrived at through negotiation between teachers and their employers. For this purpose, a number of committees has been established by Act of Parliament. Salaries of teachers in primary and secondary schools are negotiated in a "Burnham" committee, a second "Burnham" committee deals with teachers in technical colleges, and a similar committee for teachers in colleges of education is known as the "Pelham" committee. Each committee is made up of two independent panels, one of employers, the other of teachers, sitting under a neutral chairman who is appointed by the Minister of Education.[3] The employers' side consists of a representative of the Minister, and representatives of the various national associations of local authorities. The Minister himself determines which associations will be represented, and prescribes the number of delegates to which each association is entitled. The teachers' panel is composed of representatives of the unions, and here, too, it is the Minister who selects the unions and specifies the number of seats which each union can take up. Both panels are of equal size (see Tables 1 and 2). If they reach agreement, the Minister issues an official order, under the Remuneration of Teachers Act, 1965, giving statutory force to the recommendations, which are then legally binding on all local education authorities. If the panels cannot agree, the Minister appoints, or asks the Minister of Labor to appoint, arbitrators; except in specified circumstances of national emergency or economic crisis, the Minister of Education is bound to accept the decision of the arbitrators and make an order putting it into effect.

[3] Between 1899 and 1944, the governmental department responsible for education was known as the Board of Education, and the minister in charge was President of the Board of Education. The Board was abolished by the Education Act of 1944, and replaced by the Ministry of Education, headed by the Minister of Education. A further change took place in 1964, when the Ministry became the Department of Education and Science, and the Minister changed his title to Secretary of State for Education and Science. To avoid confusion, the department has been called the Ministry, and the head of the department the Minister, throughout this article, irrespective of the year under consideration.

TABLE 1. NUMBER OF SEATS HELD BY TEACHERS' UNIONS ON COMMITTEES FOR NEGOTIATING SALARIES

Committee	N.U.T.	J.F.	N.A.S.	N.A.H.T.	A.T.C.D.E.	A.T.T.I.
Burnham: Primary and Secondary	15	6	2	1	–	4
Burnham: Further or Continuing Education	2	–	–	–	–	6
Burnham: Local Education Authority Inspectors and Organizers	4	–	–	–	–	–
Burnham: Youth Leaders (Social Workers with Youths)	2	–	–	–	–	–
Pelham: Colleges of Education	–	–	–	–	12	–
Joint Negotiating Committee for Approved Schools and Remand Homes (Reform Schools)	6	–	–	–	–	–

TABLE 2. PRESENT COMPOSITION OF THE BURNHAM COMMITTEE FOR PRIMARY AND SECONDARY SCHOOLS

Chairman ⎱ Appointed by the
Deputy-chairman ⎰ Minister of Education

Management Panel		Teachers' Panel	
County Councils Association	9	N.U.T.	15
Assoc. of Municipal Corporations	6	A.T.T.I.	4
Assoc. of Education Committees	6	A.M.A.	2
Inner London Education Authority	3	A.A.M.I.	2
Welsh Joint Education Committee	2	I.A.H.M.	1
Minister of Education	2	A.H.M.I.	1
		N.A.H.T.	1
		N.A.S.	2

Joint Hon. Secretaries: Sir William Alexander—Management
Sir Ronald Gould —Teachers

This procedure makes the Minister a key figure in negotiations. There are good reasons for this: although teachers are paid by local authorities, both the amount of pay and the manner in which it is distributed are of considerable concern to the central government. Approximately 55 per cent of local authority income from taxation comes from the national exchequer, which can therefore claim to provide a large part of teachers' salaries. It is also of considerable importance to the central government that it should have a firm voice concerning all public expenditures as part of national fiscal planning. The Minister of Education, who is responsible for national educational policy, must also be in a position to channel whatever public money is available in the directions where he thinks it will do most good. Through his representative on the employers' panel, he is able to give early notice of the amount of possible increase which the government finds tolerable, and also to convey to the committee his own ideas as to how the sum should be distributed. At the same time, teachers' interests are safeguarded by the provision of machinery for arbitration. Perhaps the most disquieting feature of Burnham procedure, however, is the Minister's right to nominate the parties who sit round the table. In effect, the Minister, who is the chief employer, can manipulate the body with which he negotiates, by raising or lowering the number of seats allocated to particular unions, or by favoring certain unions to the exclusion of others. The N.A.S., for example, has only recently gained a place on the Burnham committee, after a prolonged and bitter fight. It is true that the composition of the teachers' panel, once it has been established, can only be altered by Parliament; but Parliament is also a part of the governmental machine. That the teaching unions can only negotiate through Burnham, and are barred by law from dealing independently with their employers, can be regarded as an infringement of the right of free bargaining.

Salary scales for university teachers are fixed by the Minister of Education, on advice from the University Grants Committee. The A.U.T. has right of access to the U.G.C., but there is no formal negotiating machinery. This is a matter of serious concern to the A.U.T.

After a lengthy campaign, teachers obtained a national pension plan in 1898. The basis of this plan was that throughout their working life teachers would pay a proportion of their salaries into a central fund to which employing authorities would also make a contribution. The fund had to be permanently solvent; teachers' contributions were regularly deducted from their pay, and were compulsory. Although there have been modifications in detail, the plan which is in operation today still follows the same broad lines. Teachers have consistently objected to the compulsory levy; they regard it as a reduction of salary and have consistently fought for a noncontributory plan. Their moment of triumph came in 1918, when a generous noncontributory scheme was introduced; but the new plan, though it met the wishes of the unions, failed to survive the economic crisis of 1922. Teachers' contributions were restored and have, in fact, been increased since that time.

During their long history, the unions have frequently used strikes, or the threat of strikes, in order to gain their ends. In 1907, the N.U.T. withdrew labor from schools in West Ham. Sixty schools were closed in Herefordshire in 1914, and between 1917 and 1919 militant action took place in 32 areas, including the Rhondda, where W. G. Cove (then a class-teacher, later president of the N.U.T., and a member of Parliament) brought out the whole of the teaching force. In all these instances, the dispute was about wages, and there is no doubt that the resoluteness of the N.U.T. on these occasions influenced the government and led to the establishment of national minimum scales in 1919. Since that time teachers have exercised pressure in less dramatic ways. In 1964, when a bill was introduced into Parliament for the purpose of raising teachers' pension contributions from five to six per cent of their salaries, the N.U.T. retaliated by asking its members to abstain from collecting the money which some children bring to school each week to deposit in the school's savings bank. This was too much for the Joint Four, which condemned the N.U.T.'s attitude. On the other hand, when the N.A.S. went further, and proposed a ban on collecting money for school dinners, the N.U.T. condemned the N.A.S. The unions came close to striking in 1950–51, in protest against a ruling of Durham County Council that, in future, it would only employ trade unionists. The Minister of Education intervened and directed the Durham authority to withdraw the application of this ruling to teachers; but it must seem strange to other unions that the only cause in recent history which has united the teachers' unions and driven them in concert to the brink of direct industrial action, has been their opposition to a public authority which was trying to strengthen trade unionism.

The N.A.S. has always been more belligerent than the other unions. Only one-ninth the size of the N.U.T., it has assumed the role of gadfly. There are good reasons for this. It fought against equal pay for men and women, believing that equal pay in a profession dominated by women would lead to salary scales unsatisfactory to men. Now that equal pay has been granted, it fights for more pay for more family responsibility. The N.A.S. fears that the N.U.T., with its preponderance of women members, will not enter a real fight. There is no obvious evidence that this is so; nevertheless, the

N.A.S. has continued to take a series of actions which have drawn attention to its own militancy. Its campaign culminated, in 1966, in the withdrawal of N.A.S. labor for one week, in a number of selected areas, in protest against remarks made by Sir William Alexander, Secretary of the Association of Education Committees, which the N.A.S. (but nobody else) construed as disparaging to the teaching profession.

It is unlikely that the Joint Four would ever participate in industrial action of a serious nature. The A.U.T. has occasionally considered striking in connection with delay in settling pay claims, but has never pursued the matter; it believes that few of its members would support a strike, and that university teachers owe a legal and moral duty to provide their services to students. This last point is, of course, important for all teachers. Even if they can shed their white-collar attitude toward industrial action, they are very conscious that a strike by teachers hurts children.

Since 1885, teachers have safeguarded their interests by obtaining seats in Parliament or on local authorities. The N.U.T. makes a contribution toward the election expenses of a limited number of candidates for Parliament, usually not more than four or five, and pays a small retainer to any of these who are elected. Candidates who are sponsored in this way are chosen irrespective of their party allegiance and it is well understood that acceptance of union support in no way abrogates their independence. If elected, however, they are available to assist with the passage of legislation in which the union is interested, and which they themselves support. This policy has been of advantage to the N.U.T. on more than one occasion. For example, when the Teachers' Superannuation Bill was being debated in 1925, Members of Parliament who were sponsored by the union persuaded Parliament to accept amendments which had been drafted outside the House, by the N.U.T. itself. Apart from the N.U.T., the N.A.S. is the only other union of teachers which seeks a direct voice in Parliament. The A.U.T. considered doing so, but rejected the idea.[4] The N.U.T. is also willing to

4 The 1969 Parliament contained a number of notable members who were ex-teachers. Dr. Horace King (Speaker of the House of Commons), Mr. Michael Stewart (Foreign Secretary), Mr. Edward Short (Secretary of State for Education and Science), and Miss Alice Bacon (Minister of State in the Department of Education) all had strong N.U.T. connections. Others who had taught in schools or universities included Mr. Harold Wilson (Prime Minister), Mr. Fred Peart (Leader of the House of Commons), Mr. Richard Crossman (Minister for Health and Social Security), and Mr. Anthony Crosland (President of the Board of Trade).

contribute toward the expenses of any of its members who seek election to a local education authority. Members of any political party will be supported; in theory, the N.U.T. could have a financial stake in each of the contestants for a particular seat.

Consultation

Teachers' unions are officially represented on a wide variety of committees of national importance. A few of these are listed in Table 3, which illustrates the range of union activity in this field; so many organizations seek advice from unions that it would be impossible to provide a full list here. (The N.U.T., for example, is represented on upwards of 125 bodies.) Table 3 also shows how organizations make use of union assistance. Thus, the Schools Council for Curriculum and Examinations, a governmental advisory and research body which deals with matters of common concern to all educational establishments, draws on each of the unions (except the A.U.T.) and allots representation to each in accordance with its size. On the other hand, the Central Industrial Training Council, which has national supervision over training within industry, calls only upon the A.T.T.I. By giving representation to union members, national organizations set in motion a two-way process: they gain the experience of teachers; at the same time, the unions, through their representatives, become more aware of what is taking place in the world of education outside the classroom.

Contact between the unions and governmental departments is made in a variety of ways. The Minister of Education rarely refuses to receive an official union delegation. Senior officers of the various unions soon learn their way around the corridors of power, and most of them succeed in establishing personal relationships with officers of ministries and local authority associations. It is always useful for union leaders to know how governmental officials are thinking. Unions have, however, an important formal role in the policy-making process. It is customary in Britain for governmental departments to produce trial drafts of proposed developments or changes in policy, which they circulate to interested parties, such as local authorities. This enables a Minister to test consumer reaction to his proposals and to widen the area of technical advice on which he bases his conclusions. Preliminary drafts of proposals which affect education are submitted to the teachers' union as a matter of course, and the unions are able to comment freely upon them. This practice is unofficial; there is no legal obligation upon a ministry to obtain advice from teachers. In other governmental fields, unions are usually consulted only on matters affecting wages and conditions of service. That teachers' unions are brought into consultation on matters of educational policy is probably because they are not just labor unions, but also professional associations; in this latter capacity they are the presumed repositories of technical expertise

TABLE 3. SAMPLE LIST OF COMMITTEES OR ORGANIZATIONS ON WHICH UNIONS ARE REPRESENTED, AND THE NUMBER OF SEATS HELD BY EACH UNION [a]

Committee or Organization	N.U.T.	J.F.	N.A.S.	N.A.H.T.	A.T.C.D.E.	A.T.T.I.
Schools Council for Curriculum and Examinations	11	6	7	2	4	2
National Council for the Supply of Teachers Overseas	2	2	1	1	1	1
Council for National Academic Awards	–	–	–	–	–	2
National Foundation for Educational Research	10	4	–	1	1	1
National Committee for Audio-Visual Aids in Education	8	4	1	–	2	2
Ministry of Labor National Youth Employment Council	2	1	–	–	–	1
Central Industrial Training Council	–	–	–	–	–	1
British Association for Commercial and Industrial Education	2	–	–	1	–	2
British Standards Institution	2	–	1	1	1	–
B.B.C. School Broadcasting Council	4	4	–	1	2	1

[a] Unions are frequently represented on subcommittees of organizations, even when they are not represented on the parent body. Such representation is not shown here.

which is not available elsewhere. In their advisory role, the unions have influenced educational legislation and developments, particularly on points of detail. In 1964, for example, when the Minister of Education proposed to promote curriculum development in schools through the centralized Schools Council, teachers feared that their freedom to choose what they teach was in danger, and that the new council might mark the resumption of state prescription of the curriculum—something unknown in England for more than 70 years. During the round of discussions which took place, the unions successfully insisted that majority control of the council should be in the hands of teachers, not of ministry officials; and it is safe to assume that the council will now function as an advisory body, with no powers to direct. This is an excellent instance of what teachers' unions gain by also being the recognized associations of the teaching profession.

There are, of course, topics on which the government acts for itself, without reference to the unions. In 1958, for example, the government ignored teachers' protests against changes in the method of subsidizing local education authorities from the national exchequer; money, which had hitherto been voted specifically for educational purposes, was consolidated with other subventions into a single general grant to local authorities. It was not clear at the time what effect this change would have on educational provision; it was, however, part of a larger plan of financial reform and teachers were not consulted.

Similarly, in 1965, the Minister of Education launched his plan for replacing selective secondary schools by comprehensive schools, without asking the unions to comment upon the principles involved. Segregation of children at the age of 11 into schools of different status is regarded as a social question, which the community, acting through Parliament, must resolve for itself. Once the principle has been established, there are a number of consequential matters on which teachers have much to say that is relevant. Plans for reorganizing secondary schools in a particular area should be drawn up by people possessing the necessary technical knowledge; in most areas, reorganization means that some small schools will be closed and other schools enlarged, and changes of this sort affect teachers' salaries, tenure, and status. Therefore, in his circular letter to local authorities, in July, 1965, the Minister of Education made it clear that the principle of comprehensive secondary education was one for public decision, but stressed the importance of consulting teachers on matters of implementation. It is not always easy to draw a firm line between the public province and the area of teachers' interest, but the right of the people to draw such a line is important in a democratic society.

The honorary officers of local branches of the unions work as closely as possible with their local education authorities; they are usually well known to education officers and members of education committees. Local authorities are permitted to co-opt on to their education committees men or women who have special knowledge of education, and, under this rule, it is not uncommon to find representatives of the teachers sitting as full members of the committees which employ them. The number of teachers co-opted in this way varies from authority to authority. Most education committees have at least one; some have three, representing the three stages of education—primary, secondary, and further—into which English educational establishments are divided. Teachers choose for themselves who shall represent them, and a publicly organized ballot is conducted, but, to be successful, candidates normally need the backing of a union.

Direct representation of teachers on their employing body provides a useful two-way line of communication between committees and the teachers they employ. Apart from this formal link, however, consultation tends to be sporadic, and on an ad hoc basis. Permanent joint-consultative machinery, now an established feature in English industry, is virtually unknown in education. This is partly because few teachers are aware of what happens in industry and partly because, if they know what happens, they do not consider industrial practice applicable to a profession. Labor relations within education are, therefore, mainly on a personal basis and are as good or as bad as the people involved in them.

The Quest for Unity and Status

One of the chief difficulties which faces both central and local government in their dealings with teachers is the absence of any single body which can speak for teachers as a whole. Each union was created to serve a particular sectional interest, and the formative years of institutions, no less than of individuals, tend to freeze them into postures from which they find it difficult to emerge. Even the N.U.T., which comes nearest to being a general union for the whole profession, recruits mainly from primary schools and secondary modern schools, and attracts relatively few members from grammar schools or higher education. Teachers in higher education remain firmly divided between the A.T.C.D.E. and the A.U.T.

The unions themselves are well aware of the weakness which comes from fragmentation, and some of them have made efforts to come together. The N.U.T. has joint membership arrangements not only with the A.T.T.I., but also with the Association of Teachers of Domestic Subjects, the Association of Agricultural Education Staffs, the Association of Teachers in Penal Establishments, and the Association for Adult Education. The A.T.C.D.E. and A.U.T. have a joint liaison committee for the discussion of common problems;

and, of course, the four secondary school associations are formally federated. Changes which are now taking place in the structure of English education may eventually lead to still further combinations between unions. The coming of universal comprehensive secondary education, for example, will diminish the need for separate grammar school associations. Links between teacher training colleges and universities grow stronger each year, and the reasons for teachers in these institutions to maintain separate unions are rapidly disappearing. Similarly, with the growth of colleges of higher education outside the university system, the interests of the A.T.T.I. and the A.U.T. should come closer together. The powerful forces which created separate unions in the past, however, are still at work today, and still keep the profession divided. Despite the social progress of the last 60 years, there is still a recognizable pecking-order of educational establishments. In public regard, universities are still socially superior to the teacher training colleges and institutes of technology; grammar schools are socially superior to secondary modern schools. Teachers in schools which are more highly valued by society, inevitably enjoy a higher social status which they are loth to lose. All the signs are that teachers in the autonomous universities will continue to oppose the provision of courses of university standard in colleges maintained by public local authorities and will fight bitterly to prevent further governmental interference in university affairs. Sections of grammar school teachers will continue their rearguard action against the spread of comprehensive schools. These conflicts are more social than educational, but, while they last, they deepen the cleavages within the teaching profession. It is clear that the leaders of every union will need to display the highest qualities of statesmanship and forebearance, if they are to achieve professional unity in present circumstances.

Many teachers want to administer their own profession, by controlling training requirements and entrance qualifications, by maintaining a register of those who are permitted to teach, and by exercising the right to discipline or disqualify teachers at their own discretion. From 1870, the N.U.T fought hard to obtain a registration council for teachers, analogous to the autonomous General Medical Council which Parliament had set up in 1858; but a registration movement sponsored by a union of elementary school teachers was, perhaps, never likely to succeed. An official register was, indeed, commenced in 1902, but with the government, not the teaching profession, in control. The government determined the qualifications which entitled a teacher to enrollment, and the council, which the government itself appointed for the purpose of administering the register, had little to do beyond verifying that teachers had the qualifications which they claimed. Even so, out of 12 places on the council, only one was entrusted to an elementary teacher; the others were filled by more socially acceptable men and women from schools for the upper classes. Neither the council, nor the list which it maintained, were relevant to the N.U.T.'s aspirations; the project was abandoned in 1949.

One of the reasons for the N.U.T.'s failure was lack of positive support from other unions. Self-government, on the basis of one man, one vote, implied government by teachers in elementary schools. The secondary school unions could not accept this, nor could the British government, whose members were drawn from the same social and educational class as secondary school teachers. Because of their social standing, the secondary schools associations—particularly the Headmasters and Headmistresses—have always exercised a degree of influence over educational policy-makers which is out of proportion to their numerical strength. Many teachers concluded, therefore, that if self-government was to be anything more than a dream, the unions would first have to come to terms with themselves. A profession which was divided by conflicting interests and aspirations was not likely to be entrusted with the right to administer its own affairs. Even if a central council for the profession were to be established, it could only govern for as long as its members pulled in the same direction. Further progress seemed to depend, therefore, on the construction of some overall organizational framework within which teachers could pursue matters of general concern in concert, without placing their particular sectional interests at risk. What form could this structure take?

Between the years 1924 and 1931, union leaders made a serious attempt to create a single, consolidated union for all teachers. A form of federation was proposed, under which each constituent association would retain its self-identity; a common council, comprising representatives of each association, was to be set up, with power to lay down policy and speak on behalf of the entire profession. An association which disagreed with a decision of the common council would have the right of veto, and could continue to pursue its own policy. The profession would thus show a united front on matters on which all associations were agreed, but each union was free to act in opposition. In practice, federation on these terms offered teachers nothing which they did not already possess; it did not require a formal constitution to permit unions to cooperate among themselves in areas of common agreement, and the proposed structure did little to bring unions together on issues which divided them. But it was not just the difficulty of producing an acceptable constitution which gradually led the unions to abandon the idea of a superunion. They took the view that there is an appreciable difference between the functions of a labor union and those of a professional council and that the two functions can, in fact, conflict. A professional council, which decides not only who shall teach, but also who shall be excluded from employment, exercises some of the powers of an employer; trade unions exist to give added strength to an individual who is in dispute with his employer. If a trade union is itself a component part of management, the advantage which the individual derives from union membership may be dissipated. Since the end of World War II, teachers therefore came to believe that a professional council should be separate from the unions.

In 1960, a working party consisting of representatives of the N.U.T., the Joint Four, the N.A.S., the N.A.H.T., and the A.T.C.D.E., was set up to reconsider the whole question of self-government. The A.U.T. sent an observer, and the body was also joined by representatives of the Headmasters' Conference—an association speaking for about 150 of the most famous private schools for the upper classes. The group was, therefore, completely representative. Its agreed-upon findings, announced in 1964, were that Parliament should again be asked to establish a Teachers' General Council, with similar powers to those held by the General Medical Council of the British Medical Association. This council would be an independent statutory body with which the unions could negotiate freely, as necessity arose. Unlike the registration council of 1902, however, it should be elected by teachers and be free from governmental control. It is not clear how it was intended to arrange the balance of sectional interests on the General Council, but, presumably, the unions foresaw no difficulty in maintaining their newly found unanimity, at least for the limited purposes of determining entrance qualifications and professional standards. For all industrial purposes the unions would continue to act separately. In Parliament, spokesmen for the teachers lost no time in asking the government to establish the proposed council, and, just as promptly, the Minister of Education refused to accede to the request.

The Minister's attitude was both understandable and predictable. The state respects union rights in the field of industrial relations, and already consults teachers, through their unions, on matters of educational policy. But education touches the whole community at many points; it is vital to an industrial and technological society that education should be provided in the right quantity, of the right type, and at the right levels. In a democracy, it is the province of the community to decide what is "right," and the state's ability to manipulate the number, training, and qualifications of teachers is one of its controls over the social and economic structure of the country. For a modern, collective society to hand over this power to a closed priesthood of teachers would be worse than syndicalism; it would be a return to the middle ages. Nor has the British government, in its desire to control education, singled out teachers for invidious treatment. Today, almost all of the self-governing professions are aware of increasing governmental interest in their affairs; in all areas of British life, the tendency of the times is to move away from monopolies, and to exercise a greater degree of public control over them.

From the government's point of view, the creation of an independent Teachers' General Council in 1964 might have been immediately disastrous. One of the reasons for England's seriously low level of industrial productivity is a shortage of skilled manpower; this can only be cured, in the long-term, by a program of educational expansion; but in England, as elsewhere, education itself faces serious manpower deficiencies. The Ministry of Education hopes to remedy this by an increased use in the classroom of what has come to be known as "hardware"—that is, technological aids of all types, from closed-circuit television to learning machines—combined with the employment of a new category of "ancillary teacher," who will service the machines and perform routine teaching tasks under the direction of qualified teachers. The unions have refused to accept ancillaries, claiming that they are a form of cheap labor in the schools. Under present law, teachers can refuse to work with them, and, if necessary, withdraw their own labor. A long battle may be imminent, and there will probably be some hard bargaining before the question is settled. But had a Teachers' General Council existed, teachers would have had a statutory right to prohibit the use of ancillaries. Vital as the issue is, the government would have had no *locus standi* in the dispute; a self-governing profession, which acts selfishly, can hold the country to ransom, and society has no means of redress.

But while teachers have devoted their energies to achieving self-government, in the hope that it will enhance their social status, they have also cut themselves off from one of the mainstreams of power in Britain, the workers' movement. With the recent exception of the A.T.T.I., teachers' unions have consistently declined to affiliate with the Trades Union Congress, arguing that, as professional associations, they have functions which differentiate them from organizations which are labor unions only. It is difficult to assess the consequences of this attitude. Earlier in this article, I mentioned that teachers' unions stress the importance of projecting a favorable image of the teacher. Most teachers wish to be seen as professional people, and there is a widespread belief that their chances of achieving self-government will be jeopardized if they align themselves with unions of skilled, semi-skilled, and unskilled workers. They, therefore, face the modern dilemma of all professional workers. Contemporary society needs the technocrat and makes use of him. But real power is in the hands of organized capital and organized labor. Teachers are employees; by remaining aloof from organized labor they place themselves in a limbo of professionalism, where they have middle-class respectability without political power.

The dilemma of professionalism was clearly demonstrated in 1965, when the government produced a five-year plan for national economic development, which, among other things, allocated a fixed annual growth-rate to educational expenditure. Teachers complained bitterly that, although targets for industrial production had been set after discussions with both sides of industry, teachers' views had not been sought with regard to educational expansion. But from the government's point of view, this difference of treatment was justifiable. The size of educational investment is a public matter, to be decided in accordance with national needs, national resources, and priorities; it should not be determined by a monopolistic vested interest. On the other hand, had the teachers' unions been a part of the labor movement, with seats on the T.U.C. General Council, they would not only have been a party to discussions between government and labor, but would also have been in a position to influence the attitudes and views of the T.U.C. itself. It is this latter point which has most significance for the future role of teachers' unions. By setting their sights on a Teachers' General Council, they simply assert their right to dictate how teachers should behave in situations created by public authority; operating within the T.U.C., they would be an influential voice in formulating public policy. Teachers, therefore, have to decide where their own priority lies. Do they want status, with only marginal influence? Or are they willing to join other workers on equal terms, to make their unique knowledge of educational technology available to the whole labor movement and to play a part in shaping national policy, not only on educational matters, but over the whole range of social, political, and economic activity? Britain's largest white-collar union, the National and Local Government Officers, has already chosen this latter course; in 1966, the A.T.T.I. followed the example of the N.A.L.G.O., and became the first teachers' union to be affiliated to the T.U.C. There are many who hope that other teachers' unions will follow suit, in the belief that there is mutual advantage to be gained from collaboration between teachers and those who work in other sectors of British national life.

The Ordinary Member

So far in this article we have been considering questions of organization and high policy. But what of the ordinary rank and file member? Why does he join a union, what does he expect from his membership, and how does he view his union's activities? Above all, what is his own part in those activities? Studies of industrial unions in Britain all tend to emphasize the lack of interest which rank and file members take in branch work. As one writer puts it, ". . . the major impression that post-war research into trade unionism has made on public opinion has been to reveal the extent of apathy." [5] Goldstein [6] examined the work of a branch of the Transport and General Workers Union and suggested that between 1942 and 1949 an average of four per cent of the membership attended union meetings. Roberts [7] concluded that only about one trade unionist

[5] M. Harrison, *Trade Unions and the Labour Party Since 1945* (London: Allen & Unwin, 1960), p. 110.
[6] J. Goldstein, *Government of British Trade Unions* (London: Allen & Unwin, 1952), p. 203.
[7] B. C. Roberts, *Trade Union Government and Administration, Great Britain* (Cambridge: Harvard University Press, 1956), pp. 95–99.

in 20 takes anything approaching an active part in the life of his branch. Are professional workers different in this respect? Does their higher educational level give them any greater sense of responsibility toward their colleagues? As leaders and moulders of thought in others, do they demonstrate a higher degree of involvement in democratic processes than other workers display?

We have very little precise knowledge of the behavior of rank and file members of English teachers' unions. Asher Tropp [8] pointed out that the proportion of N.U.T. members who voted in elections for their national vice-president fell steadily from 67.8 per cent in 1900, to 36.8 per cent in 1955. He also thought that there was considerable apathy in attendance at local association meetings in large cities, but that in other areas the apathy was less noticeable. "In rural and semi-rural areas and the small towns," he claimed, "meetings are well attended, and there is plenty of interest." This view appears to be based on a subjective impression, and it is one with which many informed teachers agree. It raises a number of interesting questions, but in the absence of any published figures or studies, it is not, perhaps, profitable to pursue the matter here. For the purposes of this article, however, I decided, with the help of an assistant, to take a trial boring into the attitudes of teachers toward their unions.[9]

We began by circulating a questionnaire to 200 teachers in secondary schools controlled by the City of Manchester Education Committee. The sample was chosen at random, and represented ten per cent of all secondary school teachers in that large city. Any validity which the investigation might have had was destroyed at the outset by the fact that, even after follow-up, only 66 replies— i.e., one-third of the original sample, and only 3.3 per cent of all secondary teachers in the city—were received. It was clear that those replying were not a representative sample, since all respondents belonged to a union, and 18 per cent (far more than the normal proportion) were officials or committee members of their branches. What follows, therefore, is also nothing more than an impression gleaned from the answers of 66 union members who were willing to reply to questions. Of these, 43 were men, and 23 women. Fifty per cent of all respondents belonged to the N.U.T., and 26 per cent to

8 A. Tropp, *The School Teachers* (London: Heinemann, 1957), p. 264.
9 I wish to thank Mr. Kevin Jones for the valuable assistance he gave me in making this inquiry.

the N.A.S.; the remainder were divided unequally among six other unions.

In answer to the question, "Why did you choose to join the union of which you are a member?" 60 per cent stated, as their main reason, that they supported its aims and policies. It became clear, however, from answers to subsidiary questions, that even those who joined a union on ideological grounds, were, nevertheless, likely to be influenced by other motives. Many of those who had joined one of the predominantly pro-grammar school Joint Four associations, claimed to have done so because it specialized in their particular type of teaching; nevertheless, they deplored its pro-grammar school attitude and expressed the hope that it would adopt a more progressive, pro-comprehensive school policy in the future. Twenty per cent of all respondents agreed that they had drifted into their union because the majority of the teaching staff in the school in which they were first employed had belonged to that particular union. An analysis of N.U.T. respondents showed that, almost without exception, they had been impressed by the N.U.T.'s size and power, which they thought would be helpful to them. Many joined the N.U.T. because it caters to both sexes, and provides opportunities for men and women teachers to meet together at business and social functions. Some mentioned that the N.U.T. had given them help and advice during their student days. A small number believed that it offered the best terms for buying a house.

A number of questions were asked which were designed to discover how members saw the functions of teachers' unions; opportunity was also given for them to suggest purposes which were not covered in the questions. The following table analyzes the response:

How Teachers See the Functions of Teachers' Unions

	Number of References
1. To obtain better pay for teachers	66
2. To provide benefits (insurance, etc.) for members	33
3. To obtain improved conditions in schools	20
4. To seek improved status for teachers	9
5. To give professional advice on educational questions	6

There was complete unanimity for the view that the prime purpose of a union is to obtain better pay for its members; exactly one-half of the sample still held the nineteenth-century belief that a union is a means by which workers come to the help of one another in times of financial difficulty. Less than a third thought that unions should be concerned with school conditions, although these affect teachers' working lives as well as children's welfare. Despite the long struggle for enhanced status, only nine seemed to think that this was something with which unions should concern themselves; of these nine, only six expressed the opinion, in answer to a supplementary question, that fragmentation of teachers' efforts among different unions was detrimental to success in achieving the ends which they sought, and that a single, unified union should be created. Only six out of the 66 believed that teachers' unions have a part to play in the discussion of purely educational questions.

In considering these results, we should remember the limitations of the sample from which they are derived; it may be that a wider sample, drawn from primary as well as secondary schools, and using areas more representative of the country as a whole, rather than taking in only one city, would produce a different picture. Nevertheless, the message conveyed by the sample in this inquiry comes through very clearly. No one who knows teachers would doubt that, as individuals, they are sincerely, and often emotionally, concerned with the well-being of the pupils they teach, or that their professional work is frequently a major preoccupation of their lives, but they do not see unionization as an instrument of collective action, which they can fashion and wield for themselves in order to influence what happens to children. At least for this sample, teachers' unions are labor unions, not professional associations. It would appear that the majority of those who are interested in professional matters pursue them in ad hoc associations, such as the Association for Science Education, or the Special Schools Association, rather than in the type of union with which this article has been dealing.

Lastly, how much support do members give to their local associations? Of the 66 respondents, 18 per cent said that they attended branch meetings often and regularly, 30 per cent admitted that they had never attended at all, while 52 per cent claimed to have attended once or twice, mainly out of curiosity, but had not been stimulated to renew the experience. The figure of those attending regularly may seem reasonably encouraging, but it should be recalled that officials and committee members also formed 18 per cent of the respondents; regular attenders, and officials and committee members, were, in fact, the same people. Most of the non-attenders were conscious of their apathy, but pleaded that pressure of other duties prevented them from being more active. Most of them added that they trusted their officers, and were quite content to leave union affairs in the hands of those who had been elected to deal with them. In this respect, the teacher seems to be no different from his industrial brother.

West Germany   3

Wolf D. Fuhrig

A PROFESSION DIVIDED AGAINST ITSELF

The divisions among the teachers of West Germany reflect the traditional divisions in the German educational system. Unlike most American schools which owe their existence and maintenance to local public or private initiative, most German schools have always been state institutions. In present-day West Germany, local influence upon the public schools is at best advisory. Private schools amount to less than two per cent of all educational institutions.

"Enlightened" self-interest on the part of several German princes of the eighteenth and nineteenth centuries brought public education to Germany earlier than to most other European countries. The same "enlightened" self-interest also imposed upon the schools the social and educational views of the contemporary ruling elite. Public education was designed to produce useful and loyal subjects, screened and trained for the occupations for which the state needed them. Theories of Plato, Fichte, Hegel, and Herbart [1] supported this state-centered, socially conservative approach to education.

Criticism against the prevailing conditions in public education

[1] Johann Friedrich Herbart (1776–1841) made important contributions to psychological and educational theory. His system of clearly prescribed steps in the presentation of subject matter to students prevailed among the more conservative German teachers for over a century after his death.

WOLF D. FUHRIG is Associate Professor of Political Science, MacMurray College, Jacksonville, Illinois.

arose first among progressives in general and among teachers at the common schools.[2] The latter had always had good reason to be dissatisfied because they received less favorable working conditions, less formal education, and less remuneration than the teachers at the more specialized schools. Those hostile to the social status quo also tended to acclaim more equalitarian, student-centered, and flexible approaches to education as represented, for example, by Pestalozzi, Diesterweg, and Kerschensteiner.

The sharp division of the teaching profession into two camps with antithetical social and educational principles was further aggravated by other divisions built into the German school system, mainly the divisions based upon the students' performance and religion. The social conservatism and the cult of efficiency, which so often guided the actions of Germany's upper classes, produced increasingly homogeneous groupings of students and gradually an unparalleled variety of schools and teachers. At the time of the Weimar Republic, the four-year primary school constituted the foundation for three major types of secondary schools. Which of these a student was to attend usually depended upon his record of performance and the finances of his parents. Bright students whose parents could pay tuition fees had a choice of several kinds of eight-year academic high schools.[3] For students with less academic ability and financial backing, but with an interest in a broad-based business education, appropriate secondary schools existed in urban communities.[4] The mass of students with below average and average intellectual ability, or with poor or disinterested parents, continued their education in the four-year prevocational school (the upper level of the common school) followed by several years of systematic apprenticeship in a trade and attendance of a vocational school [5] one day a week until age 18. In addition to these major school categories, most urban communities had special schools for handicapped youngsters.[6] After the age of 18, when school attendance

2 Common school: *Volksschule,* the eight-year (now nine-year) school which has traditionally been the core of the German educational system.
3 Academic high school: *höhere Schule* (today nine years), such as *Gymnasium, Oberlyzeum, Oberrealschule, Oberschule,* and equivalent schools preparing for additional education at the university level.
4 *Mittelschule, Realschule, Handelsschule,* and equivalent schools preparing mainly for careers in business.
5 *Berufsschule.*
6 *Sonderschulen, Hilfsschulen,* etc.

was no longer compulsory, graduates of nonacademic schools [7] could enter various institutions for vocational or general education provided they had sufficient time and money. The universities accepted only graduates of academic schools, but other institutions of higher education, particularly colleges for teachers at nonacademic schools, were not allowed to limit their admissions to graduates of academic high schools.

From the beginning, this tradition of educational specialization gave each kind of school a distinct social ranking. The great majority of lower class youth went through the common school and the vocational high school. Secondary schools preparing for commercial occupations attracted mainly students of middle-class background, while the upper class sent most of its children to academic high schools, and, if they graduated from there, to the university. The selection of academically superior students after only four years of schooling and the financial barrier of tuition fees made it most difficult for children of the lower class to get an academic or a business education on the secondary level.

The social distinctions among the different types of schools divided the teachers even more than the students. The more scholarly a teacher's subject matter, the higher he ranked socially and economically. The higher-ranking groups insisted that longer and more expensive academic education entitled them to higher rewards; but they opposed all demands to give the lower-ranking groups educational opportunities similar to their own. The teachers at nonacademic schools, so the argument went, taught such simple subject matter that they did not need to be trained at universities; and the skill of teaching could be learned better in in-service training than in lectures and seminars. Thus it happened that Germany had university-trained experts in the nursing of trees and the husbanding of animals long before the first common school teachers received the equivalent of a university education. Since upgrading the education of nonacademic teachers to university level meant upgrading the social status of a group much larger than any one of the professions traditionally trained at universities, the demand was opposed

[7] Nonacademic schools: elementary schools and all secondary schools except academic high schools. Although academic subjects are taught at all schools categorized here as nonacademic, their objective is not the preparation of students for a university of the German variety.

by practically the whole establishment: the *Akademiker* (the university-trained intellectuals), the rich landowners, and the commissioned military officers. The latter two groups tended to dislike intellectuals generally as a threat to their own power, while the *Akademiker* feared that a large increase of their ranks was bound to weaken their status. The nonacademic teachers usually found, much to their dismay, that the opposition to their advancement was strongest among the university-trained intellectuals including such influential groups as the ministerial bureaucracy, the teachers at the universities and academic high schools, the clergy, and leading personalities in the communication media and in community life.

Religion and the question of religious education in the public schools split the teaching profession further. Since the Reformation, the Protestant churches and the Roman Catholic church had shared control with the states over the public school system. Most schools below the university level were denominationally segregated. The age of enlightenment and nineteenth-century liberalism, however, brought sporadic but growing demands for a change to nondenominational public education, either with or without instruction in religion. While the conservative members of both major Christian denominations rejected nondenominational schools of any kind, the moderates favored them as long as time and facilities for religious instruction by church-approved teachers were provided. A minority of radical liberals unsuccessfully campaigned for the abolition of all religious instruction in the public schools. Since World War II, most Protestants have come to support nondenominational schools with denominational religious instruction. The Roman Catholic church has continued to fight for denominationally segregated schools.

The supporters of the status quo in school organization and religious education also tended to take conservative stands on other educational and political issues as characterized, for example, by opposition to coeducation, sex education, open class discussions, and student government. There has always been a segment of teachers who loyally followed the policies of their churches. For Protestants, this usually meant not more than a middle-of-the-road position in party politics, with some leeway for individual movement to the moderate right or left. The Roman Catholic church gave teachers more specific guidelines for their professional lives by urging them not only to join Roman Catholic teacher organizations but to support the political party which best represented the Vatican's interests: the Center Party before 1933, the Christian Democratic Party since 1945.

Educational philosophy, social class, religion, and political orientation were only the most prominent issues which have fragmented the German teaching profession throughout its history. Among the lesser conflicts erupting from time to time were those between teachers and school administrators and between the urban and rural segments of the profession. Since the lower-ranking groups felt more frequently aggrieved, they organized much earlier and with a greater sense of urgency. The university professors, who always ranked far above the other teachers, formed an effective pressure group only after 1945 when the gains of other professions appeared to threaten their own status. Although the majority of nonacademic teachers today opposes the status quo in education and likes to see all teachers united in one powerful pressure group, most teachers at universities and academic high schools continue to scorn this demand. They have left no doubt that they consider themselves scholars first and educators second. Increasingly, moreover, they have assailed as pretentious the rising aspirations of the nonacademic teachers.

Where class consciousness has been the cause of disunity among Germany's teachers, they have never been able to form a united front. The history of German teacher organizations shows again and again special interests separately scrambling for improvements. Sometimes these efforts benefited society as a whole, but too often the welfare of the other teachers and the general public was heedlessly disregarded.

ASSOCIATIONS OF NONACADEMIC TEACHERS

The First Rise and Fall: From the Beginnings to 1849

Although the German states took important steps toward compulsory elementary education in the eighteenth century, the common school teachers developed into a profession only in the nineteenth century. Previously they had ranked among the artisan trades whose profiles had been shaped in the Middle Ages. Common school teachers were worse off than most trades, however, because they were insufficiently trained, badly paid, condescendingly supervised by the clergy, and wholly unorganized. They also had to serve as sextons and janitors, and, in order to make a living, they supplemented their income by part-time work as tailors, cobblers, and the like. To be recognized as a profession like the teachers at academic high schools, the common school teachers needed, most of all, a guaranteed monthly salary sufficient to make outside work unnecessary, freedom from extraneous duties to church and community, and an institutionalized course of professional training.

In spite of all their troubles, few teachers thought of taking collective action, and those who joined together did so for reasons other than to campaign for redress of their grievances. Protesting against the policies of the established, "God-given" authorities was against the code of absolute loyalty in which the absolute monarchies indoctrinated their subjects. After 1794, moreover, the Prussian Land Code set the pattern by which all teachers at Germany's public schools became state civil servants. As such, they knew that open criticism of the prevailing conditions was likely to be countered by their superiors with even harsher treatment. Hence, the teachers who formed the first professional associations showed little zeal for political action. They wanted to join hands mainly for the purpose of enriching their social life. Aside from parties and outings, they developed their own glee clubs, reading circles, and study groups for self-improvement. Naturally, they also discussed ways of reducing their material plight. As a first economic action, the teacher associations usually started funds to provide members and their kin with financial help in case of sickness, death, and other emergencies. This practice of economic self-help probably attracted more new members to the associations than anything else they offered. Various insurance programs and emergency aid programs have therefore been maintained by all German teacher associations to this day.

By 1840, dissatisfaction among the nonacademic teachers had grown so intense that, in spite of the danger of reprisals by the authorities, teacher associations began to act more like pressure groups. The ruling elite opposed all educational, political, and economic change which would have raised the political maturity of the common man. As in the past, the teachers of the masses were expected to produce loyal subjects expertly skilled to take their given place in society under the undisputed control of the hereditary monarchy and the established churches. William IV, for example, considered ideologically and politically emancipated teachers an intolerable threat to throne and altar. As a show of good will, the governments of the German states granted teachers a guaranteed annual income; but everything else that common school teachers wanted met with angry, threatening rejection. Teachers stood at the crossroads of either submitting to what they considered injustice or openly campaigning for redress of their grievances even though the odds were heavily stacked against them. Only a minority of the profession chose to do the latter. These men, however, prepared the way upon which future generations of teachers were able to make progress.

The ideas which aroused nonacademic teachers in the 1840's had their roots in the young tradition of educational, political, and economic liberalism. Those who stood for its tenets became the vanguard of an emancipation movement whose arduous struggles continued into our time. The educational philosophy of this movement was strongly shaped by the disciples of Pestalozzi. They rejected schools which merely inculcated the attitudes, doctrines, and skills prescribed by state and church but insisted that public education stress universal human values and respect individual differences of interest and ability. The teacher was to be primarily an educator rather than a drillmaster. He was to have sufficient cultural knowledge and psychological judgment to choose the contents and methods most suitable for the educational situations confronting him.

These educational principles—revolutionary at that time—provided the basis for a number of bold demands for institutional reforms including the creation of a uniform, comprehensive school system with equal opportunities for all children, the abolition of all ecclesiastical supervision over public schools, teacher participation in the development of governmental policies affecting education, the establishment of courses in education at the universities,[8] and a new program of teacher preparation either at universities or at separate but equivalent institutions. In freeing the schools from all religious and political bondage and in raising teacher education to the university level, the leaders of this emancipation movement hoped to improve not only the social status but, along with it, also remuneration, fringe benefits, and the working conditions of the nonacademic teachers. Throughout their history, the teacher asso-

---

[8] Educational theory was taught by philosophy professors at most German universities throughout the nineteenth century. Regular professional chairs for education, however, have been instituted only since the 1920's.

ciations have tended to stress the needs of the student and the school more than the needs of the teachers. In the German idiom: they tried to put *Schulpolitik* (politics concerned with the school as an institution) ahead of *Standespolitik* (politics concerned with one's profession). No matter how much they were actually motivated to promote the common good or rather their own personal welfare, the efforts for the improvement of the schools ultimately resulted in tangible rewards for the profession, too.

Outside of the teacher associations, the reform movement received support only from a few liberal politicians and liberal members of the business community. The latter, in particular, began to recognize that Germany needed more and better education for the masses, the faster science, technology, industry, and commerce grew. Thus, upon the initiative of an industrialist,[9] an association for the promotion of the nonacademic schools was founded. It actively supported the teacher associations in their pleas for improved public education.

When, in March of 1848, the governments in Vienna and Berlin were forced to proclaim freedom of press and assembly, teachers in every state vented their feelings in numerous declarations telling the people in general and the politicians at the constitutional conventions in particular what reforms were needed in government and education. The famous resolution which Berlin's nonacademic teachers adopted at the Tivoli Restaurant asked perhaps for the most radical break with the past: all schools were to be run by trained teachers only; all education outside the family was to be public and free of charge; all children, not only the offspring of the proletariat, were to attend common schools for eight years; and all teachers were to be trained at universities and to be paid by a uniform salary schedule. While some of these demands must have appeared utopian to even the most optimistic progressive, the Tivoli Program served the teachers' emancipation movement not only as a model platform but also as a source of inspiration.

For a few months, it seemed as though one of the most urgent desires of the reformists was going to become reality right away: a comprehensive, representative organization of all German teachers. Friedrich Kapp, a director of an academic high school, addressed this resolution to all segments of the teaching profession in the first days of the revolution. His "Call for the Reform of German Na-

9 Friedrich Wilhelm Harkort (1793–1880).

tional Education" asked for a "united German school, freed from supervision by clergymen and jurists, without tutelage by the authorities, freely developing out of its own resources." [10] Yielding to the equalitarian spirit of the revolution, teachers from all types and levels of education soon met jointly at several cities and formed a common organization, the Allgemeine Deutsche Lehrerverein (ADLV), General German Teacher Association. The motives for this display of unity varied greatly, however. Some endorsed a united front of all teachers for nationalistic reasons; others considered it a service to education or simply sought to enhance the profession's prestige. Most academic high school teachers and university teachers opposed "fraternization" with the less educated segment of the profession; and for the few who genuinely favored such a development, it ended as quickly as the revolution.

The Second Rise and Fall: 1849 to 1933

After the abortive revolution of 1848, the common school teachers suffered more humiliation than any other professional group. Denounced by the postrevolutionary governments as "archagitators" who had caused the revolution, they were punished where it hurt most: by new restrictions of their professional freedoms and material rewards. Most states forbade teachers to join political organizations and to attend political meetings. All their activities came under closer surveillance by state and church. More than 100 of their liberal leaders were dismissed or otherwise punished. These and other repressive measures cost the teacher associations much of their membership but failed to destroy them. Only their national federation disintegrated for a few years. So the decade after the 1848 revolution saw no teachers' protests or demonstrations of consequence. The men who remained loyal to the reform movement either camouflaged their activities or met secretly. Social and self-help activities, however, continued openly and gradually drew more colleagues back into the ranks of the organized. After the victory of the German states over France in 1871, the relations between the governments and the nonacademic teachers changed noticeably for the better. Prominent politicians pointed out that, in the last analysis, the country owed its successes to its teachers. One event in particular symbolized the improved atmosphere for the nonaca-

[10] Friedrich Kapp, *Aufruf zur Umgestaltung der deutschen Nationalerziehung* (Arnsberg: Grote, 1848).

demic teachers: in 1871 they reestablished their national organization and renamed it Deutscher Lehrerverein (DLV), German
Teacher Association.

The revived teachers' organization for all of Germany attracted
mostly the liberals among the common school teachers. The teachers
at academic high schools and in higher education had come to
identify themselves so strongly with the social elite that for most of
them any permanent association with an all-inclusive teacher organization was out of the question. The more specialized nonacademic
teachers likewise tried to dissociate themselves from the common
school teachers in order to gain in social status. This is what the
teachers at the commercial schools hoped for when, in 1867, the
academic high school teachers agreed to join them in a common
professional organization. Their *mariage de convenance,* however,
lasted only a few decades, mainly because too many high school
teachers refused to make common cause with teachers who were not
university-trained. Hence, the teachers at the specialized nonacademic schools had no choice but to organize separately unless they
decided to go together with the common school teachers.

Not even the common school teachers among themselves were
able to form a united front. The widespread neglect of the rural
schools aroused some of their teachers enough to act independently
from, or even against, their urban colleagues. An association of
rural school teachers survived from the 1890's until the 1920's and
disappeared only when the German Teacher Association created in
each state a committee to represent this large segment of the profession. The young teachers without tenure and the female teachers
also maintained independent associations until they were satisfied
that there was no better interest representation for them than the
German Teacher Association.

The school principals established their own organization because
they felt that not only their special concerns but also their supervisory position barred them from joining an association of ordinary
teachers. The ministries of education, moreover, urged this view-
point upon the principals in order to maintain a good measure of
social distance between school administrators and teachers. What
the government and its school administrators did not expect, however, was the formation of a counterorganization: the German Association of Classroom Teachers. From 1906 until the end of World
War I, this group steered a much more radical course than the

German Teacher Association and often directed its attacks specifically against what it considered backward or oppressive administrative practices.

Although the intense class consciousness which characterized German society during the Second Reich had a very divisive effect upon the whole teaching profession, rival religious and political ideologies disturbed the work of the schools and their teachers even more profoundly. Prodded by their churches, Protestant and Roman Catholic teachers respectively founded the first denominationally oriented teacher associations in the first half of the nineteenth century. Since they tended to be less belligerent and more conservative than their secular counterparts, their operation suffered little from the restrictions which state governments clamped upon associational activities of teachers after the revolution of 1849. After 1870, however, the teacher associations of Roman Catholics and, to a lesser degree, of Protestants repeatedly clashed with state governments and with the German Teacher Association. In 1872, a liberal minister of education in Prussia, Adalbert Falk, moved to end the traditional church supervision over public education and tried to make all public schools nondenominational. These policies led to a power struggle (*Kulturkampf*) between Bismarck's government and the Vatican, both contending for the allegiance of the 40 per cent of the German people who were Roman Catholics. Although the denominational teacher associations gained in strength as a result of the *Kulturkampf*, the traditional church influence in public education was broken. This was an important victory for the Prussian liberals as well as for the German Teacher Association.

In view of the many divisive quarrels which plagued the teaching profession as a whole, the German Teacher Association tried hard to be a unifying force. A majority of its members supported a compromise solution for the question of religious education by advocating the nondenominational school with released time and facilities for religious instruction. In another conciliatory move in 1898, the Association passed a resolution refusing membership to any local which failed to admit colleagues owing to their religion or rank.

The *Schulpolitik* of the non-Marxist liberals always came closest to the demands of the German Teacher Association. Both groups opposed the oppressive restrictions which conservative governments had imposed upon the common school teachers; both demanded laws to clarify and liberalize the relationship between the states and their teachers; but, while criticizing the status quo, both failed to offer a sufficiently detailed and constructive program of reforms.

The Roman Catholic Center Party and many of the Conservatives to its right insisted upon a system of denominationally segregated schools with various degrees of supervision by the churches concerned. For the Center Party, which often allied itself with progressives on economic issues, *Schulpolitik* was primarily a religious concern. Some economic conservatives, however, seemed to view denominational schools primarily as a useful device for keeping the masses reasonably pious and quiet in order to ensure the maintenance of the status quo. When, in 1878, a conservative majority gained control of the government in Berlin and Robert von Puttkamer took Falk's place as minister of education, the common school teachers and their associations once again became the target of severe reprobation. In his famous "Ash Wednesday Speech," Puttkamer spoke generally for the whole conservative ruling elite when he described what he considered the failings of the common school teachers: they overestimated their abilities; they made extravagant demands; they disliked the authority of the state; they tried to destroy the bonds between state and church; they agitated in favor of political extremes; they made proposals for the whole school system even though they could not possibly assess it in its entirety; they had become morally corrupted by their involvement in party politics; and they had forgotten that their business was in the classroom, not in politics. Puttkamer and his conservative backers, moreover, raised serious doubts about the common school teachers' loyalty to the monarchy. Since teachers were civil servants, the state expected them not only to stay politically neutral but also to defend whatever official position the government took. In spite of the intimidating indictments against them, many members of the German Teacher Association made no secret of their liberal or even socialist views, all the more as the demands of the Association received support only from the parties left of center. Hence, by legislating severe curbs upon the operation of the Social Democratic Party in 1878, the conservatives were certain that they were also protecting the schools from the "treasonable" socialist or Marxist influences exerted by "disloyal" teachers.

While one segment of common school teachers stood politically left of center simply because they came from lower class homes and were dissatisfied with the conduct of the ruling elite, others, even though of similar background, supported the parties of the right because of religious convictions, monarchistic and nationalistic enthusiasm, personal opportunism, or any combination of such motives. Many of these teachers had never read anything but the literature screened for them by state and church. The conservative segment among the common school teachers grew still stronger as more and more females joined their ranks in the late nineteenth century and thereafter. Most of them, in contrast to their male colleagues, came from middle- and upper-class backgrounds; and most of them refused, just like the church-oriented teachers, to join the German Teacher Association because they disliked the relatively liberal views for which it stood.

The surge of nationalism before and after the beginning of World War I submerged much of the progressive sentiment among the common school teachers and made them forget many of their grievances. The disillusionment, however, which followed the futile sacrifices of the war led to a revival of political and educational liberalism in the decade after 1918. The constitutional assembly at Weimar, where the moderate left was strongly represented, endorsed several of the principles which, upon invitation, the German Teacher Association had recommended for inclusion into the document: 12 years of compulsory education for all children; state control over all schools; no special elementary schools for the privileged; the disqualification of supervisory personnel (particularly clergymen) without teacher training; and, as the most far-reaching innovation for the whole profession, the training of all teachers at universities or institutions with university status.[11]

In the early Weimar years, the teacher associations received a sympathetic hearing from a majority of the politicians. In line with the demands of the German Teacher Association, all public school teachers obtained more freedom from administrative direction; and the school administrators were asked to develop more personal and democratic relationships with their faculties. In other states and on other issues, however, the common school teachers soon learned that they could not rely upon mere promises by the state even if these promises were a part of the national constitution. The most important case in point was the promise of a substantially upgraded system of teacher education. Without it, no substantial improvements could be expected in the salary schedule and the social status of the common school teacher.

Contrary to Article 143 of the Weimar Constitution, the legisla-

11 Weimar Constitution, Articles 143–149.

tion which was to give the states uniform guidelines for the pro-
jected changes in public education was never passed. The highest
national court (the *Reichsgericht*) aided the conservative opposition to educational reform by ruling that the interpretation of the
teacher training clause of the Constitution devolved upon the state
governments. As a result, only the few states with progress-minded
majorities, particularly Prussia and Hamburg, reformed teacher
training as required by the Constitution. And when in 1930 the
national government cut back expenditures in response to the growing economic depression, half of the new and more expensive
teacher training institutions were shut down first. In a rare display
of unity, the German Teacher Association and most other teacher
organizations joined in condemning the government's action. The
only larger groups which failed to support the protest were, as expected, the academic high school teachers and the university
teachers.

The legal recognition of trade unions by the Weimar Republic
invited the creation of numerous new occupational interest groups
among both blue- and white-collar workers. The existing organizations, moreover, found it increasingly necessary to enhance their
pressure group potential if they wanted to exert nationally effective
influence. Although the main representative for the common
school teachers, the German Teacher Association, did gain in
strength during the Weimar years, the organizational fragmentation of the teaching profession continued; and the political rifts
among its factions deepened. Each of the major political parties
organized its own affiliate teacher association; but only the Social
Democrats and the smaller liberal parties encouraged the teachers
among their members to support the German Teacher Association.
A small number of common school teachers favored an organizational linkage with the trade union movement. Such an alliance
seemed to them the only effective way of countering the unmiti-
gated opposition of the social establishment against fundamental
improvements in the education of the lower classes. The trade
union movement, moreover, was likely to gain in social range and
respectability by allying itself with the teaching profession. The
idea, however, of having blue- and white-collar workers make common cause, perhaps even under common leadership, was still too
new in the 1920's to be easily acceptable to either side. Two teacher
associations founded right after the war did call themselves trade

unions (*Gewerkschaften*). One organized teachers with Communist and Independent Socialist leanings, the other classroom teachers (as opposed to administrators) and teachers without tenure. Both groups, however, remained small, isolated, and ineffective.

In 1921 the German Teacher Association and most other teacher organizations allied themselves with the German Federation of Civil Servants (Deutscher Beamtenbund). Founded only in 1919, this organization quickly became one of the strongest pressure groups of white-collar workers by accepting as associated members many older organizations of tenured employees. Among the larger teacher associations, only the Association of Catholic Female Teachers [12] refused to join. It opposed the right to strike which the Federation of Civil Servants endorsed at that time. The German Teacher Association had hoped that the coalition with the Federation would aid both the common schools and their teachers and win them important backing among the middle and upper classes. These hopes were not realized, however. The Federation did little for the teachers and even less for the common schools because the majority of its members opposed reforms in the educational system and the status of nonacademic teachers. It was this frustrating experience which two decades later drove the successor of the German Teacher Association into a coalition with the trade unions.

In order to lessen the organizational fragmentation of the profession, the German Teacher Association tried to give minority interests—female teachers, rural teachers, vocational teachers, teachers without tenure, school administrators, etc.—their own niche in its expanding framework without permitting any one minority to gain undue control over the whole organization. In the latter years of the Weimar Republic, the Association encountered increasingly hostile criticism from conservatives and reactionaries, especially from the German Nationals [13] and the Nazis. The growth of antidemocratic extremism on the right and on the left reflected widespread frustration with the course of events in domestic and foreign affairs. For the nonacademic teachers, most promises of the Weimar Constitution had not come true. Where progressive state governments tried to lower some of the social barriers in the school system, the

12 Verein katholischer deutscher Lehrerinnen (VkdL), Association of Catholic German Female Teachers.
13 Until its alliance with the Nazis in 1931 (Harzburger Front), the German National People's Party was the most important gathering of conservatives who distrusted the Nazi movement.

conservative forces throughout society, including many teachers, fought back and refused to cooperate. As in the past, the German Teacher Association lacked popular support and remained unable to organize a solid majority of all teachers. Excessive pride in the teachers' expertise led the Association to oppose the parents' councils created after the war. Since, by and large, the teaching profession had failed to interest the common man in the problems of education, the parents' councils frequently came under the influence of political parties; and, more often than not, the opposition to reforms and increased expenditures for the nonacademic schools prevailed.

In seeking understanding and help from the state only, the teacher associations had become victims of the same etatistic orientation which the ruling elite had fostered for over two centuries. The longer the Weimar democracy failed to satisfy its progress-minded elements, the more of them, too, fell for the impetuous promises of the radicals to the left and right. Although the Nazis offered national unity and social welfare virtually at any price, they gained enough support from frustrated liberals to get into power in 1933. Shortly thereafter, they had forced all teacher associations under their centralized control. The divisions, however, between nonacademic teachers, academic high school teachers, and university teachers were kept as rigid as ever.

What happened to public education and the teaching profession under Hitler's regime contradicted the aspirations of the German Teacher Association in every respect. Hitler, who once suggested that army corporals would make the best teachers, entrusted the primary responsibility for the nation's youth to the Party and its youth organizations. The schools ranked only third in importance, and, ideally, the teachers were to be mere tools of the Party. When the Nazis abolished the teachers' colleges and reintroduced training institutions similar to the old normal school, it became obvious that they were as unwilling to improve the intellectual education of the masses as they were eager to exploit their frustrations.

The Third Rise: After 1945

The moral and material destruction caused by 12 years of Nazi rule, the collapse of the nation's administrative and economic structure, and the four-power occupation made it impossible to continue Germany's institutional life as it had existed before 1933. After

World War I, practically all forms of German government ceased and had to be reconstructed. This break in the nation's political life forced a multitude of fundamental decisions upon both the occupation authorities and the new German leaders. Unlike the transition of power in 1918, the beginning in 1945 was much less encumbered by remnants of the fallen regime. Allied and German efforts made the revival of a Nazi-like movement virtually impossible, and the intransigence of the Soviets killed any chance for a massive swing to the radical left.

In spite of the moderate political climate which has prevailed in West Germany since 1945, the reconstruction of education encountered both new and traditional difficulties. Many schools lay in ruins, and the teaching personnel was severely reduced and badly demoralized. As so often in the past, the political leaders failed to give first priority to the needs of education. The country was first to recover economically. Yet, while this was gradually achieved, rearmament again absorbed huge funds urgently needed for the improvement of public education. The new fragmentation and decentralization of the country compounded the problem of rebuilding the school system. Each of the new states, supervised by one of the four different occupation governments, developed its own programs for educational reconstruction depending upon the political parties in power. It took years, even after the establishment of the Federal Government in Bonn, before the ministries of education in the 11 states agreed to coordinate some basic aspects of their school systems. The men responsible for the blueprint of the Federal Republic defended the new diversity as part of the price the country had to pay for the freedoms of a pluralistic society.

As soon as the schools reopened in 1945, the deep-rooted rifts between the teachers at academic and nonacademic schools, between the advocates and opponents of state-financed denominational schools, and between groups of specialized nonacademic teachers and common school teachers came to the fore again. The Nazi past and the socioeconomic upheavals of the postwar period contributed new causes of friction: conflicts between the generation responsible for Germany's disgrace and their offspring who, though innocent of the errors of their fathers, suffered most of the bitter consequences; distrust between ex-Nazis and anti-Nazis; differences between natives and refugees; tensions between those who had been trained at the old normal schools and those educated at modern teachers colleges; and problems growing out of the steadily increasing number of women in the teaching profession. These were—and still are—some of the major difficulties confronting the men who set out to build a successor organization to the German Teacher Association of the Weimar Republic.

The first local and regional teacher associations after the war appeared soon after the reopening of the schools late in 1945. They grew slowly because the political confusion in the early postwar years made most Germans hesitant to commit themselves to any politically active group. Church-oriented associations at first attracted more members than strictly secular groups. The organizations which wanted to carry on the work of the former German Teacher Association got their best start in the British Zone where the occupation government was least restrictive and the Social Democrats had their greatest strength. In January of 1947, these teacher associations joined forces on a zone-wide basis and founded the Allgemeiner Deutscher Lehrer- und Lehrerinnenverein (ADLLV), General Association of Male and Female Teachers. At the same time, two momentous plans for the future were proposed and discussed: (1) to transform the ADLLV into a meeting ground and interest representation for *all* teachers from kindergarten to university and thus to revive the idea of a united teaching profession as it was first envisioned by the revolutionaries of 1848; and (2) to affiliate this association of all teachers with the powerful German Trade Union Federation (Deutscher Gewerkschaftsbund).

The latter plan was quickly accomplished. At the 1948 convention of the ADLLV, the delegates formally affiliated their organization with the Trade Union Federation of the British Zone after the latter had invited this move. The name of the ADLLV was changed into Gewerkschaft Erziehung und Wissenschaft (GEW), Trade Union for Education and Scholarship. This label was to indicate that the new union represented not only teachers but also social workers and researchers. The term "scholarship" was addressed in particular to the teachers at academic high schools and universities who usually considered themselves scholars first and teachers second.

The successor organizations to the German Teacher Association in the American Zone also united and decided to ally themselves with the Trade Union Federation. They did not form a trade union of their own, however, but affiliated with the Union for Public

Service, Transport, and Traffic.[14] It was only a temporary solution because the road chosen by the ADLLV of the British Zone proved to be much more satisfactory. In 1949, the successor to the German Teacher Association in the American and the French Zone joined the GEW. When, in October 1949, the Trade Union Federation constituted itself for all of West Germany, the GEW became one of its founding members.[15]

The leaders of the Trade Union Federation generally approved the professional objectives of their new partners and were willing, therefore, to strengthen the pressure group potential of the GEW. The blue-collar unions knew from long and grievous experience how much their own bargaining power depended upon the size and solidarity of their membership. Yet, more than half of West Germany's teachers were not convinced that they needed to form a united front among themselves. For over 90 per cent of all teachers at academic high schools and universities, affiliation with nonacademic teachers remained as undesirable, and affiliation with blue-collar workers as unthinkable, as it had been a century ago. Many specialized nonacademic teachers also continued to favor having their interests represented by an organization of their own. Most of the support for the alliance with the Trade Union Federation came from the common school teachers. Yet, even among them, a large minority doubted the wisdom of this move or opposed it. Teachers with strong church ties criticized both the GEW and the Trade Union Federation for their allegedly noncommittal, if not agnostic, attitude toward religion. The conservatives, among them many of the older female teachers, expressed fear that any kind of partnership between ADLLV and blue-collar unions would inevitably lower the status of the common school teacher in the eyes of the general public. In Bavaria, Württemberg-Baden, and Hessen, the opposition to membership in the Trade Union Federation split the ADLLV into two groups, one joining the GEW, the other remaining outside.[16] As it became clear that the resistance to membership in the Trade Union Federation would not soon weaken, the GEW persuaded at least one of the dissident groups, the Bavarian Teacher Association, to join forces as an autonomous partner. The

14 In neighboring Austria, the main teacher association also affiliated with this segment of the trade union movement.
15 West Berlin's leading teacher association affiliated with the GEW in 1950.
16 In Bavaria, 86 per cent of the ADLLV membership refused to transfer into the GEW. The size of this dissident group dwarfed the opposition in all other states.

two organizations agreed to form the Arbeitsgemeinschaft Deutscher Lehrerverbände (AGDL), Committee of German Teacher Associations. This arrangement gave the Bavarian Teacher Association most of the advantages of membership in the Trade Union Federation but exempted it from paying dues to it, as well as allowing it to retain its separate nonunion identity. The GEW, on the other hand, strengthened its influence and bargaining power. From its inception, the AGDL has been numerically by far the strongest, though not always the most influential, of the pressure groups in education. Its membership today includes about one half of all West German teachers from kindergarten to university. The other teachers are either scattered among more than 20 smaller organizations or not at all affiliated with a professional interest group. In recent years the AGDL has won additional support in membership drives among college students majoring in education and among part-time teachers.

Individuals can become members of the GEW only by joining one of its 11 component state organizations. They administer their affairs (including their funds) independently in accordance with their common constitution. One of its rules obliges every member association to institute special committees if they are requested in any area of interest by a quarter of the members. As a result, at least ten such committees have come into being in the state organizations as well as on the national (West German) level: committees for higher education, academic high schools, commercial high schools, vocational schools, schools for the handicapped, social work, adult education, and school administration. In addition, departments for legal aid and for young people's literature exist on both levels. The national organization also maintains committees or offices concerned with beginning teachers, instruction in history, physical education, social welfare of minors, radio and television, film, international relations, international exchange of teachers and students, teachers in German schools abroad, and cooperation with the German Committee for UNESCO.

The organized nonacademic teachers who are not affiliated with the AGDL are members of denominationally oriented teacher associations, associations of female teachers, or associations of specialized teachers. Among the denominationally oriented teacher associations, three stand out: the Verband der Katholischen Lehrerschaft Deutschlands (VKLD), Association of the Catholic Teachers of Germany; the Verein katholischer deutscher Lehrerinnen (VkdL), Association of Catholic German Female Teachers; and the Bund evangelischer Lehrer und Lehrerinnen (BeLL), Federation of Protestant Male and Female Teachers. Throughout the postwar years, the membership of each of these organizations amounted to about five to ten per cent of all teachers in West Germany. Although religious allegiance is clearly the prime reason for the existence of separate denominational groups, they have also gained strength among church-oriented teachers by denouncing the GEW's leaders as agnostics who want to do away with all state-supported religious education. Compared to the GEW, the denominational associations have generally been more conservative and have shown less initiative although these characteristics have not gone uncriticized by their respective churches.

While the Association of Catholic Teachers (VKLD) and the Federation of Protestant Teachers consist only of common school teachers and their administrators, the Association of Catholic Female Teachers (VkdL) has been able to attract both nonacademic teachers and academic high school teachers. The latter organization also remains the only teacher association which emphasizes that it wants to be more than a professional interest group. Founded upon the conviction that organizations of both sexes do not do justice to the special needs of women, this association proposes to give particularly to unmarried Roman Catholic teachers an intellectual and emotional home through its meetings and publications and thus protect them from becoming lonesome. The only other organization of female teachers, the Arbeitsgemeinschaft für Mädchen- und Frauenbildung, Committee for the Education of Girls and Women, makes no such claim. As a nondenominational group composed of about 60 per cent academic and 40 per cent nonacademic teachers, it wants to gather women from all levels of education and participate in solving cultural and educational questions of special concern to women. In defending its existence, the Committee does maintain that women need their own organization because the structural changes in modern society affect women even more than men. Nevertheless, the Committee encourages its members to join the GEW, too.

More than a dozen other teacher associations serve exclusively nonacademic teachers outside the common schools or in specific subject areas, such as teachers in schools for handicapped children, vocational schools, commercial schools, etc., and teachers of history, music, physical education, etc. The GEW has been trying to accommodate these groups in special sections of its own organization. Numerous specialized associations, however, remain quite viable because their members view the general association as incapable of satisfying their particular needs and even detrimental to their special status.

Although the denominational and the specialized associations refuse to ally themselves with the powerful GEW, they are nonetheless aware of their relative impotence as pressure groups. Seven of these associations,[17] therefore, joined with the main organization of the academic high school teachers, the Philologenverband[18] in forming a common interest representation, the Gemeinschaft Deutscher Lehrerverbände (GDL), Union of German Teacher Associations. But this arrangement never became nearly as strong and effective as the AGDL, the alliance of the GEW and the Bavarian Teacher Association. The wide divergences between the views of the academic high school teachers in the Philologenverband and the views of the nonacademic teachers in the other seven organizations has made it very difficult for the GDL to operate from a sufficient basis of consensus.

Most of the associations in the GDL also allied themselves again —as during the Weimar years—with the Federation of Civil Servants. Particularly the Philologenverband, the Association of Catholic Teachers, and the Federation of Protestant Teachers[19] hoped to further their socioeconomic interests and ambitions by corporate membership in the Federation of Civil Servants. The Association of Female Catholic Teachers, however, refrained from this coalition— just as before 1933—apparently in order to emphasize its disapproval of pressure group activities per se. As it turned out in the past 15 years, hardly any group of teachers gained significantly from membership in the Federation of Civil Servants. Yet, only the Association of Catholic Teachers became so dissatisfied that it discon-

17 Comprising two associations of Roman Catholic teachers, one association of Protestant teachers, two associations of teachers at commercial schools, the association of teachers of the deaf-mute, and the association of female teachers at agricultural schools.
18 I.e., German Association of Philologists. This is a traditional name. Any teacher at an academic high school may belong to this organization.
19 The founding of this association in 1949 was, at least in part, a direct oppositional response to the formation of the GEW by the ADLLV.

tinued this relationship.[20] The others apparently rate the mere prestige value of their association with the Federation of Civil Servants higher than the alternatives of either going it alone or joining up with the GEW and the Trade Union Federation.

THE ASSOCIATIONS OF ACADEMIC TEACHERS

Most of the teachers at academic high schools and universities have traditionally opposed all changes in the educational and occupational structure which were likely to diminish the social distance between them and the groups below them in the civil service hierarchy. In the past two decades, more than ever before, numerous reform proposals and concerted political pressures by educational progressives,[21] especially by the GEW and its allies, have been putting the advocates of the status quo increasingly on the defensive. It was an urgent necessity for the latter to strengthen the organizations which represent their group interests: the Philologenverband for the academic high school teachers and the Hochschulverband (University Association) for the university teachers. Both associations organized some 80 per cent of those eligible for membership and thus succeeded much better in this respect than any association of the nonacademic teachers. An even bigger asset for the academic teachers are powerful allies most of whom are graduates of their institutions and occupy many of the most influential positions in state and society. The backing for the views which the two associations represent comes predominantly from two overlapping segments of West German society: the conservative political parties and the university-trained intelligentsia.[22]

Since the early 1950's, the Philologenverband has been confronted with growing demands for structural changes which could ultimately lead to some form of comprehensive high school in West Germany. If fully implemented, such a reform would spell the end of not only the academic high school but also the profession which the Philologenverband represents. A system of comprehensive secondary schools would certainly diminish the status barriers among

[20] In 1966.
[21] Not all West Germans whose views in politics and economics might be classified as progressive see a need for educational reform.
[22] Notable exceptions: social scientists, teachers colleges, and states with a more liberal climate, such as West Berlin, Hamburg, Bremen, and Hessen.

both students and teachers in the different tracks of study which today are segregated in different types of schools. Many conservative West Germans, however, do not consider this segregation a serious problem. To them, the system of specialized secondary schools represents a valuable tradition which gave the nation many generations of well-skilled intellectuals and craftsmen. The conservatives frankly deny that a comprehensive high school could prepare the country's intellectual elite as effectively as the academic high school. As yet, the Philologenverband and its backers have been able to prevent major changes in the system they defend. They have lost the struggle only over a few peripheral issues. All states, for example, have now upgraded the training of their nonacademic teachers; and some states are in the process of extending the common elementary school period from four to six years. In terms of remuneration, working conditions, and social prestige, the Philologenverband has successfully safeguarded all the advantages which its members traditionally enjoyed over the nonacademic teachers.

The university teachers, just like the academic high school teachers, have been jealously on guard to prevent changes in the structure and number of the institutions upon which their profession depends. Since 1945, numerous specialized institutions of higher education, such as colleges for the training of theologians, artists, administrators, and nonacademic teachers, have tried to gain university status. None of them succeeded against the massive opposition of the existing universities and their allies. In order to preserve the distinction between universities and other, allegedly lower, levels of higher education, the institutions which recognize only each other as universities [23] agreed in 1949 to join forces in a new organization, the Conference of University Presidents (Westdeutsche Rektorenkonferenz). It functions as interest representative and accreditation agency for its member institutions. Although the state governments have granted teachers colleges, art academies, and theological seminaries outside the universities some of the customary privileges of universities, such institutions simply do not rate as schools of university rank unless the Conference of University Presidents admits them to membership in its select circle. This, however, is unlikely to happen in the foreseeable future.

The Conference, like its member institutions, is financed from

[23] Thirty-five institutions in 1965.

public funds although it is practically a lobbying agency for those who control the West German universities, the full professors. Hence, the university presidents—themselves full professors and elected for only short presidential terms by their peers—could not be unaware of the danger that their organization might be criticized for serving conflicting interests, namely those of the universities as state institutions and those of the university teachers as a profession. This situation led the Conference to the decision that, at least officially, it should concern itself only with the universities' institutional problems (*Hochschulpolitik*), not with the professional problems of university teachers (*Standespolitik*). Although the presidents admitted that these two political concerns could not always be separated in practice, they thought it wiser to promote the establishment of an independent interest representation for university teachers. The new organization, the University Association, was founded in 1950 and soon formed locals in all institutions belonging to the Conference of University Presidents. Owing to their close institutional and personal relationships, these two principal pressure groups of the universities rarely disagree on the issues which confront them both. In spite of the oft-avowed difference in their purposes, their ties have remained close. Nothing demonstrates this better than the standing invitation by which each of the two organizations permits the president of the other organization to attend its executive meetings.

The University Association, just like the universities, is led and dominated by full professors who in Germany wield nearly undisputed power over the professional lives of the mass of subordinate faculty personnel. Although many of the latter do have the qualifying degrees for appointment to full professorial rank, they can get this promotion only if a few all-important incumbents find them worthy of membership in their select circle. The constitution of the University Association provides that the interests of the subordinate faculty are to be represented by six of the executive council's 15 members and by a committee dealing specifically with the problems of the lower ranks. Nonetheless, their voice in the organization is small compared to their number. In reality the Association serves their interests only insofar as these interests are identical with those of the full professors. Subordinate faculty members have never dared, owing to their dependent position, to establish a pressure group of their own even though many of them seem to feel that it is badly needed.[24]

Individually and collectively, the full professors have frequently been criticized for exclusiveness and authoritarianism in their relations with subordinate faculty, with students, and even with outsiders. Yet, they still enjoy a prestige among the German public which seems unmatched by university teachers in any other society. A 1963 opinion poll [25] showed that 30 per cent of 2,000 West Germans questioned considered the university professor the most respected man in the country. This prestige dates back to the reforms and achievements of the German academic community in the 200 years prior to the Nazi regime. The states repeatedly conceded to the profession privileges designed to create the most favorable conditions for scholarly research and teaching. When professors became part of the higher civil service, they gained all the economic benefits of this group but were gradually exempted from most of its obligations.

The most far-reaching of these exemptions was the guarantee of academic freedom which has been included in all German constitutions since 1848.[26] Throughout the German-speaking countries, academic freedom became widely understood to be a fundamental right granting professors a distinctly privileged position among civil servants and making the university corporation autonomous in academic matters. Hence, whenever professors are speaking up for their professional interests, they invariably argue that academic freedom is at stake. They took great pains to make this concept the most comprehensive and most popularized value in German university culture. The chief beneficiaries of this development have been the full professors. Their money income today is more than twice as high as that of teachers at common schools. On balance, the full professors continue to be one of the most richly rewarded and most influential professional elites in West Germany. They nevertheless

[24] Another reason for their failure to organize may be found in the common assumption, made normally by every faculty member in subordinate rank, that he will in due course be a full professor himself and, therefore, should not concern himself unnecessarily with his present transitory grievances. Once promoted full professor, the onetime subordinates seem to forget their erstwhile woes and quickly adapt themselves to the academic power elite in both attitude and behavior.

[25] By the EMNID-Institut of Bielefeld, West Germany.

[26] Excepting the constitution of the German Democratic Republic, the communist-controlled part of contemporary Germany.

consider themselves increasingly hard-pressed to hold this position as other groups in the labor market, particularly other groups in the civil service, aggressively campaign for higher rewards. Besides, the decline of Germany's academic reputation since the advent of the Nazi regime has greatly enhanced the attraction which other professional opportunities at home and abroad exert upon German scholars. Those who left the universities did so, by and large, for three main reasons: seemingly insurmountable obstacles to their professional advancement, the highhandedness of some of the full professors, and the country's lagging expenditures for higher learning in spite of its spectacular economic comeback. Few full professors acknowledge the validity of the first two reasons, but there is no disagreement about the financial needs of higher education. Particularly the professors who most vehemently oppose institutional reforms seem to be most persistent in their demands for more funds as the panacea for whatever problems beset the universities.

So the University Association is united mainly in the desire of its members to maintain their high status and to improve their working conditions including, above all, more modern facilities, more time and money for research, more assistant personnel, and sabbatical leaves. Full professors and subordinate ranks, however, do not agree about the priority of their needs. The lower ranks want primarily more economic security and more influence relative to their superiors while the latter are just as determined to maintain their advantages in the existing reward and status system.

Like the Conference of University Presidents, the University Association uses every opportunity to portray itself as an organization which transcends narrow interest politics and serves the welfare of higher learning in its entirety. The Association also clings to the profession's traditional postulate that scholars ought not to bargain and demonstrate for their needs in the uninhibited manner characteristic of blue-collar workers. This, it is alleged, would depreciate the professor's image in the eyes of the general public. When the Association was established, all but three of its founding fathers voted against the name "Association for University Teachers" and for the name "University Association" to make certain that, at least outwardly, the organization could not be identified as something akin to a trade union. Ten years later and in the middle of the profession's biggest struggle for higher incomes, one of its spokesmen reiterated this pretense by praising its president for not leading the University Association "into the wretched tracks of a pressure group" [27]—as if pressure groups were by nature morally inferior to groups not exerting organized pressure in pursuit of their objectives.

MAJOR ISSUES

Schulpolitik

Throughout the postwar period, structural reform of the educational system has been the great, persistent issue debated between the teacher associations on the one hand and the governments and the interested public on the other. The teachers certainly had—and continue to have—many material grievances; but their leaders chose to abide by the professional ethos which the German public had come to expect of them. This meant that in their dealings with the public they would go out of their way to give priority to *Schulpolitik* over *Standespolitik* and thus place the needs of society and its youth ahead of their own economic welfare. Sometimes it appeared as if the men responsible for the making of educational policies in the ministries of education would have preferred to see the teacher associations limit their lobbying to matters of direct economic concern to their members. By working for or against certain institutional changes, however, the associations showed that the welfare of their members was closely tied in with the welfare of the nation's youth. The GEW, like other educational progressives at home and abroad, argued that the pupils in the nonacademic schools failed to get their fair share of educational opportunities and that structural changes in the school system could mitigate the glaring inequalities in favor of the intellectual elite. For the teachers at nonacademic schools, moreover, substantial economic improvements, other than cost-of-living increments, depended upon an elevation of their position in the civil service hierarchy; and this in turn depended upon the enriching of the nonacademic schools and the upgrading of the training of their teachers.

The idea of broadening and extending the common school in the direction of a comprehensive secondary school system has hitherto encountered such massive opposition from the conservative establishment that it cannot be expected to come about in the foresee-

[27] Werner Weber, "Zehn Jahre Hochschulverband," *Mitteilungen des Hochschulverbandes,* August, 1960, p. 123.

able future. But the reformers are making progress with small steps
in the desired direction. The decisions to extend the common elementary school from four to six years and the total common school
to nine years, the gradual upgrading of the training of nonacademic
teachers to university level, and the expansion of the in-service
training of teachers without tenure are examples of initial victories
for the progressive alliance of GEW and Social Democratic Party
against the conservative alliance of Philologenverband and the majority of the Christian Democratic Party.

In coalition with the Free Democratic Party, GEW and Social
Democrats also face another alliance made up mainly of the Roman
Catholic Church, the Roman Catholic teacher associations, and a
large segment of Christian Democrats. In this confrontation, the key
issue is the one-half of all common schools [28] which are state-run
denominational schools. Since the Roman Catholic Church is much
more interested in denominationally segregated education than the
Protestant churches,[29] these schools predominate where Roman
Catholics are in the majority, particularly in North-Rhine-
Westphalia, Bavaria, and the Rhineland-Palatinate. Both sides in
this old controversy developed their own educational and political
theory with which to justify their viewpoints. The Roman Catholic
Church and its allies maintain that the kind of education a child is
to receive must ultimately be decided by the parents; and the kind
of schools a community is to have must be resolved on the local
level. In opposition to this claim, the GEW and its allies contend
that all educational measures must first and foremost be based upon
the needs of the child, not upon the ideological position of parents,
church, or society. Hence, teachers as professional experts on the
education of children must be considered best qualified to assist the
state in developing the appropriate institutions for the education of
its youth. The GEW, therefore, rejects not only parental and private but also local control of formal education; and where private
schools exist, the GEW opposes their support out of public funds.
While critics insist that parental and local control over public education is a necessary characteristic of democratic government, the
GEW points out that parental and local influences are frequently
quite haphazard, parochial, and prejudicial to the best develop-

[28] Fifty-two per cent in 1955.
[29] One of the most notable exceptions to this rule is the minority Lutheran
church of Bavaria.

ment of the child's potential. By favoring centralized and expert control over public education on the state level, the GEW expects to obtain a more equalitarian, cosmopolitan, and efficient school system. The teachers, moreover, hope to gain more recognition of their expertise.

Reform of the traditional German school system, as the GEW sees it, would expand the responsibilities of the nonacademic teachers or even integrate academic and nonacademic teachers into one professional stratum, thus necessitating corresponding reforms in teacher education. Instead of using the university only for the training of academic teachers, as in the past, the proposed school reform would call for a full university education and the same level of in-service training for all teachers on the elementary and secondary level. In addition, the GEW concludes, the faculties at the colleges for nonacademic teachers must be absorbed into the faculties of the universities on a level of full equality. By forcefully lobbying for this objective, the GEW not only made valuable allies among the teachers' college faculties—the only solid allies it has in higher education —it also succeeded in raising the status of the common school teachers much further in their training phase than at their places of employment. As more teachers with better and more respected training enter the profession, however, they hopefully will be able to give the reform efforts in elementary and secondary education an added impetus.

In recent years, the reform policies of the GEW have been complicated by growing shortages of teachers and by employment of substitute and part-time personnel with less than the average level of professional training. This development threatens to depreciate the socioeconomic status of the common school teachers at the very time when the GEW and its allies are hard at work to raise it.[30] Hence, stopping the use of low-paid substitute teachers in the common schools is now one of the major demands which the GEW is pressing against the state governments concerned. Both the ministries and the common school teachers as a group are faced with the difficult task of recruiting more suitable young people for a profession which suffers not only from an inferiority complex but also

[30] In contrast to the common school teachers, the university professors have long been able not only to use the shortage of men of their rank to their own advantage but also to maintain this shortage by controlling the access to faculty rank.

from a very real lack of status. This apparent dilemma, however, could turn out to be a blessing in disguise for the common school teachers if their continued opposition to substitute personnel should force the states into substantially raising their socioeconomic status.

Standespolitik

Compared to other professional groups in the civil service of the states, the teachers have generally held their own. This means that they obtained increases roughly similar to those of the other groups. Although most teachers appear to take this result for granted, they might have received less without the persistent and adroit lobbying of their organizations and allies: the GEW with the support of the Trade Union Federation and the Social Democratic Party, the Philologenverband with the support of the Association of Civil Servants and the conservative parties, and the University Association with the support of the Conference of University Presidents.

To gain higher increases than the other groups in the civil service and thus to improve a group's overall ranking is a relatively rare success for any lobbying agent. If it occurs, the government usually faces a barrage of protests from the groups not raised so that persuasive arguments are needed to weather the storm. The lobbying agents for the teachers certainly know that, under the prevailing conditions, they have little chance to improve the ranking of the groups they represent. Yet, all teachers seem to feel that their ranking in the civil service is unfair because they are included in a common salary scale with differently structured careers. While most occupations offer numerous steps to the top of the salary scale, the teaching profession has never been divided into as many comparable grades of advancement. Only a very small proportion of all teachers can be promoted to the rank of principal and beyond, while, for example, postal employees have a very good chance to rise a number of steps above their initial rank. Hence, the GEW and the University Association have long been advocating a special salary scale for teachers. Only the academic high school teachers do not seem to be so certain that such a change would work to their advantage because, compared to high school teachers in other societies, they enjoy an exceedingly high socioeconomic status.[31]

[31] Since the nineteenth century, they have ranked on the same level as lawyers and physicians.

Since the days of Bismarck, German labor generally and civil servants in particular have enjoyed comparatively adequate social security and fringe benefits. Among the improvements which teachers won in recent years are mandatory bonuses at Christmas and certain personal anniversaries of service (e.g., upon completion of 25 and 40 years of service). Grievances about working conditions are numerous, however. While most blue- and white-collar workers have gained a five-day week and a reduction of weekly working hours since the mid-50's, the teachers at primary and secondary schools continue to work on Saturdays; and their weekly contact hours with students have not been decreased correspondingly.[32] On all levels, many classes are overcrowded and facilities too small and antiquated. Although new buildings have been constructed at a vigorous pace since the early 50's, the teacher associations charge that both the states and the federal government failed to give school construction sufficient priority.

Among other issues of concern to the teaching profession, the question of codetermination, has received special attention in West Germany. Codetermination is based upon the idea that many potential controversies between employers and employees can be settled early and amicably if the law provides for representative employee participation in the formation of management policies, particularly those which directly concern their welfare. How far such participation in managerial decision-making should go, what kinds of problems should be included, and what weight the employees' vote should be given are usually settled by law but remain issues of contention in the continuing debate over codetermination. In general, the interested public appears to be satisfied with this new practice and has come to look upon it as a practical contribution to democratic and peaceful labor-management relations. Codetermination is certainly one of the reasons why West Germany has had comparatively few major strikes. Although originally designed for

32 The teachers' pleas for a free Saturday and a reduced work week have generally fallen upon deaf ears because their official weekly contact hours with students do ordinarily not exceed 30 at nonacademic schools and 25 at academic high schools. All teachers receive about 12-week vacations annually. To many persons who are not professional educators this workload appears very light. It has been difficult, therefore, to convince the general public that the sum total of all the work demanded of teachers is comparatively heavy; that their daily duties often require much more than eight working hours, particularly in a school system, such as the German, where students and teachers spend only five to six hours a day in school but many more hours on homework.

the private sector, codetermination was soon demanded by employees in the public sector, too, particularly by the lower ranks of the
civil service. In the educational system, the common school teachers
and the GEW pushed hard for representation on all three levels of
school administration: the levels of the county or city superintendent, the district superintendent, and the minister of education.
For each of these levels, representatives are elected for usually two
years. In many cases, the elections are contested between the GEW
and its chief opponents within the common schools, the denominational teacher associations. The questions in which the teachers
have gained a measure of codetermination comprise essentially matters of personnel policy: hiring and firing, tenure and promotion,
working conditions, financial and social assistance in emergencies,
institutions for the enrichment of the teachers' social and cultural
life, in-service and continuing education, administrative procedures, etc.

The rank and file reaction to this form of codetermination is
predominantly favorable but a minority remains negative.[33] By
and large, the representatives in the personnel councils, the leaders
of the teacher associations, and the politically interested members of
the profession consider codetermination a useful institution. To
dismiss the whole effort as a political game, useless for the rank and
file but often profitable for ambitious office seekers, is a reaction
most frequently reported among teachers who are not affiliated with
any professional organization.

The Pressure Potential

Civil service employment in West Germany provides a good measure of job security, social security, and middle- or upper-class status.
Yet, these advantages may be offset by some serious disadvantages:
the unmatchable power of the employer, the state; the difficulty of
airing grievances through its bureaucratic channels to those with
authority to act upon them; and especially the prohibition of the
strike. Even if the latter were permitted, teachers could hardly resort to it under present conditions. Morally, civil servants in general
and teachers in particular are faced with traditional societal expec-
tations to such a degree that any gains a strike could bring might be

---

33 This information is based upon a representative study by Ilse Gahlings, reported in her book *Die Volksschullehrer und ihre Berufsverbände* (Neuwied am
Rhein: Luchterhand, 1967), pp. 14–39.

far outweighed by a massive loss in prestige; and economically, the dues collected by the teacher associations are much too small to permit the accumulation of a strike fund. These and perhaps other considerations have kept all the postwar teacher associations from seeking the right to strike. It is doubtful, moreover, if a strike could really benefit the profession as long as it remains as divided as in the past. Although the GEW continues to solicit all teachers into its fold and appeals especially to the nonacademic teachers, one third of the latter have not yet affiliated with any professional organization; and a similar proportion of the affiliated show little or no interest in their organization beyond the (often tardy) payment of dues. It is the growing number of female teachers which constitute the main identifiable group of the unaffiliated and disinterested. Among the men, nonaffiliation and nonparticipation seem to be caused primarily by religious and political disagreement with the existing associations. But there are also others who stand aside for more selfish reasons. Frustrations and resentments may have led them to withdraw, for example, or promotions to administrative positions may have turned them into "company men."

Compared to private employers, the state confronts the bargaining representatives of its employees with substantially different possibilities and problems. Although the sovereign power of the state puts its employees at a decisive disadvantage, the various limitations on the exercise of political power, particularly the manifold divisions of government and the accessibility of its agencies to the public, give pressure groups numerous avenues for operation. Yet, where there are many agencies to which to turn for the redress of grievances, principally, the executive, the legislative, and the judicial, there may also be as many hurdles to overcome.

In West Germany, the financing of education depends not only upon the policies of each state government and the joint councils of all ten states [34] but also upon the policies of the federal government. The policy formation in each state is influenced most strongly by a handful of politicians—ministers, legislators, and political advisors—and by the top civil servants in the ministries of education and finance. The day-to-day administration of the school system, moreover, is not only shaped by the ministerial bureaucracy but also by the superintendents on the district and county (or city) level. To serve the diverse needs of their members, the pressure

[34] Not including West Berlin.

groups must be prepared to deal with all agencies from the local to the federal level. Sometimes it is not easy to decide at which point a drive for the redress of particular grievances should best be launched in order to be successful. Compared to the grievance procedures which trade unions face in private industry, the corresponding regulations in the civil service appear complicated and inefficient.

The only regular contacts between teachers and school administrators above the school level are the meetings of the codetermination councils. For the spokesmen of the associations, it is not only difficult to get the top representatives of the state to the conference table—they usually prefer written communications—but the latter invariably dictate the terms under which they are willing to confer. Often the minister and his aides do not engage in discussions at all but merely listen and ask questions; and they will state their position only at a time and place and in the manner most suitable to their own political strategy.

Short of the strike, the teacher associations have been employing most of the devices and techniques common to pressure group politics everywhere: publications and meetings to educate and, when opportune, agitate the membership; demonstrations of protest in open letters, speeches, and conventions; recruitment of big-name personalities and organizations in support of desired measures, etc. The responses which teacher associations tend to get from politicians, bureaucrats, and the general public also fall into a familiar pattern. Although the politicians' views on the major issues in public education are relatively fixed by their parties and fairly well known to the public, their answers to specific questions are often so vague that they become meaningless to the teacher associations that want to know on whom they can count and what they can get. This vagueness is the more pronounced the more a party wants to appeal to the most diverse political and social factions in society.

Discussions with ministerial bureaucrats also tend to be unproductive since, as a rule, these men are not free to commit the government in power. They usually try to appear impartial on issues contested between opposing pressure groups. It is no secret, however, that the West German ministerial bureaucrats as a group hold the views of the social establishment. As far as the public schools are concerned, the majority of them favor the status quo. Even when the university professors pressed for improved remuneration and a salary schedule of their own, it was primarily the ministerial bureaucracy which stalled and advised the politicians against the desired changes.

Appeals to the general public are even less likely to produce fast results. Although usually the GEW finds the Trade Union Federation and the Social Democratic Party on its side when it pleads for the needs of its members, there are many people in the lower and middle classes who are jealous of teachers because of their long vacations, their allegedly fewer hours of work, and their civil service status. Since the German people have always received their public education ready-made from their state governments, they tend to take their teachers for granted and care little about the profession's social and economic problems. The inertia of the public in educational matters is taken so much for granted that the teacher associations usually pursue their policies without campaigning for support from the man in the street. He becomes important only at election time. It is the grey phalanx of professional administrators below the ministers of education and finance who most frequently are the kingpins in the governmental structure which the teacher associations try to influence and activate in pursuit of their objectives.

India 4

S. Natarajan

INTRODUCTION

India, a vast country, has more than 50 million children in its elementary schools and another 17 million in its secondary schools. Given its present rate of progress, India may well have a total enrollment of 200 million pupils in her schools by 1985.

There are now nearly two million teachers employed in India's schools, whereas in 1946–47, there were only about 700,000. By the end of the Fifth Five Year Plan in 1976, the number of teachers working in all educational institutions, including universities and technical and professional institutions, may reach the four million mark.

India is a union of states each of which enjoys a considerable measure of autonomy. The states, which were formerly either ruled by the British or by princes, are mainly responsible for education. Under the constitution the central government of India is expected to ensure standards in higher and technical education.

The diversity in education in the different states and in different parts of each state has taken many forms. These have had their impact on the growth and working of teachers' organizations in India. In spite of the large number of teachers in the land, there is no effective organization of the teachers in India. The All-India Federation of Educational Associations is the federation of teacher

S. NATARAJAN is Secretary-Treasurer, Society for the Promotion of Education in India.

associations in different parts of India. It has the vast potential of bringing the teachers of India into a single all-India organization. It has, however, to contend against great odds, not the least of which is the history of teacher organizations in the country. But before examining these organizations, we will briefly examine India's educational system.

DEVELOPMENT OF THE EDUCATIONAL SYSTEM

Under the East India Company and later the British government, education was regarded primarily as an auxiliary service to produce the required number of subordinate staff to carry on colonial administration. Foreign missions which had as their main aim the spread of Christianity and inculcating the Christian way of life were encouraged to run such schools and were given aid to do so. A few schools were also run by the government. Because the purpose of education was limited, the authorities did not view with favor any effort to organize teachers; in fact, they discouraged such efforts, as did the Indian princes in those states under their control. In later years local authorities were set up and were entrusted with the responsibility of providing education. Following the example of the Christian missions, other religious bodies came forward to run schools. Thus teachers were not part of a state educational service but belonged to different categories according to the management of the school which they served. These schools included municipal, district, mission, and non-mission aided, and in some states, government schools. The diversity was further increased by the different levels or grades of the schools, such as primary, middle, secondary, and collegiate. Another division was on the basis of the religion, such as Muslim and Christian, and private and public schools. In 1921 when some autonomy was granted to the provinces and education was entrusted to public ministers, there was some expansion of educational facilities. This expansion is even more marked during recent years. In 1950, there were about 287,000 schools with more than 800,000 teachers; in 1962, there were 720,000 schools with 1,725,000 teachers.

STRUCTURE OF SCHOOL SYSTEM

There is no central legal code laying down the educational policy for the country. Even in the states there are, strictly speaking, no legal codes for education—that is, there are no rules enacted by state legislative bodies except those concerning the regulations of the state boards of secondary education which are statutory bodies. Instead, the state departments of education frame an educational code which includes rules and regulations. The grant-in-aid rules in these educational codes include regulations with regard to the service and working conditions of teachers. They also prescribe minimum qualifications and methods of recruitment and selection. Other rules in such codes deal particularly with the recognition of institutions for the purposes of grants-in-aid, which also lay down conditions that affect teachers.[1]

Teachers working in government schools are like any other civil servants and are regulated by the general rules of state service. Teachers working under the local bodies, namely district and municipal boards, are regulated by acts passed by state legislatures with respect to primary and secondary education. Teachers serving in private institutions come under the grant-in-aid rules and rules of recognition of schools framed by the state governments or by the state boards of secondary education.

Education at all stages, with two important exceptions, university and technical education, is subject to state regulation. The promotion of these latter two fields is a central government responsibility. All education in a state is under the direct control of an elected Education Minister responsible to the state legislature. The authority of the Minister in the proper organization, management, and control of education is executed through the officers of the department of education, the universities, statutory boards, local bodies, and other recognized agencies. The Minister is assisted by a Secretary and by a Director of Education, who is the executive head of the department. All policies regarding education are decided in the Secretariat of Education. Generally a state is divided into divisions consisting of a group of districts. Each division is supervised by a Divisional Inspector or Superintendent. A division is further divided into districts which are administered by District Education Officers.

The state government has direct control of education in the institutions maintained by it and indirect control, through financial

[1] The World Confederation of Organizations of the Teaching Profession in cooperation with the All-India Federation of Educational Associations conducted a study of the status of teachers in 1965–66. Much of the following material comes from that report.

assistance and inspection, of institutions which are private. In the case of institutions managed by local authorities, the state plays a vital part, since it is the main source of financial assistance. The state further does most of the training of teachers at the elementary level and to quite an appreciable extent at the secondary level. It also controls textbooks, since only books approved by the department can be used in schools. State control of education is also carried out through its inspection staffs. One of their important duties is to recommend the allocation of aid to schools and to scrutinize the expenditure incurred by them.

India has recently launched a program of democratic decentralization in a number of states by setting up units known as "Community Development Blocks." Each block consists of about 100 villages and a population of about 100,000. The total number of such blocks in the country is about 5,000. Local bodies known as *panchayat samitis* (village councils) have been created at the block level and all responsibilities of local development, including that of education, is being transferred to them. These *samitis* have *zilla parishads* (district councils) at district levels. They coordinate and supervise the work of the *panchayat samitis*. In the states where these bodies have been established, the bulk of primary education has been transferred to them.

The state sends its inspectors of schools at the block and the district levels to the *panchayat samitis* and *zilla parishads* and these officers act under the latter groups' orders. Primary school teachers, formerly working in state schools, are now being transferred to the control of the local authorities. Their recruitment, promotion, and transfer are entirely within the control of these authorities. The state, however, lays down the scale of remuneration. In certain cases it also frames recruitment rules. Where pension is provided for teachers, the state generally takes over the responsibility of paying it, as it has not been found practicable to institute separate pension funds for local bodies.

Private agencies have also played an important part in the development of Indian education. Even today their role in secondary and higher education is both extensive and significant. These agencies are broadly classified under the following categories: (1) religious organizations, (2) registered trust boards, (3) registered private bodies, (4) unregistered private bodies, and (5) individuals.

A large number of schools are maintained by various types of private bodies. The schools are controlled by a group of citizens in the locality who form a society for running the institution. They raise the necessary finances and employ teachers and other workers. Some private institutions have the life member system according to which the teachers in these institutions form the management and have a controlling voice in the affairs of the society. They take a pledge to serve the institution for a fixed number of years and accept living wages as their remuneration. There are other institutions which are run by individuals as proprietors. Attempts are being made all over the country to regulate their management.

TEACHER PREPARATION

Another important aspect of education in India involves the educational preparation of the teacher. The general trend in recent years has been to require completion of a high school course equivalent to 10 or 11 years and a two-year professional course in a teacher training institute for all those who will be teaching in the primary and upper primary schools. For secondary school teaching the minimum qualification required is possession of a first degree such as B.A., B.Sc., of B.Com. followed by one year of professional preparation in a teachers' training college. The training schools are all under the control of the state departments of education which prescribe the program of training, conduct the examination, and award the certificates. The training colleges are governed by the universities which prescribe the course of study, conduct the examination, and award the degrees.

Nevertheless, a large number of teachers who do not satisfy the minimum qualifications prescribed have been appointed as teachers. In 1965, 57 per cent of preprimary, 66 per cent of primary, 72 per cent of middle, and 66 per cent of higher secondary school teachers had the minimum training for their positions.

DEVELOPMENT OF TEACHER ORGANIZATIONS

As mentioned earlier, the expansion of Indian education took place in 1921, and that year marks the real beginning of teacher organizations. Earlier, in 1890, a group of women teachers, most of whom were missionaries, had formed themselves into a Women Teachers' Association with headquarters at Madras. The few members worked in different parts of South India in such distant places as Waltair, Nagpur, Hyderabad, Bangalore, and Trivandrum. These dedicated teachers strove to improve standards of teaching, and their work attracted attention. The men teachers of Madras also decided to form an association of teachers. For over a year they wrangled over the aims of such an organization and finally agreed that its principal aims should be the extension of education and improvement in the quality of education. The sponsors were mostly European missionaries working as teachers in the educational institutions of Madras city and senior members of the education service of the government of Madras state. A few Indian educators from colleges and high schools were also in this group. On November 2, 1895, at a meeting held in Madras and attended by more than 100 teachers from different parts of South India, they resolved to form the Madras Teachers Guild. The Guild was hailed as a significant step in the advancement of education. Its members insisted that questions of salary should not take up much of their time but that they should work zealously to build up a teaching profession that would work for improvement in the quality of education. The Women Teachers' Association then merged with the new Madras Teachers' Guild.

The Guild enjoyed official support. Soon many Indian teachers became members and centers were organized in different towns. The Madras Teachers' Guild functioned both as an association of the teachers of Madras city and as an association of teachers in South India. These dual functions created too many administrative difficulties and, as a result, efforts to organize teachers' guilds at the district levels increased. In 1908, the South India Teachers' Union was formed, made up of district teachers' guilds. Its jurisdiction was defined as the area under the political control of the Governor of Madras. The union moved vigorously, forming teachers' associations at all school centers and organizing other district teachers' guilds. Its early membership consisted largely of teachers in secondary schools and colleges. By 1928, it was able to start organizing the teachers in the elementary schools scattered in the remote villages of the state. Thus it was a union of all teachers working at all levels.

The example of the South India Teachers' Union was followed by teachers in other states. The All-Bengal Teachers' Association and the Bombay Secondary Teachers' Federation are examples of the number of associations which came into existence between 1908 and 1924.

The time appeared ripe for the formation of an All-India Association. Thanks to the initiative and foresight of two great teachers, the late P. Seshadri and the late D. P. Khattry, both of whom worked in Kanpur in Uttar Pradesh, an All-India Federation of Teachers' Organizations was organized and inaugurated in 1924 by Dr. S. Radhakrishnan, the president of the Indian Union from 1962 to 1967. Sparked by the efforts of the All-India Federation, the number of teacher organizations in different parts of the country at local, district, and state levels expanded. But unfortunately the formation of these organizations reflected the then current trend of division into castes, communities, and religions as well as into the different structures and hierarchies in the educational system. The All-India Federation of Teachers' Organizations changed its title to the All-India Federation of Educational Associations and opened its membership to all associations working for the cause of education.

There are now nearly 50 organizations of teachers affiliated with the All-India Federation of Educational Associations. Some of them cover all of India but are identified with certain phases of education. They include the All-India Science Teachers' Association, the All-India Association of Teacher Education, the Xavier Association, etc. Most of the others are state-level associations only. The South India Teachers Association is a unified teacher organization, its membership covering all levels of education and the different agencies in charge of schools or colleges.

The All-India Federation of Educational Associations steadily grew in strength and its impact on educational thinking increased in the years from its inception in 1924 until about 1948. Thereafter, it grew less and less effective as its members lost confidence in it. One reason was the teachers' economic condition, which had never been satisfactory. After India's independence, the economic situation grew even worse. The rapid expansion of education, inadequate finances, and soaring prices affected the teachers as it did other salaried employees. The teacher was hit most hard for his emoluments were in most instances below those of others with equivalent qualifications and responsibilities. The failure of the All-India Federation to solve this problem disenchanted many of its members—particularly the state associations of teachers which began to focus their attention on the teachers' economic problem.

True, state governments and the central government did take steps to improve the teachers' salaries and fringe benefits but not enough to satisfy the local teacher organizations.

THE PRESENT STATE

Another major factor which has caused the decline in the effectiveness of the All-India Federation has been its lack of financial resources. Its income is derived mainly from the affiliation fee paid by its constituent associations. This fee ranges from Rs. 30 to Rs. 100 ($4.00 to $13.33) according to the type and strength of the affiliates. The total annual income from this source is about Rs. 3,000 (or about $400). Its membership is 400,000 and thus it can provide only $.001 in service per annum to each of its members.

In addition, there is little or no direct communication between the members and the executive. The council which is the main authority of the Federation meets three times a year, and at two of these meetings it transacts organizational business. To secure a quorum for these business meetings, pressure has to be placed upon the local members to attend. Distance and cost prevent most of the associations from sending their representatives to the meetings of the council.

The Federation is unable to have full-time executive officers. The work is carried on by honorary elected officers who work full time at other employment. The main elected officers live in different parts of the country—the president in Delhi; the secretary in Calcutta; and the treasurer in Kanpur, reflecting the pressure of regional interests. As a result, they do not meet together frequently. All of these factors have caused a steady decline in the Federation's strength and effectiveness.

There are many signs of dissatisfaction. Some of the associations affiliated with the All-India Federation of Educational Associations have seceded from it and have organized the new All-India Primary Teachers' Federation. This new organization has adopted a program of action in order to invite public attention to their demands. This program included proposals for an increase in pay, parity of pay scales among teachers in different categories of schools, dearness allowances (or cost-of-living allowances) at the rates applicable to governmental employees, house rental allowance, better superannuation and retirement benefits, medical benefits, and smaller classes.

Another splinter group is the All-India Federation of Secondary Teachers. Its constitution is not clear. It claims membership from all states. Some secondary teachers' associations and some teachers in secondary schools are reported among its members. On the other hand, some of the primary teachers' associations and secondary teachers' associations which are affiliated with the new primary and secondary school organizations retain their affiliation with the All-India Federation of Educational Associations.

Another organization which has recently come into existence is the All-India Association of University and College Teachers. This too is composed of associations and individuals and some of these associations continue, at the same time, to retain their membership in the All-India Federation of Educational Associations. It will be interesting to see if such dual membership will ultimately result in the strengthening of the All-India Federation.

In addition there are a number of teacher associations whose members teach a common subject. One of the most important is the All-India Science Teachers' Association, which will be discussed again shortly. This was the first all-India subject teachers' association. It has during the ten years of its existence attempted to organize science teachers' associations in different regions or states of the country. It is slowly but steadily meeting with success in its efforts. In 1965 the Association of Mathematics Teachers of India was formed. It is now concentrating on the enrollment of members, and many teachers have shown enthusiasm for the new association. An Association of Geography Teachers is being organized now. The South India Teachers' Union Council of Educational Research has taken the lead in bringing into being these two latter organizations.

RECOGNITION BY GOVERNMENT OF THE ROLE OF TEACHER ORGANIZATIONS

The government of India has recently realized the important role that teacher organizations can play in the development of quality in education. It has tried to strengthen the teachers' organizations. The All-India Federation of Educational Associations receives an annual grant of 5,000 rupees to enable it to hold an annual conference. The delegates attending the conference are given a single fare for the round-trip rail journey. Further, during the last three years, the Federation received assistance in sending one or two delegates to the General Assembly of the World Confederation of Organizations of the Teaching Profession with which the AIFEA is affiliated. The government has nominated the AIFEA president to be a member of such important educational bodies as the National Commission for Cooperation with UNESCO and the National Council of Educational Research and Training. He is also a member of the final selection committee that recommends teachers in primary and secondary schools for the president's award for distinguished and meritorious service.

The All-India Association of Science Teachers, a part of the AIFEA, is similarly assisted by the government of India. It receives a grant to assist it in publishing its journal, the *Vignana Shiksha* (The Science Teacher); in meeting the travel costs of its executive members; and also in paying the travel cost of its annual meeting and conference. The All-India Association of Teacher Education was originally an association of principals of training colleges. Recently, it expanded its scope to cover teacher education at all levels. It also receives financial assistance in the form of an *ad hoc* annual grant from the central government.

In giving these grants, the government does not impose any conditions concerning the policies of the organizations. The idea is to help the organizations. Still, there is a risk that teacher organizations could lose their autonomy in return for financial assistance and this would be harmful to education.

The state governments, on the other hand, do not assist the state associations. There are still some feelings of suspicion and hostility between the associations and the state governments. The demands of the state associations for better pay scales and allowances have proved troublesome to many state governments. Although the old resistance to teacher organizations is weakening and a new approach of friendliness and cooperation is developing, official recognition has not been publicly forthcoming. There is, however, an increasing realization by state officials that the teachers' organizations have major manpower resources and that their work is of considerable importance in the improvement of education. The Madras government has always taken a progressive view and has recognized the South India Teachers' Union (SITU) as the body representing all teachers in this state. Its associated organization, the SITU Council of Educational Research, receives an annual grant from the state government.

The Indian Education Commission set up by the government of

India in 1964 seems to have realized that teacher organizations could play an important role in education. The Commission convened in November, 1965, a conference of representatives of both state and national teachers' organizations. Questions such as the salaries, allowances, working conditions, professional preparation and qualifications, and the role of teacher organizations in general and in special services to teachers were considered at the conference. The Commission's final report contains strong recommendations urging the government to help strengthen the teacher organizations and suggests how these organizations might design a program of action to improve the status of the teachers.

It is significant that currently the World Confederation of Organizations of the Teaching Profession, in cooperation with the All-India Federation of Educational Associations and with the help of the government of India, has undertaken a study of the economic, social, and professional status of teachers in India. This study, now completed, and the recommendations of the Education Commission, may help to strengthen teacher organizations in India.

As further evidence of the government of India's recognition of the importance of the teacher as a social force is the constitution of India which provides for a teachers' constituency in the legislative councils of the states. The teachers alone, of all the professional classes, have the right to elect their representatives to the legislative bodies. The institution of the President's Award for Distinguished Service to teachers, followed by the state governments' similar recognition by means of state awards, are further steps in recognizing the importance of the work of the teacher. A national foundation for teacher welfare has been set up by the central government to provide a benevolent fund for teachers who have retired from service. The central government, although constitutionally not responsible for financing education, has been making liberal grants, particularly to meet expenses incurred by the states in improving the salary scales of teachers.

UNIFYING THE TEACHER ORGANIZATION

The All-India Federation of Educational Associations, despite its organizational weaknesses, described earlier, does useful work. Its annual conferences are attended by teachers working in different types of educational institutions. The conference is thus an integrating forum. At its conference, there are many sectional meetings. These sections deal with different aspects of education such as pre-primary, early childhood, primary, secondary school, and university education, home, technical and vocational, physical, social, teacher, women's, and geopolitics and international education, educational research, examinations, military studies, education of the handicapped, and the education of the aborigines and the tribal people. Thus, the conference provides an occasion when the delegates can obtain a general perspective concerning the field of education. Similar opportunities are, however, not available at the state levels except in the South India Teachers' Union of Madras State. The failure to have more of these programs which help integrate education only accentuates the division among teachers, results in clashes, and weakens them as organized groups. One, of course, can hope that teachers will have common professional goals which would help unify them into a single organization. This unity, I believe, will occur despite all the forces that now keep them separate.

TEACHER EDUCATION AND TEACHER ORGANIZATION

The staffs of teacher training institutions have remained aloof from teacher organizations, although recently they have become more interested in becoming associated with these organizations. The All-India Association of Teacher Education which, as was described earlier, developed out of the Association of Principals of Training Colleges is seeking to get such teachers into a single all-India body. The government of India, its Planning Commission, and the Indian Education Commission have been stressing the importance of comprehensive teacher education institutions to provide for different levels and types of teacher education. This new association reflects the current trend toward unifying and integrating teacher education. Another movement was initiated in 1955 when the All-India Council for Secondary Education planned an elaborate program of extension services for teachers in secondary schools. As a result, teacher training college faculty members frequently visit secondary schools in their areas, hold discussions and conferences with the headmasters and teachers, and participate in refresher courses for the teachers. The activities of the extension service departments during the last 13 years have brought the training colleges into closer contact with the schools. A deeper understanding of the problems of the school has led to new thinking about teacher education.

The success of these evolving extension services to the secondary schools has caused the central and state governments to set up state institutes of education with the primary object of training extension workers who may be attached to the teacher training schools. Their job will be to organize programs of in-service training for teachers in elementary or primary schools. As the extension programs develop in the next ten years, closer liaison may well be established between the teacher training schools and the teachers in primary schools, and, since the latter group is more active in teacher organizations, their joint relationship may bring about an increased participation on the part of the staffs of the training schools in the various teacher organizations. This, in turn, will affect the involvement of future teachers being trained at the training schools.

Another trend has become noticeable since the launching of the extension project. Inspecting officers, called school inspectors or district educational officers, are taking a keen interest in the in-service programs for teachers. They advise the area teacher training institute which refresher courses are necessary. They actively participate in these courses and encourage teachers to attend them. They comment on the improvement in classroom practices as a result of such participation. Inspecting officers and the teachers can now meet as co-workers in the search for good education instead of the older relationship of faultfinder and victim. Still, educational officers and inspectors are not members of the teacher organizations in any appreciable number. There is now, however, a greater degree of friendship and sympathy than before.

TEACHERS' DEMANDS

Although all teacher associations have as their main aim improvement in the quality of education, there has been an increasing emphasis on problems related to the teacher's salary and to service conditions, which are considered poor as can be seen from Table 1. In many private teaching instituions recognized by the government, teachers have little or no security of tenure and in some states, the

TABLE 1. AVERAGE ANNUAL SALARIES OF TEACHERS IN INDIA, 1950–51 TO 1965–66

Types of Institutions	Average Annual Salary of Teachers (At Current Prices) in Rupees [a]				Average Annual Salary in 1965–66 At 1950–51 Prices
	1950–51	1955–56	1960–61	1965–66	
A. Higher Education					
1. University Departments	3,759	5,546	5,475	6,500	3,939
	(100) [b]	(145)	(146)	(173)	(105)
2. Colleges of Arts and Science	2,696	3,070	3,659	4,000	2,424
	(100)	(114)	(136)	(148)	(90)
3. Professional Colleges	3,948	3,861	4,237	6,410	3,885
	(100)	(98)	(107)	(152)	(98)
B. Schools					
4. Secondary Schools	1,258	1,427	1,681	1,959	1,187
	(100)	(113)	(134)	(156)	(94)
5. Higher Primary Schools	682	809	1,058	1,228	741
	(100)	(119)	(155)	(180)	(109)
6. Lower Primary Schools	545	652	873	1,046	634
	(100)	(120)	(160)	(192)	(116)
7. Pre-primary Schools	914	770	925	1,083	656
	(100)	(84)	(101)	(118)	(72)
8. Vocational Schools	1,705	1,569	2,041	2,887	1,750
	(100)	(92)	(120)	(169)	(103)
All Teachers	769	919	1,218	1,476	895
	(100)	(120)	(158)	(192)	(116)
9. Cost of living index for working classes.	100	95	123	165	
10. National income per head of population (at current prices)	267	255	326	424	
	(100)	(96)	(122)	(159)	

[a] 7.5 rupees = 1 American dollar.

[b] The figures within parenthesis give the index of growth on the basis of 1950–51 =100.

SOURCE: Ministry of Education, Form A. The figures for 1965–66 are estimates made in the Commission Secretariat.

conditions remain as bad as they were before India attained freedom.

Moreover, the scales of salaries are varied. Schools controlled by the central government have a higher salary scale than those controlled by local bodies. Schools receiving state aid have a still lower scale. Other benefits vary in a similar manner. Even the higher scales offered in governmental schools are inadequate and are not based on professional qualifications and responsibilities. Thus, teacher associations appear justified in formulating their demands and in submitting memoranda to the educational authorities. Teachers, like other workers, have found that the language of agitation, demonstration, and direct action stimulates the government to take quick action. Reasoned representations are considered only slowly. Hence some of the teacher organizations in Kerala, Vidharba, Uttar Pradesh, Bihar, and West Bengal have drawn public attention to their grievances by such means as fasting, hunger marches, processions, and even strikes.

The most important demands of the teachers are:
1. Better pay scale.
2. Adequate cost-of-living allowances.
3. Parity of salaries and allowances among teachers doing similar work under different managements.
4. Adequate old age and retirement benefits.
5. Better rules concerning leaves of absence.
6. Living quarters or house rent allowance.
7. Medical care and sickness benefits.

They are being met slowly but steadily because many people in and outside the government believe them just and reasonable. Madras State has granted most of these demands except living quarters and medical care benefits. Other state governments are also moving in this direction. The central government constantly keeps urging the state governments to take steps to improve the lot of the teachers. One specific demand warrants special attention—parity of pay.

The Indian Education Commission in its report mentioned earlier, reports that the demand for the introduction of national scales of pay for all categories of teachers is supported unanimously by teachers' organizations. This proposal for national scales was readily accepted in higher education because of the developments in the post-independence period. The University Education Commission recommended that the multiplicity of scales of pay which then existed in the universities and colleges should be reduced to the minimum and that an attempt should be made to adopt national scales of pay for teachers in higher education. This recommendation was generally accepted and implemented. Common scales of pay for different categories of teachers in the universities and similar scales of pay for teachers in affiliated colleges are being introduced. Attempts to achieve common scales of pay are also being made, with a fair amount of success, in engineering schools. It is true, however, that in spite of all that has been done during the last ten years, there are still considerable variations in the scales of pay of teachers in higher education. But the important point is that the overall principle of adopting national scales of pay has been generally accepted, and the problems now are to make a more determined effort to move forward on the lines already set.

Below the university level, however, the problem is more difficult because the desirability of introducing national scales of pay is itself challenged. It is argued, for instance, that as the cost of living varies from one part of the country to another, a common national scale of pay would really result in unequal pay and cause considerable hardship to school teachers in high cost-of-living areas. Critics also point out that the supply and demand position for different categories of teachers varies considerably from one part of the country to another. Women teachers, for instance, are readily available in some areas and are difficult to obtain in others. Under these circumstances, a common scale of pay would make it more difficult to recruit them in just those areas where they are most needed.

There is some force in these arguments which, however, could be met by providing local allowances in addition to basic national scales of pay. They surely do not provide grounds for rejecting the national scales of pay in order to reduce the large disparities which now exist among school teachers in different states. The Indian Education Commission therefore believes that it would be worthwhile if the government of India set minimum scales of pay for school teachers. The state should then adopt equivalent or higher scales of pay to suit their local conditions. Moreover, the remuneration of teachers having the same qualifications and the same responsibilities should have the same, or at least similar, remuneration and conditions of work and service.

UNIONIZATION VERSUS PROFESSIONALIZATION

The teacher organizations do not favor becoming unions. Some of the teacher organizations in states like Maharashtra, Bengal, Uttar Pradesh, and Kerala have registered under the India Trade Union Act. They have not, however, definitely aligned themselves with other labor unions. The Trade Union Act gives the right to an organization to represent its members in negotiations as well as the right to practice direct action. Hence, the teacher organizations, by registering under the act, do not necessarily become aligned with organized labor but rather seek the legal recognition that registration provides. Nevertheless, all teacher organizations receive a considerable measure of sympathy and support from the trade unions. There has been no noticeable pressure on teacher organizations to become part of the other labor organizations in the country.

Although almost all the teacher organizations are deeply concerned about economic aspects of teachers' work such as salary and allowances, they seem to believe that becoming a union will lessen their major responsibilities as bodies involved in the professional aspects of education. The justification for this approach is that the teacher in India is generally a dedicated person, conscientious in the discharge of his duties. His love for his pupils and his work is great. In a survey of the work load of teachers conducted by the South India Teachers' Union Council of Educational Research it was found:

1. That teachers work from 42 to 45 hours a week, which includes about 18 to 20 hours of teaching.
2. That the teacher returns from school with a sense of accomplishment. He avails himself of every opportunity provided by extension programs and services and other agencies for in-service education.

Some of the teacher organizations organize special courses and lectures on different aspects of education. All the organizations have at least an annual educational conference and educational exhibition. At these conferences, papers on selected topics are presented and discussed. Moreover, the All-India Science Teachers' Association holds along with its conference a competition among its members for presentation of new teaching methods and aids used or devised by teachers; prizes are awarded to the teacher whose method or aid is considered original and effective. It is feared by some teachers that such professional activities would be diluted or disappear if the teacher organizations became teacher unions.

TEACHER ORGANIZATIONS:
STRUCTURE AND FINANCE

Practically all the teacher organizations are financially weak except the Headmasters' Federation of the Maharashtra State, the West Bengal Headmasters' Association, and the All-Bengal Teachers Association, and these seem to be only in a slightly better economic situation than the others. In these few organizations, teachers are members of the central body and pay dues to it. This enables them to have a permanent, full-time executive staff. They also publish journals and issue bulletins, which provide some communication between the organization and its members. On the other hand, most of the other central teacher organizations have a fiscal structure which gives the national organization only a small fraction of what the individual teacher pays in dues to his local association. They have a federal type of organization in which the member belongs directly to the local association, which in turn is represented in the district, then the state, and finally the All-India body. A member pays dues to the local association. A portion of this sum is paid as affiliation fee to the district association; of this fee a moiety is available to the state association. As a result, the state association can only contribute an extremely small sum to the All-India Federation of Educational Associations. Furthermore, the teacher's salary is low and hence the individual membership fee paid in the first place to his local association is very small.

In these circumstances, none of the state organizations is able to employ a paid executive staff. Many of them do not have even a permanent office for it changes with the principal elected officer, the president or the secretary. These persons are elected to their offices, and they discharge their responsibilities in addition to their normally heavy work load as teachers or headmasters. As teachers' salaries improve, the financial resources of the teacher organizations should also improve, along with the ability to support a better administrative structure.

With very few exceptions, there is little or no communication among the members of the teacher organizations, except at the annual conferences. The South India Teachers' Union, the Mysore State Federation of Teachers, and the State Teachers' Union of Andhra Pradesh publish regular monthly magazines which keep the members informed of the organization's activities. These magazines also place before the teachers educational ideas and views. The editors are teachers who work as amateur journalists. They have neither the time nor the professional preparation for such work. But they carry it on with whatever zeal they can muster despite the difficulties inherent in producing regular educational magazines. A workshop or conference of editors of educational journals was convened at the time of the General Assembly of the World Confederation of Organizations of the Teaching Profession held at New Delhi in July-August, 1961. The Conference recommended that governmental financial assistance be given to teacher organizations for publishing educational journals.

TEACHER ORGANIZATIONS' RELATIONSHIPS WITH OTHER ORGANIZATIONS

Teacher organizations have usually remained nonpolitical. A few associations, however, have leaned toward certain political parties. This may be due largely to the personal political views of their top leaders. Such a tendency is noticeable in particular states such as West Bengal and Kerala where the political atmosphere is somewhat troubled. Generally speaking, however, whatever the political views individual teachers may hold, their organizations have been nonpolitical. They have kept on friendly terms with all the political parties. Besides not becoming tied to political parties, the teacher organizations have not generally established any relationship with labor unions or social organizations. They seem to be in isolation, concerned with their own problems and, to some extent, with general educational programs and policies.

INVOLVEMENT IN DETERMINING EDUCATIONAL POLICIES

Teacher organizations have not been involved in the formulation of educational policies and programs as such. They do offer criticisms after the government announces its decisions. Moreover, teachers are often appointed to consultative committees which may consider educational programs. But such appointments are of a personal nature in recognition of a teacher's specific abilities. They are not chosen to represent teacher organizations.

One reason that teacher organizations are not effective in shaping educational policies may be the division among the organizations. Also, facilities for teacher education are still limited. They were even worse before 1946. Today about 45 per cent of the practicing teachers have had no professional training. Further, about 35 to 40 per cent of the teachers in most of India's elementary schools have had only seven or eight years of schooling. Thus, many teachers are not qualified to offer advice on educational policies. Another and a more important factor is the perhaps narrow view that the teachers and their organizations take of their responsibilities in developing educational policies. A high sense of professional responsibility for helping in the formulation of educational goals and policies has yet to be developed. Perhaps the increasing interest which the governments are taking in teacher organizations may lead to an improvement in the status of these organizations, and as a result they may become concerned with over-all educational policies.

In this connection, it should be noted that India is an emerging country making progress in the different fields of industry and agriculture. The preoccupation of the leaders so far has been and will be for some time in developing economic self-sufficiency. But now there is a growing realization that education is basic to progress, and increasing attention is being paid to it. It cannot yet be said that there is a national policy for education with clearly defined goals. India is still only carrying on the system that prevailed before independence, despite frequent criticisms that it was designed to produce clerks, that it develops only the ability to do what one is told to do, and that it stifles imagination and initiative. Though several commissions and committees have dealt with aspects of education, only recently has a commission been set up to study the entire field of education and to recommend measures to be taken in order that education may serve the varied needs of the nation. Teacher organizations were invited by this commission to submit their views and to tender evidence before them, which they have done.

TEACHER ORGANIZATIONS AND EDUCATIONAL RESEARCH

The SITU Council of Educational Research is the only organization of teachers that has the goal of conducting research and studies in education. This was organized by the South India Teachers Union at a time when it realized that the struggle for better pay would preoccupy them. It, however, understood the importance of research in education in improving the quality of educational service rendered by teachers. It has undertaken studies in curriculum, carried on experiments in new methods and techniques of classroom procedures, and has surveyed laboratory facilities available in schools for the teaching of science and library service in schools in Madras state. Its work is having an impact on education in Madras and is attracting attention in other parts of India. It is a voluntary organization of teachers in schools and teacher training institutions. It is receiving financial assistance from the National Council of Educational Research and Training (set up by the Ministry of Education in 1961), from the government of Madras, and from the Universities of Madras and Annamalai which have each nominated a representative to the organization's executive board.

THE FUTURE

This joint effort in educational research is a hopeful sign of better professional cooperation between the practicing teacher and educational authorities. An increase in such cooperation in other fields of education would help not only the teacher, but also his organizations and education in general. The report of the Education Commission may strengthen such cooperation. The government of India has supported many of the educational recommendations made by the joint UNESCO-International Labor Organization's experts meeting on the status of teachers. A spokesman of the Indian government has said that the government will take suitable action along the lines of the recommendations of these experts to improve the professional, economic, and social status of the teachers.[2] The present conflict between unionization and professionalization of teacher organizations may resolve itself in favor of professionalization if the UNESCO recommendation is followed that statutory negotiating bodies be set up and consist of representatives of teacher organizations and educational authorities. Then the Indian teacher, with his traditional love for teaching and dedication to the child, will be able to concentrate on his professional responsibilities as a teacher while the teacher organizations will

2 See Chapter 10 herein.

become increasingly involved in the development of an educational philosophy and in formulating educational policies and programs.

It is interesting to note that the Indian Education Commission has recognized that teachers' organizations have a great role to play in Indian education. It suggests a number of functions for teacher organizations.

1. To secure for their members, individually and collectively, their rightful status—social, economic, and professional.
2. To safeguard their professional interests and to secure satisfactory conditions of work and service.
3. To secure the professional growth of teachers through refresher courses, seminars, publications, library service, and research.
4. To work for the improvement of education in response to the challenge of the ever-changing socioeconomic situation.
5. To improve the teaching of subjects through the establishment of subject-teachers' associations.
6. To establish a professional code of conduct for teachers and to ensure that it is followed by members.

It has been further recommended that professional organizations of teachers fulfilling the above functions and having a responsible and representative body of members should be recognized by the central and state governments. Such recognition should entitle them to the right of being consulted on all matters relating to school education, general and professional education of teachers, and salaries and conditions of work and service.

Backed by such recommendations, teacher organizations may grow stronger and, as a result, the All-India Federation of Educational Associations may become a true federation of all teachers' organizations in India, bringing about the unification of the teaching forces of the country and becoming a more powerful factor in the development of the country.

Japan 5

Solomon B. Levine

Teacher unionism in postwar Japan is intimately bound up with the profound economic, political, and social changes that have occurred in that nation since 1945. The dramatic upsurge of the general labor movement immediately following World War II represented a major alteration in Japan's institutional landscape. From the outset, teacher unionism became an integral part of organized labor, comprised one of its major sectors, furnished some of its most articulate leadership, and spearheaded its growth in becoming the third or fourth largest labor movement in the democratic countries. In providing critical links within the movement as a whole, the teacher unions have welded together an unusual alliance between white- and blue-collar workers.[1]

Despite numerous difficulties which have confronted teacher

[1] Solomon B. Levine, "Unionization of White-Collar Employees in Japan," in *White-Collar Trade Unions,* ed. Adolf Sturmthal (Urbana and London; University of Illinois Press, 1966), pp. 205–260.

SOLOMON B. LEVINE is Professor of Economics and Business and a member of the Industrial Relations Research Institute and the East Asian Studies Program at the University of Wisconsin, Madison. For assistance in gathering and preparing materials used in this study, the author is indebted to Toshiaki Izeki, Ryuji Komatsu, Yasumi Miyamoto, and Yoshihiro Mizuno, former Graduate Fellows at the Institute of Labor and Industrial Relations, University of Illinois, as grantees supported by the Keio-Illinois Research and Exchange Program in Industrial Relations. I also wish to thank Professor Hisashi Kawada, Keio University, and Kazutoshi Koshiro, Yokohama National University, for helpful comments.

unionization in Japan, the unionized teachers have maintained this vital position to the present and may be expected to continue to do so for the foreseeable future. Although Japanese teacher unions have continually encountered government restrictions, public antagonism, and internal disruption, their viability rests on providing the teachers—for the first time in Japanese history—with an important, if not sole, means for achieving professional status, exercising political power, and gaining economic improvements. This hybridization of functions and objectives—expressed principally through the more than half-million-member nationwide teacher organization, Nikkyōso [2]—has assured teachers a permanent and prominent place in the Japanese trade union scene. The strengths and weaknesses of the organized teachers reside in this hybrid combination.

Today, almost one of every 15 unionists in Japan is a teacher. About 80 per cent of the nation's more than 900,000 employees in educational services are unionized. Nikkyōso, probably the largest nationwide teachers' union in the free world, has the second largest membership in Japan [3] and is affiliated with the 4.2 million member Sōhyō,[4] Japan's biggest national labor center. Teacher unionism pervades Japan; local units or branches are organized down to the hamlet level in almost all the more than 3,000 public school districts.

This study probes the reasons for and the consequences of the unusual role teacher unionization has played in postwar Japan. It focuses upon the salient characteristics of Japanese teacher unionism that have evolved since World War II, especially those features that appear useful for comparing Japan's experience with other nations. Because of space limits many details are omitted; for example, relatively little attention is given to relations among and between teachers and school administrators, content of teacher training, or teacher salary structures and levels, although no doubt such matters are important facets of any analysis of teacher unionism.

First, to depict the conditions in which Japanese teacher unionism arose, the study traces the evolution of modern education in

---

[2] Or, Nihon Kyōiku Shokuin Rōdō Kumiai (Japan Teachers Union). The official abbreviations for trade unions are used in the text; the full name and translation into English are given in footnotes.

[3] The largest is Jichirō (or, Zen Nihon Jichi Dantai Rōdō Kumiai), the All-Japan Perfectural and Municipal Workers Union, with close to 800,000 members.

[4] Or, Nihon Rōdō Kumiai Sōhyōgikai (Japan General Council of Trade Unions).

Japan, beginning with the Meiji Restoration and culminating in the profound reforms instituted by the Allied Occupation. It then turns to the emergence of teacher unions—the organization, growth and spread, and extent of membership—contrasting the brief and limited prewar experience with the almost total unionization after 1945.

Next, the analysis takes up the motivations, objectives, and philosophy that underlay the efforts to organize the teachers and led to the formation of Nikkyōso. This is followed by discussions of union structure, membership scope, factionalism, and rival unionism, which in turn lead into sections on relationships with the general labor movement, notably Nikkyōso's affiliation with Sōhyō, and programs for political and economic action. The study concludes with a review of major public policy issues regarding teacher unionization, especially as seen in the running confrontation between Nikkyōso and the central government and in the prolonged conflict over Japan's ratification of ILO Convention 87 on Freedom of Association. These issues serve to depict such problems as the appropriate "professional" conduct of teachers and their role in shaping educational development in the New Japan.

EDUCATION IN JAPAN'S PREWAR DEVELOPMENT [5]

A principal ingredient in Japan's emergence as a modern economy and political state almost a century ago was the rapid spread of formal educational institutions. By the turn of the century, the Meiji educational system provided six years of compulsory elementary schooling for all children, laid the foundations for an economically functional, multiple-track tier of secondary schools, and established a small set of high quality, elitist universities. These developments were part of Japan's response to real or imagined threats of Western invasion and colonialism, and, at the same time, they were the release of long-accumulated internal forces for organizing human talents and abilities already present within Japan's crumbling but dynamic premodern society. Education was tied inti-

[5] Unless otherwise noted, the data in this section are drawn from Ronald P. Dore, *Education in Tokugawa Japan* (Berkeley: University of California Press, 1965); Herbert Passin, *Society and Education in Japan* (New York: Columbia University, 1965); and Japanese National Commission for UNESCO, *The Role of Education in the Social and Economic Development of Japan* (Tokyo: Ministry of Education, Japan, 1966).

mately to a nationwide determination—based upon wide popular consensus, buttressed by a highly homogeneous culture, and led by an energetic oligarchy—to embark upon rapid economic growth, industrialization, and militarism which would place Japan in the ranks of the leading world powers. Japan reached this objective within a generation, the first non-Western nation to do so.

Whether by conscious design or not, education functioned to universalize values and norms crucial for modern development and also preserved a particularistic stratification reminiscent of the pre-modern social structure. Key to this educational dualism was the training of appropriate numbers of teachers who could be at one and the same time both modern and traditional in outlook. Actually, Japan entered the modern era relatively well-endowed with a supply of experienced teachers. Teaching had long been a respected career. The very word for teacher, *sensei,* commanded reverence. In transforming Japan, the Meiji leadership first chose to rely upon this group, even though it was not well prepared, for carrying out instruction until new training institutions could generate replacements.

Until 1868, official concern of the shogunal government and the feudal clan lords had been almost exclusively focused on the career preparation of samurai, who, as a class comprising about five per cent of the total population, were expected to assume responsibility for public administration. Increasingly, samurai education had emphasized intellectual attainment, especially in the context of Tokugawa Japan's isolation from the rest of the world and the prolonged 250-year era of relatively peaceful conditions within Japan. However, while the shogunal and clan governments did not actively oppose or support commoner education, schooling at this level had also grown rapidly after the middle of the eighteenth century largely as the result of local and private efforts. For commoners the most notable educational development was the spread throughout cities and villages of the *terakoya* (literally, "temple" or parish schools) , which tended to be secular and stressed teaching of the three "R's" and homely ethics. In systematizing and extending elementary education, the Meiji government relied upon this *terakoya* base. For establishing the tiers of secondary and higher education, the government transformed the officially sponsored shogunal and clan schools and utilized privately operated academies (*shijuku*) which also had become widespread.

The private academies, which at the end of the Tokugawa era enrolled more than 150,000 students, were especially important for the molding of education in Meiji Japan that would combine both traditional and modern elements. As independent centers of learning, usually based around a single master-teacher, these schools often experimented with new knowledge and ideas which supported social, political, and economic change. They were among the forerunners in introducing Western studies, particularly science, and produced some of Japan's most respected teachers and able students. Significantly, the *shijuku* did not limit enrollment to samurai, but were open to all who showed aptitude for learning in *terakoya* or fief elementary schools. Thus, in addition to providing the base for secondary and higher education, they were significant in providing a heritage of academic freedom and professional independence.

These sources of educational development in modern Japan stressed both regimentation and self-dependence—two principles which have remained in conflict throughout Japan's modern period. At first, the Meiji leadership hoped that the established schools could be readily converted with little added investment to embrace the aims of the New State. In fact, however, habits and techniques in education did not change rapidly.

When a Ministry of Education was first established in 1871, it drew up highly ambitious plans for establishing the world's first nationwide school system. A Code for Education, promulgated in 1872, called for the immediate creation of 53,760 elementary schools, 256 middle schools, and eight universities, and a universal requirement of four years of compulsory elementary education. To administer the system the Ministry adopted the French model of local financial responsibility subject to centralized supervision and urged use of pragmatic American-style teaching methods.

However, this comprehensive plan took much longer to achieve than anticipated, and indeed the number of elementary schools called for does not exist even today. The combination of local financial responsibility, central supervision, and pragmatism in teaching failed to catch fire. By the end of the 1870's barely half of the elementary schools planned were in operation; most were still carryovers of *terakoya* and fief schools. In 1879, largely as the result of local resistance, compulsory education was reduced to 16 months for children between the ages of 6 and 14. By 1880, only ten per cent of the schoolteachers had graduated from the newly established normal schools, also created by the Ministry's plan. Local communities provided far too low compensation to attract able persons into the profession as full-time teachers so that the pre-Meiji teachers, many of whom were deposed samurai, remained the principal corps of instructors, usually committed to traditional methods of education.

By the mid-1880's the government ceased to rely upon the French administrative model. In the name of restoring Japan's "traditions," the government began to introduce a much higher degree of regimentation in the schools. In particular, major targets were the training of schoolteachers, their assignment to the various schools, and their teaching duties. In the decade from 1885 to 1895, education policy was completely reshaped and set the pattern for the next 60 years. Only in higher education and in the scattered private schools was academic liberalism permitted to persist.

The process of centralization and regimentation began with an Imperial Rescript in 1879 which called for a return to Confucianist principles in education. A year later, a traditionalist took the helm of the Educational Ministry and ordered that all schools teach Japanese "morals" and replace all "foreign" textbooks with indigenous materials. For the first time, moreover, and contrary to earlier pronouncements, the new Minister declared that all teachers were public servants, not independent scholars, and issued orders forbidding teachers to participate in political activities.

Final shaping of Japan's modern educational system came under the leadership of Mori Arinori, who after returning to Japan from his post as Minister to England in 1884, was appointed Minister of Education the following year, a cabinet rank for the first time. Mori brought to the post an interesting mixture of attitudes which stressed a revival of traditional Japanese values combined with the efficiency of Western institutions and techniques. Probably as much if not more than any other single individual in the Meiji period, he represented the apotheosis of the slogan, "Western Science, Japanese Culture." Although Mori was assassinated by a fanatic in 1889, his four years in office were the turning point in Japan's modern educational development, striking a stable balance between a small dash of liberalism and a large dose of regimentation, between the pragmatic efficiency of Westernization and the emotionalism of Japanese nationalism.

Mori succeeded in imposing a uniform curriculum in the elementary schools and ordered the return to four years of compulsory education. The Ministry issued standardized textbooks, systematically introduced Germanic pedagogy and required the famous course on Japanese ethics in every school. At the same time, under Mori's leadership, the concept of a multiple-track secondary school system was firmly established, while Tokyo University, now renamed the Imperial University, was further consolidated as the pinnacle of Japanese education. School uniforms, symbolizing the "spirit of morality and nationalism," became mandatory for all students. It should be noted that, even though the universities were permitted to retain considerable academic freedom, the regimentation imposed on all school children, plus the difficulties of rising up a highly competitive educational ladder, insulated centers of higher education from radical "excesses."

Mori's strictest measures dealt with the training of the teachers. The chief aim was to inculcate devotion to the state and to buttress Japanese nationalism. Normal schools were consolidated and set apart as a distinct secondary educational track, and the content of the curricula increasingly stressed morality, harmony, and obedience. Military drill became compulsory for teacher candidates, who were now required to live together in army-type barracks under the supervision of ex-military officers. As wards of the state, these students received financial support from the government. No longer was there any question of whether the teachers, now placed under prefectural jurisdiction, were state servants or independent academics.

In the wake of Mori's reforms, the teaching profession was completely transformed. An entirely new generation entered teaching careers, displacing the pre-Meiji independents. Commoners, rather than ex-samurai, now made up the teaching corps. With this changeover, there was a notable decline in the social status of teachers, especially for elementary school instructors, although for a peasant family acceptance of one of its members into a normal school represented a distinct improvement.

The capstone of the new system was the Imperial Rescript on Education, proclaimed on October 30, 1890, soon after the adoption of the Meiji Constitution. The Rescript reaffirmed Japan's traditional Shinto-Confucianist values and demanded filial piety, obedience to superiors, and primary duty to the state on the part of all subjects. Until 1945, every schoolchild was to learn by heart the wording of this document.

Full achievement of the educational system launched by Mori took another 15 years. By the time of the Russo-Japanese War, compulsory education, about to be extended from four to six years, was virtually universal. Increasingly, the central government took over direct financing of the schools from the local communities; the charging of tuition completely disappeared. Now, each prefecture supported at least one middle school and one normal school. Secondary education was on the verge of rapid proliferation, based on multiple tracking, while quasi-vocational programs and institutes were mushrooming in response to the needs for trained manpower in the fast-growing industrial development. At the level of higher education, the comprehensive Imperial University in Tokyo was the model for several additional imperial universities, and for the growing number of private colleges and universities. From the early years of the present century until 1945, this educational structure remained fixed, but expanded enormously, notably leaping ahead during World War I. Within the context of the multiple track system, an individual's career possibilities were determined early, usually by the time he was 14 years old or younger.

When militarists ascended to power in Japan following the Manchurian Incident in 1931, the military quickly seized upon the educational system as a chief means to assure its control. The transition was easily accomplished, since there were few elements, outside the university centers, who saw much difference from the control pattern that had long been in operation. Increasingly the schools carried out ultranationalistic indoctrination as part of the technique of "thought control." In 1941, as the Pacific War was to become World War II, a leading Army general became Minister of Education, and the schools became an integral part of the military establishment.

Throughout this 50-year period, the Japanese government considered the public school teacher a major key for achieving national unification, for inculcating the young population with the desired ideology and moral values, and for guiding the children into needed career patterns. The teacher was the "first line of Japanese nationalism" and at the local hamlet level was required to perform functions which had long been reserved to family heads and village elders. He usually played a dual role: an obedient servant of the state, subject to the closest scrutiny of his personal life and placed at the lowest rung on the civil service hierarchy; and a respected counselor and man of wisdom at the local community level. This dualism reflected the government's dilemma of "creating a powerful, modern state" and at the same time "permitting unrestricted social change." It was within this context and in view of the lingering notion of the independent teacher that the government felt compelled to exert close control of teacher activities. In instituting the compulsory course on morals, the government asserted that "the teacher must himself be a model of these virtues in his daily life, and must endeavor to stimulate his pupils along the path of virtue." Minister Mori was even more direct: "In the administration of all schools, it must be kept in mind, what is to be done is not for the sake of the pupils, but for the sake of the country."

Inculcation of the teacher depended heavily upon regulating his training. In the 1880's, the state systematically expanded its operation of normal schools, establishing the Tokyo Higher Normal School as the model for prefectural schools. Those accepted into the normal schools committed themselves for life to teaching. In the late 1880's, in fact, the Ministry of Education specified a minimum of ten years of service after graduation.

As a distinct secondary education track, normal schools began to mushroom following the mid-1880's, when there were approximately 80 such training establishments. Although fewer than 1,000 students were enrolled in normal schools in 1900, the enrollment had more than doubled by 1920. And in 1945, almost 75,000 students were in teacher training programs.[6] The rise of teaching as an occupation is reflected in the ratio of primary and secondary teachers per 10,000 population since Japan's modernization began. In 1880, this ratio was 5.5; by 1905, it had grown to 21.2. The peak was reached during the 1920's when the ratio was almost double the latter figure. It then leveled off as the educational saturation point set in.[7] In the prewar era, the pattern of teacher training reached full development in the 1920's. For the preceding 30 years, the structure of the normal schools and content of their curriculum underwent numerous changes, which culminated in the adoption of

6 John E. Blewett, ed. and trans., *Higher Education in Postwar Japan* (Tokyo: Sophia University Press, 1965), pp. 150–151.
7 Hisashi Kawada and Solomon B. Levine, *Human Resources Development in the Industrialization of Japan* (unpublished manuscript).

the Universities Act of 1918. With this legislation, normal school training became uniform.[8]

These developments signified that, as in other areas of professional and technical education, the training of teachers had become highly channelized. Virtually all new teachers for Japan's schools now came through a system closely controlled by central government authorities. Furthermore, the teacher candidate was not exposed to the intellectual freedom of the university, although in 1943, in an effort to enhance the prestige of teachers and to cope with increasingly complex subject matter, the Ministry of Education took direct charge of all prefectural normal schools and raised their status to that of the technical college—a step that was a forerunner of the Occupation reforms. Except for this gesture, however, teacher training was not considered a part of Japan's prewar system of higher education, but a specialized institution limited to directly serving the aims of the state.

THE POSTWAR REFORM OF EDUCATION AND UPGRADING OF TEACHERS

The initial aim of the Allied Occupation was to transform defeated Japan into a peaceful nation, incapable of waging war and restructured to foster a democratic society. Almost immediately, General MacArthur, as Supreme Commander of the Allied Powers (SCAP), initiated a set of drastic reforms which affected nearly every field of human activity. The most prominent were the purging of ultranationalists from public life; abolition of the military (including war crime trials of government and military leaders); adoption of a new national constitution that de-deified the Emperor, instituted representative party government, and provided a "bill of rights" of unprecedented scope; redistribution of landholdings to eradicate tenancy; dissolution of the *zaibatsu* cartels; encouragement of a widespread labor movement; and an increase in years of compulsory education and widening of educational opportunity. Here, of course, the focus is primarily on the last.

Equality in educational opportunity was the principal theme. This meant abandoning the multiple track system, instituting coeducation, and establishing comprehensive schools. It also meant

[8] Ronald S. Anderson, *Japan: Three Epochs of Modern Education* (Washington: U.S. Department of Health, Education, and Welfare, 1959), pp. 156–158.

a drastic revision in curricula at all levels and a wholesale change in teacher training. At the same time, the reform called for the end of central government control over education. Autonomy was to revert to the local community which, within the guidelines set by the new constitution and Occupation policy, was to be responsible for the basic educational process.

The Occupation's implementation of these aims followed the recommendations of the U.S. Educational Commission to Japan issued in 1946, although in the interim steps were taken to purge ultranationalists from the schools, eliminate the teaching of Japanese ethics, introduce new materials and textbooks, and encourage the formation of teacher unions. Despite expressions of doubt and fear, the Japanese government, hardly in a position to thwart Occupation desires, embodied the recommendations in the new national Constitution and subsequent legislation. Article 26 of the Constitution, which went into effect in May 1947, declared: "All people shall have the right to receive an equal education correspondent to their ability. . . ."; while Article 19 specified: "Academic freedom is guaranteed. . . ." Already in March 1947, the new School Education Law and the Fundamental Law of Education began to spell out the details of these provisions.

Specifically, the reforms immediately extended compulsory education from six to nine years, with a common core curriculum and coeducation of the sexes. They consolidated all secondary school above the ninth grade into a tier of three-year high schools, also on a coeducational basis, open to all on the basis of competitive examinations; and set up a system of four-year universities and two- to three-year junior colleges, which absorbed all the pre-existing professional and technical institutes, including the normal schools.

The enormity of this change was staggering. School buildings and facilities, destroyed or damaged by bombing or allowed to deteriorate during the war, had to be rebuilt or newly constructed in the face of burgeoning school attendance. Most Japanese saw in education the best means for enhancing their career chances. In particular, to meet this demand, there was the pressing need to create new colleges and universities. In 1942, only 49 institutions of higher education existed; by 1955, there were 245 universities and 320 junior colleges. In 1947, fewer than 90,000 students enrolled in universities, with faculties numbering less than 8,500; ten years later, the university and college student body had grown to almost

650,000 and the faculty to 55,000. These growth rates, it should be noted, have continued to the present.[9] Still another index of dramatic educational change was the increase in the ratio of primary and secondary school teachers per 10,000 population. By 1950, it had almost doubled over the level ten years earlier to 71.8; by 1960, it reached 74.5.

This growth signalled a revolution in teacher training and the status of the teacher in Japan. With the normal schools incorporated into the new single track 6-3-3-4 system, officially required preparation for a teaching career, as in some other professions, lengthened by as much as five years. This created a large gap between the new candidates and the teachers who were carried over from the prewar system. Thus, in addition to bringing teacher training into college and university curricula, it was also necessary to embark on a large-scale program to upgrade the existing teacher force. Under the National School Establishment Law adopted in 1949, 51 of the 71 national universities then in existence were required to provide four-year teacher education programs. At the same time, the Ministry of Education launched retraining programs for the 600,000 active teachers who did not then meet the new requirements for certification.

Actually, more than a decade was required to bring the teaching force to the level of preparation necessitated by the reforms. Although minimum standards were set in the Law for the Certification of Educational Personnel of 1949, it permitted the issuance of temporary and emergency certificates and the substitution of previous years of experience or in-service training for university study. In the spring of 1947, for example, it was estimated that, while there was a shortage of more than 100,000 qualified teachers, at the same time 80,000 unlicensed instructors were employed in the elementary schools and another 28,000 without certification in the middle and high schools. In 1951, the year temporary certification ended, only one-fourth of the elementary school teachers and one-tenth of the middle-school teachers met the requirements even for temporary certification. Another ten years elapsed before the demand for new teachers was met by those who had the legally-required qualifications, although as late as 1963 only about 40 per cent of the 56,000 newly certified teachers recruited that year were graduates of the postwar education programs of universities and colleges. Nonethe-

[9] Blewett, pp. 139, 153.

less, the upgrading of the teacher force made teaching a far more attractive career than it had been earlier. The numbers of students seeking entrance into education curricula rapidly increased, doubling for example between 1952 and 1955 from 40,000 to 80,000. Lack of facilities held down the actual acceptances, however; and, only after Japan entered the great boom period following 1955 did competition from other promising career fields reduce the number of applications. The evening of supply and demand also resulted from a drop in teacher turnover, which in 1948 had been as high as 11 per cent a year; by 1952, this had fallen to six per cent, and has remained at this level until recently.[10]

It should be emphasized that these changes in the Japanese teacher force were taking place in a revolutionary context which saw (1) the administrative decentralization of education (although, as discussed later, partly reversed by the mid-1950's) ; (2) drastic revision in the content of school curricula, notably the dropping of the ethics course (although also partially revived in recent years) and military training, introduction of social studies, and the rise of general, comprehensive education in place of specialized tracking particularly at the secondary school level; (3) immense increase of freedom for teachers, who, although still in civil service status, were now being prepared in the liberal setting of universities and had rights, even though eventually restricted, to organize themselves for economic and political purposes; and (4) rapid re-emergence of Japan's economy, demoralized, disrupted, and chaotic from 1945 to 1949, as one of the fastest growing and most advanced of the world. All of these factors contributed to the development of a totally different role for the teachers than they had played in Japanese society prior to 1945.

TEACHER UNIONIZATION: PREWAR AND POSTWAR

Despite the strict control over teachers initiated as early as the 1880's, some self-organization among teachers did emerge prior to 1945. Although these teacher unions were extremely small and short-lived, they represented the undercurrent of professional independence that traditionally had characterized the Japanese teacher. By keeping this undercurrent alive, the prewar unions imparted a

[10] *Ibid.,* pp. 59–60, 63.

heritage which the teachers seized upon to justify in part their widespread organization following World War II.

Although the government in the 1880's expressly forbade teachers to participate in political activity (and in 1893 issued an edict denying them the right to speak publicly on political matters), individual teachers had been among the organizers of the earliest trade union and socialist movements in Japan around the turn of the century. Teacher unionism as such made its initial appearance at the end of World War I.[11] At that time, rampant inflation, food shortages, and the events of the Russian Revolution were at the basis of Japan's first experience with widespread unionization. Civil servants such as teachers, living on low-level fixed incomes and aspiring for higher status, bore the brunt of the deteriorating economic conditions. In 1919, a small group of public school teachers in Saitama Prefecture near Tokyo founded the Keimeikai [12] and demanded immediate salary improvements and relaxation of controls over their personal lives. The Keimeikai was even bold enough to participate in the first May Day parade a year later. While teacher unionization did not catch fire, similar small organizations sprang up in other parts of Japan, notably in Kobe, where left-wing influences were the strongest. As expected, the government's response to these movements was stern condemnation, although it immediately took steps to increase teacher salary scales. After this, the teacher unions crumbled, although the Saitama group managed to remain alive as late as 1928.

Again in 1932 teacher unionism made an overt appearance—on the occasion of the government's announcement of pay reductions as an economy measure. These unions also proved short-lived, especially when the government threatened to arrest most of the 300 teachers who had formed a Marxist study club in Nagano Prefecture. Ever since the amendment of the Public Peace Protection Act in 1926, the government had kept a sharp eye upon alleged "subversive" activity among the teachers, and sporadic jailings had occurred. After 1932, if there were organized efforts among the teachers, they were underground. The militaristic government's continuing concern that this might be the case no doubt made the teachers even more furtive. Following the Shanghai Incident in

[11] Levine, "Unionization of White-Collar Employees in Japan," pp. 226–320.
[12] Or, Nippon Kyōin Kumiai Keimeikai (Japan Teachers Union Founding Association).

1938, the government issued another stern warning against attempts by teachers to form their own organizations or to engage in any agitation or protests.

Repression of teacher self-organization was probably the most extreme of the restrictions in general placed upon a barely-tolerated trade union movement during the prewar era. Efforts during the "liberal" years of the 1920's to enact trade union laws which would accord labor movement recognition had failed, and after 1931 there was no hope that labor's rights would be achieved. Trade unionism penetrated only a small portion of the general industrial labor force, reaching a height of eight per cent of the total number of organizable workers in the mid-1930's. Within this context, it could not be expected that teacher unions would account for more than the tiniest fraction of the membership.

Moreover, the prewar labor movement was marked by continuing internal battles over ideology, splitting the unions from the early 1920's on into warring groups of anarchists, socialists, and communists. In turn, the unions that did form and survive were deeply suspicious of white-collar workers such as teachers, so that few efforts were made to bring the latter into the labor movement.

On the other hand, intellectuals predominated in the leadership of the movement, and among them were prominent professors and former teachers. Their role left a legacy of radicalism, although few of these spokesmen later re-emerged to take the helm of the teachers' drive to organize after 1945. In all likelihood, they kept alive widespread, if unexpressed, grievances among the teachers that they were politically suppressed, socially downgraded, and economically deprived.

The outburst of teacher unionism that followed Japan's surrender to the Allied Powers provided an amazing contrast to the feeble efforts at self-organization in the prewar era. Within two years, Japan's largest national union had unified almost all the public teachers and comprised a major component of the general labor movement. Whereas teachers had been the "first line of Japanese nationalism," in the New Japan their role was to spearhead social reform and promote democracy. For this, teacher unionism received the blessings of the Occupation.

Certainly also, one of the immediate reasons for widespread organizing success among the teachers was the motivation that unionism would assure their rising social and economic status. Not only were there to be radical changes in the role of education and up-grading of the teaching profession, but also the reforms were pro-posed at the very time the economy was in a state of chaos and not likely, so it appeared at that time, to provide more then bare subsis-tence to a rapidly-growing population on a set of small, crowded islands lacking in natural resources. As did all other industrial workers, teachers experienced the ravages of rampant inflation and shortages of essential goods. Thus, coupled with protecting newly won social status, was a drive for economic security, especially threatened by the plans to upgrade qualifications for certification and to purge ultranationalistic elements from the schools. Indeed, on the latter count alone, by 1947 one-fifth of the 600,000 teachers were ordered to leave the profession. Joining a union not only could demonstrate the teacher's acceptance of the reforms, but also was a means of escaping the purge itself.

This "mix" of political, economic, social, *and* professional drives also provided a leading role for teacher unions and unionists in the general labor movement itself, for they brought together most dra-matically the variety of reasons for the sudden mushrooming of labor organization throughout Japan in the immediate postwar period.

A series of fast-moving events following Japan's surrender set the stage for teacher unionization. In October 1945, SCAP not only ordered the release of 3,000 political prisoners from Japanese jails, but also gave its blessings to unrestricted organizing activities among workers, including teachers. At the same time, General Mac-Arthur gave instructions to eliminate all traces of militarism and ultranationalism from school curricula and to establish machinery for investigating, screening, and certifying educational personnel and for purging ultranationalists and collaborationists. By mid-December, 1945, the Occupation banned religious instruction (essentially, State Shintoism) from the schools, and at the end of that month eliminated the long-established "ethics" course. In the meantime, courses on Japanese history and geography were revised, old textbooks destroyed, and new texts written. The purge of 120,000 teachers began in earnest in January 1946.

Among the first steps in the Occupation reforms was the legal guarantee of the right of all workers to organize, bargain collec-tively, and engage in strikes, including protection against unfair labor practices. By December, the Japanese government had adopted the new Trade Union Law, which followed the model of the U.S. Wagner Act. This went into effect the following April. Now only firemen, police, and prison guards were denied basic trade union rights. Teachers were as free as any other employees, public or private, to establish their own autonomous trade unions— virtually without restriction as to their scope, structure, and affiliations. While the law required trade union organizations to direct their activity primarily toward economic objectives, it did not rule out political action as a legitimate function. Passage of the Labor Relations Adjustment Law in September, 1946, further encouraged unionism by providing tripartite machinery at both national and prefectural levels for dispute settlement through mediation, conciliation, and voluntary arbitration. While this act set a limitation upon the strike rights of workers in public utilities,[13] a similar proposal applying to school teachers failed to pass—due probably to the liberal attitude of Occupation officials. Still another enactment —the Labor Standards Law, adopted in April 1947—required minimum work standards, thereby underwriting many key demands then being put forth by the new unions.

Moreover, the underlying spirit of all these acts was embodied in the new constitution, adopted at the end of 1946 and placed in effect in April 1947, which in its Article 28 guaranteed the right of workers to organize and to bargain and act collectively. However, it should also be duly noted that Article 15 stated that all public officials are servants of the whole community and not of any subgroup. Open encouragement by the Occupation of virtually unrestricted trade unionism continued until early 1947, when, following a general strike threat, a process of policy reversals began that led to new legislative acts and amendments in 1948 and 1949.

It was during this liberal period from 1945 to 1948 that Japanese teacher unionization, along with the labor movement in general, leaped ahead and reached a level which, except for short periods in 1950 and 1959, has since been maintained. As shown in Table I, by June 1947 the teachers had formed more than 1,450 basic unions at the local level including a total membership of at least 440,000. The dramatic spread of teacher unionism continued into 1949 when the number of basic unions reached more than 1,800 and membership 576,000. Despite slight drops in total membership in 1950, 1959, and

---

[13] Solomon B. Levine, *Industrial Relations in Postwar Japan* (Urbana: University of Illinois Press, 1958), pp. 148–49.

TABLE 1. NUMBER OF UNIT UNIONS AND UNION MEMBERSHIP IN EDUCATION SERVICES, JAPAN, 1947–1966 [a]

	Number of Unit Unions [b]	Membership
1947	1,463	440,447
1948	1,624	516,239
1949	1,812	576,176
1950	1,573	572,926
1951	1,588	586,311
1952	1,656	591,392
1953	3,309	609,006
1954	2,883	631,609
1955	3,777	634,803
1956	2,803	680,257
1957	2,762	695,979
1958	2,806	709,726
1959	2,746	698,902
1960	2,898	703,359
1961	3,014	725,749
1962	3,027	722,505
1963	3,106	724,471
1964	3,146	748,039
1965	3,277	755,809
1966	3,282	758,511

[a] As of June 30.
[b] A unit union is defined as the most local organization, with its own constitution, in conformity with legal requirements for recognition as a union or personnel organization.
SOURCE: Japan Ministry of Labour, *Year Book of Labor Statistics, 1949–1965; Rōdō Kumiai Kihon Chōsa Hōkoku, 1966.*

1962, each year from 1949 to 1965 saw increments from 5,000 to 45,000, essentially maintaining the rate of organization at a constant level. The number of basic unions doubled from 1952 to 1953 and has since leveled off at around 3,000, varying mainly with school district consolidations.

FORMATION OF NIKKYŌSO

The objectives and guiding philosophy of Japanese teacher unions may be traced through the events that led up to unification in 1947. Unity did not come readily. At the very outset, competing ideological, political, and professional interests divided the unionized teachers. However, unlike other major parts of organized labor in Japan which from the outset split into rival communist, socialist, and "neutral" camps, the teachers succeeded in combining the diverse groups within their own ranks into a single entity. It is important to sketch this process as the "diversity-within-unity" theme has continued to characterize Nikkyōso's objectives and philosophy to the present.

Within a few days after Japan's formal surrender in September, 1945, teacher unionists began to develop plans for forming their own nationwide organization. By the end of October a group of politically conservative teachers had founded a national union, the Nihon Kyōikusha Kumiai.[14] Early in December the Marxist left-wing had established Zenkyō.[15] Attempts to bring the two groups together utterly failed.

Immediately Zenkyō demanded full collective bargaining rights and higher wage levels, purge of all militaristic and ultranationalistic elements from education, and a "democratic" educational system. It gained a measure of recognition when the then Minister of Education, Maeda Tamon, agreed to negotiate on its demands. In concrete terms, these included (1) an immediate 500 per cent salary increase, (2) uniform nationwide salary schedules, (3) establishment of school lunch programs, (4) abolition of the Ministry's school inspectorate, and (5) teacher election of school principals and administrators. While these first meetings were inconclusive, they did set the stage for protracted negotiations at the national, rather than local, level.

At the same time, the right-wing groups further consolidated and in July, 1946, formed the Kyōin Kumiai Zenkoku Remmei,[16] in out-and-out rivalry with Zenkyō. The latter had been especially successful in organizing those teachers who held only temporary certificates and feared dismissal under the new educational system for lack of qualifications. By mid-1946, Zenkyō claimed 100,000 members.

With this step-up in unionization and the sharp rivalry among the competing teacher groups, the Ministry of Education warned that union organizing activity must not interfere with teaching. The Ministry, however, did confirm the right of teachers to engage in political action. Further affirmation of this new freedom found

14 Japan Educational Personnel Union.
15 Or, Zen Nihon Kyōin Rōdō Kumiai (All-Japan Teachers Labor Union).
16 National League of Teachers Unions.

full expression in the recommendation of the U.S. Educational Commission, which issued its report to SCAP in March, 1946. In its deliberations, the Commission welcomed consultation with the teacher unions and actually met with Zenkyō representatives.

Zenkyō's list of demands to the Ministry of Education now lengthened. Added were provisions for menstrual leaves, school building construction and use of idle factories as schools, teacher control over curricula, and establishment of a national board of education on which teachers would have representation. Confronted with these, the Ministry of Education, now headed by Tanaka Kotaro, and the conservative Yoshida government balked at dealing with the teachers, particularly the left-wing Zenkyō. Declaring that teacher unions should refrain from focusing on political issues and engaging primarily in political activities, the national authorities held that Zenkyō did not conform to the definition of trade unionism under the new Trade Union Law. Thus, the government withheld recognition of Zenkyō at the very time teacher unionization was growing at a rapid pace and the educational reforms were about to go into full swing.

The government's attitude in all likelihood increased the left-right rivalry within the teachers' unions. By early June, 1946, splits began to appear in local Zenkyō units of elementary and secondary public school teachers in Tokyo, where Zenkyō had major strength. These defections followed a refusal by the union leaders to obey administrative orders issued by the Ministry of Education and the Tokyo Municipal Education Bureau and to accept supervision by the officially appointed school superintendents and inspectors. As moves toward independence from the government authorities, the Zenkyō unions had announced they would directly operate school lunch programs, develop new textbooks, and, especially through the new P.T.A.'s, enlist parental cooperation with the unions in running the schools. Such union control over school administration was actually achieved in several instances, notably outside Tokyo (for example, in Ibaraki, Kanagawa, and Tochigi), and even included holding of school entrance examinations and conducting graduation exercises.

By this time also, Zenkyō began to take leadership among all public employees in developing a united "struggle" against the government. The public worker's economic position, perhaps more so than other employees, had severely deteriorated with the galloping inflation and failure of the government to grant pay increases. Still another basis for protest was the proposed Labor Relation's Adjustment Law with its provisions to limit work stoppages in public utilities and welfare industries and to prohibit them altogether among government employees, including teachers. As a result, the public employee unions now resolved to unseat the conservative party government then in power and replace it with "progressives."

From the summer of 1946 to February 1947, the public employees, especially the teachers, carried on a continuing skirmish with the government. Although it was largely the pressure of organized labor which prevented adoption of the proposal to prohibit teacher strikes, such restrictions were enacted in September, 1946, for public non-manual welfare and utility employees and all branches of the civil service. This fanned the growing unrest, although teachers at that time were not affected.

In early October, 1946, the Ministry of Education, furthermore, announced its intention to institute salary scales for teachers which would continue the prewartime policy of regional pay differentials and thus ignore the union's demand for a uniform nationwide salary schedule. It was on this last issue in fact that the first signs of reapproachment between the right- and left-wing teacher unions appeared. As a result, a new coordinating organization, the Zenkyōkyō,[17] was formed in December, 1946, for the main purpose of bringing the rival teacher groups together and to direct their "struggles" in conjunction with other public employee unions.

Throughout the fall of 1946 grievances of the government workers provided a rallying point to achieve unification of organized labor, up to that time sharply split among the communist-led Sanbetsu, the right-socialist Sōdōmei, and "neutral" groups. This widespread agitation and unrest helped to precipitate a cabinet crisis in December and January, which in turn afforded the opportunity to establish a joint labor strategy committee to direct the efforts for overthrowing the conservative Yoshida government. On January 15 the joint committee announced its intention to call a general strike on February 1, which was averted only by the direct prohibition of SCAP a few hours before the announced deadline. General MacArthur's intervention marked the beginning of what eventually was the reversal in Occupation policy toward the labor movement, al-

17 Or, Zen Nihon Kyōin Kumiai Kyōgikai (All-Japan Council of Teachers Unions).

though formal modification, especially affecting public employees, did not come until a year-and-a-half later. This was enough, however, to impel the teachers toward unification.

The general strike prohibition and impending restrictions upon civil servant unions made it apparent that, barred from exerting direct pressure on the government, the teachers would now have to seek direct representation in the national Diet and attempt to secure centralized collective agreements with the Ministry of Education. These objectives were especially pressing in view of the imminent adoption of the new school reform laws, and, at the same time, the call for the general elections in the spring of 1947. The teachers unions, through Zenkyōkyō in particular, now concentrated their energies on supporting candidates from their own ranks, and, in the accession of Japan's first and only Socialist-led government, succeeded in winning three seats in the Lower House and eight in the Upper House. In local elections held shortly afterwards, teachers could claim 70 seats among the various prefectural and municipal legislatures.

A hallmark development in the meantime came in the signing of the first formal collective agreements with the Ministry of Education. On March 8, 1947, the joint Zenkyōkyō group and the Ministry concluded a pact which set forth the principles of establishing a nationwide teacher salary schedule, a new structure for teacher personnel administration, a national budget for the education system, the right of the teacher unions to negotiate automatic dues checkoffs, and the specification of various working conditions. In addition to establishing collective bargaining at the national level, it was agreed to encourage negotiations on a systematic basis also between the prefectural teacher union branches and their respective prefectural governments. Immediately the separate right-wing groups, now consolidated and reorganized under the name of Kyōzenren,[18] demanded similar recognition and on March 11 succeeded in obtaining the identical agreement from the Ministry.

The conclusion of these identical agreements furthered the drive toward teacher union unification. While the pacts were actually denounced as illegal "political" acts by the government-sponsored Education Reform Committee, a body set up at the suggestion of the U.S. Educational Advisory Commission, the government viewed them as a means to stabilize relations in this sector of public em-

---

[18] Or, Kyōin Kumiai Zenkoku Remmei (Teachers Unions National League).

ployment at the very moment the profound changes in the Japanese educational system were about to take place and considerable unrest continued among government workers. With the union-government agreements concluded, the new education reform laws were promulgated on March 31, 1947. These agreements and laws, although still to be implemented in detail, provided common ground for the rival teacher unions.

It should be noted here, also, that as in the case of other Japanese labor organizations, the teachers felt closely identified with their respective local employing units—a characteristic traceable to historic economic and social factors and labeled "enterprise consciousness." [19] In all likelihood, the new legislation and collective agreements not only reinforced this localized identification but also provided a common set of specific economic and social interests among the local units which overrode the sharp ideological differences. In this context, two factors were of critical importance. First, most school superintendents, principals, assistant principals, and other administrative personnel also had joined the local teacher unions—partly from the strong sense of identification with their school groups and partly from their recognition that failure to join threatened their own status or raised questions about their acceptance of the reforms. Indeed, a sizable proportion of the initial union leadership and spokesmen came from these officials. Second, the great uncertainty surrounding the application of new high qualifications for certification and the threat of the purge prompted teachers and administrators alike who were long employed in the old school system to seek security through union membership.

Furthermore, unity was enhanced by the weakening of the central government's control over the education system. There now appeared a vacuum as to who would set educational policy and determine its administration. The teacher unions, coalescing around their common interests, felt strongly that the teachers themselves were qualified to direct the new system, especially in view of the aims to promote both democratization and decentralization of education.

For these reasons, many teacher unions officially opposed SCAP's advisory commission's recommendation for popularly elected local school boards, based on the American model. The teachers protested that such boards would merely perpetuate prewar education

[19] Levine, *Industrial Relations,* pp. 89–107.

practices, since in all likelihood they would fall under the control of the traditional local "bosses." Most teacher unions preferred instead national and prefectural boards of education with ample representation for the teachers themselves, in order to assure uniformity of treatment. However, despite their opposition, the educational legislation adopted in 1947 provided for popularly elected local boards, although it allowed teachers the right to become candidates for election. This political issue also contributed to bringing the teachers together into a single national organization.

All these developments culminated in the establishment of Nikkyōso on June 6, 1947. Except for minor segments of the profession, Nikkyōso's membership was all-embracing, bringing together Zenkyōkyō, and Kyōzenren, and the then independent union of public university professors. For the first time a single major national union had been formed in spite of deep internal ideological divisions. Moreover, while Nikkyōso shared certain organizational characteristics common to most other Japanese unions, it was the only important union which had a strong occupational orientation as its base.

INTERNAL UNION STRUCTURE AND MEMBERSHIP SCOPE

Although unification of the various teacher unions in 1947 established Nikkyōso as the single national organization for teachers, from the beginning its internal structure has reflected both the basic political jurisdictions and the tendency for teachers to identify closely with their respective employing units. Nikkyōso, formally, is a federation of prefectural unions. The 46 prefectural unions, in turn, are made up of branches each of which is identical in scope to the jurisdiction of the more than 3,000 municipal, town, and village school districts. It is the branch that is considered the basic union unit, although it may be composed of subbranches at the school level. One result of this structure is that there are wide variations in the size of prefectural union membership, with the heavily populated prefectures such as Tokyo, Hyogo, Osaka, Kyoto, and Nagoya (Aiichi) as the leading centers of union activity.

Selection of the prefecture as the basic component of Nikkyōso's structure was due not merely to the administrative divisions of Japan (and, thus, the prefecture by law is the employer), but also because in turn each prefecture has tended to exhibit special characteristics of its own in terms of economic interests, cultural background, and social relationships which, despite Japan's history of governmental centralization, have exerted important influence upon governmental policy and administration. Regional identification, moreover, was fortified during World War II by prefectural and local groupings promoted by the wartime patriotic associations. This regional identification is not unlike "enterprise consciousness" among Japanese industrial workers.

In the immediate postwar period, the heritage of regionalism fitted easily with both the Occupation insistence upon equalitarianism and the leftist demands for working class solidarity. As a result, the teacher unions opened membership to all personnel engaged in educational activity, private as well as public, non-teaching as well as teaching—with the prefecture as the key structural component. A member of a branch or subbranch of a prefectural teachers union, unlike most other national labor organizations in Japan, at the same time automatically became a member of the national organization, Nikkyōso, under its constitution. Until recent changes in the law, usually a union embraced all members of a given school or school district; partial organization has been rare, as in the case of most enterprise unions in Japan.

Teacher union membership grew apace with the expansion of the number of teachers until the late 1950's when the percentage of unorganized, particularly among elementary and junior high teachers, rose slightly and is now about ten per cent. Also, there has been relatively little success in organizing the 85,000 full-time teachers in private schools, almost half of whom are at the senior high level. A major reason for the recent slowdown in the increase is that females account for a growing percentage of the teaching labor force. Women now constitute somewhat more than one-third of all school teachers and almost half of those in elementary schools. However, in the junior high schools they still comprise only one-fourth, and in the high schools, less than one-fifth.

Actually, Nikkyōso's organizing success has been mainly among the teachers in the public elementary and junior high schools. In 1964 Nikkyōso claimed a membership of about 80 per cent of the 727,000 teachers who were employed in more than 53,000 public schools, but the rate of organization among the 575,000 public elementary and junior high teachers was somewhat higher than this, probably at least 85 per cent. In fact, nine-tenths of Nikkyōso's membership falls in these two groups. Most of the remaining ten per cent is drawn from the public high schools and public special schools, where, as will be explained later, Nikkyōso's rates of organization are relatively low—respectively 45 per cent and 70 per cent. It has as members only minor proportions of the private school teachers and the 97,000 public and private higher education teachers. Only two per cent of Nikkyōso membership is made up of clerical workers in schools, two-thirds of whom are organized.

As of 1964, there were more than 45,000 principals of public schools, 32,000 of which were at the elementary and junior high levels.[20] Most of the latter—perhaps as much as 70 per cent—had remained members of Nikkyōso despite the passage of the various laws and amendments from 1947 to 1952 which discouraged supervisors from joining rank-and-file unions and despite numerous defections especially since the issue regarding teacher merit-rating erupted in 1957. They accounted for almost eight per cent of the total membership until forced to withdraw by new revisions in the law in 1966.

It is estimated that since 1960, as much as 20 per cent of all newly hired public school teachers have not joined unions upon employment. Until then, membership rates among new teachers had been running as high as 95 per cent. Of those who do join, a declining percentage enters Nikkyōso. Especially high rates of nonunionization obtain where conflict with government authorities has been severe, for example in Ehime, Saga, Aomori, Chiba, and Tokyo. In these cases, whole branches or subbranches have defected. Nikkyōso, however, claims that the rate of membership depends upon the period of the year, and, since most new teachers are still on probationary status when official membership figures are gathered in June, failure to affiliate then seems high. In actuality, Nikkyōso claims, once the usual 6-months probation is over, in the fall, the new teachers do seek membership.

Despite these problems, Nikkyōso, in attempting to develop itself as a unified national union, has probably succeeded in this respect more so than any other major labor organization in Japan (with the exception of the seaman's union). Although Nikkyōso's membership base also depends upon strong identification with the local

[20] Government of Japan, *Education in 1964* (Tokyo: Ministry of Education, March, 1966), pp. 42–43.

school or district and the prefectural regions, the origins of the national union—especially its initial successes in organizing on a national scale, gaining recognition for collective bargaining from the central government, and achieving successes in national level politics—have stamped Nikkyōso with a greater-than-average national outlook in contrast with other major national unions which are essentially loose federations of enterprise or government agency-level units. Nikkyōso's continued insistence upon centralized negotiation, plus standardization of government policies affecting the training, employment, and compensation of teachers, has fortified a "profession-orientation" unique in Japan.

This objective, however, should not be overstressed. Like most other national unions, Nikkyōso depends upon its members' compartmentalized "enterprise" consciousness at the local level, drawn from long-ingrained tendencies for personal identification with the immediate organization, even though this is attenuated by a degree of intra- and inter-prefectural mobility among teachers. Nikkyōso, thus, "pays the price" of diluting the "union" consciousness it strives for as a national organization.

Each of Nikkyōso's 3,000 local units has by-laws which conform to the requirements set forth in the laws to qualify as trade unions or personnel organizations. The number of such units has about doubled since the founding of Nikkyōso, particularly multiplying in 1953 when the Local Public Service Law was adopted, permitting recognition of certified personnel organizations to negotiate with appropriate local government agencies. This law led to the subdivision of local units to meet the new legal stipulations. A typical public school district is likely to contain ten or more school attendance centers, although each of the latter is a subbranch. It is these unit unions which in a given prefecture combine to form a prefectural teachers union (or kenkyōso).

At the national headquarters level, Nikkyōso has developed an elaborate organizational structure. The annual convention, composed of representatives from the prefectural unions, is the supreme ruling organ and elects a central committee, also on the basis of prefectural representation, to hold policy meetings three times a year between national conventions. To conduct day-to-day activities, the convention also elects an executive committee which is required to include representatives not only from each prefecture but also the chiefs of Nikkyōso's staff departments. It is this committee which elects the full-time officers of Nikkyōso, comprised of the national chairman, two vice-chairmen, the secretary-general, two assistant secretary-generals, the treasurer, and the auditor. These officials serve one year terms but may be reelected.

At present, most of Nikkyōso's staff departments are structured according to professional or occupational interests—Kindergarten, High School, College and University, Special Education, Private Schools, Teaching Nurses, and Nonteaching School Personnel. In addition, there are two departments, designated Youth and Women, which cut across the occupational groupings. Until 1955, there was also an Elementary and Junior High Department, but it was abolished, since the affairs of this predominant group inevitably came to occupy the central attention of Nikkyōso.

Thus, the internal organization of Nikkyōso as a national body attempts to combine both geographical, occupational, and special functional interests. At the prefectural level, organization virtually parallels that of the national headquarters, and the prefectural staff departments work closely with their counterpart national departments. In addition, the prefectural unions of Nikkyōso have organized formal intermediate groupings, combining as many as ten prefectural unions each in an attempt to strengthen regional interests within the national organization.

Several other formally-organized special-action bodies have existed within Nikkyōso. In 1954, after Nikkyōso began to turn its attention to the "professional" problems facing Japanese school teachers, it sponsored so-called Educational Research Conferences (Kyōiku Kenkyū Taikai) to enable its members to examine such issues as the efficiency of the 6-3-3-4 system, development of night schools, teacher research opportunities, academic standards, class-size and teacher-pupil ratios, teaching methods, classroom planning, school-community relations, education for handicapped children, status of students in the society, prekindergarten programs, vocational training, and "peace" education. While the Japanese government labelled these conferences as propagandistic and political devices, out of them came the establishment in 1957 of a permanent but separately incorporated Research Institute for National Education (Kokumin Kyōiku Kenkyūshō).

Also, in 1951, Nikkyōso created consumer cooperatives to provide teachers with everyday necessities at discounted prices and to publish textbooks for use in school curricula. Although these cooperatives have since become independent, principally serving teachers, they, too, have been a target of government criticism for engaging in political and nonprofessional activities.

Beginning in 1952, Nikkyōso launched the separately-organized Japan Teachers Political League (Nihon Kyōshokuin Seiji Rennmei) to facilitate direct teacher participation in political campaigns as permitted within the laws. Later, the name of this body was changed to the Japan Democratic Education Political League (Nihon Minshū Kyōiku Seiji Remmei).

Despite Nikkyōso's success in achieving national organization, it has failed to embrace and retain all of the teacher groups. The heavy concentration of public elementary and junior high teachers in Nikkyōso has made it difficult to achieve a tightly organized national union. A wide diversity of school-level interests have plagued teacher unionization from the beginning; and, although Nikkyōso achieved a high measure of formal unity, breakaway and rival unions have formed and persisted.

The most important of the rival groups are the Nikkōkyō [21], or Japan High School Teachers Unions, which originally formed as a single organization and in 1962 had about 58,000 members, drawn mainly from the public senior high schools. In 1963, Nikkōkyō split into separate left and right groups, each with the same name, and in 1967 they claimed 38,000 and 23,000 members respectively. Together, their membership is probably as large as the senior high component in Nikkyōso. Neither the right nor left Nikkōkyō is affiliated with a national labor center, although the Left is closely allied to Nikkyōso.

A second significant competitor is the Nikkyōren,[22] or Japan Federation of Teachers Organizations, with almost 20,000 members drawn almost entirely from the public elementary and junior high schools. Nikkyōren was formed out of an earlier organization, established in 1962, known as the Zenkyōren,[23] or National Federation of Teachers, which brought together a number of independent local teachers' unions as a protest against the militancy of Nikkyōso. It, too, is unaffiliated with a national center. Nikkyōren stresses the "professional" status of teachers, eschews politics, and organizes research units for studying the "normalization" of education.

In addition there is a scattering of independent local unions,

21 Or, Nihon Kōtō Gakkō Kyōshokuin Kumiai. Until 1950, this group was called Zenkōkyō (or, Zen Nihon Kōtō Gakkō Kyōshokuin Kumiai), the All-Japan High School Teachers Union.
22 Or, Nihon Kyōshokuin Dantai Rengōkai.
23 Or, Zenkoku Kyōshokuin Dantai Rengōkai.

mainly among public elementary and junior high teachers but usually led by principals and assistant principals who quit Nikkyōso at various times especially since 1957–58. Major examples occurred in Nagasaki and Shimane prefectives in 1960. In total, their combined membership at present is approximately 60,000. The largest is the *Nihon Kyōshokuin Rengokai,* or Japan Federation of Teachers and School Personnel formed in 1967 with 16,000 members. Also, now in their formative stages, are new organizations of principals, assistant principals, and administrative personnel prohibited by law in 1966 from joining unions composed of practicing teachers.

TEACHER UNION RELATIONS WITH
THE GENERAL LABOR MOVEMENT

Nikkyōso has been a key component of the Sōhyō federation since the latter's inception in 1950. From 1947 to 1950, Nikkyōso refrained from officially affiliating with either the communist-led Sanbetsu or the socialist Sōdōmei, the two competing national centers at that time, although it cooperated with national unions, especially public worker groups,[24] in each center in carrying out various economic and political activities. Nikkyōso's all-encompassing structure made untenable sole affiliation with either camp.

On the other hand, Nikkyōso was in a sense a forerunner, or model, for a national trade union organization which accommodated opposing ideological and political viewpoints. When Sanbetsu began to collapse in the late 1940's as the result of Occupation pressure, reversals in government labor policy, and democratization movements within the unions themselves, Nikkyōso undertook a major role in launching a new national labor center which would stress economic rather than political activity. The new center, Sōhyō, also hoped to be all-embracing and drew upon major elements of Sōdōmei, national unions which had defected from Sanbetsu, and other national unions which had formally remained neutral in the ideological struggle between Sanbetsu and Sōdōmei. Affiliation of the teachers' union was a critical element in this endeavor not only because of its size and neutralism but also because of its articulate leadership and ubiquitousness.

Actually, however, Nikkyōso presented a structural anomaly for

[24] However, Nikkyōso did join with other government worker unions to establish the so-called Kankōrō, or Public Employees' Joint Action Council.

Sōhyō, which proclaimed as one of its major objectives the development of "pure" industrial unionism that could match the bargaining power of management oligopolies. Nikkyōso did not fit this prescription, given its occupational base, except insofar as it might reach out to organize the "education" industry. Rather it was an amalgam of professional, regional, and local groupings, which, however much it demanded centralized negotiations with the national government, was actually highly fractionated in collective bargaining and economic interests.[25] Despite the initial economic stress of Sōhyō, in fact, Nikkyōso as a national organization was tempted increasingly toward political activities as the major means for holding together the diverse groups within it. This was especially the case when the government placed restrictions on the right of public employees to organize and carry on bargaining.

Under these conditions, it was not likely that Sōhyō itself could long remain politically neutral, devoted primarily to economic trade unionism. When Sōhyō was formally established in July, 1950, it had succeeded in gathering in only about half of organized labor. Various unions preferred to "wait and see," while others felt either that from the outset Sōhyō had compromised the principle of industrial unionism or that they would sacrifice their own organizational base in joining the new center. Furthermore, despite the Communist dénouement under threat of the "red" purge, reversals in Occupation and government policy, and internal trade union revolts, the political coalition representing labor remained highly precarious. The socialists at that time had achieved but an uneasy unity and suffered from left-right rivalry that had been exacerbated by failures of the socialist-led governments in 1947–48, the Occupation's economic stabilization policies under the Dodge Plan in 1948–50, revisions of the labor laws, and the impending peace and security treaties.

Soon after Sōhyō's founding, it was apparent that it would abandon its initial pronouncements of ideological neutralism and economic emphasis. While a special Sōhyō convention, with Nikkyōso support, immediately condemned the North Korean invasion of

[25] In this sense, Nikkyōso has paralleled another major component of Sōhyō, the 800,000 member All-Japan Perfectural and Workers Union (Jichirō), which Nikkyōso itself helped to organize in the early 1950's when it became clear that local civil servants and public workers would be placed by law in organizing jurisdictions separate from the national government employees. The two national unions together have comprised about one-fourth of Sōhyō's total membership, and, with other government worker union affiliates, well over one-half.

South Korea and upheld the U.N. action (but without involving Japan), this proved to be a short-lived position. A year later, again with Nikkyōso support, Sōhyō policy had begun to shift; and by July, 1952, at its third convention, Sōhyō came out in favor of Japanese neutrality as a "third force" in world politics.

In 1951, moreover, the socialists had formally split into separate right and left parties. The left opposed a peace treaty with the West excluding the Soviet Union and insisted upon no Japanese rearmament, no foreign bases on Japanese soil, and Japan's neutrality— the so-called "four principles of peace." After heated right-wing opposition, Sōhyō endorsed this stand in March, 1951; and at the July, 1952, convention Shōyō condemned the proposed San Francisco peace treaty. This signaled the end of Sōhyō's political neutralism and precipitated a series of defections, particularly by national unions in the private industry sector. In turn, these events led to the founding of the rival right socialist labor federation, Zenrō, in 1954, under the leadership of the textile workers, seamen, and Sōdōmei unions.

In the course of these events, Nikkyōso intensified its identification with Sōhyō, now abandoning its "third force" concept and embracing a "peace force" position. Faced with a series of restrictions upon its activities and attacks from rival right-wing unions, Nikkyōso sought close support from the other affiliates of the national labor center as well as from the Sōhyō headquarters. This took the form not only of protesting against the treaty and security agreement, but also in mounting attacks against the conservative government's "reverse course" in labor legislation and antisubversive activity measures. Specifically, these were tied together with the increased restrictions placed upon teacher unionism and changes in the educational system, such as the abandonment of locally elected school boards, proposals for teacher merit-rating, reintroduction of ethics courses, and the like.

On the other hand, while the main thrust of Sōhyō and its chief affiliates such as Nikkyōso was being directed at unseating the conservative government, a struggle within the national labor center, particularly following the withdrawal of the right-wing unions, saw a gradual submerging of the "peace force" faction and re-emergence of the "third force" group. A similar contest was occurring within Nikkyōso and in most other major Sōhyō affiliates. Within Sōhyō, this culminated in ousting Takano Minoru from the Secretary-

Generalship. He was leader of the "peace force" faction in the Sōhyō convention of July 1955, and was replaced by Iwai Akira, a "third force" advocate. By the 1956 Sōhyō convention, with the election of Ota Kaoru to the chairmanship of Sōhyō, the "third force" position again clearly became the mainstream of the national center, and has remained so to the present.

In the years since 1954, Nikkyōso's ideological and political position has virtually paralleled, although lagging behind, the Sōhyō development—gradually increasing emphasis upon economic demands but holding to a vociferous political role. However, the process within Nikkyōso took several years longer, the turning point coming around 1959 or 1960.

In 1952, the moderate Miyanohara Sadamitsu, who had been a deputy secretary-general, became secretary-general of Nikkyōso, probably the most powerful post at the national headquarters. A year later, similarly moderate Kobayashi Takeshi assumed the chairmanship (or presidency) with Miyanohara as one of the two vice-chairmen, but Hiragaki Miyoji, a prominent left-winger and close associate of Takano, the leader of the "peace force" faction in Sōhyō, assumed the secretary-generalship. In an uneasy truce, this combination remained in office until 1958 when Miyanohara once again took over the post of secretary-general from Hiragaki, placing the mainstream faction in virtually full command. This followed upon the growing strength of the Ota-Iwai ("third force") leadership in Sōhyō, but also resulted from internal divisions within Nikkyōso especially over the question of teacher merit rating then being proposed by the government. In 1962, Miyanohara succeeded Kobayashi as chairman and has remained in that post to the present.

When Nikkyōso first affiliated with Sōhyō, like the latter, it quit the World Federation of Trade Unions (WFTU) and resolved to join the newly formed International Confederation of Free Trade Unions (ICFTU), becoming a member in 1950. However, especially following the ICFTU endorsement of the U.N.'s action in the Korean War, this affiliation became very tenuous; and in 1958, despite Nikkyōso's shift toward moderation and, perhaps as a concession to the still forceful left-wing, Nikkyōso quit the ICFTU and its affiliated International Federation of Free Teachers Unions. From 1953 on Nikkyōso, largely under the influence of Hiragaki, sent observers to the conventions of the WFTU-sponsored World

Federation of Teachers Unions (FISE) and continued to do so until as late as 1965, although Nikkyōso, in line with Sōhyō's policy of neutralism, had not reaffiliated with the WFTU. Over the years, however, since 1951 Nikkyōso has maintained membership in the WCTOP (World Confederation of Organizations of the Teaching Professions), alongside such conservative groups as the U.S. National Education Association.

The close interdependence between Sōhyō and Nikkyōso derives basically from their common aspiration to establish a political base for the labor movement. Sōhyō relies upon Nikkyōso to exert political influence in behalf of the Socialist Party especially at the village grass-roots, where conservative forces have long had their greatest strength. Lacking effective means for bargaining at the local level Nikkyōso looks to Sōhyō as the primary means for confronting the national government in its economic "struggles." Thus, there is a close wedding of the two organizations which stems from the drive both to redevelop the political system and to strengthen an occupational group, in this case the teachers, in attempts to win economic improvements. Nikkyōso's aggressive policy in making demands for increases in the national budget to improve the educational system (including teacher pay and benefits) conjoins with Sōhyō's general onslaught upon the conservative government's social and economic policies in both domestic and foreign spheres. It is difficult, under these circumstances, to separate away the political and economic aspects of the teachers' union.

POLITICAL AND ECONOMIC ACTION

From its beginnings, Nikkyōso has made broad appeals for the support of the teachers and the general public. It has attempted to stand as a force for political and ideological reform, as a means for enforcing educational standards, and as the bargaining agency for improving the economic position of school personnel. In all these respects, the organization has stood as the complete antithesis to the status of the Japanese schoolteacher in the prewar era. To accomplish this, it has stressed the teacher's identification with the national organization rather than only his local unit, although for legal and social reasons mentioned, Nikkyōso is composed of locally oriented prefecturewide units.

In its founding platform, Nikkyōso called for the thorough

democratization of Japanese education. It not only supported nine years of compulsory education, but also urged its extension through the 12th year, open to all on a free basis, and proposed expansion of publicly supported nursery schools. It demanded guarantees of academic freedom and the continued purge of ultranationalist and fascist elements from the education system. It advocated a "bright, healthy" culture and as the major social investment, construction of new schools and school facilities.

At the same time, Nikkyōso announced that it would continue to seek a national level agreement with the Ministry of Education which would provide a minimum guarantee of subsistence wages for the teacher, protected by price stabilization; improvement of teacher salaries based on a uniform nationwide scale; and retention of the rights to organize, to conclude collective agreements, and to engage in strikes.

Formation of Japan's first socialist-led government in the spring of 1947, shortly after Nikkyōso's founding, provided an exceptionally favorable climate for Nikkyōso to achieve its demand for recognition at the national level. The period from mid-1947 to mid-1948 saw a number of agreements reached at national and prefectural levels which have since determined some of the basic working conditions for the Japanese public school teacher. For example, these negotiations established a uniform 42-hour work week; 20 days with pay each year for the teacher's independent study; maternity leaves; three-year leaves of absence for tuberculosis recovery; joint teacher-supervisor committees to decide transfers, promotions, discharges, salary adjustments, injury compensations, and welfare benefits; and consultation with the unions on appointments, discharge, and transfer of superintendents and principals. Further, the agreements recognized the teachers' rights to engage in political activity, guaranteed that teachers elected to full-time union office would retain their civil service status (at first with full-pay), and provided for negotiation of automatic dues checkoff.

These gains, however, were abruptly curtailed after mid-1948. The "reverse course" in Occupation and government policy became visible following the spring elections of 1948 when the conservative party regained control. With the onset of the "Cold War" it was now clear that Japan's economic reconstruction to become a reliable industrial ally of the West would have priority over social and political reform. Aside from measures to assure economic stability and growth, restraints on political radicalism—particularly through the "red" purge—got underway. A major target was the trade unions—through revision of the various labor laws that would constrict organizing activity, reduce involvement in political movement, and narrow, if not eliminate, the scope of collective bargaining.

Actually, as early as June, 1947, the central government, apparently with SCAP approval, began to question if not ignore the provisions that had been negotiated with the teachers' unions. In one incident, the union vigorously protested a unilateral order of the Ministry of Education requiring all public school teachers to enroll in Ministry-sponsored "retraining" courses. Nikkyōso held that the Ministry's failure to consult the union in advance violated the agreements made. Again, in the summer of 1947, the cabinet declared it would not pay the salaries of full-time teacher union officers still on civil service rolls despite understandings to the contrary. It further demanded a reduction in the agreed-upon number of union officials permitted to serve under this arrangement. A number of cases also came to light, especially in Tokyo, of the appointment of high school principals without prior consultation with the teacher unions. In April, 1948, SCAP itself forbade the Saitama prefectural union to renew a contract which stipulated continued payment of union officer salaries from public funds and, when the union refused to comply, summarily ordered the election of new officers for this prefectural union.

After a year-long series of skirmishes on issues such as these and increasing unrest, including a rash of local level walkouts among public employees in general, SCAP moved in July, 1948, to redefine the trade union status of the public workers. In a famous letter to the Japanese Government, General MacArthur stated that civil servants should be denied the right of collective bargaining, arguing that it was incompatible with the principle of state sovereignty and disruptive of the stability of the government administrative machinery. This, of course, was in addition to the prohibition of strikes among public employees that had been issued on the occasion of the aborted general walkout on February 1, 1947.

Upon receipt of the MacArthur letter, the Ministry of Education immediately notified Nikkyōso that it would no longer engage in collective bargaining with the union, would remove all full-time union officers from public payrolls, and would mete out punishment to any teachers who engaged in stoppages. The Ministry further declared all existing agreements null and void. A Cabinet order codified these actions for all civil servants.

Amendments to the National Public Service Law, at that time applicable to the local public school teachers, were passed by the end of 1948. As revised, the act became the model for the Local Public Service Law, later adopted toward the end of 1950. About one-million civil servants as a result were removed from the coverage of the original Trade Union Law and placed in a special category which provided limited organizing and "negotiating" privileges but no rights to conclude collective agreements, engage in work stoppages, or take part in political activities except the right to vote.[26]

The National Personnel Authority was now empowered to determine whether an organization of civil servants met legally-set qualifications to "negotiate" conditions of work. Essentially, to gain this "recognition" a union—or in the terms of the law a "personnel organization"—had to confine its membership to the employees of a designated agency and elect its officers from this membership, a matter which was to become a major source of contention ten years later.

At the same time the Diet adopted a series of laws implementing the new educational system. The most important of these was the enactment in July, 1948, of the Board of Education Law which, in addition to creating comprehensive autonomous school districts and ending direct Ministry of Education controls,[27] established an American-type system of popularly-elected school boards at local and prefectural levels. This meant, of course, that teachers' unions now had to seek recognition and negotiating rights from these agencies and that national-level negotiations were to cease. Although the original bill included a flat prohibition against electing teachers to school boards, after considerable commotion in the Diet over this issue, the final version permitted teachers to become candidates on the condition they resign their positions.

[26] In addition, in late 1948, special legislation was enacted concerning employees in central government-owned corporations and enterprises—also replicated for similar local government operations in a special law in 1952. These laws prohibit the right to strike but allow the right to organize and to bargain collectively subject to limitations.
[27] Also, a new Ministry of Education Establishment Law was adopted in June, 1949.

This act affected Nikkyōso in two other ways. First, it increased the union's emphasis upon seeking control over the school system through political means; and second, under the principle of comprehensive school districts, which by itself represented a radical departure from the pre-war multiple-track approach, it led to further consolidation of the teachers' unions at the prefectural and local levels. When the first school board elections were called in October, 1948, Nikkyōso threw all its efforts behind "teacher" candidates, who accounted for about one-fourth of more than 1,500 aspirants seeking school board seats. This drive proved relatively successful in that more than half the "teacher" candidates were elected, giving the union "representatives" on nearly all boards and in some cases majority control.

The conservative government reacted to this development with consternation and, over the next five to six years, it made a series of proposals both to eliminate the popularly elected school board system and to reduce the influence of teachers upon the boards. A first step in this process was the classification of school teachers as local rather than national government civil servants through adoption by the Diet, in January 1949, of the Law for Special Regulations Concerning Educational Personnel (reconfirmed later in 1950 by the Local Public Service Law). While Nikkyōso protested the implications of the act, in actuality its resistance was feeble. By this time, the reversal of Occupation policy was in full force—the "red" purge, economic stabilization measures, and abandonment of plans for *zaibatsu* dissolution. The labor movement itself, moreover, was in disarray and entering a process of ideological realignment, as the internal democratization movements spread within most major unions, especially those affiliated with the communist-led Sanbetsu center. These groups demanded the end of adherence to radical ideology, decentralized union control, and emphasis upon economic rather than political action by unions. Nikkyōso did not escape these developments, particularly since it was itself an amalgamation of left- and right-wing groups that earned it the popular title of the "red-headed white crane." A rash of defections occurred within Nikkyōso. The Kyoto City union, for example, split in two, and 700 members organized an independent body. In 1951, 15,000 high school teachers withdrew from Nikkyōso to establish the Zenkyō-kyō, although as much over dissatisfaction with the predominance of the elementary school teachers as over ideological issues.

Further, the "red" purge was in full swing by 1950, and by May, 1950, more than 1,000 teachers had been dismissed, approximately one-tenth of those driven from posts in public agencies and hence from their unions. Some of the most vocal elements among the teachers were among those discharged.

Nonetheless, despite the attempt to contain, or perhaps disrupt, Nikkyōso as the "reverse" course policies unfolded, the teachers' organization remained firmly bound together. The basis upon which the teachers had found common ground for unification remained essentially unshaken. The unity, however, was not necessarily solid. As an omnibus organization, Nikkyōso harbored such a wide diversity of ideological, political, economic, and professional interests that its positions were necessarily couched in general pronouncements and ideals. In this context, Nikkyōso sought allies outside the teaching profession, and, given the long history of teacher maltreatment, control, and suppression, Nikkyōso sought justification in close affiliation with the mainstream of the Japanese labor movement, especially to protect itself against the now uncongenial government and Occupation policies.

Moreover, once the peace treaty was consummated and the conservatives continued to control the government, the "reverse course" resumed on the grounds that various Occupation reforms had not proved suitable to the "realities" of existing Japanese conditions. With regard to organized labor particularly, the government moved to enact further restrictions on the exercise of trade union rights in publicly owned enterprises; [28] provisions for handling "emergency" disputes; prohibition of strikes in "vital" private industries, specifically coal mining and electric power (following a near disastrous strike in these industries in the latter part of 1952); and antisubversive activities legislation, which union groups claimed was merely a revival of prewar "thought control" and police surveillance. This series of new laws and revisions fanned Sōhyō opposition and led to growing political involvement of the labor movement. Nikkyōso's activities were especially visible on all these issues.

By 1953, furthermore, the government began to prepare additional legislative proposals aimed directly at curbing teacher activ-

[28] These included the new Local Public Enterprise Labor Relations Law and amendments to the Trade Union Law, Labor Relations Adjustment Law, Public Corporation and National Enterprise Labor Relations Law, Labor Standards Law, National Public Service Law, and Local Public Service Law, all in July, 1952.

ity in the political sphere. In 1954, a bill was proposed to designate public school teachers as national government civil servants as a means to control the teachers, but failed to pass partly because of the opposition aroused by Nikkyōso. The government did set up a commission to study "neutralism in education," on the heels of a highly publicized incident—the so-called Yamaguchi case—in which it was revealed in a pupil's school diary that his teacher, highly active in the union, was instructing students to view the United States as the aggressor in the Korean War. Shortly thereafter, the government succeeded in changing the law for educational personnel so as to prohibit teachers from becoming school board candidates in districts where they were employed (although allowed to run elsewhere), engaging in political campaigning, and espousing "political" biases in classroom instruction. The opposition, however, blunted the new legislation by obtaining only minimal penalties for violations. This skirmishing between the government and Nikkyōso had by this time turned into a full-fledged confrontation that, despite recent attempts to change the relationship, has continued to the present.

The confrontation between Nikkyōso and the government inevitably meant that the union's concern would be directed toward political action. Not only had the government increasingly imposed restrictions upon political activity, but also there were only limited opportunities for the teachers' union to engage in economic negotiations. Thus, a vicious circle of retaliation upon retaliation set in, which was certain to confound economic and political activity and to erase any distinction between them. The principal issues regarding the teachers since the end of the Occupation amply illustrate this point.

MAJOR POLITICAL ISSUES

For almost two decades, Nikkyōso has been in the center of a continuing series of heated policy debates. Ever since 1948 when the government renounced the centralized contracts with Nikkyōso and refused thereafter to recognize Nikkyōso as a negotiating agent, the prime moving issue for the teachers has been to regain these bargaining and representation rights under the law. Only in 1965 following the International Labor Organization (ILO) investigation and revision of labor legislation for public service personnel did there appear any signs of a change in the increasingly restrictive state of affairs for the teachers.

Until the government recently "softened" its position toward Nikkyōso as the result of the issue over ratifying ILO Convention 87, to be discussed shortly, for more than a decade the government, speaking usually through the Minister of Education, repudiated Nikkyōso's demands, thereby feeding the animosity that existed.

Following the 1954 revisions of the legal status of the public school teacher, the conservative government set out to abolish elections for local school boards. While this proposal was rationalized on the grounds of achieving greater efficiency for the school system and enforcing uniform educational standards, it was also an obvious attempt to decrease the influence of the teachers unions and to limit further Nikkyōso's political role. The government's plan was to empower prefectural governors to appoint all local school boards —prefectural, municipal, town, and village—with the consent of the local government assemblies. Nikkyōso and Sōhyō, of course, interpreted this as an attempt not only to eliminate teacher representatives on the boards but also to undermine the still tenuous local political organizations which the opposition parties had managed to develop. The proposal was greeted with vigorous protest that it was tantamount to a return of control over the school system directly to the Ministry of Education.

Enactment of the bill in 1956 after three years of debate had the effect of shifting the confrontation between the teachers' organization and governmental authorities increasingly to the national political level. With the central government, through the Ministry of Education, providing the prefectures with half the funds for teacher salaries and other educational expeditures, Nikkyōso reiterated its demand for bargaining with the Ministry over the fundamental terms of teacher employment in the public schools. While the Ministry continued to "negotiate" or discuss issues with Nikkyōso, it steadfastly refused to recognize the union as a bargaining agent. In the events leading to the revision of the law in 1956, however, Nikkyōso waged a massive campaign in opposition, including mass demonstrations, sit-downs, and hunger strikes—tactics which while they failed probably induced prefectural governors, now empowered to appoint board members, to include teachers on many of the school boards.

A second major issue concerned the teacher's "professional" behavior. In 1952 Nikkyōso formulated a code of ethical principles for teachers which the government immediately condemned as additional evidence of left-wing, revolutionary domination of the unions. The code generally called for "defense of peace," academic freedom, and equal opportunity in education, and further declared that teachers were members of the working class, entitled to a suitable standard of living and the right to autonomous self-organization, including alliances with parents and other groups to solve the problems of youth and construct a "bright new culture." To the government, this was not a professional credo but merely a pronouncement of political aims, and as a countermove, the Ministry of Education proposed the introduction of compulsory "morals" instruction in the schools and concommittant changes in social studies curricula.

The importance of the teachers' code was that it challenged the government's control over educational policy. Nikkyōso declared it would not accept the government's attempts to "dictate" the content of education and to eliminate teacher union influence in deciding upon that content. Refusal to abandon the code strengthened the government's determination to abolish popularly elected school boards on which teacher union influence might prevail. In turn, this threat, culminating in the revision of the law in 1956, prompted Nikkyōso to reaffirm the code as a necessary step against the revival of the prewar system of educational controls.

The code has been a continuing issue to the present, contributing to the Education Minister's refusal even to confer with Nikkyōso representatives between 1960 and 1965. The government insisted that any recognition of Nikkyōso was in part dependent upon abandoning the code. Nikkyōso's retort has been that the government's insistence upon rescinding the code constituted an interference in internal union affairs and, in turn, an attempt to control the behavior of an independent and autonomous professional group.

Coupled with the debate over the teachers' code of ethics was a proposal for instituting teacher "merit rating." Given the far-reaching change in teacher preparation and qualifications for certification, the Ministry held that salary advancement, promotions, assignments, and retention should at least in part relate to evaluation of the teacher's performance. Nikkyōso's perception of merit rating was that it would be merely a method for controlling teacher behavior and undermining the teachers' unions. Following considerable public discussion during the early 1950's, the Ministry set forth a uniform, nationwide plan for teacher merit rating in 1957, which it urged public school districts to adopt for promotions, salary adjustments, and discharges. The plan set forth guidelines and rating criteria which would be applied by superintendents and principals without necessarily any rank-and-file participation or consultation with the teachers' unions.

Again, Nikkyōso protested vigorously. In its view, not only did merit rating violate its notion of uniformity of treatment of teachers and uniform pay-scales, but also abrogated principles of agreements already made for joint determination of school personnel matters. Further, the plan would drive a wedge between school principals and teachers, increase competition among the latter, and destroy union solidarity at the school level which was a key for the success of unionization in the first place. Finally, some of the criteria for rating appeared highly subjective, with the implication that the system could revive surveillance over the teacher's personal life and moral behavior as well as impose penalties for union activity.

Nikkyōso itself was being wracked by internal ideological dissension which came to a head over the merit rating issue. The extreme leftists refused to accept any part of merit rating, while the moderates were willing to accept the plan provided there were negotiations with the union in advance and consultation over application. Of all the issues which contributed to the confrontation between Nikkyōso and the government, merit rating was probably the most disruptive, leading to frequent protest demonstrations and walkouts. In one instance in 1958, the government arrested Chairman Kobayashi for violation of the strike-prohibition clause of the Local Public Service Law, while thousands of teachers were subjected to disciplinary measures if not outright dismissal. Although merit rating gradually gained acceptance, the agitation over this and other issues was so severe that in 1960 the Ministry declared that it would no longer meet with the representatives of Nikkyōso even for purposes of "discussion."

Still other heated issues in the confrontation between Nikkyōso and the government have concerned pupil testing, class sizes, and teacher study conferences. In 1961 the Ministry of Education proposed an extension of achievement testing of pupils, then given only at the senior high school level, to both elementary and junior high students. Nikkyōso strongly objected on the grounds that such testing violated the notion of providing equal educational opportunity and also revived central government control over career choices. The union demanded instead the availability of free schooling up through the high school level for all who wished to attend. It also condemned achievement testing as still another device to undermine Nikkyōso vis-a-vis its membership, since such testing would not only place increased pressure upon the schoolchildren but also add to the work loads of the teachers themselves.

By the early 1960's, moreover, the Ministry was taking the position, in view of the drop in the birthrate and, hence, the size of the school population, that there should be a reduction in the number of elementary school teachers. Such a proposal not only hit at the bulk of Nikkyōso's membership, but also again posed the issue of control over working conditions, in particular class sizes. Apparently, the government felt little necessity for a reduction of pupil-teacher ratios, while Nikkyōso had long insisted upon this as a major desideratum in educational policy.

Finally, the competition between Nikkyōso and the government centered on in-service teacher training. The Ministry of Education, as earlier mentioned, in the 1950's began to conduct educational research conferences for teachers in rivalry with meetings conducted by Nikkyōso's Research Institute for National Education. Local boards implicitly were encouraged to reward teachers who attended the Ministry's meetings and to disfavor those who went to Nikkyōso's. Similarly, the Ministry issued its own list of approved textbooks, implying disapproval of Nikkyōso-recommended texts. On these matters, Nikkyōso, of course, has held they are "union-busting" devices and attempts to destroy teacher independence.

The tie between policy issues and economic bargaining, of course, looms most prominently in the annual debate in the National Diet over the budgetary appropriation for support of public education, especially the size of the subsidies for equalizing educational costs among prefectures and for payment of teacher salaries. By law the national government provides up to half of the public teachers' pay through its budget. The debate begins in the spring and becomes the focal point of both political and economic pressures. Once this budget is determined, the teachers' union finds it necessary to exert pressure upon the national and local personnel authorities when they make their annual recommendations for pay increases and upon the Ministries of Finance and Education in shaping budget requests to the Cabinet and Diet. The National Personnel Authority (NPA) sets the process in motion, since under the law it conducts an annual survey of wages in private industry for purposes of comparing the pay status of public employees and, in fact, must make recommendations for adjustments if it finds a differential of five or more per cent between the two sectors. This procedure is fraught with debatable items: survey techniques, choice of groups compared, the amount of adjustment recommended, etc. Since the NPA recommendations reverberate throughout the economy, the Authority is subject to pressures from virtually all segments of industry, private and public alike.

These activities reinforce the close alliance between Nikkyōso and Sōhyō, especially with the other affiliated public employee unions which confront the government with demands at the same time. The annual drive for wage increases and semi-annual campaigns for wage bonuses bring these unions together for coordinated action under the aegis of the Kankōrō, the council of public employees unions formed within Sōhyō. These also become the occasions for combining political activity with economic demands; and the so-called spring, fall, and year-end "struggles"—waves of scheduled slow-downs, demonstrations, and short-stoppages—stress such problems as the abolition of the U.S.-Japan Security Treaty, return of Okinawa to Japanese control, expansion of trade with China, end of Japanese rearmament and ban on nuclear weapons, stopping of visits of U.S. nuclear-powered warships to Japan, opposition to the treaty with the Republic of Korea, and most recently the Vietnam War. Nikkyōso is usually in the thick of these political movements, as well as participating in election campaigns. Using the seasonal struggle as a springboard, furthermore, Sōhyō attempts to wheel private industry unions into coordinated courses of militant action, strikes, and demonstrations. Thus, Sōhyō's strategy is to develop a nationwide involvement in labor issues. Perhaps even more than the other government employee unions (such as the national railways, telephone and telegraph, postal operations, national monopoly corporations), Nikkyōso chooses to devote most of its energy to the political sphere.

Nikkyōso's political emphasis also appears to be the product of relatively limited opportunity to engage in direct collective bargaining even with local public authorities. What local bargaining there has been since 1948 has tended to lack uniformity, varying with local organizational strength and political influence upon governors and mayors. The Nikkyōso branches often find themselves shunted from the local to the prefectural educational boards and back, unable to locate the appropriate agency which has clear authority to carry on negotiations. This situation arises, of course, from the kaleidoscopic legal arrangements for allocating funds for public education and for determining policy regarding the educational system. In part, then, the inability to pinpoint where in the governmental structure effective negotiations may be undertaken has increased Nikkyōso's reliance upon political action, as well as the demand for centralized bargaining. Under these circumstances, Nikkyōso and its branches became ready targets for accusations that they are neither professional nor trade union organizations.

Under the law, in fact, there are no legal rights for the unions of public school teachers to bargain at the local level, but they may attempt to "negotiate" or make representations to the school boards. Much of the discussion that does go on, in those instances where the local board is receptive, revolves around local personnel issues particular to the given school district or schools within the district. Few of the basic problems—general wage adjustments, hours of teaching, classroom sizes, etc.—are entered into directly. Under these circumstances, it is especially important for the local branches to have close relationships with supervisory personnel, especially principals and assistant principals, in order to work out the day-to-day solution of personnel administration problems. Membership of these supervisors in the union, of course, facilitates these adjustments. Before the laws were changed in the late 1940's, most teachers were covered by collective bargaining agreements executed formally by the basic union units. Today there are only scattered contracts for private school teacher unions.

To the extent that bargaining relationships do exist, they tend to be informal and unsystematic and are entwined with the political situation in the given locality or region. In general, the locus of the bargaining is at the prefectural government level where the Kenkyōso negotiates with the prefectural school board and/or personnel commission. Here, because of taxing powers and receipt of subsidies from the national government, there is often leeway for setting policy for the prefecture as a whole on salaries, benefits, working conditions, and matters of personnel administration. As a result, school boards and unions at the municipal, town, and village level usually relay their positions to the prefectural authorities, so that local level negotiations are confined to merely immediate problems such as individual grievances and complaints. In certain prefectures, such as Ibaraki, Tokyo, Kyoto, and Osaka, the teachers' union has achieved considerable success in obtaining access for negotiations at the various levels. In others, however, there have been notable failures. Fundamentally, the degree to which negotiations are established depends upon the local political influence the teacher's unions are able to exert. It is often a subtle and frustrating process, with much behind-the-scenes maneuvering and ambiguous and variable outcomes that contribute to differential wage and working conditions of teachers from one locality to another.

Despite these limited bargaining opportunities, greatly improved economic conditions since the middle 1950's have favored increasing attention of Nikkyōso to the teachers' economic status. Even though public school teachers largely depend upon national government enactments for welfare benefits as well as wage increases, Nikkyōso has moved in the direction of developing its own economic welfare programs, such as providing funds for dismissed or disciplined teachers and developing mutual life and fire insurance schemes. These developments, aided by the dominance of socialist leadership since the late 1950's (and the decline of communist influence), derive in part from the growing shortages of new teachers to enter the profession. As in other fields requiring modern skills and education, the supply of teachers has tightened with the widespread needs for trained labor in other sectors of the rapidly expanding economy, with Japan's falling birthrate, and with requirements of greater education to enter a variety of new occupations. One result of this squeeze has been the shift to increasing use of females in teaching, which up to the postwar period had been largely a male occupation. The recruitment of females, however, as in other nations has increased Nikkyōso's difficulties in enlisting new members, thus making it all the more imperative to obtain legal recognition of its right to represent the teachers in negotiations, preferably at the national level.

By the late 1950's it was apparent that major sectors of the Japanese labor movement, especially principal Sōhyō affiliates which claimed they received the brunt of the government's "reverse course," would no longer rely only upon their own resources to protect the rights and advance the interests of the Japanese trade unionists. The main upshot was to turn to foreign support to bring pressure upon the central government. This took the form of demanding Japan's ratification of ILO Convention 87 on Freedom of Association and ILO condemnation of the failure of the Japanese government to do so. The Japan Teachers Union has been a major principal in this debate, which began with the lodging of formal complaints in 1958 and culminated in an on-the-spot ILO investigation in Japan in 1965, although the issues involved have not been fully resolved despite Japan's subsequent ratification of the convention.

THE ILO 87 ISSUE [29]

The stiffened position of the government toward the teachers' union in 1960 prompted Nikkyōso in October of that year to join with other public employee unions, notably the postal workers, the national railway workers, and the local and municipal workers, in filing complaints with the International Labor Organization that the Japanese government was violating the guarantees for freedom of association under ILO Convention 87.[30] Nikkyōso specified that the government contravened the convention in denying the right of strike to teachers, punishing striking teachers for engaging in union activities, refusing to negotiate with duly-elected representatives of the teachers union, and arbitrarily withdrawing the civil service status of teachers elected to union office. These actions, the union held, violated the principles of the right of workers to organize and to select representatives of their own choosing.

Nikkyōso directly entered the ILO 87 debate following the Ministry of Education's refusal to continue the established practice of holding discussions with Nikkyōso. Although the national government had refused after 1948 to negotiate with Nikkyōso, the Ministry of Education had been willing to discuss with representatives of the union matters affecting the economic status of teachers. However, as the acrimony heightened between the government and Nikkyōso throughout the 1950's, soon after assuming the office of

[29] International Labour Office, *Report of the Fact-Finding and Conciliation Commission on Freedom of Association Concerning Persons Employed in the Public Sector in Japan* (Geneva, 1965, mimeo).
[30] The first formal complaints were filed by the Postal Workers in April 1958, although the National Railway Locomotive Engineers' Union had lodged a protest earlier.

Education Minister in 1960, Araki Masuo flatly declared that such consultative meetings would cease because he alleged Nikkyōso was nothing more than a political organization which should seek redress through the Diet. Araki further affirmed that any negotiations as permitted under the law had to be carried out at the prefectural or local levels, since the central government possessed no authority to negotiate with local government civil servants. Araki's declaration, it should be noted, came on the heels of the antisecurity agreement demonstrations in 1960 which had forced the cancellation of President Eisenhower's visit to Japan. It also occurred at the height of the heated controversy over the Ministry's proposal to extend achievement testing to elementary and secondary school pupils and while merit rating was causing widespread dissension within Nikkyōso.

In 1962, Minister Araki declared his willingness to reopen the consultative meetings only if Nikkyōso revised its organizational structure to exclude principals and other supervisors, abandoned its political activities, and amended its code of ethics by dropping ideological statements contained therein. This was to remain the government's official attitude toward Nikkyōso until the ILO investigating commission succeeded in inducing a reopening of discussions in mid-1965.

Following some five years of investigation and debate in Geneva, the ILO early in 1964 decided to establish a Fact-Finding and Conciliation Commission to conduct an on-the-spot inquiry in Japan. This decision was reached only after the failure of the Japanese government to effectuate its own repeated declarations, beginning in November 1958, that Japan intended to ratify ILO 87 and to revise her domestic labor laws accordingly. While a series of bills had been taken up in the Diet during this period, all had foundered—not only as the result of differences among the major political parties but also within them—on the question of the appropriate revisions of the labor laws, particularly the scope of organization to be allowed the teachers' union, requirements for the public worker unions to register, right of full-time union officers to retain civil service status, scope of subjects permissible in negotiation, continuation of compulsory dues checkoff, and right of teachers to engage in work stoppages and conclude collective bargaining agreements. The ICFTU itself had joined the chorus of voices in the ILO demanding that the Japanese government promptly meet its oft-proclaimed promise, while Sōhyō and Nikkyōso exploited the issue in their political activities and seasonal "struggles."

Basically, from the legal point of view, the chief stumbling block for adopting ILO 87 and revising the pertinent labor laws lay in the restrictions that had been written a decade or more earlier in the Public Corporation and National Enterprise Labor Law, the Local Public Enterprise Labor Relations Law, the National Public-Service Law, and Local Public-Service Law that officers of government worker unions had to be selected from the membership. Thus, if these officers were dismissed from their government jobs for engaging in illegal activities, their unions would automatically lose recognition. Although originally most of the Japanese trade unions had accepted this restriction as a means to eliminate radical left-wing, particularly communist, infiltration, and to achieve solidarity on the basis of "enterprise" identification, by the late 1950's a series of episodes allegedly involving illegal stoppages had led to the temporary withdrawal of recognition of such major unions as the Postal Workers and National Railway Workers. Thus, the complainants pointed out that not only had Japan failed to comply with ILO 87 but also actually had violated ILO Convention 98 on the Rights to Organize and Collective Bargaining which Japan had indeed ratified as early as 1953.

In its defense, the Japanese government argued that no union officers had been dismissed for engaging in union activities but only for violating the laws pertaining to the operation of public agencies. Nonetheless, in its promise to ratify ILO 87, the government declared it would also attempt to clarify the provisions of the various laws to achieve consistency with the Convention. By 1962 the ILO had issued appeals on at least nine occasions to the Japanese government to ratify ILO 87. Japan's adoption of the Convention came three years later, only after further appeals and the on-the-spot investigation.

The report on the hearings and investigation conducted by the ILO Commission clearly reveals the complexities of the issues surrounding the unionized public employee in Japan. Here we shall deal only with those issues of direct relevance to the teachers' unions.[31]

The complaining unions objected to: (1) restriction of elected officers to the civil servants in the union unit, (2) proposed elimination of retention of civil service status by those elected, (3) refusal

31 See ILO *Report*, especially Chapters 15 and 39.

of government authorities to engage in bargaining collectively, (4) proposed end of the automatic dues checkoff system, (5) restriction of the freedom of local units to federate with other units, and (6) denial of the right to strike without compensatory procedure for settling disputes, processing grievances, and providing adequate payment. Nikkyōso submitted a long list of its own specific complaints pertaining to the teachers, which included individual episodes and examples of discrimination against union members, refusals by authorities to negotiate, interference in local union affairs, and restrictions upon affiliation of teacher unions beyond local and prefectural levels. In each instance, the government denied the allegations or argued they did not contravene the existing laws.

The ILO Commission began its work in Geneva in the spring of 1964 and proceeded to Japan in January, 1965. A few weeks later it issued a preliminary report after completing hearings in Japan and in July, 1965 produced a lengthy final report. In the interim, the Japanese government had ratified ILO 87 in June, initiated the first of a proposed series of regular discussions with Sōhyō, and promised to bring the Minister of Education and Nikkyōso together again for an exchange of views. Deliberations in the Diet also resumed, leading to agreement to appoint a special tripartite Advisory Council on the Public Personnel System to study the issues and formulate proposals which would bring the domestic laws into conformance with the ILO Convention.

Throughout the hearings, it became clear that one of the main bones of contention between the government and Sōhyō was the question of reinstituting discussions between the Ministry of Education and Nikkyōso. However, the teachers' union insisted that, given the nature and history of the educational system, the only sensible and meaningful solution was to centralize collective bargaining at the national level mainly because, it alleged, the Ministry exercised effective control over budgets, salaries, working conditions, class sizes, hours, etc. Nikkyōso conceded that it was prepared to accept an end to retention of civil service status by union officers but asked for a prolonged period in which to make the transition because of the large number of full-time union officials who fell into this category.[32]

Again, the government, for its part, contended it had little or no power over local and prefectural school boards in any of the above-

[32] Full-time officers in Nikkyōso in recent years have numbered close to 1,000, of whom more than one-fourth had served in their posts five years or longer.

mentioned matters. The Ministry of Education and the Ministry of Finance, in its view, merely provided guidance which the local governments could choose to ignore. Since the law specifically excluded bargaining at the national level, there was no choice for the unions but to seek recognition to negotiate from the prefectural, municipal, and local units of government. The government, furthermore, denied all charges that it encouraged the local boards to discriminate against Nikkyōso members and to urge teachers not to join the union, to set up rival organizations, and to establish separate unions for principals and supervisors.

The chief result of the hearings and subsequent reports was that, aside from the steps to ratify the Convention, launch mutual discussions, and establish machinery for revising the laws, a period now ensued in which there was a relaxation of the tensions that had mounted over the years between the government and the labor movement.

In essence, the ILO Commission urged simplification of the web of laws that had come to characterize Japan's labor scene. Its report implied that a return to the original Trade Union Law was desirable, but at the same time appealed to Sōhyō and its affiliates, especially Nikkyōso, to abandon their preoccupation with political activities. More specifically, the Commission proposed that the Japanese government make a distinction between its function as a government and an employer; and therefore, it recommended that future policy designate which public services are "essential" and "nonessential," develop a compensatory dispute settlement system for the former, and permit the right to strike for the latter.

With regard to Nikkyōso, the Commission did not urge outright centralized collective bargaining, but asked that teacher organizations be guaranteed a voice in appointing members to local personnel and equity commissions and access for both the unions and individuals to be heard by such commissions. Thus, the Commission did not advocate that the teachers be granted the right to strike but held it of utmost importance to establish systematic dispute machinery and to provide "full and prompt implementation" of Commission recommendations.

A major root of the problems, the Commission held, was that Japan had built an overly complex legal structure for industrial relations, so that the location of authority and channels for negotiations were inevitably obscure. In the case of the teachers, for example, there was a large and intricate network of legalities emanating from the Local Public Service Law, the various laws on education, recommendations of the National Personnel Authority, Cabinet orders, Ministry of Education policies, bylaws of thousands of local governments and their commissions, as well as conflicting court decisions. The result was that any government body could take refuge behind the mass of rulings and claim that other bodies had jurisdiction.

At the same time, the Commission concluded, the teachers' unions (and others such as the local and municipal government employees) not only frittered away resources and energy in attempting to locate authorized bargaining counterparts, but also ran the risk of organizational atomization in the process. In turn, as a means of preserving unity in policy and structure, it held, the teachers tended to place power in their central union organization, which, because of the fragmentation of procedure and dissipation of energy at local levels, was likely to emphasize extremist action. The fact, furthermore, that Nikkyōso enjoyed no legal status could readily give rise to charges of irresponsibility. In light of these complexities, the Commission urged that, with the ratification of Convention 87, the parties begin their relationships anew with a clean slate, dropping all existing grievances and sanctions (for example, even during the midst of the ILO Commission developments, the government had disciplined 195,000 public workers from January to June, 1965).

Although the Commission felt that special legislation for the teachers was unnecessary and that centralized bargaining should not be mandatory, it recommended that it would be appropriate to recognize Nikkyōso as a negotiating party at any level. To do so, the government was urged to decide that decisions made at the central level would be binding upon the local authorities, and in the event actual bargaining was left to the latter, they should have "real freedom to negotiate." In any event, in the Commission's view, it was up to the government to determine which matters were to be handled at the national and which at the local levels.

Even before the Commission issued its final report in July, 1965, the Japanese government had moved to initiate discussions with Sōhyō. While Sōhyō rejected the Commission's initial recommendations in January, mainly because of the failure to include centralized negotiations for the teachers, the first of a series of government-labor discussions did begin on May 18th. Those attending included the Prime Minister, nine cabinet members, and Shōyō leaders.

In the meantime, the Diet ratified the Convention in April, with the socialist legislators joining the conservatives in supporting its passage. Simultaneously the Diet adopted a set of revisions for the relevant labor laws to bring them into conformity with the Convention, although the implementation of the amendments was put off for a year while a Diet-established tripartite advisory council debated other issues that remained unsettled. After the upper house of the Diet gave its approval, Geneva received the instrument of ratification in June, 1965.

Despite its willingness to meet with Sōhyō, the government continued to balk at having direct talks between the Ministry of Education and Nikkyōso. At this point, Sōhyō refused to meet further with the government. In August, 1965, however, the government conceded the point and discussion resumed.

The heart of the problem now lay in the revisions of the labor laws. Under both the National and Local Public Service Laws, the amendments adopted in April provided for five major changes: (1) a widened definition of "managerial" personnel in public service and a stipulation for separate organizations of supervisors should they exercise their right to organize; (2) election of union officers by a majority of those voting rather than of all members as previously required; (3) permission to form unions including employees outside the given governmental unit (including those dismissed); (4) dropping the restriction that union officers must be elected from employees of the government unit but providing for loss of civil servant status for those that were; and (5) limitations on the government's authority to cancel a union's registration. Unsettled issues left to the new tripartite advisory council included (1) appropriate scope of public employee unions; (2) adoption of a uniform law for both national and local public employees; (3) the right of public employees to strike; and (4) the transition from retention to loss of civil service status for full-time union officers. The council was composed of 21 members, nine of whom were "neutral," and the remainder divided between government and unions. Of the six unionists appointed, five were from Sōhyō.

Actually, it took until November before the advisory council held its first meeting. Considerable maneuvering attended the appointment of its membership and then over the question of the agenda.

When the body first met officially on November 1, the Sōhyō representatives refused to attend, but they did appear on November 18 upon receiving certain minor concessions on procedure.

Meanwhile, the historic meeting between the Minister of Education and Nikkyōso took place on August 26, 1965—the first official discussion of its kind in five years. Nonetheless, the government held to its earlier points: Nikkyōso must abolish its code of ethics, observe neutrality in politics, and abstain from striking and obstructing school operations. Nikkyōso replied that these demands again constituted an attempt to interfere with its internal affairs and repeated its insistence upon centralized negotiations for wages, working conditions, and educational policy. Further strain arose over the question of how often these discussions were to be held, the government refusing to meet on a regularly scheduled basis. By October, after a few additional meetings which saw merely reiteration of these issues, the two parties were at a complete impasse.

By this time, the focus turned to the deliberations of the tripartite advisory council, which finally convened as a full body on November 18, 1965. A series of hearings through the winter produced few fruitful results. Only by February, 1966, did the council reach discussion on substantive issues, and by June 13, when the labor law amendments adopted the year before were to take effect, it had held 16 sessions. Although the Sōhyō representatives again walked out at this juncture, the "public" members announced that they favored immediate enforcement of the revisions except those regarding the loss of civil service status for full-time union officers. Immediately the Cabinet issued an enforcement order to this effect extending the civil service status question for another six months.

By February, when the council had turned to substantive issues, the Minister of Education and Nikkyōso agreed to renew their discussions. The principal issues of these meetings revolved around questions of increasing the number of senior high teachers, establishing a retirement system for local civil servants, reducing overtime for teachers, and determining eligibility of principals and head teachers to become and remain union members. Little agreement had been reached on any of these matters by the time the council recommended enforcement of the amendments.

With the promulgation order issued by the Cabinet, it was now left to the National Personnel Authority and its local counterparts (personnel and/or equity commissions) to define the scope of "managerial" employees for the purpose of establishing the eligibility for union membership of principals, assistant principals, head teachers, and other school supervisors. The revised law did, however, permit persons so excluded from teacher union membership to form their own personnel associations. Nikkyōso's immediate reaction, as could be expected, was to exert pressure on the National Personnel Authority for a tight definition of "managerial" personnel out of fear that the loss of principals and other supervisors (totalling 80,000) would spell destruction of the union as an effective organization. Resolution of this issue came with the adoption of amendments by the Diet which, in addition to excluding principals and certain staff (such as night school administrators and nurses) from teacher union membership, permitted local authorities to decide whether assistant principals and other school administrative personnel could continue to belong to teacher unions.

At the same time, the socialists and other opposition party groups in the Diet resorted to parliamentary maneuvers to delay implementation of the revisions and to exact further concessions favorable to Nikkyōso's positions. Protest against eliminating supervisors from the union and limiting the civil service status of officers and demands for wage increases for the public employees were at the economic heart of Nikkyōso's participation in Sōhyō's annual fall "struggle" in October, 1966, that also in general condemned the Vietnam War. In the course of the "struggle," the inevitable demonstrations and brief walkouts occurred, leading to a police search of Nikkyōso's headquarters and to the discipline and arrest of teacher union officers and members for engaging in illegal stoppages under the Local Public Service Law. On December 21, 1966, in fact, the police brought charges against Chairman Miyanohara and General Secretary Makieda for instigating the strikes.[33] This counteraction, it should be noted, occurred as the nation prepared for new general elections for the Diet at the end of January, 1967. Then, on December 24, 1966, in the face of Sōhyō requests that action on the revisions be further postponed until the tripartite advisory council made its final recommendation, the government announced enforcement of the amendments.

Paradoxically, while the ILO 87 problem had led to a much clearer pronouncement than had existed on the right of public

---

[33] This occurred despite the ruling of the Japanese Supreme Court on October 26 that work stoppages on the part of public employees were not "criminal activities." See *Japan Labor Bulletin,* December, 1966, pp. 1, 3–4.

employees to self-organization and selection of representatives of their own choosing, it appeared to have been accomplished at the expense of eroding, if not actually destroying, the basic principle of Japanese union organization—the tight-knit, close identification of all members of an employing unit with the unit's union. In the general context of enterprise unionism in Japan, this could spell a serious decline in the importance and effectiveness of Nikkyōso. Further, it could accentuate the political and ideological role of the national leadership to compensate for an increasing lack of unity among the rank and file as the result of growing apathy, increased mobility, and a notable gap at the local level in union consciousness between older and younger teachers. The exact outcome at this writing is not known, but it is apparent that the struggle that has been in process since 1948 over the status and organization of the teachers' union is far from over.

CONCLUSIONS

The history of teacher unionization in Japan reflects a hybridization of political and ideological motivation, advancement of economic interests, and a drive to achieve professional status. Traditionally, the teacher in pre-Meiji Japan was an agent of innovation and independent thought, but once modernization began he was largely an instrument of state policy, subject to close control by the authorities as to selection, training, assignment, and duties.

Japan's defeat in World War II called for abandonment of these controls, and the Occupation policy immediately permitted a sudden release of the teacher from long-standing constraints. One result was widespread teacher organization, represented mainly by Nikkyōso, through which teachers attempted not only to achieve an independent professional status but also concomitantly to reshape the society, through radical reform, which would reinforce their new status. Seemingly "unprofessional" in its activities, Nikkyōso joined with the bulk of the labor movement which itself embraced social revolution as its goal.[34]

Japan's government and the Occupation reacted to this with the

---

[34] Especially with the present exclusion of principals from teacher union membership, Nikkyōso has stressed the teacher's status as a worker to counter government demands for "professional" behavior. Nikkyōso, for example, has been insisting upon overtime pay for performing teaching functions beyond the hours established by the Labor Standards Law, while the government has sought to provide special salary "allowances" instead.

imposition of restraints upon the labor movement, and probably these restraints fell most heavily upon the teachers, since the opportunity for participation in the formal machinery of decision-making was particularly denied to them. The ILO 87 episode fully illustrates the degree to which Nikkyōso found itself hamstrung in the consultation and decision-making process at national and local levels. It may be said that Nikkyōso's reaction by continuing and perhaps increasing its political and ideological emphases resulted from the blocking of the very channels which might have otherwise facilitated a "professional" role for the teacher. Given their intellectual qualities, the teachers through Nikkyōso have been even more shrill than most parts of the Japanese labor movement in protesting and demanding a revamping of society.

On the other hand, basic cultural, economic, and historical conditions further restrained an emphasis upon pure "professionalism" among teachers. Although after World War II, teacher training was drastically revamped, the civil service status of the teacher constantly reinforced the prewar notion of being state instruments. This was embedded in a compartmentalism that has long characterized Japanese society at the village and city ward level, so that identification as professionals on a national scale would inevitably be especially weak. Further, the labor movement itself, of which Nikkyōso is a major component, has long been characterized by localism, especially as expressed in the structural phenomenon of "enterprisewide" unionism, a trait that is as apt for government worker unions as in the private sector. If the political authorities were to tolerate unionization among teachers, it was likely to be only on this basis.

To a large measure, this combination of circumstances may explain the hybridization of themes found in Nikkyōso, for while the average rank-and-file member may remain passive, so it appears, the organization embraces the various aspirations of a new society and the new status most teachers hold. The alternatives to the teachers' union do not appear especially attractive, even though there have been defections (perhaps under subtle threats) and some separate unionism (such as the high school teachers). The modernization of Japanese society has yet to reach the point where teachers may exert an independent influence through established administrative and political machinery which recognizes their distinctive professional role. Until far more of this is achieved—and the ILO issue may have been an important opening in such a direction—it is difficult to envision a drastic change in the hybrid organization which Nikkyōso represents. Also, it is difficult to predict an early end to the continuing sharp confrontation between the government and Nikkyōso.

The demand for education in Japan, supported by rapid economic growth, however, may become a critical factor in changing the mix of themes. This plus the new constraints and opportunities placed upon teacher unionism in Japan could eventually reshape Nikkyōso toward greater autonomy, less compartmentalization, and increased emphasis on economic issues. A difficult transition awaits, and adverse economic and political events could spell the destruction of Nikkyōso. Nikkyōso has its strand of aspiration for professionalism but the extent to which it can be attained (limited in most societies) is bound up with the admixture of old and new, which is the stuff modern Japanese democracy is made of.

Mexico 6

Victor Alba

Mexico is one of the few countries of our time which has carried out a successful and far-reaching revolution. It is also one of the very few underdeveloped nations in the world whose economic growth has exceeded its growth in population, even if slightly. Although Mexico belongs to the Latin American community in which pre-Colombian culture mixes and struggles with the Spanish inheritance, its national personality is more distinctive than other Latin American countries possibly because the mixture of these two basic elements is more advanced than elsewhere in Latin America.

These facts—the revolution, the integration of the two cultures, and the rate of economic growth—make an exceptional case of Mexico, one which is not representative of Latin America. Therefore, the history and characteristics of organizations of Mexican teachers differ greatly from other Latin American teachers' organizations. One of the characteristics of this history—the struggle between the church and the state and its repercussions on education and therefore on the activity of the teachers—does not seem likely to be repeated in the other Latin American countries or, in general, in other countries in the process of development because of recent changes in the Catholic Church. The theme of our study, then, is peculiar, without parallel in the past, and possibly without parallel in the future.

Victor Alba is Professor, Kent State University, Kent, Ohio. He is former Director, Centro de Estudios y Documentación Sociales, Mexico.

THE ROLE OF TEACHERS IN MEXICAN HISTORY

The monopoly on education by the church, first established during the colonial era (and which, in fact, already existed in Aztec society before the conquest) continued after independence. Even though there were attempts to separate the church from the state after independence, the liberals, who were the ones favoring the change, were not able to destroy church monopoly until they reached power and promulgated the so-called Laws of Reforms (leyes de reforma) and the constitution of 1857. The latter established the separation of church and state and the former deprived the church of its properties.

The liberals, who were fighting to free education from the control of the church, had already founded in 1833, when they were first in government, an office of public education to put their ideas into practice; at the same time the first night schools and two teachers' colleges were set up. Antonio López de Santa Anna a few years later ended these programs. Free education and academic freedom were reestablished as principles in 1856 by the liberal government and the following year were included in the constitution. It was, however, already understood that it was not enough to start schools: it was also necessary to eliminate the social conditions—poverty in the cities, serfdom in the country-side—responsible for a "shortage of pupils," as pointed out by Benito Júarez.[1]

After the war against Maxmillian, the liberal group in power established public schools with lay teachers, even though the parochial schools continued to exist and were more prosperous and better accepted than the public schools. In general, public schools were poor and teachers had deficient training. Anyone who had some education and who was willing to accept a miserable salary and to confront the clergy and the upper class in small cities could be a teacher. In the villages there were no schools, and the *hacendados* (large land-owners) never worried themselves with the education of the sons of their *peones*.

A change took place, however, when Gabino Barreda (1818–1881), a young liberal who had studied in Paris under August Comte, came back to his country and was named Director of the Escuela Nacional Preparatoria (the first Mexican college) by President Benito Júarez. Barreda reformed the educational system and

1 Alberto Bremauntz, *La educación socialista en México* (Mexico, 1943), pp. 29, 30, 34.

introduced positivism, which during those days had spread through-out Latin America and had become the philosophy of the new urban bourgeoisie. Some private schools utilizing modern methods were established in the cities, but the teachers were still persons without special training. Public instruction was under the Secretary of Justice. Some advances were made, but the only beneficiaries were those groups in the city who were already well-off. Rebsamen, a Swiss, introduced new methods at that time and foreign scholars were invited to teach in the country; later specialized schools were established. In 1903 there were 9,620 public schools with 666,723 pupils and 576 private schools (mostly parochial) with 43,720 pupils.[2]

Justo Sierra (1848–1912), under the regime of Porfirio Díaz, who served as president for 30 years until 1910, increased the number of teachers' colleges, modernized the teaching methods in the large cities, and established the modern university. He did little, how-ever, for schools in rural areas.[3]

During this same period, the first *mutualidades* (mutual aid soci-eties) of craftsmen and workers appeared in Mexico as did a few unions. In some cases these groups established schools for their members' children. These schools had self-trained teachers with ten-dencies for utopian ideas. In 1866 a Greek tailor by the name of Plotino Rhodakanaty established in the city of Chalco a school of a rationalistic type (name given by anarchists to their schools) several alumni of which became leaders of the Mexican labor movement. The school was dissolved when one of its students, the peasant Julio Chávez, led an armed movement against the government in 1869 and after four months of fighting was captured and shot in the backyard of the school of Chalco.[4]

Many teachers of that era (who taught for a short time until they were able to find better paying jobs) participated in the political and social struggles. Many were liberals who used their positions to pass on their political ideas. And more than a few teachers died, some in combat, others executed by the Imperial forces or by the "*rurales*" (ranger police during the Díaz regime). Frequently,

2 C. Trejo Lerdo de Tejada, *La educación socialista* (Mexico, 1935), pp. 24, 68.
3 Leopoldo Zea, *El positivismo en México* (Mexico, 1953), p. 55; and Agustín Yáñez, *Don Justo Sierra, su vida, sus ideas y su obra* (Mexico, 1950), p. 65.
4 Alfonso López Aparicio, *El Movimiento obrero en México* (Mexico, 1952), p. 116; Manuel Díaz Ramírez, *Apuntes históricos del movimiento obrero y cam-pesino de México 1844–1880* (Mexico, 1954), pp. 35–36.

groups of people, stirred by the Sunday sermon, would lynch, wound, or expel the public school teacher from the community. After the Laws of Reforms, the church intervened in Mexican politics (including both civil wars which the clergy promoted from 1858 to 1861 and from 1864 to 1867) mainly to recover the monopoly of education.

THE ROLE OF TEACHERS DURING THE REVOLUTION

The participation of teachers in the political struggles of the country had become widespread during the years preceding the revolution of 1910. A new liberal party founded in 1906 by Ricardo Flores Magón (1873–1922) was the first party to try to attract the teachers and to organize them. However, his purpose was not to promote the teachers' interests, but rather to use them as a means of political education and propaganda. Teachers in provincial cities were among the few informed people who read books and newspapers. Because of their low social standing they frequently felt frustrated and tended to become involved in activities which at the time were considered subversive and had to be carried out illegally. Organizers of the liberal party, during their secret trips, often were lodged in the homes of sympathizer-teachers, and the teachers were frequently engaged in the distribution of literature against Porfirio Díaz. Many teachers lost their jobs and were jailed because of their activities. Such teachers, of course, were in the minority.

During the revolution which followed from 1910 to 1917, the teachers played a meaningful role. Since the revolutionary forces were made of people from the provinces—middle-class and peasants —who, in general, had little education, the teachers acted often as advisors to the leaders of the guerrilla groups. In certain places, the teachers themselves organized guerrillas or else developed local political groups. The famous head of the southern agrarianists (the guerrillas fighting for a land reform), Emiliano Zapata (1873– 1919), at the beginning of the turmoil had a teacher from Tlaltizapan, Otilio Montaño (1877–1917) as an advisor. Montaño had already been known for his campaigns in defense of Indians and in support of the survival of the pre-Spanish culture. At the beginning of the guerrilla war he helped Zapata in the wording of the "Plan de Ayala," which quickly became the agrarian platform of the revolution and which also had a decisive influence on

Mexican agrarian policy. In 1917, Montaño, who had been part of the Socialist group, was executed on orders of Zapata himself when the teacher made a public statement concerning his doubts of victory for agrarianism.[5]

Plutarco Elías Calles (1877–1945), an historic figure of the revolution, had been a teacher in Sinaloa state. He abandoned teaching to join the constitutional army, in which he became general and later the president of the republic from 1924 to 1928. He was also a counselor for presidents who followed and founder of the party in which the different revolutionary forces settled (PNR, then PRM and later PRI). Calles, who knew through his own experience the problems of education, supported strongly a campaign dedicated to building schools and preparing teachers initiated during the presidency of his predecessor, General Alvaro Obregón (1880–1928). During these early years of the 1920's, writers and teachers from other countries in Latin America were brought to Mexico (e.g. the Chilean teacher, Gabriela Mistral, who at that time was not famous, but later became a Nobel Prize winner in literature, and the Dominican professor, Pedro Henríquez Ureña). New schools were established; urban and rural teachers' colleges were organized; and special schools to prepare teachers destined for those regions inhabited by Indians were initiated. José Vascoucelos (1882–1959), Secretary of Education, was the man who led all of these activities.

The number of teachers thus increased markedly and a teachers' union was organized. Conditions were favorable for its organization. Workers had not participated much in the revolution because their organizations were headed by those with anarcho-syndical leanings who considered the revolution as a clash between different bourgeois factions. When the workers realized their error, they took sides, joining the constitutional army (the moderate wing of the revolution) or the Red Batallions, organized by la Casa del Obrero Mundial in Mexico City. They fought the Zapatistas, an action which produced a division between the urban workers and the peasantry.

The alliance between the constitutional group and the labor organizations was finally realized because of Obregón. When he became president in 1920, the labor organization CROM (Mexican Regional Labor Confederation) was most influential. This influence

[5] Rafael Ramos Pedrueza, *La lucha de clases a través de la historia de México* (Mexico, 1941), p. 103.

continued during the presidency of Calles, when the CROM leader, Luis N. Morones, became Secretary of Industry and Commerce, which included under its jurisdiction labor problems also. A new constitution, written at the end of the revolution in 1917, spelled out the rights of the workers to associate and to strike. Procedures for conciliation and arbitration of labor-managerial disputes by government officials were also established.

The law did not permit the organization of government workers (which had to wait until 1935 and even then without the right to strike). An exception, however, was made in the case of the teachers since it was thought that it would be convenient to have them organized and in this fashion influence them. The government and the revolutionaries believed that the teachers should carry out an important role in the fight against the influence of the church. The government supported and protected the teachers' union as it grew in strength, particularly when the struggle between the state and the church came into the open.

THE TEACHERS AND THE CHURCH

Regardless of the educational campaigns for free, public education, there were still many private schools in Mexico after the revolution, the majority of which were religious. In these schools, education was in the hands of priests, friars, or nuns, the majority of whom did not have college degrees. Although many of the lay teachers had not pursued professional studies, several teachers' colleges were operating and a new teacher had to receive a degree from such a college. The lay teachers viewed the religious teachers as competitors without proper qualifications, somewhat like a worker views a "scab." Furthermore, in the small towns, there was the traditional rivalry between the lay teacher and the priest (who frequently ran the school in the church) in trying to secure the larger number of students and to gain the greater influence in local politics.

After independence from Spain was secured, the church had great power, more than during the colonial era. With the power came great wealth in land and buildings. As a result, the church received the brunt of liberal attacks during the nineteenth century. When the liberals reached power, first in 1833 and later in 1857, laws were enacted to deprive the church of its wealth. In 1833 the liberals were thrown out of office without a fight, but in 1857, led by Benito Júarez and a group of active intellectuals, they faced the conservatives in several civil wars and beat them. A stable liberal regime was established which ended with the dictatorship of the once-liberal General Porfirio Díaz. He became friendly toward the church and allowed her to regain property. When Díaz was ousted by the revolution of 1910, the church lost its properties again, not for religious reasons, but because many peasants occupied the church's haciendas. The church, however, did not lose its schools, which had been built in large numbers during the Díaz regime when the state was slowly establishing its own schools.

After the revolution, the church did not focus its main efforts on trying to regain its wealth but rather on maintaining and increasing its influence over the people through education. The government campaign to expand public education alarmed the church. Moreover, the church had opposed the revolution and latter attacked the agrarian reforms of Obregón and Calles. From the pulpits, the priests criticized government policy. Even the small town priests (who on certain occasions took sides with the revolutionaries, regardless of the official opposition of the bishops) opposed the arrival of lay teachers resulting from the expansion of public schools. The church believed itself to be powerful since the great majority of Mexicans were Catholic, but it did not realize that the bulk of the people, though deeply religious, did not support the church as an institution. The people saw the church as an economic and political organization more than as a spiritual one. The church, for example, declared that to be a member of CROM was a capital sin, but this did not reduce membership in the labor organization.

The bishops became restless and decided to react against the revolution, believing that they had best do it before they lost the influence they thought they still had with the peasants. In 1926, the press (all of which opposed the revolution), following the suggestion of the Archbishop of Mexico, published an old pastoral letter in which the constitution was condemned. The government reacted to the letter as a provocation and Calles ordered that all the articles of the constitution regulating the freedom of religion be put into effect, since up to that point they had not been applied. He also ordered the deportation of foreign priests and the registration of the Mexican priests. He also set out to close those private schools where teachers lacked a teacher's degree. A prompt response came from the bishops who ordered their priests not to register, and if the order was not revoked, to stop performing mass and giving the sacraments; namely, to go on strike. During a period of 36 months, the churches were, in fact, abandoned by the priests, but the parishioners, encouraged by the government, organized committees for the care of the temples and kept them open. The church learned then that the people cared more for the presence of an image of a certain saint than for the presence of a priest at the altar.

The Vatican supported the church and condemned the government. The people, however, took such a passive position that not even Calles was able to organize a national church as he wanted, nor were the Catholic guerrillas who ran into the hills backed by the peasantry. Three years later, a new president made things easier for the church, which accepted the laws, and since then there have been no important struggles between the church and the state.

The teachers found themselves in the middle of the three-year struggle between church and state because Catholic propaganda was focused on making the people believe that the government's purpose was to "dechristianize the children" using the public teachers. In the towns and small cities, active Catholics looked upon the teacher as the representative of the Antichrist—the name given to Calles. For this reason, the teachers suffered much during this period. Whenever the Catholic guerrilla fighters entered a town, the first thing they did was to search for the teacher. Sometimes they hanged the teacher in the main square of the town; at other times they tortured him, covered him with tar and feathers and left him tied up in the middle of the countryside, or else cut off his ears or tongue. Furthermore, they burned many schools.

The teachers' organizations pressured the government to send troops to protect those teachers who had been threatened by the "Cristeros," the name given to the Catholic guerrillas. At the same time, these organizations backed the government in the struggle with the church and acted as a propaganda machine against the "Cristeros." The newspapers carried numerous pictures of teachers who had been tortured or murdered. For a period of time, these stories took the place of murders and rapes in the yellow press.

At the same time, the teachers were becoming more radical. Up to this time, they had generally supported the revolution. The revolution, however, had become for them empty of doctrine; it was only a simple series of hazy principles in defense of the constitution and its laws. Probably in no other time have school children studied the constitution of their country more than the Mexican children attending school at that time. The struggle with the church made teachers militants. Many Catholic teachers had to face the dilemma of losing their jobs or their faith, and the great majority lost their faith.

About the same time, namely, during the religious conflict, members of the new generation who had not taken an active part in the revolution were beginning to project themselves into politics. Their ideology was more precise than that of the old revolutionaries. They had discovered Marxism and wanted to make a socialist country of Mexico. They were not Communists, because the Mexican communist party, small and bureaucratic, followed slogans which did not fit the reality of the country. For example, when some generals rose against Calles and fighting broke out, the Communists went into the streets, not in support of the government, but rather to proclaim the soviets, in a country where almost nobody had any idea of what the soviets were. All of this was in accordance with the slogans of the Communist International. Nevertheless, though this new generation acted still within the framework of the revolution and worked with the government, it ideologically accepted many objectives of the Communist movement.

Teachers naturally felt exasperated at persecutions by the "Cristeros," and they were willing to capitalize on these events for the benefit of their profession and their bureaucratic status. They found a point of identification with the new generation, which gave them not only ideology, but respect, social consideration, and acceptance among the intellectual groups.

Teachers, as victims of the reactionaries' wrath and as instruments of the revolution's hopes, were frequently well-treated by the government, not so much with regard to salaries, which were still low, but with regard to other considerations and influence. The technical officers of the Ministry of Education were chosen from among the teachers. Little by little, it became a prerogative (acquired and not written) of teachers to occupy these offices. The educational system was reorganized, new positions were opened to substitute for the numerous religious schools closed by the government, and new positions of inspectors were created, making the professional hierarchy more complex.

At the same time these changes were taking place, the teacher began to see himself as the voice of revolutionary purity, to act in the small cities and towns (since in the large cities he was lost within the crowd and his personality did not stand out) as the conscience of local politicians and, in general, as a decisive element in the radicalization of the younger elements among the minority of people active in politics. The school often became a center of propaganda and of ideological formation. Certainly all teachers did not accept the same ideology. But among the most active of this group, the ideology was a mixture of anticlericalism and rationalism on one hand, and Marxism, sympathy for Russia, and anti-Americanism or anti-imperialism on the other hand. This did not mirror the convictions of the persons in power but it satisfied those within the framework of the revolution who hoped to succeed them.

During these years, nobody removed or suspended a teacher, and this implied *de facto* job security and tenure which became *de jure* in 1935 when President Lázaro Cárdenas passed a legal ordinance for civil servants. But it must be remembered that the most important benefits and improvements in teacher status came about because of the persecutions by the "Cristeros" and governmental policies and less as a result of actions of their organizations. The organizations alone would have produced little, no matter how much effort they made, if it had not been that the "Cristeros" considered the teachers a symbol of the regime they were fighting.

THE FIRST UNIONS

Since the beginning of the teachers' union movement, there has been what may appear to be a class division. One group was made up of teachers in the federal capital who considered themselves privileged and influential in that they were close to the central government and therefore able to interview officials from the Ministry of Education and to put pressure on them. They also received higher salaries than did the teachers in the other parts of the country, and they had the cultural advantages of urban life. The other group was made up of the rural teachers in the provincial cities and towns, far from the central government, whose highest ambition could only be to become influential in local and state governments. They received lower salaries than their counterparts in Mexico City, were culturally isolated, lived in a constant struggle with the priests, and frequently faced the risk of being attacked and killed.

Some of these rural teachers became advisers of local politicians, for whom they wrote speeches and documents; or else, in a very few cases, they became regional political leaders or formed part of the local government, either through election or as part of the political machinery in the region. The majority of the rural teachers, however, lived a limited life, which quite often had missionary or apostolic characteristics.

This division was reflected in the professional organizations. On one hand, the Confederación Mexicana de Maestros (Mexican Confederation of Teachers) represented the rural teachers. This organization affiliated itself with the CROM (Mexican Regional Labor Confederation). The teachers in the capital organized the Federación de Maestros del Distrito Federal (Federation of Teachers of the Federal District), which also extended its influence outside the capital and in which there was an internal struggle for control among teachers of different ideologies: Communists, anarcho-syndicalists, Cromists (pro-CROM). The Communists became highly influential because there were better possibilities in Mexico City for propaganda and more intellectual groups there willing to be influenced. The Communist teachers or those who followed the Communist line were able to mix with the intellectuals. This gave them personal satisfaction and social status which in turn helped keep them within the orbit of Communist influence.

During this same period of the 1920's, these organizations won the prerogative that the state directors of federal education, the inspectors, and the principals of the urban and rural schools had to be members of the teachers' unions. In fact, if a teacher were not a member of one of the two teacher organizations, he could not hope to advance within his profession.

These two national organizations were made up of state or area organizations to which, in turn, belonged local unions in the various cities and in some schools. The principal activity of these two organizations, especially for the Mexican Confederation of Teachers, developed during the "Cristeros" era. The Confederation was strong enough to maintain a permanent delegation at the nation's capital. These delegates placed pressure on the government for military protection for those teachers located in regions where the "Cristeros" were active, and also sought to secure compensation for the families of those teachers murdered by the "Cristeros."

At the same time, these organizations backed the government in its struggle and tried to influence the parents of their pupils as well as public opinion by depicting the "Cristeros" and the church as enemies of education and murderers of teachers. The Confederation was effective in this respect and, due to its efforts, an anti-Cristero atmosphere was created in certain regions of the country which, due to the people's cultural background, might otherwise have been expected to be pro-Cristero.

During this period, a union made up of employees at the Ministry of Education was created, the majority of whom were residents of Mexico City. It included nonteaching staff who received a salary from the Ministry, such as secretaries, museum administrators, and school employees. It was named Sindicato Unico de Trabajadores Administrativos, Técnicos y Manuales de la Secretaría de Educación Pública (Union of Administrative, Technical, and Manual Workers of the Ministry of Public Education). One of the general secretaries of this union at one time was a lawyer, Adolfo López Mateos, who later on became Minister of Labor and then President of the Republic from 1958 to 1964.

The administrative workers' union and other similar ones in the various states, the two teacher unions, and other small groups of educational specialists around 1935 formed the Agrupación de Organizaciones de Trabajadores de la Secretaría de Educación (Association of Organizations of Workers of the Ministry of Education). It was this central group which dealt directly with the Ministry; teachers had great influence in this association and participated fully in its leadership.

In spite of all the organizational activity, the unions were weak, had few really involved members (even though the majority of the teachers belonged) and the leaders and active members paid more attention to politics and the struggle among the different groups (Communists, anarcho-syndicalists, non-Communist Marxist, Mexican revolutionaries) than to their professional problems. The situation changed shortly after General Cárdenas became President.

LEGAL CHANGES UNDER CÁRDENAS

General Lázaro Cárdenas (b. 1895), who had had a dull military history during the revolution, became a governor and then a minister because of the support of Calles, the statesman and stabilizer of the revolution. Cárdenas also owed the presidency to which he was elected in 1934 to Calles, but once in office he wanted to be rid of Calles' influence and sent him into exile. Then, to consolidate his own control over the instruments of power, he had to follow an apparently radical policy. At the same time he changed the course of the regime's orientation. On the one hand, he tamed parliament and on the other he backed the union movement (in 1936 partially united in the Confederación de Trabajadores de México—CTM—founded and directed then by Vicente Lombardo Toledano [1894–1968]), and linked the unions with the government in such a way that they have never regained their independence. He also changed the course of the agrarian reform, which was initially based upon the *ejido* as a transitory institution for the education of the new property owners. Cárdenas transformed the *ejido* system into a permanent institution, now bureaucraticized, and in some cases collectivized.

In the process of reinforcing his position, Cárdenas tended to bureaucratize the revolution also, and the number of civil servants increased considerably during his presidency. As means of obtaining the support of this bureaucracy and, at the same time, satisfying the demands of the labor movement, Cárdenas, as mentioned earlier, guaranteed job security for the civil servant and promoted the formation of unions of bureaucrats in the federal government and in the different state and local structures. He also grouped them in a Federación de Sindicatos de Trabajadores al Servicio del Estado (FSTSE), established in 1938. All these steps became formalized in the Legal Statute of Civil Servants (Estatuto Jurídico de los Trabajadores del Estado.)

This statute was written by a commission made up of representatives of the government and the civil servants and was enacted in 1938. Article 55 recognized FSTSE and gave it the right to represent the civil workers. Estatuto Jurídico recognized also the right of public employees to present claims and to raise demands, but it did not give them the right to strike to back these demands. Instead, an arbitration court was to resolve such conflicts. It is interesting to note that since 1938, the word "bureaucrat" in Mexico has no longer been considered derogatory and sarcastic as it has been in the other Spanish-speaking nations.

Although Vicente Lombardo Toledano was once Secretary General of a teachers' union of the Federal District and later on became Secretary General of the Teachers' Federation, he did not try, even from his powerful post of Secretary General of the CTM, to affiliate the FSTSE to the CTM, although the Federal Districts' teachers' union did affiliate with it. FSTSE declared itself independent and has never tried to change this status. It has, however, become an accepted practice that FSTSE's Secretary General, or else some other prominent member of the organization, will become a candidate for Congress and sometimes for the Senate within the structure of the PRI (the official party of the government) in all elections, and as an official candidate of PRI, he will normally be elected side by side with the leaders of the CTM and other minor labor federations.

The FSTSE names a delegate at the arbitration court as established by the Estatuto Jurídico. In 1939, Professor Ignacio Villanueva, a member of the teachers' federation, became secretary general of the FSTSE, and, in 1941, he became a member of the arbitration court. This shows how important the teachers' organization was during the first years of life of the FSTSE. This influential position, however, has lessened since the era of Cárdenas, even though the number of teachers has increased constantly and in greater proportion than the other bureaucrats. Logically, it should have maintained its influence within the FSTSE. That this was not so (since 1941 no teacher has become a prominent leader of the FSTSE) indicates that something has been happening in the teachers' organization.

THE TEACHERS AND THE THIRD ARTICLE

What has happened is that both the local and national organizations of teachers found themselves in the midst of ideological struggles that divided and weakened them. The first manifestation of this was over the struggle to change the third article of the constitution of 1917 which requires that all education be supervised by the state. The church objected to this article. This was the real motive for the fight between the church and the government during the Calles regime because the third article established if not *de facto,* at least potentially, a state monopoly of education. The militant Catholics demanded freedom of education; that is, the possibility of establishing Catholic schools at all levels, just as the liberals had demanded freedom of education when the church had monopolized the schools.

On December 13, 1934, Congress amended the article and declared that education should be socialist. The revised wording of the third article was, in its final form, as follows: "La educación que imparta el Estado será socialista . . . combatirá el fanatismo y los prejuicios, creando en la juventud un concepto racional y exacto del Universo y de la vida social." ("The education given by the state must be socialist; it should fight fanaticism and prejudices, producing in the young a rational and exact concept of the Universe and social life.")

Moreover, private schools had to receive authorization to operate from the government, which had the privilege of revoking the authorization at any time if the schools did not apply the principles established in the amended article.

Several organizations were formed with the idea of supporting and establishing socialistic education, and many of them were made up of teachers, or with teachers in them, namely, Committee for Educational Reform, Union of Revolutionary Teachers, Teachers League of Revolutionary Action, Teachers Left Block, and even a Student National Party for Cárdenas. The Communist teachers in the beginning opposed the revised amendment since they felt that "in a bourgeois regime socialistic education cannot exist," but later they changed their attitude.

Naturally, the conservative and religious organizations were against the changed article, and committees supporting this point of view were formed. Opposition to the change, however, came not only from religious and conservative forces. Others feared that the change would result in a loss of academic freedom. Thus, the rector (president) and the faculty of the National Autonomous University of Mexico and many student organizations opposed the change. Interestingly, the supporters of the amended article used the same arguments that the church had once used against the liberals when the latter group had fought for academic freedom in the previous century.

One reason many teachers opposed the socialist school idea of Article 3 was that the supporters of the changed article considered it necessary to revoke the law giving job tenure to teachers. They feared that many teachers could not or would not, due to ideological reasons, provide a socialist education. The supporters of Article 3 also favored more male teachers, since they felt that women (who made up the majority of the teachers in grammar schools and rural areas) had not been "assimilated to the revolution."

A new outburst of violence greeted the passage of the amendment. Thirty-two teachers were either killed or mutilated in the small towns by Catholic groups. The violence, however, lasted a short period of time, which should give us some idea of how many victims there were among teachers during the earlier "Cristero" revolt which lasted much longer and was far more violent.[6]

In a country which had had a nationalistic revolution and was directing its society toward capitalism, this expression of socialism in Article 3 provoked major controversies. Those teachers who were Communists (and they made up one of the most active groups in Mexico) interpreted the socialist doctrine as inspired by the international Communist movement. Several textbooks of a pseudo-Marxist type were published, and certain subjects were introduced such as History of Social Revolutions and Dialectic Materialism. Economics and other disciplines were taught following the simplified philosophy which was being passed off in Russia as Marxism. Even some Russian textbooks were translated at the time.

But all this remained superficial. Most teachers had been educated in the traditional liberal school and considered Marxist philosophy as alien to the Mexican revolution. Of course there were some militants and fanatics who tried rigidly to impose the "socialist" doctrine on teachers and students, but only rarely did they succeed.

Although the majority of teachers had approved the amendment to the third article, the approval was, in most cases, just a formality. Most thought the change was merely propaganda, only to be used as a balance against religious influence on education. They did not think that it could be put into practice. Many teachers with a real social conscience utilized this amendment to focus their teaching in a more realistic way on the society of their time, criticizing the type of society that was being formed without making these viewpoints doctrinaire Marxism. When the Communists and their fellow travelers tried to use their union offices to impose textbooks, programs, and sectarian educational guidelines, there were revolts and protests among the teachers.

I have called the group that prepared the amendment to Article 3 the "Halfbreeds" (*Mixtos*). It was made up of those who were trying to reconcile the type of Marxism propagated by the Communists with the principles of the Mexican revolution. (The best known

6 Bremauntz, pp. 206, 213, 329.

representative of this group is Vincente Lombardo Toledano.) This group had a great deal of influence in the upper levels of the bureaucracy and induced the Board of Inspectors and Principals of Federal Education in 1932 to propose that rural education try to transform the system of production and distribution toward an ultimately truly collective system. A Congress on Education, held the same year in Xalapa, resolved that "the communities should be prepared to take an active part in a socialized utilization of the wealth for the benefit of the working classes." In 1933 the National Student Congress passed a resolution which stated that "the University and the higher education centers of the country must produce men who will contribute to the formation of a socialistic society." [7] However, all this was nothing but a repetition of recommendations made several times before and was never practiced by the teachers during their everyday professional life.

Those teachers who opposed the amendment—and more importantly, its application—used, among other things, phrases from a former president, Abelardo L. Rodríguez, who said that the amendment "would replace the priest by the public leader" and would lead to a "sectarian monopoly of education similar to that of Italy or Russia."

Many teachers believed that a socialistic education should not be taught, but rather that the main objective of education should become that of preparing "people capable of continuing what the revolution had started and transforming it into a socialist revolution." For some, socialistic education must supply what the revolution had not contributed in the field of general culture. However, education "proved to be incapable of overcoming the deficiencies of the revolution." [8]

After Cárdenas finished his term and even during the last years of his presidency, nobody tried seriously to enforce the amendment. During the government of his successor, General Manuel Avila Camacho (1940–1946), nobody mentioned the article, and education came back to its normal course, even a number of religious schools were allowed in a more or less indirect manner. Finally, on December 30th, 1946, just before the new president, Miguel

---

[7] Cited in Victor Alba, *Las ideas sociales contemporáneas en México* (Mexico, 1960), p. 237.
[8] Bremauntz, pp. 190, 240; Octavio Paz, *El laberinto de la soledad* (Mexico, 1950), p. 156.

Alemán (1946–1952) was inaugurated, Congress again changed the third article, substituting the expression "Socialist" with that of "Scientific progress." This time there were no struggles or arguments among the teachers. It was quite evident to everybody that so-called socialistic education had never become part of the reality of Mexican life.

THE POLITICAL DIVISIONS

As has been mentioned before, not all the people who opposed the amendment of the third article were Catholics or reactionaries. Generally, the young teachers favored the amendment, while the old ones who had struggled before and during the revolution were opposed to it. The latter were men of liberal background, some of whom had evolved from anarcho-syndicalist groups and who opposed any form of dogmatism in education.

These divisions showed up in the structure of the labor movement. While Cárdenas was president, the union leaders changed. Former president Calles, who put General Cárdenas in office, had been sent into exile by Cárdenas because Calles opposed the social policy supported by the young group around Cárdenas. Along with Calles, Luis N. Morones, the main leader of CROM, also went into exile. With the support of the new President in 1936, CTM (Confederation of Workers of Mexico) was founded under the direction of Vicente Lombardo Toledano and became the main center of unionism in Mexico. Toledano, however, never could unite all unions and therefore some small federations survived along with the CTM. Lombardo, having been one of the leaders of the union of teachers of the federal district, was able to get this union to adhere to the CTM.

Just before this, the Union of Workers in Education of the Mexican Republic (Sindicato de Trabajadores de la Educación de la República Mexicana-STERM) had been formed and was soon controlled by the Communists. Naturally, this union supported the government in its attempts to enforce the amendment to the third article of the constitution. It was possible to form this union because the preliminary propaganda used in preparing the amendment inclined many teachers to listen to the Communists, who had come to accept the philosophy of the new third article. This also was the period in which the Communists were applying their new theory of popular front, which favored the penetration of Communists in the labor movement and cooperation with other left-wing groups. This approach received a good deal of support among the teachers.

Teachers frequently lived in close contact with the poverty of the masses, were somewhat better informed than the common public with regard to world affairs, and had more of a background to understand ideologies. They were thus more receptive to ideological propaganda. The Communists succeeded in attracting a good number of teachers. They were, however, never capable of obtaining a majority of the profession, although they often were able to dominate assemblies and meetings due to the discipline among their members and the lack of coordination among their opponents. The non-Communist teachers finally united when the Communist control of the Union of Teachers of the Federal District and later of STERM became intolerable.

A group of discontented teachers formed the Confederación Nacional de Trabajadores de la Enseñanza (National Confederation of Workers in Teaching—CNTE), controlled by liberal elements faithful to the ideals of the Mexican revolution. After a period of mutual attacks and accusations, the Communists, being afraid that CNTE might appeal to the great majority of teachers and professors, tried to make a deal with the new organization. Both groups signed a pact in which the two organizations distributed among their leaders some important offices in the administrative apparatus of the Ministry of Education, thus allowing each union to protect its members. For instance, the director of rural education belonged to STERM, while the deputy director came from CNTE; the director of elementary education belonged to CNTE, and the deputy director belonged to STERM. It must be remembered that these organizations were made up only of public school teachers, since those working for private schools had never been organized, although in certain private schools there were independent unions (or, in fact, company unions).

Because of the agreement between the two organizations, the liberals quieted their distrust, thereby allowing the Communists to obtain direct or indirect control, depending on the individual case, of the teachers' union movement. One teacher characterized the situation in the following way: "The union movement of the teach-

ers was encouraged and directed by leaders who were outsiders, as
well as by the officials in the Ministry of Education who used it to
satisfy their own and very personal political ambitions; they had
more interest in controlling the union than in developing education." [9]

The teachers' unions, regardless of the group in control, continued to allow the authorities in the Ministry of Education to influence them. This influence came not so much from the Minister, but
from the high officials in administration or inspection, who were
teachers and members of the unions. They used this influence by
granting concessions and favors to those who helped them, and punishing or suspending from employment those who opposed them in
the internal policy of the union.

The unions, whatever their ideology, are made up of sections
which elect their own governing boards and act with relative autonomy. Making use of their influence with high officials, the Communists have been able to place some of their own members in
certain territories until they have enough members there to control
the meetings and therefore the section. This trick does not require
large numbers since most of the teachers do not care much for the
union and/or do not bother to attend the meetings. At times, often
by chance, some courageous liberals oppose and destroy the Communist control. When such an event occurs, those high officials who
want to use the union will take advantage of any pretext to remove
or displace those teachers who oppose the Communists, so that
Communists, who are easier to handle, will recover the control of
the union's section. When the high official has democratic convictions or has struggled in the past with the Communists, he utilizes
the same maneuvers to remove the Communists and help the liberal
group. This situation causes many teachers to lack interest in the
union for they recognize that they really have no voice in the
union's operation. Moreover, many parents of school children mis-
trust the motivations and manipulations of the unions. Finally,
many teachers are not protected by the union unless they agree
politically with the group in power. Those who are protected are
not aided through trade union tactics but through political favors.
Therefore, the union rarely assists those teachers who are displaced,
fired, or demoted because of political reasons.

[9] Rubén Rodríguez Lozano, *El Sindicato Nacional de Trabajadores de la Educación. Su Proyección histórica* (Mexico, 1958), p. 14.

Another result of this situation was and still is, but to a lesser degree, the one described by the teacher previously cited:

The efficiency and prestige of the Mexican rural school started to decline, practically losing the meritorious efforts of distinguished teachers. The existence of the teachers' organizations was threatened by its own congenital vices, due to the intransigent doctrinary differences of those who were part of their leadership, as well as to the personal ambitions of many of the leaders who had abandoned their positions in the union struggle and had become, abruptly, officials in the Ministry of Education and were serving the political plans of either Vicente Lombardo Toledano or else Hernán Lobarde. These two figures struggled between themselves for the control of the teachers' organization through the CTM and the Communist Party, respectively.

In that huge propaganda effort it was easy to violate the rules of promotion in the profession and utilize these to reward the followers of either group. The different union offices were distributed without regard to the will of the teachers. Fabricated conventions and meetings were held and directed by remote control by groups of individuals representing one of the groups. The differences between these two groups were always solved through a distribution of offices either in the government or the union.[10]

The teacher also noted that in this era of the popular front euphoria, the word "comrade" was generally used between teachers, authorities, and pupils as a demagogical manifestation of equality. "The Comrade Minister and the Comrade Vice-Minister discussed educational problems with Comrade Lombardo or Comrade Laborde, and from these secret sessions came the appointment or dismissal of a teacher regardless of his professional merit." [11]

Despite all this comradeship between the union and the Ministry, when in 1937 a group of Communist teachers decided to strike, seeking a raise in salary as well as in fringe benefits, public officials were violently opposed and President Cárdenas declared that he would not allow any walkout of teachers. This statement was enough immediately to calm down the Communists.

The generation of Mexicans educated during the early 1930's is now more than 40 years old and does not reflect the Communist influence as might have been anticipated. This indicates that the communism of many teachers was not always carried to the schoolroom but was more of an opportunistic doctrine which led to promotions or security and, consequently, appeared only in meetings and demonstrations.

10 *Ibid.*, pp. 14–15.
11 *Ibid.*, p. 16.

As expected, this situation had two natural consequences. As parents became more and more discontented with the political manifestations within the public schools, private schools increased and public schools generally were restricted to educating only those students whose families did not have the economic resources to send their children to private schools. The other result was that the already divided union organizations grew even further apart. A simple list of the different teacher organizations of that time (none of which lasted very long) points out how disintegrated the teacher's labor movement had become. There was the Frente Revolucionario de Maestros (FRM), which was a liberal organization, including part of the members of CNTE; STERM (which finally absorbed another part of CNTE) affiliated to CTM and controlled by Lombardo Toledano; SUNTE (Sindicato Unico Nacional de Trabajadores de la Educación) controlled by the Communists under the direction of Hernán Laborde (1894–1956). (Laborde, expelled from the Communist party in 1940 after being its general secretary, nevertheless continued as a loyal follower of Stalin even after his expulsion.) Furthermore, within STERM there was already a division similar to that within CTM itself—namely, between the pro-Marxist followers of Lombardo and the non-Marxist elements such as Rodolfo Piña Soria and David Vilchis, the latter being one of the leaders of STERM.

The struggles among the different groups created a number of peculiar situations. STERM and SUNTE joined forces and obtained the resignation of a minister, Octavio Véjar Váquez, who refused to play their political game, and FRM secured the resignation of another minister, Luis Sánchez Póntón, who too openly supported Lombardo and Laborde.

During the presidency of General Manuel Avila Camacho (1940–46) the government considered these divisions a real obstacle in dealing with the professional problems of the teachers. It, therefore, intervened discretely to change this situation and to get rid of the best-known Communist elements. To achieve this goal, the government asked a teacher, Leopoldo Kiel, to start new unity negotiations. With this purpose in mind, a Congress was held in Querétaro, and SMMTE (Sindicato Mexicano de Maestros y Trabajadores de Educación) was created, but it could not unify the various groups; it became still another separate group. The president of the official party, PRI, Antonio Villalobos, then intervened and after a series of talks, struggles, quarrels, and reconciliations, a new union was formed in which all the different groups were brought together—the Sindicato Nacional de Trabajadores de la Educación (SNTE) or the National Union of Workers in Education.

THE SNTE

SNTE thus was not formed spontaneously because of the initiative of the teachers, but rather it was a creation of official political pressure. This fact has characterized its existence and, as a result, has linked it with the government.

The first national committee of SNTE was made up of representatives of the different ideologies; nonaffiliated Marxists, Communists, liberals, etc. The Secretary General was Luis Chávez Orozco, a Marxist historian who opposed Lombardo Toledano. He was succeeded by a Communist teacher who had been a congressman, Gaudencio Peraza. Afterwards, the different presidents were members of the government party, PRI, eliminating in this way the Communist influence from the national committee, but not from a number of its sections. Jesús Robles Martínez who succeeded Peraza as Secretary General of SNTE also held prominent offices in FSTSE and in politics. However, his successors, Manuel Sánchez Vite, Enrique W. Sánchez, Edgar Robledo, and Félix Vallejo, did not participate actively in politics.

In the interim, the educational policy of the country had changed. The era of rural education that followed the revolution, and the era of socialist education during the presidency of Cárdenas, was followed by an era of nationalist education during World War II. Finally, since 1946, when the country moved into a period (continuing to the present) of civilian presidents, beginning with Miguel Alemán, the policy in education became similar to the philosophy of government: it tends to be Mexicanist, that is nationalist, not in obedience to a political ideal, but rather as an affirmation of national values. At the same time, the government has tolerated private education, thereby permitting an important expansion of religious schools. Actually there are now religious high schools and even a university owned by a religious order, though this religious order does not appear as its legal owner. There also has been a rapid growth in private nonsectarian elementary, high, and commercial schools. Some of these are military academies; others are sponsored either by foreign governments or citizens, such as the German, American, and French schools. Furthermore, there is a university sponsored by American businessmen. This increase of private education is due to different factors: distrust of the political bias of some public teachers, poor facilities of public schools, and growing numbers of the middle and upper classes.

The postwar era was also characterized by campaigns against illiteracy, and for increased school construction. Moreover, much more attention was given than before to universities and professional schools. The annual budget for education has been increased every year since 1917 not only in absolute figures, but also proportionately, both in state and federal expenditures. Furthermore, since 1935, education has taken the second largest amount from the national budget.[12]

These changes in educational policy certainly affected teachers. The different ideological groups which existed during the post-World War II decade tried to influence educational policy. For example, the Communists have tried to have books prepared by them used in certain disciplines such as history and economics. Those teachers with liberal ideology have not been as active, since their point of view coincided with the official policy and they had the impression that they did not have to fight anymore. This attitude gave the Communists and their sympathizers, who were often far more efficient than those who did not belong to their party, a free hand in many places.

These ideological differences have influenced the life of SNTE. There has been a continuous struggle among persons and groups of the different ideologies and in these struggles the officials in the ministry have indirectly participated, particularly those lower ministry officials who originally came from the union and still feel themselves linked with it, and to which they often owe their positions. Certainly this political influence is not legal, but it exists and serious consequences result from it. Many members have lost confidence in the union because they feel that it is easier to obtain promotions and transfers or to avoid punishments and loss of their jobs by being linked to any of the political groups or officials within the union rather than as a result of fairly-administered union rules and regulations. With the loss of confidence, it was easy for a

12 C. Lerdo de Tejada, p. 251.

teacher to feel that the union was useless and that the payment of dues (which is automatically taken from his salary) was just another tax.

Nonetheless, the union was able to obtain certain improvements in the working conditions, mainly in the field of social security and retirement programs. It also obtained, at least in written form, a number of guarantees concerning job security and rules for promotion. The teachers have also secured a number of dwellings in the large cities. These houses are constructed by the state for civil servants. Nevertheless, the Mexican bureaucracy, including teachers, is poorly paid, with no improvement forseeable in the near future.

The fact that civil servants have no legal right to strike has not prevented the teachers from striking on certain occasions. In such cases the officials in the Ministry of Education have followed a tactic which, though not always effective, is common in Mexico. It tries to avoid the confrontation in the beginning through the personal influence of high officials. If this influence does not prevent the conflict, the authorities let the situation worsen and even reach the streets through strike action. This gives the President of the Republic, with all the power and prestige of his office, a basis for ending the dispute. Of course, the protestors do not obtain all they demand; but they frequently receive some benefits—as an appeasement to them—and in this way the Minister of Education need not fear that he has antagonized any group.

SECTION IX AND THE TEACHER'S COLLEGE

During 1957 and 1958, close to the end of the presidential term of Adolfo Ruíz Cortines (1952–1958) a movement for honest leadership in the labor movement began, under Communist inspiration, within several unions where the liberal and bureaucratic leadership had degenerated and had become corrupt. Because of dissatisfaction with corrupt leaders, the Communists, often without attracting attention, were able to secure control of certain labor organizations (railroads, national oil company) or important local sections of other unions. In the case of the teachers the Communists secured control of Section IX (which covers the Federal District and is the largest and most influential section of SNTE) where they had been relatively strong. The former leadership did not yield willingly to the Communists; as a result, the section divided. A series of strikes, demonstrations, and acts of violence organized by those unions in which the Communists had obtained the leadership then took place. Communist teachers and sympathizers actively participated in these events and in a general teachers' strike in Mexico City. The leader of Section IX, Othón Salazar, was arrested and found guilty of *disolución social,*" [13] a crime spelled out in the penal code during World War II as a measure to fight possible Nazi infiltrations. This action, plus the energetic attitude of the officials in the Ministry of Public Education, allowed liberals to regain the control of Section IX. But the liberals did not use the control positively, and, in 1964, the Communists again were influential in Section IX. This time, however, they were more discrete, perhaps because they were now isolated from their allies in other unions who, unlike the teachers, were not able to regain the power they had secured in the labor organizations six years before. By 1967 they again lost the control of Section IX.

To understand teacher unrest in Mexico, it is necessary to remember that every six years, at the same time the new president takes power, a new Secretary of Public Education also takes office, and other changes will follow in the Ministry. As a result, groups are formed to back individual teachers for specific offices. Sometimes there are strikes and public demonstrations, either to support the political aspirations of a teacher or else to destroy the chance of another teacher seeking to secure a post in the Ministry.

For the Communists, the possibility of having a sympathizer in a high post is not only important from the purely political standpoint, but since Communists and fellow travelers frequently receive invitations to attend international meetings and courses, it is convenient for them to have someone in the Ministry who will authorize leaves of absences and permits. For example, Othón Salazar, freed by the new president in 1960 in order to establish a peaceful climate among the teachers, attended, in 1965, a congress of Communist teachers in Algiers, as the only Latin American delegate.

A common practice used by the Communists is to utilize the parents of their pupils to back their demands. During the strike of 1958, they organized the parents to support their program and later to demand the discharge of those teachers who did not join the movement or were opposed to Salazar. During the strike, the union

---

[13] Similar to disorderly conduct. It literally means "social dissolution" or instigating the destruction of the society.

demanded higher salaries, but even more important, they demanded union control over such things as appointments and promotions. They were thus trying to capitalize on the discontent among the teachers with the educational bureaucracy and, as a result, secure the right to decide, in an indirect manner, the future and the career of teachers. This would have probably made Communist control permanent. The authorities did not accept these conditions.

Another source of Communist strength among teachers is in the teachers' colleges, mainly in Mexico City. The teachers' colleges, since the foundation of the first one, have been centers of political activity but never have played an important role in the union movement. In the teachers' college of Mexico City, the Communist influence in the last 30 years has been most powerful, particularly in its graduate school where high school teachers are prepared. After the Communists were able to obtain certain administrative and academic positions in both colleges, they were then able to attract other Communist teachers, utilizing without hesitation course grades to help friends and to eliminate from a teaching career those who opposed them.

In the last ten years, the students of the teachers' colleges have frequently gone out on strike. At times, the goals sought have been professional: scholarships, or distribution of posts to the new graduates. But frequently the goal has been political. In 1958, for example, there was a strike at the Normal Superior (the teachers' graduate college) which lasted for a year amidst frequent violence. And in 1960 another strike of the new graduates of the Escuela Normal (Mexico City teachers' college) affected the activities of the college for several weeks and culminated in a combined demonstration of teachers and students in street rioting.

After the students finish their teachers' degrees, they join the union and frequently continue the same political activities in their profession that they had displayed as students. This is one of the toughest problems to be solved by the authorities in the Ministry of Education because of its political consequences, and particularly since some of the subordinate officials at the Ministry are linked with the political groups causing the trouble. During the last few years the economic condition of teachers, though poor, has improved through increases in salaries and other benefits. As a result, there appears to be a tendency toward decreased political activity and the number of teachers who practice a type of political neutralism seems to be increasing.

The old concern of the teacher about the priest in the private school has now been replaced in the young teacher by an indifference toward the private schools. Many young teachers, in fact, work in private schools after they finish teaching in the public schools in order to earn some extra pay. For these teachers, who spend several hours with overloaded classes (in the cities the public schools often have two and three shifts of four hours each since there are not enough teachers or schools to cope with the children of school age), a private school class with a reduced number of children, for one or two hours, is often considered a rest period.

Nonetheless, on May 15, 1966, during the celebration of the holiday known as the Día del Maestro (The Day of the Teacher), the secretary general of SNTE, Professor Edgardo Robledo, publicly asked the authorities to put into effect what the third article of the constitution declared with regard to the lay character of education in the private schools. In reality, what he was asking for was a larger market for lay teachers.

The improvement of the economic status of the teachers mentioned has been reflected in the raised social prestige of the profession. This has been achieved to a great extent through the union activities. Some figures will help to complete the picture. In 1955 there were 83,000 teachers in grammar schools (public and private); by 1962 there were 126,000 of which 42,000 were college graduates. The increase in teachers in this period was 51.8 per cent, but the increase in registered pupils was 62.5 per cent. In 1955 there were 41 pupils per teacher; in 1962, 44 per teacher. (See: *Estudio Social de América Latina, 1963–1964,* Pan American Union, Washington, 1964.) There are no exact figures available on salaries, but from personal interviews, it can be estimated that a grammar school teacher, after five years of service, has an annual salary of around $2,000 to $2,500 excluding special benefits and extras.

ORGANIZATION AND FUNCTIONS OF SNTE

A declaration of principles was published in 1951 by SNTE. It states that the ideology of the union is that of the Mexican constitution of 1917 and that SNTE will accept as members all individuals of all ideologies as long as they are willing to comply with the resolutions of the majority and follow the decisions of the legally-elected executive board.

In the field of education, SNTE supports unbiased and free access to all levels of education, from the elementary school up to the university level. It also advocates the intensification of rural education and literacy campaigns and declares itself against any changes in the third article of the constitution. SNTE will fight for the improvement of the teachers' working conditions and for the unity of the Mexican workers. It also declares that it will have relations with all the international organizations of teachers, and it does, as we shall discuss later.[14] The declaration of principles is written in such a way as to keep everybody happy and to avoid taking sides in the ideological struggles.

SNTE states further that teachers should sustain high professional efficiency, participate in the formulation of the education policy, maintain the confidence the society has in their work, and be loyal to the nation and to democratic principles. They have the right to security in their jobs without being persecuted because of their own beliefs as long as they stay within the confines of the third article of the constitution. They also have the right to associate freely, to receive a high-caliber professional education, to secure assistance in improving their education, to be made technically competent, and to work in adequate classrooms and with sufficient materials regardless of the economic means of the pupils. Research should be carried out to test new methods of teaching. Finally, in the field of salary and fringe benefits, the teachers want a working contract (from the Ministry of Education, state government, city government, or private institutions), which will contain the following: job security, pay high enough to allow the teacher and his family to have a decent living, and salary on the basis of equal pay for equal type of service (without discrimination because of sex). The payment of differentials and supplemental salaries should also be made without any discrimination. SNTE also wants teachers to have free medical services and medicines, full payment and benefits during sickness, a yearly vacation with full pay, and retirement after 30 years of service without age limit and with full salary. Teachers, they state, should also receive a pension equivalent to full salary in those cases where the teacher is retired from his job because of mental or physical illness. The pension should be adjusted in accordance with changes in salaries. The union also supports an automatic increase of ten per cent of the basic salary every five years of service, a legal grievance procedure to be used in disciplinary cases,

14 Lozano, pp. 35 ff.

life insurance, and for women, full maternal care. The union has negotiated and obtained the great majority of these rights. The teachers receive an annual salary increase similar to that of all civil servants, which is usually about ten per cent. In addition, union leaders are kept busy trying to protect individuals who are victims of arbitrary acts.[15]

Long ago the union obtained medical services for the teachers. In 1956 the federal government created a committee to administer such services, supported financially by contributions from the teachers, the Ministry of Public Education, and the local governments. These contributions were also used to build special clinics for teachers. More recently, this service has been integrated into the Instituto Nacional de Seguridad Social para los Trabajadores del Estado (National Institute of Social Security for Federal Employees) when this institute was founded.

Aided by the federal government, the union was able to construct a building and an auditorium in Mexico City which has become the home of the national organization as well as headquarters for sections of the union in the Federal District. In several states, buildings have frequently been constructed with help of the local governments.

In its Third National Council (or Convention), SNTE set up its structure. According to its rules, SNTE is to be headed by a National Executive Committee which must be elected by the National Council and will be made up of a Secretary General (who will represent SNTE) and the following secretaries: Grievances, Organization, Finance, Social Planning, Propaganda, Social Activities, Relations, and Promotion and Construction. Besides these officers, there are special commissions: a political commission in charge of relations with the nation's political organizations, a commission of education which deals with technical problems of the profession and relations with the Ministry of Public Education, and a women's commission which deals with the specific problems of women teachers.

The local unions, called sections and designated by a roman numeral, are organized in the same manner as the national union. The delegates from these sections make up the National Council, which then elects its directors and is the supreme authority.

15 *Ibid.*, pp. 45 ff.

THE ACTIVITIES OF SNTE

The national union and its sections do many things, some related directly to education as a profession, some to the improvement of conditions for its members, and some involve participation in the life of the community. The second type of activities are the ones which consume most of the union time, effort, and money. Still, examples of the range of SNTE activities may be seen from the following examples:

1. The Mexican Constitution establishes in its Article 123 that private enterprises must furnish schools for the sons of their employees, but this article has only seldom been enforced. SNTE started a campaign in 1953 to induce companies to comply with the law, but the results have not been satisfactory. More recently, SNTE proposed, without success, an amendment to Article 123 to make it clear that the obligation to build and support schools for the children of their workers is not only the responsibility of those factories located in rural areas (as it had been interpreted by the courts), but also the responsibility of those in urban areas.

2. According to a statement made by Enrique W. Sánchez, Secretary General of SNTE in 1959, the 120,000 workers in education have obtained new benefits from 1953 to 1958 equivalent to a gross value of 210 million pesos ($17 million) and an increase in salary during that time of 80 per cent.[16] During this period a single administrative and pay system was achieved for all the public teachers. This was not true for private teachers who in general have not been willing to organize and, as a result, are generally paid less than teachers in public schools.

3. The union also has a publishing house (Editorial del Magisterio) where it prints materials for the national SNTE and its local sections, as well as some books. It also has food stores and cooperatives formed with government subsidies.

4. Efforts have been made in the past by SNTE to enlarge the federal institute for training teachers (Instituto Federal de Capacitación del Magisterio) to include not only rural teachers, but all teachers. The institute was created in 1944 after the law of the professions was passed. This law prevented people from practicing a profession without proper accreditation. Up to that time in Mexico, a person could practice any profession as long as the person would

16 *Ibid.*, p. 68.

state on his stationery that he did not have a college degree. As a result of the changed law, he now needs to have a college degree to practice a profession and the function of the institute was to prepare degreeless teachers so they could obtain degrees. The activity of the institute so far, however, has been limited to rural teachers.

5. Several campaigns, such as those for the construction of schools, traffic education, forest conservation and development, have received support from SNTE. With regard to the construction of schools, SNTE proposed the establishment of a bank with government assistance which would give credit to those teachers who wanted to start new private schools. This proposition was not accepted.

6. SNTE maintains relations with all the international organizations of teachers, but is a member, even though not very active, of the World Federation of Teachers' Unions, a part of the Communist World Federation of Trade Unions. Possibly, when SNTE affiliated with the WFTU, it was believed that this international affiliation would keep the Communists in the union quiet. However, as mentioned before, in the 1957–58 period Communist elements were in control of the powerful Section IX. Since that time the relations between SNTE and WFTU have cooled off, but have not been broken.

CONCLUSIONS

Since 1935 the Mexican labor movement has had close relations with the state and generally follows the policy of the government. Its former aggressiveness has disappeared and its present accomplishments are simply concessions from the government.

The teacher' unions which never were aggressive followed a pattern similar to the rest of the labor movement, linking themselves to the officialdom in the Ministry of Education, while the rest of the labor movement became an integral part of the official political party. After an era of deep ideological differences, the movement united under official pressure and since then it has been an organization which deals with negotiations of benefits and the solutions of bureaucratic problems.

The changes in the role of the teachers' unions are similar in a way to those changes in the role of the teacher in Mexican society. The teacher has gone through the following evolution: from promoter of unrest to defender, mostly in the small towns, of Mexican revolutionary principles and lay education; and from a revolutionary into civil servant with no other function than teaching. In this way, the Mexican teacher has followed the same pattern as that of the teachers in highly industrialized countries, with the exception that the society in which he lives still needs the stimulus which traditionally came from the teacher.

Nigeria 7

John P. Henderson

Beginning in July, 1967, the Republic of Nigeria became involved in a civil war, as the oil-rich Eastern Region seceded, evoking for its name that of the ancient city of Biafra. Undoubtedly the social and economic disruptions which the war occasioned will be long lasting, if not permanent. In the event the Federal troops, dominated by the Hausa and Kanuri peoples from the Northern Region, are successful in preventing secession, the former eastern territory will not have the importance which it enjoyed in the years following Nigerian independence. The only major ethnic group that migrated to all regions of the country, the Ibos of the Eastern Region would be greatly restricted, both politically and economically, in any reconstituted Nigeria that might emerge. On the other hand, should the Biafrans succeed with their separatist movement, the Balkanization of sub-Sahara Africa would have been carried one step further.

The War of Biafran Secession marked the ultimate and final stage of a political and economic disintegration that was inevitable when Nigeria won independence from the British in October, 1960. The basic disunity of a territory loosely joined for 60 years by the superstructure of colonial administration was quick to erupt in a series of major and minor crises, each bringing the nation nearer disaster. The trial, conviction, and imprisonment of major political leaders for treasonable felony; the creation of a new state in the midwest; a

---

JOHN P. HENDERSON is Professor of Economics, Michigan State University.

state of emergency in the Western Region; two nationwide general strikes; heated political controversy over the population census; accusations of rigged election; clandestine misuse of government funds by party leaders; and finally, the two successive military coups which resulted in wholesale slaughter of thousands of Ibos in the Moslem North, effectively ended a federation which had never had a strong indigenous base, either culturally or economically.

Nigeria was never in a position to display the strength that was expected of her. Although the British had established the ceremonial trappings of an open society in all regions of Nigeria, instituting representative assemblies, the ballot box, and an independent judiciary, they had left untouched the real processes of community life throughout the territory. The political struggle for power that has dominated independent Nigeria's brief history is but the surface manifestation of fundamental difficulties that stem from the fact that, contrary to widely accepted opinion, no attempt had been made to integrate and unite the economy of the British Protectorate of Nigeria.

The strategy of British colonial administration in Nigeria was indirect rule, a system whereby indigenous socio-political structures were retained as control units. The system originated in the north and worked best utilizing the absolute authority of the Moslem emirs who ruled the Hausa-Fulani people dominant in that region. In the south, the system had to be adapted to less autocratic forms of tribal organization, but it nevertheless worked through indigenous political institutions.

Accordingly, Nigeria's 200-odd linguistic groups retained as many local governments, each representing a separate social system and a traditional economy that was largely uncoordinated with that of its nearest neighbors. British traders extracted palm oil, groundnuts, cocoa, rubber, and other primary products without interfering either with local authority or with traditional systems of production and distribution. The result was that no overall integration of economic activity took place. The Ibo cash-crop system of palm production was more coordinated with the European economy than with groundnut production in Hausaland or with cocoa farming in Western Nigeria. Diverse and conflicting social systems remained intact, their traditional economies operating separately within the framework of colonial control.

The various disciplines of the social sciences provide a number of tools for interpreting and analyzing the causes of Nigerian disunity. A psychologist might find the subconscious a useful concept to explain the diverse responses to the market economy,[1] while political scientists might stress the structural defects in the federal-regional relation.[2] But whatever the basic orientation might be, one of the common denominators would be Western education and the role it has played in the acculturation process (sociology), development of a labor force (economics), awakening of nationalism (political science), and detribalization (anthropology). In each instance, the researcher's discipline would undoubtedly shape and direct the way in which Western education would be evaluated as a vehicle of transition to modernity. Nonetheless, there would be general agreement that the availability of Western education, or its absence, has been the most crucial variable in the modernization process.

Education has always been the most vital concern of the Nigerian people, particularly those living in the southern areas. Although the colonial government consistently allocated very little to education, preferring to rely upon the missionaries, individual Nigerians sought, and valued, education opportunities above all else. The schools that were available were never sufficient to meet the demand and as a consequence there was continual pressure to increase the educational budgets and to improve the curriculum, and each of these campaigns tended to increase the demand for teachers, especially those of better quality.

The very important role of education, as well as the ever increasing demand for its product, has made the Nigeria Union of Teachers the largest as well as the oldest trade union in Nigeria. The Union had a reported membership of 60,000 in 1965, the largest by far of eight unions with over 5,000 members. Furthermore, the Teachers' Union has always been considered an ideal trade union organization, especially with respect to its internal affairs, tactics, and philosophy of labor relations. Both the British colonial administrators and the leaders of independent Nigeria praised the Union's stable organization and endorsed it as a model which other unions should emulate, eulogizing its leadership for refraining from the vituperative outbursts, wildcat strikes, and "general trouble-

[1] Robert A. LeVine, *Dreams and Deeds: Achievement Motivation in Nigeria* (Chicago: University of Chicago Press, 1966).
[2] Richard L. Sklar and C. S. Whitaker, Jr., "The Federal Republic of Nigeria," in *National Unity and Regionalism in Eight African States*, ed. Gwendolen Carter (Ithaca, New York: Cornell University Press, 1966), pp. 7–136.

making," a phrase typically used to characterize the Nigerian labor movement.

In contrast to most trade unions in Nigeria, the Teachers' Union has "gone it alone" and has not participated very actively in the political strikes and boycotts that have played such an important role in Nigerian trade union history. Essentially it is the fact that the teachers primarily have been concerned with the problems of the industry in which they earn their living that sets the Union apart from the typical trade union activity. Their interest in joint consultation and collective bargaining among teachers, school districts, and the private entrepreneurs who dominate primary and secondary education, stamps them as a business union and more like unions in the developed nations than those in Nigeria.

To some extent the differences between the Nigeria Union of Teachers and the other Nigerian unions stem from the universal aspiration of teachers to be viewed as something more than just workers. In large part, this is a consequence of the special importance of education in the country and the fact that it has a number of special problems which sets it aside from the typical political orientation of the majority of unions. The proper perspective for viewing the structure and policies of the Teachers' Union is from an analysis of the crucial role of education and of the nature of trade union activity in Nigeria.

THE DEVELOPMENT OF EDUCATION IN NIGERIA

The first aspect of any evaluation of the role of Western education in Nigeria concerns the contrasting policies which developed in the North and the South. Beginning in the 1840's Christian missionary societies started educational institutions in the southern territories, several decades prior to the English conquest. Why the missionaries did not push farther northward is difficult to say fully, but certainly the prevalence of the Moslem religion was the principal deterring force. In addition, funds were always scarce, and there were millions of pagans in the coastal regions around Lagos, Bonny, and Calabar. But whatever the reason, by 1900 when Lugard [3] conquered Nigeria's northern provinces and established British au-

[3] Lord Frederick Lugard was the officer of the Royal Niger Company (1862) who conquered Northern Nigeria for British imperialism. He later became Governor-General of Northern Nigeria (1907) and of Nigeria (1914).

thority, there were no mission schools in the territory. Moreover, Lugard made a commitment to the emirs which guaranteed that no Christian missions would be permitted in the Moslem areas, which at the time accounted for 65 per cent of the population of the Northern Region. With respect to the pagan pockets in the North, Lugard's agreement did not exclude them from contact with the Christian missionaries, but for the next several decades the number of schools was minimal. As early as 1920, all Protestant evangelical activity in the northern pagan areas was being carried on by African clergy, as white missionaries temporarily abandoned the territory.

British colonial strategy played a major role in excluding the Christian schools from the Moslem portions of the North. Lugard, as the major architect of British rule, was extremely fearful of the corrosive effects of a Christian egalitarian philosophy, since it might be interpreted as advocating the "abolition of class distinction." Having come to Nigeria many decades later than the missionaries, Lugard was determined that the mistakes of the Southern Regions not be repeated in the North. The principal mistake, so far as he was concerned, being the "poor" education responsible for the "discontent, impatience of any control and an unjustified assumption of self-importance" of Nigerian youths.[4] Accordingly, Western education in the North was rigidly controlled and restricted in order to foster the principle of indirect rule; no education in English was available as it inevitably led to "utter disrespect for British and native ideals" and interfered with the colonial administration.[5] In his report on the "Amalgamation of Northern and Southern Nigeria," published after he retired in 1919, Lugard attributed a large portion of the failure of indirect rule in the South to the fact that the missionary schools had produced youths who were "ill-educated, unreliable and lacking in self-control."[6]

For pragmatic reasons, the colonial government operated only through the indigenous authority, the exclusive contact with the native population. Too much Western education, Lugard thought, would make the task of the traditional authorities more difficult, for indirect rule only could be successful if traditional authority was

[4] Alan Burns, *History of Nigeria*, 5th ed. (London: George Allen and Unwin, Ltd., 1955), p. 258.
[5] James S. Coleman, *Nigeria: Background to Nationalism* (Berkeley and Los Angeles; University of California Press, 1963), p. 137.
[6] Burns, p. 258.

rigid, well defined, and enforceable. Under no circumstances should the colonial regime permit an educational system to develop that could possibly undermine the authority of the emirate power structure. As a first step, there should be no Westernizing influences. As British mercantile activities gathered momentum and became more complex and integrated, a need for the traditional authorities to increase their knowledge and skills would develop, as they would be required to adjust to the needs and desires of the commercial enterprises. The sons and heirs of the indigenous rulers, the elite of the traditional society, would have to acquire some Western education to permit them to administer the demands of this expanding commerical empire. But there would never be any need for mass education. Accordingly, the education that Lugard advocated was designed exclusively for the "proper people," a system calculated not to disrupt the traditional society. The Moslem religion and Arabic were primary to the curriculum, as all of the customary forms of deference, including prostration, were rigidly respected. "In short," Coleman says, "every effort was made to adapt the educational system to the environment and thereby avoid a repetition of the southern pattern." [7]

Undoubtedly, the primary motive behind the emirs' decision not to permit the establishment of missionary schools was religious, especially because of the all-prevailing influence of the Islamic creed. In addition, there was the possible eroding effect which Western education could have upon the emirate political and economic power base. Therefore, even if an alternative to the Christian schools had existed, the emirs would not have permitted their establishment. Western education, as taught by the missionaries, meant not only Christianity and egalitarianism, but an exposure to English, non-Islamic philosophy, history, and values. The emirs did not object to the British, so long as they did not disrupt their traditional power base. By refusing to allow formal and systematic instruction in a foreign tongue, both the potentially subversive influence of Christianity and the possible wage employment of their subjects was avoided, thus preserving the source of their power and wealth.

In the southern territories, the missions were firmly entrenched before Lugardian ideas could have any influence. The predominate religion in the South was paganism, and there also was no emirate

[7] Coleman, p. 138.

hierarchy to prevent the spread of the Christian religion and with it Western education. Accordingly, the southern areas gained an advantage over the North which was never lost, and as the years went on the differential grew larger and larger. In 1914, when the two administrations of Northern and Southern Nigeria were amalgamated to form the Protectorate of Nigeria, there were approximately 36,000 pupils in missionary schools in the southern territories, and none in the Moslem North; approximately 1,000 were in attendance in the pagan areas of the North. The total population numbered about 15 million at the time. In 1926, when the colonial government reluctantly commenced its partial subsidization of education, 138,000 pupils were in attendance in the South and 5,000 among the pagan tribes of the lower portion of the North. The effects of these contrasts were apparent in 1952, when census data showed that 16 per cent of those over seven years of age in the Eastern Region were literate, 18 per cent in the Western Region and only 1.4 per cent in the Moslem North; 3.3 per cent of those seven and older in the Middle Belt were literate. Approximately 5 per cent of the Moslems were literate in Arabic in 1952.

Despite the continuing increase in the percentage of school-age children in primary education, people in the southern areas were not satisfied, and they continually agitated for the colonial government to aid education, either by grants-in-aid to the mission schools or by constructing new government schools. The dissatisfaction centered on a number of issues, of which poor instruction was the major. From a missionary standpoint, the purpose of mass education was mass conversion and only enough of the three r's was taught to make the fourth "r," religion, palatable. The quality of education in the majority of these schools was certainly inferior, but it was better than nothing. A second difficulty concerned the stress upon primary education. The missionaries could see no need for secondary schools, and it was only in 1961 that the Roman Catholic Mission changed its exclusive emphasis upon primary education. As the years passed, the British began to realize that government would have to take a hand in education, for the poor quality of the missionary educational system was causing difficulty, and "half educated" youths, as Lugard called them, were voicing discontent.

The big change came in 1926, with the establishment of a system of grants-in-aid to the mission schools and an official recognition of mission education but with government registration of teachers.

Although the new policy did not mean anything in the Moslem North, it did in the South, since the amount spent on education more than doubled. In 1929, the government spent 4.3 per cent of its budget (£ 263 thousand) on education; in 1925, 2 per cent (£ 116 thousand) had been allocated for education.[8] For the decade 1926–1937, there was a 59 per cent increase in primary school enrollment, and during the next decade the increase was 146 per cent, reaching a southern total of 538,391. Secondary enrollment in the South also rose, from 518, in 1926 to 9,657 in 1947; by contrast there were 251 students in secondary schools in the North in 1947. The 1926 Education Code had its effect in the pagan areas of the North; in 1926 there were only a little over 5,000 primary school enrollees; by 1947 the enrollment had climbed to approximately 71,000.

The group that benefited most from the new government policy, in addition to the new enrollees who could find places, were the teachers in the mission schools, since the greatest part of the grants-in-aid went to pay the salaries of qualified instructors.[9] In addition, the government began to stress quality and the need for better qualified teachers, with the result that it raised the standards for teacher qualification. At the same time that the government was attempting to raise the qualifications of the teachers, it cut grants-in-aid in 1931, because of the depression. It was this issue that brought the Nigeria Union of Teachers into existence, for the demand for better qualified teachers coupled with the cut in grants meant that salaries fell as the cost of qualification rose.

All the members of the new Nigeria Union of Teachers were employed in mission schools, since there was no place else for them to teach, and there were numerous complaints lodged against the employers. The Union, however, did not attempt to deal with the various voluntary agencies in a typical employer-employee relation, but instead directed all of their attention to the colonial administration. In other words, even though the government was not the primary employer, the Nigeria Union of Teachers acted as if that were the case. With the government supplying most of the money for salaries, as a consequence of the grants-in-aid, the Union cor-

8 *Ibid.*, p. 134.
9 David B. Abernethy, "Nigeria" in *Church, State and Education in Africa,* ed. David G. Scanlon (New York: Teachers College Press, Columbia University, 1966), p. 210.

rectly looked upon the colonial administration as the real employer and began to think of themselves as near-government employees. The teachers not only adopted this attitude with respect to salaries and qualifications, but also in regard to the government's educational philosophy, as policy became more and more centralized in Lagos. The Union's first president, I. O. Ransome-Kuti, claimed, "It is the duty of the government to foster education and to look after the welfare of teachers, and no amount of whatever the missions can say or do can exonerate the government from final responsibility." [10]

The voluntary agencies continued to be the primary employers, as teachers continued to work in the mission schools, but after 1926 the real employer became the government as grants-in-aid steadily increased. Abernathy has described the relation thusly,

With each passing year, in other words, the government became increasingly committed to supporting a voluntary agency educational system, while the voluntary agencies grew increasingly dependent upon government for the maintenance of the system. A major explanation for this development was that the government was economy-minded—particularly during the Depression—and by operating through the voluntary agencies it saved itself the administrator costs of managing and inspecting a large body of schools. For their part the voluntary agencies were happy to accept government funds provided the administration did not imperil their religious activities within the schools.[11]

The link between government and the mission schools, the individual employers in education, was similar to the link between government and private enterprise which prevailed in other sectors of the Nigerian economy. The Nigeria Union of Teachers looked upon the government as the teacher's employer because of the intimacy which existed between government and all commercial activity in the country. The essence of this economic activity was mercantilism, not free enterprise capitalism. The purpose of English control in Nigeria was trade: the extraction of cocoa, groundnuts, oil palm products, tin and gold, and the sale of cloth, sugar, spice and other consumer requisites. The essential economic unit was the expatriate trading firm such as the United Africa Company, John Holt, the United Trading Company, Commerce Français de l'Afrique Occidentale, and Société de Commerce d'Outre-mer en Afrique. Private interests were synonymous with the public interests

10 *Ibid.,* p. 211.
11 *Ibid.,* p. 209.

of the colonial administration that granted the monopoly rights, and supplied the judicial and political institutional superstructure. Nigeria was an economic system in which private capital was nurtured, assisted, controlled, and utilized by the government, with the open approval of the business community, for the financial benefit of the trading companies. The normal course of business activity was to lean more and more upon a generalized system of state intervention, aid, and protection. Colonialism and commercial capitalism became closely identified, as both expatriate and indiginee recognized the marriage of government to business. For almost half a century, as Berg has said, there were ". . . price-fixing arrangements, government-bestowed monopoly privileges, restrictive wage and labor market policies, forced labor—all dependent on an alliance between colonial governments and private enterprise." [12]

Accordingly, there never was a sharp differentiation between public and private interests. To the native Nigerian, the major distinction between the United Africa Company and government was that officials of the former wore white "knickers" and the latter wore khaki. To the expatriate there was also little difference, since salaries, post allowances, and other emoluments were competitive; the relationship of government to the trading companies, under mercantilism, was that the former was dedicated to serving the latter. To the Nigerian, educated and uneducated alike, there was no difference between Barclay's Bank D.C.O. and Her Majesty's Government, or the U.A.C. and the Governor-General; there were no differences among the United Africa Company Ltd., G. B. Olivant Ltd., Kingsway, and the African Timber and Plywood Ltd., each a division of Unilver. Economic policy in Nigeria was monopoly oriented, paternalistic, and against free enterprise. Because of the mercantilist relation between the colonial government and the trading companies, business followed the flag in all matters of economic policy, and this process extended to the labor market.

When the grants-in-aid to the missions commenced in 1926, it was quite natural for the Teachers' Union to look upon government, rather than the voluntary agencies, as the employer. The few shillings which the numerous missions collected from each of their parishioners to run their schools, and to pay the teachers' salaries,

[12] Elliot J. Berg, "Socialism and Economic Development in Tropical Africa," *Quarterly Journal of Economics* (November 1964), p. 554.

was inadequate to the task of an expanding educational system. In addition, such an income base could provide only for very low salaries; the grants-in-aid were necessary to raise salaries to a level which would attract more qualified personnel.

With the beginning of grants-in-aid, the Nigeria Union of Teachers began a long struggle to raise salaries to a level that would approach salaries in the government. In the government operated schools which were opened as a supplement to the mission schools, the salaries paid teachers were considerably higher than in the older institutions. As a result, a church-state schism developed, the salary differential between the two groups of institutions being the most important trade union issue. Actually there were two differentials that the Nigeria Union of Teachers struggled to eliminate: (1) the differential between the wages paid government teachers and the wages of other government employees, and (2) the differential between the wages the missions paid, even with grants-in-aid, and the wages of teachers in government schools.

At least 98 per cent of the teachers in Nigeria, even as late as 1960, were employed in mission schools, or those run by local village or city authorities or private entrepreneurs,[13] the other two per cent teaching in government operated schools. For most teachers, therefore, the problem was not to raise salaries to parity with other government employees, but to reduce the differential between salaries in the mission schools and those operated by the government. In 1937, for example, primary teachers in the mission schools earned between £ 30 and £ 60, while government teachers started at £ 36 and advanced to £ 72. The first part of the Union's campaign was directed at having the government fix the wage level in all schools, a goal that has never been accomplished because of the continuing influx of "uncertified" teachers.

The large number of "uncertified" teachers, running as high as 40 per cent in the primary schools, was the result of a number of circumstances. In the first place, the educational structure has al-

[13] Grants-in-aid have been available to any school which met certain minimum requirements with regard to teacher certification, and the ratio of training graduates to untrained personnel. Because of the great demand for education, and because the missions did not increase the supply rapidly enough, the void has been filled by private entrepreneurs opening schools to make a profit. Usually operated by politicians, who could receive grants-in-aid even when they did not meet the qualifications, such institutions have always showed an extremely high profit rate.

ways concentrated on primary education, and never less than three fourths of the budget has been allocated at this level. After primary education, beginning in the 1930's, the second largest item in the education budgets of government was higher education, first training colleges and grammar schools and later universities. The secondary schools have never received more than ten per cent of any educational budget, and this fact has been one of the major shortcomings of the Nigerian educational system. The very small number of secondary school students has meant that most looked to the government and commercial labor markets, and a limited number thought of education as a possible career. Moreover, not all of the graduates of the teacher training colleges and grammar schools had stayed in education, since a certificate from one of these institutions opened doors to government and commerical opportunities for employment, and only a small percentage were fed back into primary and secondary schools. As a result teaching positions in the primary schools were filled by anyone with a minimum of a primary school certificate and hopefully one or two years of secondary schooling.

As the number of primary school children increased, with over two million in attendance in the southern areas by 1952, the number and percentage of "uncertified" teachers greatly increased as well. Given an education structure that placed so little emphasis upon secondary education, a peculiarity of all of tropical Africa, there was no opportunity to reduce the percentage of unqualified teachers. The problem was compounded by the fact that the rapid growth of the government and commercial infrastructure absorbed a higher and higher proportion of the graduates of teacher training colleges, grammar schools, and technical institutes, not to mention the university graduates. As a consequence, the teaching profession in Nigeria largely became composed of poorly trained, but highly dedicated, teachers. The Nigeria Union of Teachers made constant demands that the teaching occupation be viewed as "professional," and on a par with physicians and lawyers, but as long as the majority were poorly qualified, the "professionalization" campaign was not very successful.

The difficulties associated with the high percentage of poorly qualified teachers prior to 1955–57 were compounded by the campaign for "universal primary education." Adopted in the Western Region in 1955 and in the East two years later, this crash program to raise the literacy rate epitomized the Nigerian emphasis upon education as a solution to all social, political, and economic difficulties. Universal primary education had as its goal compulsory free education for all primary grades; when it was introduced 35 per cent of the six to fourteen year olds in the West were enrolled, and 43 per cent of those in the East. With the new policy, enrollment in the West jumped to approximately 66 per cent of the eligible enrollees and 75 per cent in the East. Most of the new teachers were primary leavers, those who had completed only the primary six grades, with four weeks training, and some "uncertified" teachers and discards from the mission schools. Although the new employment opportunities were a great boon to unemployed primary school leavers, the number of uncertified and unqualified teachers was doubled, and the effect upon standards was drastic. In addition, the experiment placed education more and more in the hands of the regional and local governments and this had the effect of destroying the Nigeria Union of Teachers' campaign to establish a nationwide salary schedule, as well as any hope of raising the level of wages to parity with the federal government. In 1961, the Banjo Commission, appointed to evaluate the educational standards of the Western Region, observed,

The teaching profession has been termed a sick profession. The minimum qualification for entry has been very low. The salary scales are not comparable with those of other types of employment like the Civil Service. There are very few promotion possibilities and these can only be obtained by passing examinations. The teacher's professional efficiency hardly affects his career. Many teachers instead of teaching efficiently are busy working hard to "uplift" themselves, or running price coaching practice to increase their income. Many of those who succeed in "uplifting" themselves find it more worthwhile to get out of the teaching profession altogether and join the Civil Service where they will be paid a higher salary. It is reasonable to say that the most basic weakness in the primary education systems of Southern Nigeria lies in the quality of the teachers.[14]

By 1959, the Western Region had 4,252 trained teachers and 26,000 untrained, and was spending 41 per cent of its total budget on education, while the Eastern Region was spending 43 per cent.[15] Both governments realized that it was impossible to continue to allocate such a high portion of their budgets to education, especially in view of the extreme capital shortages for other types of economic development. Accordingly, in 1960 a new system of "local

[14] James O'Connell, "The State and the Organization of Elementary Education in Nigeria: 1945–1960," p. 9 (mimeographed).
[15] *Ibid.,* pp. 5, 9.

contributions" was introduced, whereby mission schools, and those recently constructed by local communities, would have to absorb a large share of the primary education cost. In addition, only the first three grades were now free, and there was a drastic reduction in the number of enrollees. In the relatively short period of five years, there was a tremendous increase in the number of schools, students, and teachers, but as the financial burden of universal primary education became too great, there was also a great drop in the number of teachers, enrollees and classrooms.

One serious consequence of the rise in fees and fall in the number of pupils during these years was that many teachers, mostly probationary ones, were declared redundant and dismissed. These dismissals were one more blow against the status of teachers who tend more than ever to become a semi-intellectual proletariat. Poor salaries, bad conditions of service and little enough official acknowledgement of their services have militated against young people of ability choosing a teaching career or staying in the profession once the opportunity arose to leave it.[16]

To a very large degree teachers in Nigeria were not very much different than any group of semiskilled workers, for the very large percentage of poorly qualified teachers meant that any claims of professionalism were viewed as pretentious. Because they were a "semi-intellectual proletariat," trade unionism was an accepted way to protest the low salaries and poor working conditions. Except for the pretensions of professionalism, the Nigeria Union of Teachers was composed largely of unskilled workers, and the reason the Union grew to be by far the largest of all unions was due to the ever accelerating demand for the services it produced. Because the problems of the education industry were no different than those in transport, commerce, or the mines, the Nigeria Union of Teachers adopted the same political trade unionist philosophy that other unions adopted, namely to attempt to negotiate all their trade disputes with the colonial government, not with the individual employers for whom they labored.

NIGERIA'S TRADE UNIONS

There are several ways in which a trade union movement may be considered to be politically oriented. Most frequently it is assumed that political unionism suggests union efforts to affiliate with one of

[16] *Ibid.*, p. 9.

several political parties or to form a political party representing union interests. This, of course, Nigerian unions never did; moreover, the Nigerian unions avoided any direct association with the political parties because they were dealing with a "foreign" government and not one that was controlled by indigenous parties.

The Nigerian brand of political unionism consisted of a reliance upon political bargaining to gain economic objectives. Whatever their tribal, religious, political, or regional orientation, Nigerian workers, of course, were primarily interested in their economic well-being. Like workers the world over, they sought, in their union activities, to achieve economic goals. But they did so by political means, for they negotiated with the colonial government rather than private employers. Nigerian workers desired higher real wages, shorter hours, and better working conditions, but very few were in a strong enough position to obtain these objectives by means other than by government fiat. Too weak to gain economic objectives by means of economic tactics, Nigeria's trade unions have relied upon the general strike, the threat of political boycott, and collective political action that cuts across tribal, industrial, and craft lines to win, from government, the wage increases which have come about every five years since World War II.[17] Even before the breakout of hostilities there was almost a complete absence of collective bargaining contracts.

Having played an important role in the struggle for independence, providing its organized mass movement, the trade unions began to see their influence wane in the early 1960's. In the drafting of the Six Year Plan (1961–1967) they were not even accorded lip service, and, as the first full blush of independence began to fade, the rapprochement between the political elite and organized labor rapidly disintegrated. When the federal and regional governments refused to grant a wage increase in 1963, for example, the unions resorted to the threat of political boycott, a tactic they had resorted to under the guise of nationalism when the British were in control. The pressure was exerted by means of a general strike in September, 1963, strategically called on the eve of Nigeria's appearance as a Republic. The general strike disabled the entire modern sector, sufficiently hindering government operations and the impending

17 W. M. Warren, "Urban Real Wages and the Nigerian Trade Union Movement, 1939–1960," *Economic Development and Cultural Change* (October 1966), pp. 21–35.

political celebrations to achieve its objective. No action was required of private employers, as employees merely reported for work but would not perform any duties. It was the federal government that finally succumbed to the workers' demands and agreed to appoint the Morgan Commission, whose responsibility was to conduct an inquiry into the wage structure of the entire economy. The Commission's assignment was:

(a) To investigate the existing wage structure, remunerations and conditions of service in wage-earning employment in the Country and to make recommendations concerning a suitable or new structure, as well as adequate machinery for wage review on a continuing basis.
(b) To examine the need for:—
    (i) a general upward revision of salaries and wages of junior employees in both Government and Private Establishments;
    (ii) the abolition of the daily wage system;
    (iii) the introduction of a national minimum wage.
(c) On the basis of (b) (i)–(iii) above, the Commission should make recommendations.[18]

The Morgan Commission issued its findings in April, 1964, but the federal government refused to grant the wage increases it recommended. On June 1 of the same year a second general strike tied up the economy; the federal government finally capitulated to the workers' demands for a wage increase. The strategy of both general strikes was to gain wage increases in the government sector which would then be extended by private employers, and to try to eliminate regional wage differentials. The pattern followed in 1964 was the same as in 1959, 1952–1954, and 1946; each time the unions forced the colonial government to grant wage advances at a national level, and in each instance the private employers followed suit.

There were, of course, some very good reasons for the reliance of the Nigerian trade unions upon political rather than economic strength to gain their objectives. In the first place, the government was the country's single largest employer and certainly the highest paying one. In 1963, for example, the federal and three regional governments accounted for over 60 per cent of all skilled manpower, and these were the workers most actively involved in trade union activity.[19] In 1961 the federal and three regional govern-

18 *Memorandum on Salaries and Wages Review*, submitted to the Morgan Commission by the Electrical Workers' Union of Nigeria.
19 *Nigeria's High-Level and Skilled Manpower, 1963–1968*, submitted by Nigerian Manpower Board, Seminar on Manpower Problems in Economic Development with Special Reference to Nigeria (Lagos, March 1964), Table I. It is

ments accounted for 23 per cent of all wage earners working for establishments employing ten or more people, and the local governments and public corporations accounted for another 29 percent.

Secondly, expatriate employers historically have followed the government's lead in wage matters. Before independence, increases in the private sector were always granted when the colonial regime revised the wage structure in the civil service, but only then.[20] The same pattern prevailed in 1964 and 1965, with private employers accepting the wage increases recommended by the Morgan Commission once these were granted in the government sector.

The third reason for the reliance upon political bargaining was the weak financial position of almost all trade unions in Nigeria. Very few could have successfully carried out a prolonged strike against an individual employer. Especially was this the case, since unemployment was conservatively estimated at about 25 per cent. On the other hand, it was relatively easy for workers to join other unions in a brief but dramatic political demonstration or general strike.

The strength of the Nigerian trade union movement was a legacy of the struggle for political independence and the strongly mercantilist orientation of the British colonial regime. Colonial economic expansion in Africa was the handmaiden of neomercantilism with the growth of commerce limited to a few companies, such as the United Africa Company and John Holt; and control over markets, prices, and wages was an essential goal of the various colonial governments. With the development of a bureaucratic approach to economic activity came labor regulation: the Trade Union Ordinance of 1938, the Workmen's Compensation Ordinance of 1941, and the Labour Code Ordinance of 1945. Each ordinance fostered and gave legal sanction to the trade unions, so that the leaders and memberships could be under the surveillance of the colonial authorities. As part of the mercantilist colonial mentality, the institutionalization of the labor market went hand in hand with the growth of political unionism.

As one of the few legal and effective mechanisms by which Nigerian workers could give expression to their desires for independence, since the political parties were limited and confined to the various ethnic groups, trade unions played an active role in bringing about

estimated that there are about 83,000 persons skilled or in a professional category, in Nigeria, exclusive of teaching and research staff.
[20] Warren, p. 23.

the end of the colonial regime. Many of the leaders of the independence movement owed their political strength to trade unions, and the 1944 trade union dispute in the Eastern region was used by nationalist leaders as a rallying point for independence. The killing

TABLE 1. TRADE UNION MEMBERSHIP IN NIGERIA, 1940–1964

Year	Number of Unions Registered at End of the Year	Membership in Unions Registered at End of the Year
1940	14	4,629
1941	27	17,521
1942	80	26,275
1943	85	27,154
1944	91	30,000
1945	97	41,000
1946	100	52,747
1947	109	76,362
1948	127	90,864
1949	140	109,998
1950	144	144,358
1951	124	152,230
1952	131	143,282
1953	152	153,089
1954	177	165,130
1955	232	175,987
1956	270	196,265
1957	298	235,742
1958	318	248,613
1959	347	259,100
1964	540	367,200 [a]

[a] Estimate of Nigerian Employers Consultative Association

SOURCE: T. M. Yesufu, *An Introduction to Industrial Relations in Nigeria* (London: Oxford University Press for the Nigerian Institute of Social and Economic Research; 1962), Table 4 for 1940–1944; *Annual Report of the Federal Department of Labour, 1958–1959* (Government Printing Office, Lagos) for 1945–1959.

of Enugu coal miners by the police, in 1949, was advanced from the realm of a labor dispute to one involving the struggle for political independence. The colonial government continually associated the growth of trade unions with "political demagogues" and independence leaders, and not as arising from worker dissatisfaction with wages, hours, and working conditions.

Table I shows the growth of the trade union movement from 1940 through 1964, when the Nigerian Employers Consultative Association estimated that there were over 367 thousand trade union members, a figure that was undoubtedly inflated. Nonetheless the increase in the reported membership was impressive, and in 1960, at least half of all the employees in establishments with ten or more workers belonged to some union. In the early 1960's there were an estimated two and one-half million wage earners in the money economy and another million market women. Since women and men both are engaged in growing crops for both subsistence and cash, there were approximately 30 million persons in the agricultural labor force, in peak months.

The current political and economic chaos of Nigeria results from serious undercurrents in that troubled country, not the least of which has been the inability of the economy to supply the employment levels, wages, and working conditions which the trade unions believed would flow from political independence. The same politicians who fanned the flames of trade union growth before 1960 to gain support for the independence movement, were quick to urge the unions to act responsibly and to hold their demands in check once independence had been attained.

Meanwhile, the leaders themselves and the upper echelons of the indigenous government service showed no inclination to practice the austerity they urged upon the wage earner. It was the unions who pointed out, in 1963, that:

The excessive upper income salaries in Nigeria have little or no genuine economic incentives. They are a carry-over from the colonial days. A colonial administrator earned a much higher income in Nigeria than he would have earned in Britain because men had to be encouraged to enlist in the colonial service. Moreover, the colonial government paid all sorts of allowances, such as 'Entertainment Allowance' purely for prestige reasons. Prestige factors certainly entered in a large way into the determination of the salaries of 'senior service' personnel. When Nigerians became Ministers of State and Parliamentarians they argued that they should maintain a social status at least equal to that of the top colonial higher civil servants. Again, when Nigerianization started, Nigerian Officers insisted on not being paid any income lower than those of their expatriate equivalents. Since the firms had to attract graduates and other educated Nigerians into their services, they too had to pay higher salaries. Thus was the colonial structure of executive salaries maintained even for Nigerians. As for the lower income groups they had to be satisfied with starvation wages under the colonial regime. There was a pronounced master-servant relation expressed not only in a prestige income structure but in social snobbiness. All this has been carried over into the new period.[21]

21 Joint Action Committee of Nigerian Trade Union Organizations, *Nigerian Workers Memorandum to Morgan Salaries and Wages Review Commission 1963* (Lagos, 1963), p. 14 (mimeographed).

Accordingly, the general strikes of 1963 and 1964 were not exclusively trade union tactics to improve wages and working conditions. The strikes also mobilized a widespread protest against the economy's drift. Following independence in 1960, employment had not increased and may even have declined on an absolute basis. Real wages also declined in the face of sharply rising living costs. Unemployment in the rural areas became Nigeria's number one economic problem, and discontent among wage earners greatly was aggravated by the enormous contrast in the living standard of the political elite.

The professionalism which the leadership of the Teachers' Union sought steered their followers away from the broader struggles and bellicose tactics of political unionism. Typically, the Nigerian trade unions engaged in political, rather than business unionism, because they had little choice. Collective bargaining and economic boycotts against individual employers were of little value in an economy whose productivity base could not support the workers's demands for an improvement in their economic status. If there is little or no basis for an annual improvement in labor productivity, which typically is a result of technological progress, there can be little economic reason for increasing wages. Thus, Nigerian workers have sought, by political means, a larger share of the national output by negotiating and struggling with the national government, rather than with attempting to bargain with individual employers. Their demands were the same that business unionism would promote, but their tactics were geared to national bargaining and to influencing the power structure.

Even though the Nigeria Union of Teachers did not engage in many of the tactics of the majority of Nigeria's unions, and officially the Union refrained from participating in the 1963–1964 general strikes, it nevertheless looked to the national government for relief. Following the establishment of the 1926 Education Code and the beginning of the grants-in-aid, the Teachers' Union attempted to bargain at a national level and to represent itself as a national union, advocating industry-wide action, rather than bargaining individually with the various voluntary agencies, local authorities, and private entrepreneurs. By its tactics, the Nigeria Union of Teachers utilized political unionism, but without the bellicose practices of the other unions. To a very large degree, the Union's relatively peaceful career was due to the very important role assigned to education in Nigeria's southern cultures, for it has been difficult for the workers in education to deny that strikes in their industry would be against the public welfare. This attitude was reinforced by the relatively conservative attitude of the Union's leadership and the social position of the voluntary agencies. One of the unique features of the relation of the teachers to education in Nigeria has been that while the national government contributed the substantial portion of the wage bill in the industry, the control over the actual working conditions, including hiring and firing, was administered by the voluntary agencies and local authorities. The reason the Union was so large was because education was so important and employed so many, and because wages were established by bargaining with the national government, not local employers. Although the Union was never able to gain the objective of having the same salary schedule in all schools, nor parity in salaries of the voluntary agencies with government schools, it was not because it did not try, but because the trend of economic decision making was away from the national government toward the regions and local authorities.

There were many indications that independence from the British would fracture the myth of unity which had existed under the guise of nationalism. The political parties, for example, were regional, if not ethnic, in origin and strength; economic growth at four per cent required rural development, not just expansion in Lagos, Port Harcourt, and other metropolitan centers. The indigenous economic and political power base was located in the local communities, and the idea that policy would be determined at the federal level was waning, especially given the overpowering influence of emirate control from the North. With independence the reins of the national government passed from the British to their heirs, the emirs. The tendency for decisions to be made at the local level had been apparent since 1954, when the Macpherson Constitution was abolished in favor of a new one which gave the regions greater autonomy; the 1957 constitution and independence carried the process a step further, and the War of Biafran Secession finally resulted.

Nigerianization from the very beginning has meant not the consolidation and solidification of the political, economic, and social life of the numerous communities and ethnic groups, but the exact opposite. Division and disintegration have been the major characteristics since 1960. The trade union movement, on the other hand, has always advocated more power at the center and continually has pushed for national solutions to the problems of wages, employment, and working conditions. The reason for this union attitude, contrary to the trend of events, is largely a reflection of the fact that it was a child of the movement for independence. The Nigeria Union of Teachers was no exception.

THE NIGERIA UNION OF TEACHERS

The Nigeria Union of Teachers was founded in July, 1931, and registered under the provisions of the Trade Unions Ordinance of 1938, when it came into effect in 1939. The origins were economic; the reduction of government subsidies to education, caused by the world depression, and the imposition of more rigid qualifications for teachers, combined to arouse the approximately one thousand workers to collective action. The expressed aims and objectives of the Union were:

1. To unite the teachers of Nigeria and to extend the influence of the teaching profession.

2. To strive to obtain grants-in-aid from the colonial government, as well as suitable conditions.

3. To establish a provident fund for members of the teaching profession.

4. To provide a vehicle for settling disputes between employers and teachers.

The Union's first success came in 1936, when the Church of Scotland Mission in Calabar attempted to reduce salaries by 15 per cent. A strike was called in March, and "the teachers demonstrated such unity of purpose and firmness of action" that they were successful in requiring the Mission to restore the lost wages. A major ally of the Union, in this particular instance, was the Colonial Government of Lagos which threatened to withdraw its grants-in-aid from the Scotish Mission if it persisted in its attempt to cut wages. The 1936 strike, therefore, was an important victory, not only because it prevented the wage reduction, but also because it brought the government to the side of the teachers and indicated that grants-in-aid were the primary ingredient so far as salaries were concerned.

From the beginning the union was multitribal, the first President was a Yoruba, I. O. Ransome-Kute (1931–1955), the Vice-President an Ibo, A. Ikoku, and its only General-Secretary an Efik, E. E. Esua. The General-Secretary was the real power in the Union and was its leading spokesman and representative in Lagos. Organized along industrial lines, the Union membership included graduate teachers, both at the primary and secondary level, teachers holding certificates, and the great mass of uncertified instructors that dominated Nigeria's educational system. One of the largest industries in Nigeria, in 1961 there were 67,337 teachers, with 55,223 belonging to the Nigeria Union of Teachers, or 92 per cent of the eligible members.[22]

TABLE 2. MEMBERSHIP IN NIGERIA UNION OF TEACHERS, 1949–1965

Year	Membership
1949	22,327
1950	24,112
1951	26,542
1952	28,628
1953	31,213
1954	33,525
1955	37,153
1957	44,126
1958	47,526
1959	51,236
1960	53,462
1961	55,223
1962	56,671
1965	60,000

SOURCE: Nigeria Union of Teachers

Initially the Union's membership was restricted to Lagos, later including teachers in the hinterland of the east and west, with regional or provincial headquarters established in the late 1930's. It was in the post-war period that membership soared, as shown in Table 2, and in addition to the nationalist movement that accounted for the growth of all trade union activity, the Teachers' Union benefited greatly from expanding enrollments in both primary and secondary schools (Table 3). In 1956, for the first time, the Northern Teachers' Association affiliated with the southern

22 Nigeria Union of Teachers, *30th Annual Conference Report* (January 1961), p. 21.

dominated Nigeria Union of Teachers, and in 1959 the Union had 259 locals scattered throughout the country. By 1963 there were 356 locals.

TABLE 3. PRIMARY AND SECONDARY WESTERN EDUCATION IN NORTHERN AND SOUTHERN NIGERIA, 1906–1962

| | Northern Nigeria | | | | Southern Nigeria | | | |
| | Schools | | Pupils | | Schools | | Pupils | |
Year	Primary	Secondary	Primary	Secondary	Primary	Secondary	Primary	Secondary
1906	1	0		0	126	1	11,872	20
1912	34	0	954	0	150	10	35,716	67
1926	125	0	5,210	0	3,828	18	138,249	518
1937	539	1	20,269	65	3,533	26	218,610	4,285
1947	1,110	3	70,962	251	4,984	43	538,341	9,657
1957	2,080	18	185,484	3,643	13,473	176	2,343,317	28,208
1960	2,600	41	282,848	6,334	13,103	842	2,629,770	129,100
1962	2,568	50	359,934	7,995	13,018	1,106	2,474,076	187,504

SOURCE: Coleman, Table 14, p. 134 for 1906–1957; *Annual Digest of Education Statistics, 1962*, Series No. 1, Vol. II (Federal Republic of Nigeria, 1962), Tables 1–2, pp. 17–19 for 1960–1962.

NOTE: Population in 1931: 19,930,000; in 1952–1953: 31,180,000; in 1963: 55,671,000.

Despite its rapid growth, the Union had its difficulties as the General-Secretary, E. E. Esua, reported:

On paper the Union is made up of 308 Branches many of which were not active. This moribund state of many of our Branches was due to several factors. One was the failure to appoint the right type of people to hold offices in the Branches especially the office of branch Secretaries. Another was the failure to introduce such activities in the Branches as will enlist the members' interest. A third was the type of people admitted to the profession. Many of them are not well educated enough to appreciate the value of a professional association of teachers.[23]

The stress upon the professsional aspects of the Union was a matter that caused considerable conflict between the aspirations of the leadership in Lagos, particularly as viewed by Esua, and the problems of the great mass of uncertified teachers. One of the central difficulties was that universal primary education placed a tremendous financial burden on local communities. When the Eastern Government had to cut back on its subsidization to these communities and request local contributions to make up the deficits, many

[23] *Annual Conference Report*, 1963, p. 43.

areas were not capable of meeting the new obligation. As a consequence, hundreds of teachers in the Eastern Region were not paid; the difficulty was compounded by the fact that most of the unpaid teachers were also uncertified, and the professional orientation of the Lagos leadership made it not too sympathetic to their needs. There were, accordingly, a number of splinter groups in the East and at one time it appeared that the Teachers' Union would lose a large percentage of its Eastern Region membership. A compromise over policy was adopted, finally, as Esua and his followers came to the defence of the uncertified teachers.[24]

The relation between the General-Secretary and the locals was never very strong, particularly in the East. The one occasion for national decision-making was the annual conventions, to which the locals would send representatives, if they wished. In 1959, 18 out of 297 were represented at the convention; in 1960, 19 out of 289, and in 1961, 23 out of 324 locals. In addition to locals and the national executive, there were also Regional Area Executive Committees, which tended to have more decision-making responsibility than the headquarters in Lagos. Like the great majority of Nigeria's unions, dues collection was the major problem for the Teachers' Union; success in this area was the key to the strength of individual locals and regional executives.

In addition to the bargaining over wages, which took place every time there was a national review of wages by a commission of inquiry, the Teachers' Union engaged in some activities directed at improving the quality of its members. From 1962 to 1964, for example, it arranged for hundreds of uncertified teachers in the Eastern Region to attend a ten-week session at the University of Nigeria, Nsuhha. Classes in English, arithmetic, science, and history were conducted by University personnel, Peace Corps Volunteers, and expatriates, in an attempt to raise the level of competence of the uncertified teachers in attendance.

The program to raise the qualifications of uncertified teachers was a most outstanding one which clearly recognized the needs of Nigerian teachers. The issue of salaries, however, always was the major problem so far as officials of the Union were concerned. Essentially, the conflict within the Union revolved around the problem of wages, as the national officers and government teachers

[24] Lagos, *Daily Times,* December 27, 1963, p. 1.

sought to raise the salaries of the better qualified, while the majority of teachers were concerned with improving their qualifications in order to advance in scale. The overall policy of the Union, however, was not concerned with the large base, but with increasing the salaries of those at the top of the scale, not the bottom.

NATIONAL JOINT NEGOTIATING COUNCIL

Salaries in the federal or regional government schools in Nigeria were considerably higher than the schools run by the voluntary agencies and local authorities. In part this was because the salaries of government teachers reflected the higher wages of all government employees and partly because the agencies and local authorities took advantage of the supply and demand conditions. Although government teachers never attained parity with other government officials, they nonetheless were among the highest paid employees in the country, and they benefited from the dual wage economy that existed in Nigeria. The dual wage economy, in turn, was a result of the application of expatriate salary levels to indigenous personnel, since Nigerianization meant not only equality in occupations but income as well. Government teachers were never able to attain parity, but only because the government would not pay the equivalent of a 12-month salary to teachers who worked only nine. The government also claimed that emoluments should not be equal, since the cost of city living to teachers was not as large as for other government employees. Whatever the size of the differential between the salary of government employees and government teachers the income of both groups was among the highest in the country. The salaries of government teachers were tied to the salaries of expatriates, not to the great majority of teachers in the mission schools.

Expatriates were paid salaries and given fringe benefits to compensate them for living in a malaria-ridden and tsetse-infected country. In almost all instances the income of the colonial administrators, no matter at what level of service, was considerably higher than they could earn at home, and a hundred times the income of any part of the indigenous population. But in addition to money income, the colonial administrator also received guarantees which included a social security system, minimum wage laws, trade unions, three- and four-week vacations, employment agencies, and retirement pay. Although the impetus for the development of this vast structure was the desire of expatriates to receive abroad the same economic guarantees they would enjoy at home, and they instituted such practices for their own benefit, it was not long before the practices were applied to indigenous workers. The most telling incidence of the transfer of expatriate benefits to indigenous personnel was the extension of the expatriate salary scale to indigenous workers. As Nigerians began to perform the same work as expatriate personnel, in teaching, government service, or the skilled trades, they expected equality in pay and the same fringe benefits. As Ehrlich has observed, in speaking of Uganda, "In a country where the mass of the people receive a cash income of less than $20 per annum, an indigenous professional *elite* is being trained to expect salaries, based originally on expatriate scales, which compare favorably with those earned in the richest countries in the world." [25]

As a consequence of the application of the expatriate salary scale to the indigenous worker, Nigeria developed a dual wage structure. On top, in posts formerly held by expatriates, were the elite whose wages and salaries carried a differential many times larger than any productivity allowances could account for and explain. The Joint Action Committee of the Nigerian Trade Union Organizations, in a 1963 memorandum to the Morgan Commission, claimed that:

. . . employees of the Federal Public Service, the Lagos Town (now City) Council, the Public Corporations, Missions or Commercial firms employing 10 or more persons, 1,200 persons earned more than $810 per annum, whereas 5 $\frac{1}{2}$ times their number or 1/9 of the total employed by these entities earned less than $90 per annum. A total income of $1,000,000 is earned by the uppermost 1,200 employees, an average earning of $1,000 per annum per person. But a total income of $2,400,000 or twice the first, is shared among 23,300 persons, or an average of $103 p. a. per employee. The same picture is repeated among the category of small employers and self-employed.[26]

Problems arising from the presence of a dual wage structure, largely having to do with the existence of a "double" standard for an otherwise democratic culture, were compounded as more and more members of the wage economy were granted wages comparable to those paid in the developed economies. As a greater percent-

[25] C. Ehrlich, "Some Social and Economic Consequences of Paternalism in Uganda," East Africa Institute of Social Research, 1959, p. 13.
[26] "Nigerian Workers Memorandum to the Morgan Salaries and Wages Review Commission 1963," *Joint Action Committee of Nigerian Trade Union Organization* (Lagos, 1963), pp. 12–13 (mimeographed).

age of the wage earners moved to the top of the wage structure, receiving not only higher wages but in addition allowances for automobiles, houses, and their childrens' education, retirement schemes, and "home leave" vacations to England, the system became top heavy.

The presence of the dual economy permitted those at the top to develop strong habits of conspicuous consumption of imported goods and services, not only for automobiles, radios, and wool suits but also for movies, records, and education abroad. As a high percentage moved up the wage scale, the number demanding foreign goods increased and the employment benefits of the expanding money economy were felt in London, Bristol, and Pittsburgh, rather than in Lagos, Port Harcourt, and Kaduna. Teachers in the government schools benefited from this escalation.

For 98 per cent of the teachers, however, the problem was not this differential, but the differential between the government teachers and those employed by voluntary agencies and local authorities; for two decades the Union campaigned for a narrowing of the gap between government and nongovernment salaries, by bringing the latter into line with the former.

The Union has always argued that the salaries for teachers in the voluntary agencies should be regulated and controlled through a national negotiating council composed of employers and teachers with an independent chairman. The purposes of such a plan were twofold, (1) to reduce regional and rural-urban wage differentials, and (2) to raise the level of wages in the mission schools and those administered by local authority. The voluntary agencies and local authorities, of course, resisted these proposals and insisted that the differentials only reflected differences in living costs in various parts of the country and that earnings of government teachers were already too high, given the realities of the Nigerian economy.

Before the adoption of a new federal constitution in 1954, the machinery for fixing wages in nongovernment schools was by a joint negotiating panel, chaired by Professor W. Hamilton-Whyte of the University College at Ibadan, and composed of teacher and employer representatives. The purpose of the Hamilton-Whyte panel was to "regulate teachers' conditions of service for the whole of Nigeria," [27] and its industry-wide approach reflected a general phi-

[27] "The Teachers' Case," Memorandum prepared by the Nigeria Union of Teachers for presentation to the National Joint Negotiating Council. (Yaba, 1964), p. 6.

losophy of the "Macpherson Constitution," which held that Nigeria was "an essentially unitary state with specific powers devolving from the center to the regions." [28] So long as Nigeria was controlled and administered by the British this was perhaps an appropriate vehicle, since all authority was derived and executed from the top. From a British standpoint, Nigeria was a single administrative unit and the colonial office applied the same wage schedule in Keffi, Calabar, and Sapele as it did in Lagos. A single wage schedule was a great aid in moving expatriate personnel from one locality to another, and it provided the colonial with extreme flexibility in administration. Given this background it was quite easy to assume that the same procedure was applicable to education. The major fault with such a policy was that it did not take into consideration that the salary schedule for indigenous teachers needed to be adjusted to local conditions.

With the abolition of the Macpherson Constitution in 1954, because it did not give enough autonomy to the three major ethnic groups in their respective regions, the Hamilton-Whyte panel was dissolved in favor of three regional panels, the Udochi Committee in the West, the Nibbert Committee in the North, and the Ibiam Committee in the East.[29] The Union, of course, was displeased with the new arrangement and campaigned to restore the machinery of the Hamilton-Whyte panel. The Union pushed for a national joint negotiating council, industry-wide bargaining, and wage equity in all areas for all teachers. To attain these ends, it favored a strong central government with little power left to the regions, and a continuation of the wage schedule as administered by the British.

Running through the political life of Nigeria has been a definite pull toward a strong central government, with urging for a weakening of the tribal-based regional governments that have always been controlled by the respective regional parties. The trade unions, and in particular the Teachers' Union, favor a strong central government and a weak regional structure, as have most of the intellectuals and the army officer corps. The short-lived Aguiyi-Ironsi regime, January to August of 1966, was crushed primarily because it attempted to bring into existence such a strong federal constitution and eliminate the old autonomous regional structure. The Fulani-Hausa emirates, their allies the NPC (Northern Peoples' Congress Teachers) and the North-dominated battalions of the army in the

28 Coleman, p. 371.
29 "The Teachers' Case," p. 6.

wake of the August coup, reaffirmed the hegemony of the regional regimes. Had the Aguiyi-Ironsi regime been able to stay in power, there is no doubt it would have received the backing of the trade unions, like the Teachers Union, for a return to a Macpherson type constitution. Arguing for the establishment of a national joint negotiating committee, the Teachers Union claimed,

One of the defects (of the 1954 Constitution) was that the different salary scales, which were agreed upon by the various Regions, differed widely from the other, so much so that the National Council of Establishments subsequently attempted to iron out the sharp differences, but no change was effected in the end. Another object . . . was that they (Regional Committees) were purely advisory bodies whose recommendations the Government was in no way bound to accept. This made them very different from the Hamilton-Whyte Committee whose recommendations were not modified by Government.[30]

Several factors accounted for the reluctance of the various regional governments to take the advice of the teachers' panels to eliminate zonal differences in wages. Most important was the establishment of universal, compulsory primary education. As the great step to eliminate illiteracy, the scheme for free primary education was abandoned as the discussion earlier indicated. The plan, even if it had to be reduced in scope, nonetheless left the wage schedule in the hands of the local areas and reduced the influence of the central government. Another reason for the reluctance of the regional governments to agree to a nationwide wage scale was that such a system would elevate the significance of the central government and thereby reduce the authority of regional and ethnic political parties and their respective administrations. In addition, the Northern and Eastern wage scales were considerably lower than those of the Western Region, and these governments argued in favor of zonal differentials.

EDUCATION IN TRANSITION

Over the years, the comparative isolation from the rest of the trade union movement which the Teachers' Union imposed upon itself has had a number of consequences. By concentrating upon the problems of education and the particular controversies associated therewith, the Union has been able to maintain an active and stable membership and to attain considerable status as a "reliable"

[30] *Ibid.*, p. 7.

organization. The stability of membership, in turn, has been a major factor contributing to the Union's financial strength. While no Nigerian union was ever financially solvent, measured by standards in the advanced economics, the Teachers' Union was one of the few that was able to function independent of the several Nigerian trade union counsels supported either by the WFTU (World Federation of Trade Unions) or ICFTU (International Confederation of Free Trade Unions). This independence was reinforced by the very important role of education, since the increasing demand provided a buoyancy to an expanding membership. Nevertheless, the Union always took a conservative attitude with respect to educational philosophy in that it supported what Azikime called education for "alphabetists." The top leadership, moreover, was more concerned with raising the salary of the few government teachers to parity with other government salaries than with the plight of the thousands of poorly qualified and uncertified teachers in the schools administered by the missions and local authorities. The Union had a quality bias, meaning that it was constantly concerned with raising the teacher's standards of performance as applied to an elite, with the result that it usually was in the camp of the accommodationists. The main body of Nigeria's trade union movement, on the other hand, was more radical and played a very active role in the nationalist movement.

The aloofness of the Teachers' Union to the political struggles which absorbed the other major unions relegated it to a generally conservative role, disassociating the leadership from the aspirations and activities of the great majority of the country's workers. The characteristic of separatism is something the Nigerian teachers share with teachers in other cultures. Until quite recently teachers have thought and acted differently from workers engaged in production or in subprofessional and unskilled services. They have been alienated from the aims and tactics of other occupational and skill groups by customs, mores, aspirations, and by the nature of the industry in which they labor.

The particular set of circumstances which, in a given society, differentiated the teacher from other workers was primarily a function of the prevailing socioeconomic conditions. In the advanced economies, the teacher's self-image was one in which he saw himself as carrying the major responsibility for transmitting societies' norms and values to the youth. His role, therefore, was to maintain the status quo; his values were middle class, his aspirations professional and administrative, and his politics conservative. He willingly assumed responsibilities which other workers did not share and he did not identify with them or embrace their trade union tactics. Historically, for example, the American teacher has looked upon collective bargaining as a socially disruptive practice and not worthy of his professional participation. Acting through various "education associations" the teachers have resorted to political lobbying to bring improvements in working conditions through changes in legislation. The American teacher has been restricted to interpreting and disseminating, rather than formulating, educational policy.

Teachers in a country such as Nigeria, have had to operate under a quite different set of circumstances. They, too, have transmitted society's values to youth; in a society in transition, however, the role has been that of agent provocateur. While the teacher lived by the old order, he expounded the new. As an employee of the voluntary agencies and committed to teaching as a means to conversion, he could not transmit the traditional norms and values, for the classroom and the teacher-converter are symbols of a new order. Meanwhile, the teacher's living and working conditions, and those of his pupils, continued to be those of the old culture, little changed by the knowledge and the norms of the new religion and way of life. Perhaps for this reason, he was politically conservative, seeking neither to formulate nor to interpret but merely to transmit an educational system that had little relevance for that segment of the masses reached by primary and/or even secondary education. The great realization that the white man did not live by the code of his own religion was something the Nigerian's grasped very early and is part of the reason that Christianity had so little influence on their daily lives.

Nigeria's educational policies were formulated by the colonizing power and its spokesmen, the clergy. The system was designed to produce a politically conservative clerical class, subservient to the administrative functions of a colonial power. Western education, transmitted with a static rigidity to the Nigerian child of the southern regions disrupted the satisfaction with a traditional culture, but did little to shape a new culture in which the various ethnic groups were equipped to participate in the crucial decisions of state. The conservatism of the leaders of the Teachers' Union, and the policies they helped formulate, reflected the even greater conservatism of portions of the Nigerian elite who attained higher education in the universities of Europe and America. Alienated from their heritage, the elite sought to maintain their positions of prestige and economic advantage and to impose the ceremonial trappings of a so-called democratic and open society. The failure of Western education in Nigeria was due to the hypocrisy of those who taught and of those elite who received the most of it. Emulating the living standards and status symbols of Western culture, Nigeria's educated elite retarded rather than fostered the shaping of a new culture. Their tragedy was that they learned nothing of the needs and difficulties associated with the "great ascent," as they were incapable of providing the necessary leadership. The "chop politician," concerned more with his own advantage than with the country's rate of growth, had been alienated from the values of his traditional society by Western education.

Nnamdie Azikiwe protested, in 1937, that Nigeria's educational system had failed to produce "the moral courage which is the basis of dynamic leadership," encouraging instead "the existence of a privileged class of alphabetists" and facilitating "the claims of Uncle Toms to leadership." [31] The course of events since independence has borne Azikiwe out, evidencing that neither Western education nor the participation in colonial governmental administration prepared Nigerians to formulate or run an independent government in which progress and change are key ingredients.

The function of government during the British regime was mainly a policing operation, as exemplified by the "district order"; record-keeping and codification were the means and practices of government. With independence, however, the role of government changed; and administrators, politicians, and advisors were required to develop and foster a development program which could enlarge and expand the economy's modern sector. The task not only required a knowledge of engineering, biology, agronomy, demography, and economics, but also forward planning and an investment scheme designed to disrupt the status quo. Not only had the educational system failed to provide a curriculum equal to the new task, but more important, it had produced a mental attitude that was antagonistic to the needs of a developing economy. Those who fell heir to political control looked upon government activity as a record-

31 Nnamdie Azikiwe, *Renascent Africa* (Accra, 1937), p. 135.

keeping and administrative function. Having achieved, through independence, a place in the power structure, they viewed change as a threat to that structure, and to the advantages they would derive from it.[32]

The strong literary bias of Nigeria's educational system also contributed to the difficulties which the system had in shifting to rural and technical development. For many decades the agricultural sector will be the major employment outlet for the expanding population, and continuation of a system that was developed to lure people to the urban centers has many repercussions. Moreover, the problems of an emerging economy require an educational system that aids, rather than deters, in their solution. An example of the way in which the old educational system has contributed to the difficulties is urban unemployment, undoubtedly Nigeria's major economic problem before the War of Biafran Secession. The same system Azikiwe criticized, and the one the majority of teachers transmitted even after independence, produced thousands of "alphabetists" who flocked to the urban centers, disdaining the agricultural sector because their "education" instilled aspirations it could not fulfill. Primary education of a literary bent should not be expanded beyond a certain ratio to the foreseeable intake of the secondary system. Otherwise the primary school "leavers" will flock to the overcrowded cities where they will only swell the rising unemployment that occurs because the number of openings in the wage economy does not expand rapidly enough. Possessing few skills, if any, the primary school "leavers" were educated by a system devised to satisfy the needs of a colonial administration that had no desire to alter any of the traditional societies of the rural areas in Nigeria. The old educational system drove the primary school "leavers" out of the agricultural sector, where economic development was most necessary if the modern sector was to develop and expand. The increasing column of urban unemployment was in the 1960's testimony to the fact that the requisite development was not occurring, in either sector, as well as the fact that the education system alienated the youth from the agricultural economy. The first six-year plan (1961–1967) hypothesized the need for a four per cent

[32] For a discussion of the difficulties caused by the failure of the various government agencies to produce viable and feasible projects suitable for foreign aid, see: Edwin R. Dean, "Factors Impeding the Implementation of Nigeria's Six-Year Plan," *Nigerian Journal of Economic and Social Studies,* Vol. 8, No. 1 (March 1966), pp. 113–128.

growth rate and discussed the major problem of overcoming the shortages of labor and manpower. The planners did not envision the possibility of increasing unemployment, and stressed the problem of shortages of manpower. By the time of the drafting of the second plan, in 1966, the only mention of manpower as a guide post was the need for a "rapid solution of the present unemployment problem." The education system, one of the root causes of urban unemployment, had added to Nigeria's difficulties rather than helped to alleviate them.

The imposition of a British-type educational system upon the Nigerian economy, with all the *accoutrements* of the "sixth-form" and General Certificate of Education did not prove satisfactory to the task of economic development. Academic or literary education, with its emphasis upon the creation of an elite corps of specialists, was Nigeria's claim to the heritage of political and religious experience of mankind.[33] It was necessary, in a sense, because it opened the doors of the universities of the West to the competent Nigerian student. Without the "sixth-form," the graduate of a Lagos academy could not have entered the Univerity of London, let alone Oxbridge. But when Nigeria extended education to a broader base, using the same type of education that was utilized to produce university graduates, the system was found to be defective.

For a small elite group, the alienation from Nigerian cultures which a literary education produced was not of great consequence, since the few were easily absorbed into professional, business, and political activities. But when this system was extended to a large percentage of the school-age population, frustration, unemployment, and discontent resulted. Little or no attention was given to the question of what the primary and secondary school leavers would do when they finished their studies, as the educational system turned out thousands of youths eager to escape the rural sector. The country needed more rural employment and rising productivity in agriculture to finance the expansion of the modern sector, and this could not be achieved without a broadly based educational system that was designed for these purposes.

The Nigerian teacher, and his trade union, the Nigeria Union of Teachers, was involved in an educational system that was both alien to his heritage and daily life and out of tune with the needs of a developing and expanding society. So long as Nigeria was a Brit-

[33] Guy Hunter, *The New Societies of Tropical Africa* (New York: Praeger University Series, 1964), p. 246.

ish colony, the educational system was adequate to its purposes, for it fed the need for junior clerks to transfer papers from the desk of one colonial administrator to another. Given independence, the tasks were different, but the same system continued and the teacher became an anachronism trapped by the system, and his leaders were not very interested in changing his role. Heretofore, he had been the bridge between the traditional societies and modernity. His services were demanded only if suitable jobs were available for the type of students he trained. The door to success for those with an education closed very quickly, however, when a larger percentage of the population was trained than the modern sector could absorb.

The paradox was that the traditional, rural sector provided the education, and paid for it, but the training was designed for and usable only in the modern sector. The teacher himself was the exception. His locus of employment remained "in the bush" from whence his pupils came. His life was not unlike that of the peasant farmer, for though he was differently occupied and earned a money wage, it did not provide him with the amenities of the city or change, basically, his way of life. He ate the rural diet, lived in a traditional mud house, and followed the local ritual and customs. Yet he did not participate, as a producer, in the village economy. Instead, he was the purveyor of an intervening culture which rewarded endeavors quite different from those of his village brothers.

Thus, the teacher's position in a country in transition is an awkward one. He is both a part of the village community and yet set apart from it by his role as an educator. Nor has he a less tenuous place in the new culture. Here, too, he is a member, is indeed its spokesman, but he is more truly set apart from the new culture than from the old, participating in it collectively only. Approximately 80 per cent of all Nigerians still live in rural areas, and it is here that Western education takes place. The typical Nigerian teacher continues to be a rural village master, not a city dweller.

Unlike the urban wage earner, who is a city dweller, the village teacher's daily life is rural. He does not observe the pleasures and material advantages of city life, even though he might aspire to increase his share of them. This is neither to say that Nigerian teachers are devoid of material aspirations, nor that they are ignorant of the modern world. But the teacher's standard of living, relative to the village community, is high. He is not subject to the daily contrast provided by the homes, automobiles, clothing, clubs, and food-stuffs displayed by expatriates and the indigenous elite of the urban areas.

Nor is he in close or frequent contact with the educated segment of Nigerian society, associating freely with the commercial and professional classes. Before the War of Biafran Secession, he occasionally attended an educational conference of a meeting of the Teachers' Union and perhaps at these times he felt a part of all that the city represents. But he could not be thoroughly at ease in the unfamiliar surroundings of a hotel or rest house equipped with modern plumbing and frequented by the educated elite. These occasions primarily served to bring him together with other rural teachers to discuss the professional aims and problems relating to an educational system designed for city life, even though he normally lived in comparative isolation.

Although the leadership of the Teachers' Union in Lagos had greater contact and communication with the government, the rural teacher had little opportunity to gain a broad awareness of political and economic issues. Standing as he did with one foot in the new order and one in the old, both his knowledge and his experience were limited to the educational system itself and to the curriculum he agreed to transmit. He did not question the content of that curriculum nor the function of an educational system in a developing society. Simply, he had a job to do, and as a semi-intellectual proletariate, he wanted more wages and better working conditions.

The city worker readily assessed the inequities of his position and identified the difficulties of unemployment and low wages with political inaction and inefficiency. He looked to the government to alter the political and economic system under which his standard of living had declined since independence; the workers' opportunities dwindled in the face of increasing wealth conspicuously concentrated in the hands of the few. Individually, he was powerless to improve the conditions of his life; collectively he had little economic bargaining power in an economy dominated by large numbers of unemployed. His demands were made in the political arena where pressure was brought to bear on the decisions which only maintained the status quo.

But the rural teacher was a part of that status quo and was not oppressed by it. His professional status and his money income gave him both prestige and high standard of living in a rural setting, identifying him with the modern culture as he identified his self-interest with government policy. His role, politically, was to maintain and expand the system which he served. He had neither the means of changing it, nor any reason to do so, and that is why he was politically inactive and voted not to participate in the general strikes of 1964.

The rural environment of the great majority of Nigeria's teachers, the professional orientation of the leadership, and the educational system of which they were a part, each contributed to the isolation of the Union from the aims and tactics of the Nigerian trade union movement. Historically this isolation was an asset, both to the Union and to its members, as they benefited from the harmonious relations with the colonial government and the negotiation of their problems. But the social and political unrest that disrupted Nigeria threatens to destroy the teacher's ivory tower, for Nigeria will not be a united economy for many years to come. The trend, even before the outbreak of the current hostilities was toward division of authority and responsibility, and the old control at the center in Lagos was disappearing. This development will, undoubtedly, fractionalize the field of education, even more than was the case prior to 1967. The Nigerian teacher's role, as he has known it, may be in jeopardy and likewise the Nigeria Union of Teachers may be in peril.

Thailand 8

David K. Heenan and Stanley P. Wronski

SCHOOL AND SOCIETY

The educational system in Thailand, like that of any society, is the product of the social forces in which it is immersed—namely, the major social institutions in Thai society. These institutions frequently differ to a significant degree in form, substance, underlying purpose, and direction from those found in Western society. It is not within the scope of this chapter to analyze in detail these social institutions. But it is useful—indeed imperative—to identify those facets of various institutions which relate to, impinge upon, or influence the educational enterprise in Thailand.

The primary and most pervasive influence in the educational system in Thailand is Buddhism. The manifestations of Buddhism in education are myriad. They range from the overt and obvious to the subtle, value-laden actions that can be explained only by the individual's personal interpretation of what Buddhist tenets should dictate under the given situation. The Western observer of Thai education is soon confronted with most unlikely and initially surprising manifestations of the close relationship between religion and education. Nearly every formal meeting of teachers, administrators, or other governmental officials is begun with a so-called "opening ceremony." It is a quasi-religious activity in which from one to several Buddhist monks take an integral part. Both religious and lay leaders of the ceremony pay respects to the Lord Buddha

DAVID K. HEENAN and STANLEY P. WRONSKI are Professors in the College of Education, Michigan State University.

whose status always adorns the omnipresent ceremonial altar. There is no wall of separation between church and state here. Not only are the two tolerated together; it is unthinkable to the Thai that they be separate.

Examples of the obvious relationship between religion and education in Thailand are ubiquitous. What is even more important is the interaction between the two in matters of values and beliefs. Teachers or students, for instance, frequently ask the Prime Minister some version of the question, "What can we do to assist you and our nation in its program of development?" His normal reply has become almost a national symbol: "Do good, do good, do good." As with many verbal symbols it appears vague and platitudinous. But such an interpretation would not do justice to its impact on the Thai people. It is merely the contemporary application of the admonition laid down by the Lord Buddha over 2500 years ago. Contrary to the connotation that the phrase conjures up in the Western —especially American—mind, the "do-gooder" in Thailand is a person to be respected, not scorned.

The question may be seriously raised as to whether Buddhism— or any other religion, for that matter—which has such a pervasive impact on the educational system is a stultifying force on educational development. Criticisms have been voiced of some Buddhist teachings which appear to be in conflict with social and ethical practices accompanying the rapid social and economic changes of the past few years. But working out a viable accommodation to conflicting patterns of beliefs and values is one of the redeeming traits of the Thai people. They would prefer to accept and emphasize the areas of common agreement rather than to dwell upon the schisms. Thus it appears that for the foreseeable future the schools and the temples can work hand in hand in promoting such generally agreed-upon virtues as diligence, thrift, respect for parents and elders, benevolence, and moderation.

Buddhism has still another attribute which, if not unique among religions, is still unusual and is a factor which facilitates its close affiliation with education. Unlike most other religions Buddhism invites, welcomes, and even insists upon critical evaluation of its own philosophical tenets, for faith alone is not sufficient for acceptance of the Buddhist religion. This religious concept has enormous significance for education in Thailand. Whereas in many societies faith may present an obstacle to the search for truth, in

Thailand it is a potential facilitator. Of course, a given individual may privately hold beliefs which impede his learning. Buddhism is so permissive a religion that this could readily happen. But it is unlikely that in Thai society there would be the head-on clashes between, for example, science and religion which have been so frequently the case in Western civilization.

The second major social institution that impinges on education in Thailand is the government. And in Thailand when one speaks of the government, one speaks of the monarchy. For the salient political fact of life about the Royal Thai Government is that it is indeed a monarchy—albeit a limited or constitutional one. (The word "constitutional" may properly evoke some righteous disagreement. The constitutional assembly, after several years of delay, finally promulgated a written constitution in 1968.) The King appears genuinely well-liked and almost universally respected—even revered. The close relationship between the government and religion is augmented in that the King is also the patron of Buddhism. This relationship is extended to the schools in that they are required by law to set aside regular periods for religious instruction, to hold appropriate ceremonies on certain religious holidays, and to observe the King's birthday as a holiday. In the minds of the Thai people not only has the King earned merits, he deserves what he has earned. It is not surprising, therefore, that pictures of the King and Queen are prominently displayed in nearly every room of every school in the kingdom.

A third major institution is that of the economy, but the relationship between the schools and the economy in Thailand is indirect and less apparent than in the case of religion and government. The base of the Thai economy is agriculture. Eighty-two per cent of the population is engaged in agriculture; about 70 per cent of the Gross National Product emanates from the agricultural sector. One obvious relationship between the economy and the schools emerges from this pattern: the vast majority of the students ultimately become farmers or are employed in some phase of agriculture. This fact directly influences the thinking of many Thais about the schools and the function and purposes of education. Why should a child be educated beyond acquiring the elementary ability to read, write, and do simple arithmetic? Many would answer that additional education is superfluous and wasteful. They argue that education beyond the fourth grade is not necessary for one who will spend most

of his time working in a rice paddy. Indeed, the greatest dropout
rate at the present time occurs after the completion of *Pratom*
(Grade) 4 (see Figure 1). It is true that the officially stated policy
of the Thai Ministry of Education is to implement the Karachi
Plan—which calls for universal public education at least through
the seventh grade. But it is extremely unlikely that this goal will be
achieved even within the next 20 years. A second relationship between the economy and the schools arises because, with such a large
part of the population engaged in agriculture and with the widespread diffusion of this population throughout the nation, schools
are widely separated and have relatively small enrollments. The
consequences of this arrangement are the usual concomitants of
small rural schools: crude physical facilities, inadequate instructional materials, and poorly paid and poorly prepared classroom
teachers. The third and probably most significant relationship between the economy and the schools, as far as teacher organizations
are concerned, arises out of the relatively small industrial sector
within the total economy. In most industrialized nations, whether
in the East or the West, the process of industrialization has been
accompanied by certain identifiable social and economic developments, among these are social welfare legislation, specific legislation
affecting wages and working conditions, and labor unionism (which
is sometimes aided and sometimes impeded by legislation). But
industrialization is still relatively new in Thailand, in spite of what
the casual visitor to Bangkok may surmise, and labor unionism has
developed even more slowly. Several reasons may be given for the
slow growth of unionism in Thailand (see the latter part of this
chapter), but regardless of reasons the net effect has been to deprive
teachers of either a model for organizing themselves or an on-going
vehicle to which they could attach their own organization.

The pattern of family life in Thailand is another social institution which exerts a subtle but pervasive influence on Thai education. In a real sense the schools may be looked upon as an extension
of the influences acting upon the child from the informal ones of
the home to the more formally structured ones of the school room.
The most binding common ground for both of these loci of influence is again the Buddhist religion. But an important secular factor
also affects the relationship between family and school. It is the
phenomenon of social class. Whether in an up-country village or in
metropolitan Bangkok, a subtle social scale develops on which any-

FIGURE 1. THE PYRAMID OF ENROLLMENTS 1964

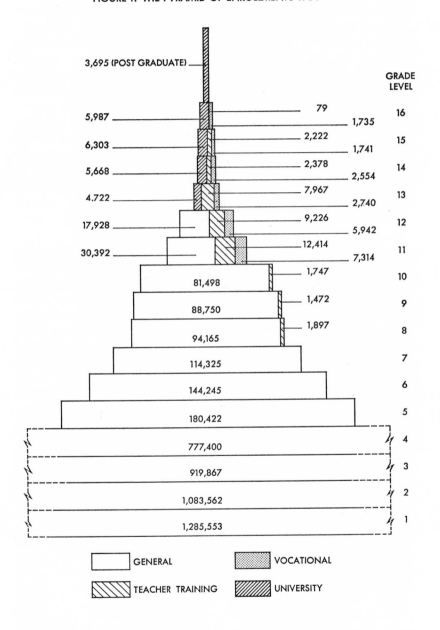

body who aspires to be anybody is placed. The typical social class determinants operate: occupation, income, heredity, and other visible symbols of affluence such as type and location of home, chauffeur-driven automobiles, membership in the "right" clubs, and friendship patterns. The children of parents in the higher social class will have more ready access to schools, will probably get preferential treatment within the schools, will be able to afford private secondary schools, and upon graduation from a university will have greater access to positions in the private or public sector of the economy. In addition to the social class factors, Thai society is also characterized by a hierarchy based on royal titles, which result in caste as well as a class structure. The interrelationship of caste and more especially class determinants within the total family patterns in Thailand results in a latent power structure of enormous influence. A chart depicting the formal organization of a governmental agency, for example, may show two individuals as far removed from each other in the chain of command. In fact, the two may have very close and frequent interaction because they are close personal friends, they are relatives, they are both friends of a third person, or because of many other reasons which are not or cannot be expressed on an organization chart. The net result is that the entire bureaucratic power structure—including that involving the educational system—is a complex blend of personal, aristocratic, and official relationships.

The Structure of Thai Education

Out of the social forces and conditions of Thai society, a distinctive educational system has emerged. An understanding of the structure of this system contributes to an understanding of those organizations concerned with teacher welfare. Figure 2 depicts the organization of the Ministry of Education in Thailand.

As with most other nations outside the Western Hemisphere, Thailand has a centralized system of education. The American concept of local control and authority is nonexistent.[1] The central government in Bangkok is the source of almost all funds for education. The Ministry of Education is the main policy-making agency in matters pertaining to education. This Ministry is one of eleven

[1] As this is being written, the Thai government has announced its intention to transfer elementary education from the Ministry of Education to the Ministry of Interior—ostensibly to promote local control.

FIGURE 2. MINISTRY OF EDUCATION ORGANIZATION

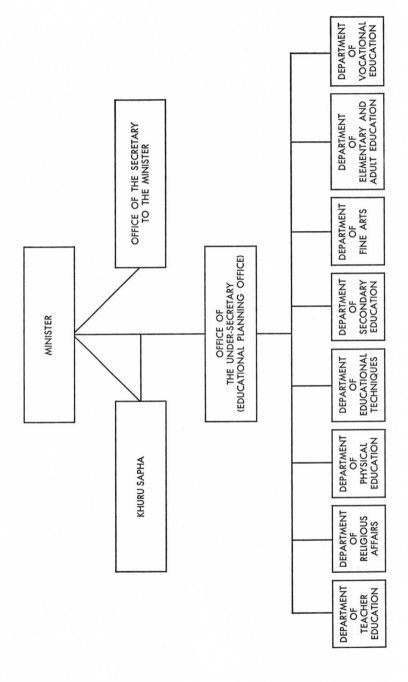

FIGURE 3. ARTICULATION CHART OF THE THAILAND SCHOOL SYSTEM BY LEVEL AND TYPE OF COURSE

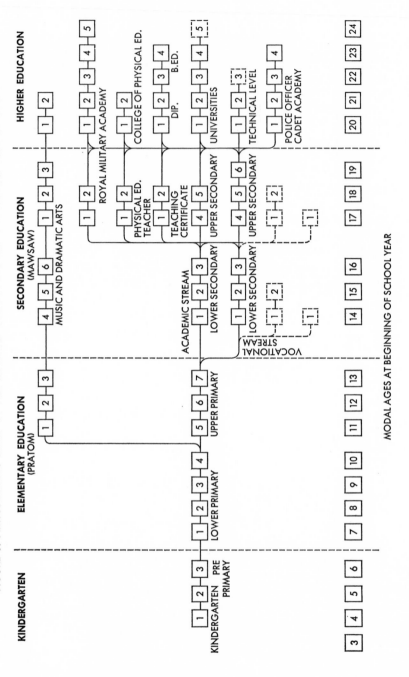

such Ministries. The heads of these Ministries plus other key government officials constitute the Prime Minister's Cabinet. As with all such centralized forms of government, there are some inherent advantages. Curriculum changes, for example, can be decided upon, promulgated, and implemented in a relatively short time. There is no necessity—although it may be strategically desirable—to secure local approval. It should also be noted from Figure 2 that the Khuru Sapha, the most influential teacher organization in Thailand, has quasi-official standing within the Ministry of Education. This organization will be discussed in greater detail later in this chapter.

Figure 3 depicts the various components of the school system within the Ministry of Education. It shows the types of schools by tracks (or "streams" as they are referred to in Thailand), the relationship of grade level to age levels, and the dividing points between elementary, secondary, and higher education. Although Figure 3 shows a large number of possible paths from elementary to higher education, the most significant categorization is between the academic and vocational streams. Most students who have survived *Pratom* (Grade) 7 are faced at that point with the decision to choose to pursue either the academic or vocational stream. Those who do not make the decision at that point are forced to make it at *Matayom Suksa* (abbreviated *Maw Saw* or *MS*) 4, i.e., the beginning of the eleventh grade. This sharp demarcation between academic and vocational streams is frequently reflected in teachers' organizations, which also tend to consist of academic or vocational teachers but not both. The Khuru Sapha is an exception to this rule because all teachers are required by law to be members.

The Educational Pyramid

Still another characteristic of the Thai educational system which has a bearing on teacher organizations is the pattern of enrollments from primary grades to higher education levels. This pattern is most effectively depicted by the so-called educational pyramid. The one for Thailand is shown in Figure 1. An examination of this figure reveals the following significant observations concerning the "productivity" of the system in Thailand.

1. There are two levels in the educational ladder where there are substantial numbers of dropouts: after *Pratom* 4 and *MS* 3.

2. The largest number of dropouts, in both absolute numbers

and percentage, occurs after *Pratom* 4. Approximately four out of every five pupils completing *Pratom* 4 do not continue their schooling and are absorbed into the economy.

3. The attrition rate at *MS* 3 is of such magnitude that only about one out of two pupils continues to *MS* 4. These students are at an age (about 15–16) when they would normally enter the labor force. Most of them will have pursued a program in the academic stream rather than a vocational program.

4. For the secondary school grades alone, the productivity of the system is such that for approximately every five pupils entering at *MS* 1, only one pupil will complete *MS* 5 or 6.

This sharply peaked educational pyramid has significance also for teacher organizations in Thailand. Most important of all is that the overwhelming majority of teachers are in the elementary schools. Their own level of preparation is low (an average of about 11 years of schooling) as are their professional aspirations. The concept of professionalism is ill-defined for most of them. Even further removed is the notion of banding together with their associates for the purpose of improving their professional position. Most teachers' organizations in Thailand consist of those with special subject matter interests, those who teach in private schools, or those in higher administrative positions. These categories normally do not include elementary teachers.

THE KHURU SAPHA

By far the most influential and inclusive teacher organization in Thailand is the Khuru Sapha. It is a unique association blending governmental paternalism, individual self-interest, and professional aspirations. That it is established by law and that membership in it is compulsory for all teachers immediately connotes a kind of "company union." But it would be a mistake to apply this analogy too literally. It should be kept in mind that all public school teachers in Thailand are civil servants. The various obligations and prerequisites associated with membership in the Khuru Sapha are viewed by the typical teacher as an extension of the larger pattern of civil service regulations covering job description, pay, allowances, leave, fringe benefits, and the like.

The Khuru Sapha came into being with the Teacher Act of 1945 (Buddhist Era, or B. E. 2488). It succeeded a previous teacher association called Samakayacharn Samakom, which has been referred to as combining the functions of in-service training and an "amusement center" for teachers. The Khuru Sapha was intended to improve the low morale of teachers after World War II. Its major functions may be grouped into two categories: (1) the promotion of teacher qualifications, and (2) the promotion of teacher welfare.

Activities Relating to Teacher Qualifications

Although the Teacher Training Department within the Ministry of Education is mainly responsible for teacher improvement, the Khuru Sapha carries on many significant in-service training programs. In carrying out these programs, Khuru Sapha frequently uses personnel and physical facilities of the Teacher Training Department and other agencies of the Ministry. It prepares, plans, and executes such programs. These programs consist of (1) those carried on during the summer vacation period, and (2) those carried on during the regular school year.

Summer Programs

The normal school vacation period in Thailand falls approximately between March 15 and May 15. The main Khuru Sapha headquarters building, located within the Ministry of Education compound, is a busy place during this time. Teachers and administrators from all parts of the country are there. The key programs carried on by Khuru Sapha in Bangkok and elsewhere are the following:

1. Study groups. Meetings are held in conveniently located large communities where teachers may gather. These study groups may listen to lectures, go on tours, or engage in discussion of various teaching problems. In addition to improving their professional knowledge, the teachers participating in these study groups gain a better understanding of their fellow teachers from other parts of the country.

2. Professional lecture program. Khuru Sapha sends out teams of lecturers—about four or five to a team—to various parts of the country. These teams usually stay for about one week in any given locality. The lectures deal with matters pertaining to professional education and academic disciplines.

3. Tour groups. This program enables teachers to gain a knowledge of the geography and culture of a locality, a region, or a

foreign country. Khuru Sapha has provided inland tours by bamboo raft along the Ping Tributary in the north and by boat along the east and west coast of the country. Foreign tours have been made to Burma and Malaysia.

4. Training courses for promotion examinations. One of the most popular programs is the course that assists and prepares teachers for the qualification promotion examination. By passing these examinations a teacher may obtain a higher diploma or certificate. These, in turn, enable the teacher to be promoted in rank and salary. Such courses are offered in Bangkok and throughout the country. Tuition fees are nominal.

Continuing Education Programs

Throughout the school year Khuru Sapha conducts programs for the professional improvement of teachers. These programs include the following: (1) Lectures, delivered over an educational radio station; (2) low cost pamphlets dealing with educational topics and distributed nationwide; (3) a circulating library, made available to teachers so that they may borrow books for as long as one year; (4) two educational journals—one emphasizing elementary education, and the other secondary education; and (5) (in the Bangkok-Thonburi area) various lectures, discussions, and movies, scheduled throughout the year.

Activities Relating to Teacher Welfare

The Teacher Act of 1945 stipulates that the most important function of Khuru Sapha is the promotion of teacher welfare. There is little doubt that the organization has taken this charge seriously. It has initiated a wide range of activities affecting the teacher's life from pre-service days until death. Many of these activities are the type that social welfare agencies in other countries would normally carry out. They include the following:

1. Land settlement for teachers. Khuru Sapha has purchased a large tract of land in Samutsakorn (about 40 miles from Bangkok) and has subdivided it into 1,103 parcels. Teachers have an opportunity to purchase this land on an installment plan basis for 74 *baht* (approximately $3.75) per *rai* (approximately one-half acre).

2. Assistance to teachers whose homes have been destroyed by fire. Fires in the highly flammable Thai houses are a frequent occurence. Khuru Sahpa provides a 500 *baht* grant for the purchase of clothes for teachers whose houses were burned.

3. Teachers' dormitory in Bangkok. Teachers from up-country frequently find it necessary or desirable to visit Bangkok. Dormitory rooms at modest cost are provided for such teachers.

4. Tours of Bangkok. In addition to dormitory space, the Khuru Sapha also arranges tours and provides guides for teachers visiting Bangkok.

5. Assistance in furthering the education of teachers' children who intend to become teachers themselves. Khuru Sapha issues certificates to children of teachers who in turn present them to schools they plan to attend. Although these certificates do not guarantee admission, they do facilitate the process and enhance the probability that the student will be accepted.

6. Operation of a commercial store. Khuru Sapha has its own store at which teachers may trade. Prices are generally lower than those prevailing in privately operated stores.

7. Health clinic. A Khuru Sapha operated health center is available to teachers. Fees are generally lower than those charged by private physicians.

8. Death benefits. Khuru Sapha levies a flat 50 *satang* (about 2½ cents) assessment on each teacher. This money is used primarily to pay for the cremation ceremonies. If any amount is not used, it reverts to the children of the deceased.

The number and breadth of activities carried on by the Khuru Sapha suggest a vigorous and aggressive organization. To some extent this is so. But there are still drawbacks to its effectiveness as an agency which ought to have the immediate and long-range best interests of the teachers at heart. One of the most significant of these drawbacks is that it is legally an entity within the framework of the Thai government. Aside from whatever advantages may accrue to it because of its position, there is the undeniable consequence that government officials rather than classroom teachers or even school administrators dominate the organization. A second drawback is the teachers' own lack of knowledge about the organization. Up-country teachers know about it only in the vaguest way. This lack of knowledge breeds indifference, noninvolvement, and noncommitment to the profession. A third deficiency is illustrated by the remark of a high Khuru Sapha official who was describing the various programs carried out by the organization—lectures, conferences, tours, study groups etc. When asked what the Khuru Sapha had in mind when the current series of programs was completed, he thought for a while and then replied, "Well, I guess we would then start all over with more of the same." There was little or no concern with new programs, new approaches, new concerns. Particularly lacking was a feeling of greater aggressiveness on behalf of teacher welfare and teacher autonomy. Finally, and probably most significant of all, is the near absence of many attributes of professionalism in most teachers in Thailand. Their low salaries and low positions in the civil service have had the inevitable consequence of placing them far down the list of prestigious professions in Thailand. Although the Khuru Sapha is making valiant and conscientious efforts to improve the situation, the status of the teaching profession with respect to other occupational groups in Thailand has not significantly improved over the past several years.

OTHER TEACHER ORGANIZATIONS

Two primary factors provided the impetus for the establishment of a large number of teachers' organizations after World War II. First, the setting up of the Khuru Sapha was very important because it demonstrated to teachers the value of having an agency which could speak on their behalf both in extending teacher benefits and making their desires known to the policy-making bodies in the government. The Khuru Sapha also pointed out the uniqueness of teachers in the society by showing that their common concerns and interests could best be served by banding together in their own organization.

The second impetus came from an external source, i.e., new ideas from abroad. Prior to World War II the educational system of Thailand was patterned after the British system, adapted, of course, to the traditions, customs, and needs peculiar to Thailand. One can get a notion of the conservatism and parochialism in the educational system by reading *Anna and the King of Siam* (unfortunately, the main source of information about Thailand to many people in the Western world). An unusual sequence of events during and after the war brought the Thais into closer contact with the West, particularly the United States; these events brought many changes in the educational system as well as other institutions—private and public. During World War II, Thailand was occupied by Japanese troops, and the Thai government even declared war against the United States and Great Britain. In the late stages of the fighting, when it was apparent that Japan was going to be defeated, a new group of political leaders came into power, and sought to gain favor with the Allies. This group, supported by the very active Free Thai underground that had helped the Allies and harrassed the Japanese during the war, was able to convince the United States that Thailand should not be treated as one of the defeated nations. The United States, on its part, was eager to have friends and contacts in Southeast Asia in the post-war years and, consequently, treated Thailand leniently after the war.

Shortly after the struggle ended, the United States began an extensive program of aid to encourage technological development as well as to promote a better understanding and mutual cooperation between the two nations. Part of this program included sending outstanding Thai teachers, administrators, and governmental officials to the United States for further training and advanced educational degrees in the American universities. One of the important by-products of these visits was exposure to many new experiences and ideas which had relevance for and could be adapted to the educational institutions and system in a developing country such as Thailand. Included in these experiences were new methods of learning, emphasis on quality in education, teaching aids, and teacher organizations. American practices and philosophies of education have had a great impact on the educational system of Thailand. Several thousand Thais have been sent to the United States and many now hold positions in the government or other policy-making agencies or institutions.

Many scholars and officials who returned to Thailand were impressed with the teachers' organizations they found in the United States and were instrumental in founding organizations which would help improve the quality of and extend educational opportunities to young people. These organizations do not act primarily as bargaining agents for teachers but are more concerned with improving teachers' social and intellectual well-being. Now, in addition to Khuru Sapha, a number of these organizations are established and are providing teachers with a collective voice to improve the educational system. A short description of a few of these organizations will help to show their nature and functions.

Education Society of Thailand

One of the organizations initiated by teachers returning from abroad is the Education Society of Thailand. This society is an exclusive (honorary) organization which includes some of the most distinguished teachers in the kingdom. In 1965 it had only about two hundred members; new members are nominated and elected by the existing membership. Its primary purpose is to bring together dedicated educators who are concerned with improving the quality of education at all levels and instilling in teachers a greater awareness of their professional responsibilities. A limiting factor to the effectiveness of this group is the lack of adequate finances. Initiation fees supplemented by some funds from the Asia Foundation and the World Confederation of Organizations of the Teaching Profession (WCOTP) enable the group to issue a few publications, permit members to travel to give lectures or conduct seminars for teachers or parent-teacher groups, purchase time for radio and television broadcasts, etc.—all of which is done without remuneration to the members. The Education Society has carried on a number of significant activities which have contributed to the improvement of teaching, and hence, the education of Thai children. Some examples of the work they do include special training courses for teachers to prepare them for the examinations required for certification; publication of the *Education Center Magazine,* which carries articles on diverse subjects such as different philosophies of education, the role of the teacher in society, new developments and research in education, counseling of students, and the use of school libraries. Members of the society are expected to help write textbooks for the elementary and secondary schools.

The Education Society of Thailand has made a number of significant contributions to the educational system of Thailand, mostly by bringing attention to the need to improve educational standards and instruction. While they recognize the need to increase teacher salaries and other teacher benefits, they do not consider this need an appropriate function of their organization.

Epsilon Pi Tau

A second honorary teachers organization, which was initiated in the post-war years, is Epsilon Pi Tau. The membership of this group is by invitation from the existing members and includes leaders (teachers and laymen) in the fields of industrial arts, vocational and technical education, industry, and labor administration. This is a branch of an international society which has its headquarters in the United States. Although it is primarily concerned with the teachers in industrial arts and vocational education, it does bring together people who are not directly involved in education but who have a common interest in research and developments in various technological areas.

Epsilon Pi Tau is set up within and is under the jurisdiction of the Ministry of Education—its officers are government officials. With this kind of administrative structure the group is not able to negotiate or bargain for its members and, necessarily, directs its efforts to programs which involve improvement of teaching and research. This organization sponsors seminars, lectures, and publications which are available to teachers and others who have an interest in the improvement of technical education in Thailand. Because of their association with an international organization they have resources to support research by teachers and technical experts and to publish the results. These publications have been helpful in disseminating knowledge and generally improving the teaching of vocational and industrial subjects.

PRIVATE SCHOOL TEACHERS' ORGANIZATIONS

As mentioned earlier in this chapter, a large percentage of the children in Thailand are educated in private schools. Because some of the problems of private schools differ greatly from those of the public schools, private school teachers could be expected to need special organizations. In the period after World War II three private school organizations developed: the Private School Teachers Association, the Private Schools Association, and the Education Cooperative Association.

Private School Teachers Association

The Private School Teachers Association includes both teachers and administrators. While it is very much concerned with matters related to salaries and improving the economic well-being of teachers, it does not attempt to be primarily a negotiating agent to deal with owners of the schools. In its statement of purposes it says that it offers assistance to individuals or groups who request its support in securing justice or additional aid for teachers who have been wronged—but few cases are known when this help has been sought. Like its counterparts in the public schools, the Private School Teachers Association devotes most of its efforts to such things as in-service training for improving classroom teaching, preparing teachers for the certification examination, assisting teachers in finding funds for additional training either in Thailand or abroad, and encouraging the improvement of the quality of instruction. Scholarships and financial aids are not as readily available for private school teachers as they are for public school teachers so the securing of this assistance is a very important part of the work of the Private School Teachers Association.

Private Schools Association

The Private Schools Association is comprised of owners, administrators, and teachers in the private schools. Internally, it serves both teachers and administrators among the member schools in matters related to the improvement of teaching and school programs. Externally, it represents the member schools in negotiating with the Ministry of Education for government subsidies, handling complaints, or dealing with problems arising from deviations from the law. Since all schools are under the jurisdiction of the Ministry of Education, they are obliged to comply with rather stringent regulations described in the Private School Act. If a school were accused of violating a regulation, the Private Schools Association might be called in to mediate the case between a school and the governmental authorities. If a teacher (or group of teachers) wished to present a list of grievances, a hearing might be held by a committee from the Association; if not settled there, it would be passed on to the Department of Secondary Education for a final decision. This organization has sought more support from the government to improve the salaries of teachers in the private schools. The Association is concerned because of the high attrition rate of the private school teachers and it feels that the government has a responsibility to provide additional subsidies to private schools because of the large proportion of Thai students attending such educational institutions. The Private Schools Association also works through international organizations such as UNESCO to secure funds to enable teachers to receive further training. Similar to other teacher organizations, it sponsors seminars, lectures, etc., as well as social events to further the quality and community of teachers.

Education Cooperative Society

A third organization for private school teachers is the Education Cooperative Society. Membership is open to all teachers in the private schools who care to join. This society has carried on a number of important research projects to improve education for Thai students, and its publications are distributed to people who have or should have an interest in the subject. Help is offered to teachers for improving instruction techniques, evaluating student performance, setting course objectives, etc. The society also offers low-cost tours for teachers to encourage them to broaden their horizons and perspectives. Some in-service training programs are available for teachers who are preparing for certification examinations and who wish to improve their classroom teaching. The organization also supports special interest clubs for teachers and provides a clearing house for such groups throughout the country. While it is primarily designed to serve the needs of private school teachers, it also attempts to further the cooperation and unified action of both private and public school teachers to further the cause of education.

In addition to the general teachers' organizations, many special interest groups also have been organized in the past 20 years. Teachers have welcomed the establishment of teachers' organizations in specialized areas and have actively participated in their meetings and conferences. These organizations have played an important role in improving teaching and extending the quality of education at all levels.

Pre-School Education Association of Thailand

One of these specialized groups is the Pre-School Education Association of Thailand. Initially set up by a group of kindergarten teachers, its membership now includes parents and other lay people concerned with improving this level of education. Although its primary purpose is to collect and distribute materials to kindergarten teachers, it has also served as a bargaining agent dealing with manufacturers and business houses to obtain better prices through large-scale buying. The Association also offers teachers in-service training, arranges educational tours, conducts seminars, and sponsors conferences; it also conducts public relations activities to publicize the programs offered by kindergartens. Using radio, television, and newspapers, the organization has increased public interest in pre-school training. This program has enabled the Association to solicit funds which have been used to send teachers abroad for further training. The kindergarten program in Thailand has been greatly extended and improved, and certainly much of the credit belongs to the Pre-School Association.

Thai Library Association

Another group which has made important contributions to aid educators and education in Thailand is the Thai Library Association. This organization has attempted to strengthen the whole library program in Thailand—but has had a special concern for the school libraries. Its membership includes both professional librarians and teachers, and it has helped to bring about a better understanding of libraries in schools. To people in the Western world this achievement may sound rather strange because libraries have always been considered standard equipment in any school. In Thailand, however, traditionally children were taught through the lecture (rote learning) method, but in recent years a concerted effort has been made to encourage self-education through independent study. As a result, schools have had to be provided with sufficient library materials and facilities, which has encouraged the promotion of reading by students. The Thai Library Association has been instrumental in furthering this program. In addition, the Library Association has established facilities for training new librarians and has a center for keeping librarians informed of new research and developments in the field. It has published several books on library science, and it sends regular bulletins and a journal to schools and librarians throughout the kingdom. The Association also offers services to reorganize established libraries and has helped new libraries by giving advice on cataloging, selecting new books, care and maintenance of books, etc. The Association has maintained an active public relations office to make the people and officials of the government more aware of the value of and need for good libraries. Through this program it has been able to raise money and find sponsors for the acquisition of more library materials. It has started another ambitious project to establish a union card catalog to facilitate locating library materials available in Thailand. This group has been organized for only a few years but already it has shown its effectiveness by coordinating the work of the schools and the library committee in the Ministry of Education.

Special Professional Organizations

Several more professional organizations have been established by special interest groups in the field of education. Two or three examples will suffice to show the recent development to establish a closer community among people with common interests. The Science Society of Thailand was established in 1948 by a group of professors and lecturers at Chulalongkorn University, but it has since opened its membership to teachers at all levels of education. It carries on a variety of activities to encourage research and the dissemination of knowledge to improve the teaching of science. It subscribes to scientific journals and other publications which are distributed to schools. The Science Society has become involved in the translation of science books and has published several textbooks. The Society has also sponsored science clubs, a science fair, and has provided lecturers for in-service training of teachers. It also publishes the *Science Magazine Monthly* which has a wide circulation. The Science Society of Thailand has played an active and important role in improving science education in Thailand.

In 1956, the Mathematics Association of Thailand was started as part of the Science Society—but a year later it became a separate entity. As its name suggests, the Association's concern is in a very specialized area. It has been instrumental in conducting and distributing research findings on new developments in mathematics and new techniques in teaching. It has maintained a close working relationship with similar organizations in other parts of the world and has sponsored lectures by distinguished mathematicians to various schools and universities in the kingdom. The Association directs an annual competitive examination to discover talented young people in this area. It publishes a monthly bulletin which is distributed to schools and members. It, too, has a program for training teachers in mathematics and statistics.

Another organization which has had a great impact on education in Thailand is the Home Economics Association of Thailand. This group was organized at the suggestion of a professor from the United States at an in-service training session for home economics teachers held at the Ministry of Education in 1955. Its membership includes teachers, housewives, and other people who have an interest in home economics. Attached to the Ministry of Education, it has an opportunity to make suggestions and recommendations which can be implemented by the officials of the Ministry. The Association collects and publishes information which would be useful to teachers in the field, and maintains a close relationship with the teachers' training colleges to help provide better training for people who plan to enter the teaching profession. The group also sponsors an annual fair to display new ideas and devices in the field of home economics. Members are frequently asked to give lectures and demonstrations to groups or on radio or television, and they organize regular training sessions for teachers and housewives. Monthly meetings are held to enable teachers to exchange ideas and to make plans for future projects.

ASSESSMENT

The purpose of describing these various teachers' organizations is to give the reader some notion of what has and has not been done in one developing country. An overall assessment of the effectiveness of teachers' organizations is extremely difficult because frequently there is a considerable difference between what the leaders of the organizations aim to accomplish (their stated goals) and the work that is actually done. The leaders of the various teachers' organizations, especially those who have traveled abroad, are completely aware of the low economic status of the teachers in Thailand, and often one finds in the statement of objectives of these organizations that they wish to "attempt to better the economic well-being of teachers." The problem of what can be done about low salaries for teachers is frequently discussed by the teachers' organizations but few people have even given serious thought to trying to unionize teachers or to carrying on collective bargaining to force the government or owners of the private schools to improve the economic status of the members of the teaching profession. Often people in the Western world find it difficult to understand why, in a relatively prosperous country such as Thailand, workers in all professions do not follow the pattern that has worked successfully in the West to demand more economic benefits. To understand this failure to act, one needs to understand the difference between the value systems, the political organization, and certain customs and traditions that determine living patterns in various cultures. There is no doubt that most leaders in Thailand are very much interested in (or at least they give lip-service to) increasing industrial growth, improving the economic standards and conditions of the people, extending democracy, as they see occurring in the prosperous West. Although they want the end, they are not ready or willing to adopt the means used in the West to achieve these ends. Thus, the notion of dealing with matters such as improving teachers' salaries ration-

ally and aggressively is repugnant to the average Thai. Unlike
people in the West, Thais do not tend to equate economic standing
in one's society with the degree of a man's success in life.

While some efforts have been made to establish labor unions, this
movement has not won widespread and enthusiastic support. Most
Thai people dislike aggressiveness and the Western concept of collective action to serve social or economic benefits and, to them,
unionization includes both of these as component parts. Traditionally, a "good Thai" attempts to live harmoniously with his fellow
man and rarely would he do things which would draw attention to
himself as an individual. In talking with leaders of teachers' organizations, one gets the impression that most teachers would refuse to
join any kind of teachers' union because a union would have the
effect of lowering the high social position enjoyed by the teachers to
the same level as that of a common laborer. It is probably for this
reason that the existing teachers' organizations have tended to emphasize the "community of teachers," quality of education, improvement of instruction, etc., and have de-emphasized collective
bargaining as one of their functions.

All public school teachers are, of course, under the Civil Service
System. Occasionally one hears complaints (especially from university instructors) about the failure of this system to take into
account the difference in performance and in the contributions of
individual teachers, but, on the whole, most teachers seem to enjoy
the security and regularity the system offers. Once a teacher (or any
other government worker) enters the Civil Service he can expect
regular salary increments and regular promotions, which are determined primarily on the length of service. The idea that teachers
should be promoted on the basis of merit is generally discarded as
impractical. A typical Thai teacher would not expect—or want to
be promoted before a senior colleague. The reverence for seniority
and authority makes people quite willing to accept what senior
officials and administrators decree for them. This principle applies
not only to teachers but within families, political life, religion,
etc.

There is another factor which has deterred the development of
labor unions in Thailand—even if teachers earnestly wanted them,
i.e., the present military and political insecurity in the whole region
of Southeast Asia. Government officials carefully watch the organization of any groups that might tend to upset the political tranquil-

ity. If one wanted to establish a new teachers' organization, for example, he would be obliged first to register this plan with the police. Any group having any affiliation with an outside power which opposes the existing government would, in all probability, be refused the right to organize. Individual members joining such a group would be checked for their loyalty and integrity. Meeting times and the organization's objectives must be approved by the appropriate governmental agency.

All these factors have contributed to the peculiar nature of the teachers' organizations in Thailand. Probably the best way of summarizing the role of teachers' organizations in Thailand is to say that they have been instrumental in helping teachers gain a greater awareness of their responsibilities and importance in the development of their country. Through their efforts to improve the quality of instruction and in their support of educational innovations they have effected important changes in the educational system. As these organizations continue to expand in numbers and provide more services to the teachers and nation they should become more effective agencies in guiding policy-makers in the government of Thailand.

United States 9

Michael H. Moskow and Robert E. Doherty

INTRODUCTION

Teacher organizations in the United States have undergone a dramatic change since 1962. They have turned to collective bargaining or variations thereof as methods of making demands to their employers for determining salaries and working conditions. In prior years, state teacher organizations concentrated most of their efforts in lobbying, while local teacher organizations did little more than present proposals to their boards of education. Now the trend is for local organizations to negotiate formal written collective bargaining agreements with boards of education and for state and national affiliates to lobby for legislation requiring boards of education to negotiate. The affiliates also continue to supply research and personnel services to the local organizations. From 1965 to 1967, nine state statutes were passed requiring boards of education to engage in collective bargaining with teacher organizations; only one, Wisconsin, had a negotiation statute prior to 1965. The number of teacher strikes reached an all time high in 1967 and 1968. New York City teachers strikes involved over 40,000 teachers, and a state-wide strike closed most of Florida's schools for almost two weeks. There also has been a proliferation of institutes, textbooks, and university

MICHAEL H. MOSKOW is Research Associate Professor of Economics and Education, Temple University, Philadelphia, Pennsylvania.

ROBERT E. DOHERTY is Professor of Industrial and Labor Relations, Cornell University, Ithaca, New York.

courses on negotiations in public education; and in recent years it has become the major topic in educational literature and at board of education and school administrator conventions and meetings.

After a brief introduction to the United States' educational system, this chapter will focus on the teacher organizations and their policies and activities in negotiations with boards of education.

THE UNITED STATES' EDUCATIONAL SYSTEM

Responsibility for guaranteeing the establishment and maintenance of a system of public schools in the United States is given to each of the 50 states. The actual operation of the schools is delegated locally, however, and 21,704 local school districts presently exercise this delegated responsibility. Each school district has a governing board, usually called a "board of education" or "school board," which is given administrative powers by state statute. The local school board is legally an agency of the state, but it is also the instrument by which local control in operating the schools is maintained.

The United States' educational system is based on lay control. In fact, teachers and administrators employed in a school district are specifically prohibited from serving as members of that district's board of education. The board consists of local citizens usually elected by the constituency of the district. About 15 per cent of the boards of education, mostly in large cities, are appointed by the mayor or municipal governing body. Most boards of education consist of between seven to twelve members who serve without compensation. The board is supposed to be a policy-making body; the implementation and application of its policies are delegated to the school superintendent and his administrative staff.

Each state regulates its local school districts by constitutional provisions or legislation. The most common state regulation of school covers such areas as: minimum length of the school terms, compulsory school attendance, required elementary and high school programs, course offerings, textbooks, teacher certification and minimum salaries, school facilities, pupil personnel services, and transportation of pupils.[1]

There is considerable variety among states in financing public

[1] Arthur W. Foshay, ed., *The Rand McNally Handbook of Education* (Chicago: Rand McNally and Company, 1963), pp. 21–31.

education, but the majority of funds usually comes from local sources. In recent years, the state governments and federal government have increased their share of financial support for public education to 40.3 per cent and 7.7. per cent respectively [2] (see Table 1). The fiscal structure of local school districts varies: some boards of education can set their own budget as well as levy and collect taxes to obtain the necessary income; others must submit their budgets to a local city council or mayor for approval. In many states, boards of

TABLE 1. PERCENTAGE DISTRIBUTION OF PUBLIC SCHOOL REVENUES, 1957–58 TO 1967–68

	Per Cent of School Revenue Derived From:		
School Year	Federal Sources	State Sources	Local and Other Sources
1957–58	4.0	39.4	56.6
1958–59	3.6	39.5	56.9
1959–60	4.4	39.1	56.5
1960–61	3.8	39.8	56.4
1961–62	4.3	38.7	56.9
1962–63	3.6	39.3	57.1
1963–64	4.4	39.3	56.4
1964–65	3.8	39.7	56.5
1965–66	7.7	39.2	53.1
1966–67	7.9	39.1	53.0
1967–68	7.7	40.3	52.0

SOURCE: National Education Association, Research Division, *Estimates of School Statistics, 1967–68* (Washington, D.C.: The Association, 1967), p. 18.

education are required to submit their budgets to the electorate for approval at a special referendum. Most boards are free to set their own debt budgets and tax levies within state limitations, while the majority of large city boards of education are subject to budgetary review by a city council or other local agency.

School districts vary widely in terms of grade levels. Most school districts include grades from kindergarten through twelfth grade. Some school districts, particularly on the West Coast, include junior college grades thirteen and fourteen while others are limited to either elementary grades (grades K to 8) or secondary grades (grades 9 to 12).

[2] National Education Association, *Estimates of School Statistics, 1967–68* (Washington, D.C.: The Association, 1967), p. 18.

Student population also varies widely among districts. New York City has the largest school district in the United States with over one million students, while many districts enroll fewer than 100 students. Approximately 20 per cent of the school districts in the United States enroll over 75 per cent of the total student population. The number of teachers and school administrators almost always varies directly with the student population because of virtually fixed pupil-teacher ratios.

Most school districts have a superintendent of schools who serves as executive officer of the board of education. In larger districts, the superintendent has a staff of administrators and specialists in areas such as curriculum, personnel, and budgets. Each school has a principal who is normally a full-time administrator of a specific school. Secondary schools usually have department chairmen who teach part time.

Approximately 70 per cent of all teachers are female, but the percentage of male teachers has increased in recent years. Men now constitute a majority in the high schools and have recently made strong inroads into the lower grades as well.[3] The average level of teacher preparation is increasing; turnover rates, however, remain high at about 14 per cent. Male teachers hold second jobs more frequently than almost any other occupational group in the United States.

A large number of teachers, particularly unmarried females in their 20's and 30's, are not committed to teaching as a career. Male teachers frequently move into administrative positions or to other occupations because of the relatively low maximum salaries for teachers. In fact, male teachers ranked 32 of 49 professional-technical groups in a 1960 study of median earnings.[4]

TEACHER ORGANIZATIONS

There are two national organizations representing teachers in the United States: The National Education Association (NEA) and the American Federation of Teachers (AFT). This section describes the organizations and some of the recent developments in their policies.

[3] National Education Association, *NEA Research Bulletin*, vol. 43, no. 3, p. 68.
[4] U.S. Census of Population, 1960, *Subject Reports, Occupational Characteristics*, Final Report PC (2)—7A, Table 25. Reprinted in William J. Baumol and William G. Bowen, *Performing Arts—The Economic Dilemma* (New York: The Twentieth Century Fund, 1966), p. 104.

National Education Association

At the national level is the National Education Association with over one million members consisting of "classroom teachers, school administrators, and specialists in schools, colleges, and educational agencies which are both public and private." Classroom teachers in public schools constitute over 85 per cent of the total membership. One of the major beliefs of the NEA, however, is that since education is a profession unique unto itself, membership in associations should not be limited to classroom teachers. Therefore, most state and local affiliates accept both teachers and administrators as members. In fact, several state associations will not accept local affiliates unless they are open to both classroom teachers and administrators.

According to the *NEA Handbook.*

The NEA is an independent, voluntary nongovernmental organization available to all professional teachers. It believes that all educators, regardless of position, rank, or authority, are workers in a common cause. It cooperates with all groups in American life who seek to improve education. It works for better schools and, to further that end, for the improvement of the professional status of teachers. Under such policies, the National Education Association has become the largest professional organization in the world and the only over-all professional association for teachers in the United States.[5]

The NEA has 33 departments (Table 2), 25 commissions and committees, 17 headquarters divisions, and a staff of over 900 persons to carry out its policies. It has a research division staffed by 20 professional and administrative personnel and about 35 skilled clerical, secretarial, and statistical workers. It has a state-level affiliate in each of the 50 states and a local affiliate in over 8,000 school districts.

The 33 departments reflect the wide diversity of the activities of the NEA. The largest is the Department of Classroom Teachers which includes approximately 800,000 teachers in elementary and secondary schools. School administrators are members of departments such as the American Association of School Administrators, the National Association of Secondary-School Principals, and the Department of Elementary School Principals. Other departments include art education, educational research, foreign languages, and speech.

[5] National Education Association, *NEA Handbook* (Washington, D.C.: The Association, 1965), p. 13.

The state education associations with almost 1.6 million members, representing 89 per cent of the instructional staff, have had a substantial impact on education in the United States. McKean [6] documented the power of the New Jersey teachers' lobby in the 1930's; Blanke [7] found that chief state school officers perceived education interest groups (the state NEA affiliates were prominent in these groups) as having about average influence with legislators.

TABLE 2. DEPARTMENTS OF THE NATIONAL EDUCATION ASSOCIATION

Thirty-Three Departments	
1. Administrative Women	17. Industrial Arts
2. Art Education	18. Journalism Education
3. Audiovisual Instruction	19. Mathematics Teachers
4. Business Education	20. Music Educators
5. Classroom Teachers	21. Public School Adult Education
6. Colleges for Teacher Education	22. Retired Teachers
7. Driver Education	23. Rural Education
8. Educational Research	24. School Administrators
9. Educational Secretaries	25. School Librarians
10. Elementary-Kindergarten Nursery Education	26. School Public Relations
11. Elementary School Principals	27. Science Teachers
12. Exceptional Children	28. Secondary-School Principals
13. Foreign Languages	29. Social Studies
14. Health, Physical Education, Recreation	30. Speech
15. Higher Education	31. Supervision & Curriculum Development
16. Home Economics	32. Vocational Education
	33. Women Deans & Counselors

SOURCE: National Education Association, *NEA Handbook, 1965–66* (Washington, D.C.: The Association, 1967), p. 12.

"Each legislative session in each state finds state association lobbyists working feverishly for passage of teacher welfare bills. Elaborate mechanisms for enlisting grass roots support for all kinds of educational legislation have been perfected. Local associations and individual members are kept well informed on activities of legislatures and legislators. Score cards and progress charts are maintained and success is measured in terms of bills passed or defeated." [8]

6 Dayton David McKean, *Pressures on the Legislature of New Jersey* (New York: Columbia University Press, 1938).
7 Virgil Blanke, "Educational Policy Formulation at the State Level by Chief State School Officers" (Ph.D. diss., University of Chicago, 1961).
8 Ronald F. Campbell, *et al.*, *The Organization and Control of American Schools* (Columbus, Ohio: Charles E. Merrill Books, Inc., 1965), pp. 268.

On the other hand, until recently local education associations were usually weak organizations. Although the number of full-time staff members working for local associations has increased rapidly in recent years, less than 100 local associations have a paid staff. In 1960, Lieberman [9] described the local association as typically engaging "in futile efforts to improve their conditions of employment. Other than this, they give teas for new teachers in the Spring, and perhaps listen to a few travelogues in between."

The American Federation of Teachers

The American Federation of Teachers, affiliated with the AFL-CIO, the national federation of American trade unions, was formed in 1919. The stated objectives of the AFT are as follows:

1. To bring associations of teachers into relations of mutual assistance and cooperation.
2. To obtain for them all the rights to which they are entitled.
3. To raise the standards of the teaching profession by securing the conditions essential to the best professional service.
4. To promote such a democratization of the schools as will enable them better to equip their pupils to take places in the industrial, social, and political life of the community.
5. To promote the welfare of the childhood of the nation by providing progressively better educational opportunity for all. [10]

With approximately 450 local affiliates, the AFT has approximately 140,000 members most of whom are concentrated in large cities. The AFT permits locals to decide on an individual basis whether they will accept principals as members; school superintendents are prohibited from membership by a constitutional provision. Separate locals for administrators are now prohibited, but prior to 1966 they were permitted providing the local AFT affiliate approved. The AFT constantly emphasizes that it is the only organization specifically devoted to the interests of the classroom teacher.

Although the NEA and the AFT have been in competition since 1919 the struggle gained new impetus in December, 1961, when the United Federation of Teachers, a local affiliate of the AFT, was elected bargaining agent for 44,000 New York City public school

9 Myron Lieberman, *The Future of Public Education* (Chicago: University of Chicago Press, 1960), p. 192.
10 Constitution of the American Federation of Teachers (correct as of October, 1964), p. 3.

teachers. The UFT received nearly three times as many votes as the NEA's hastily formed contender—the Teachers' Bargaining Organization. More important though, was the fact that for the first time the labor movement gave active support, in the form of personnel and financial resources, to a local of the AFT. Shortly after the victory, the AFT joined the Industrial Union Department of the AFL-CIO, which had been the major contributor to the UFT.

Since that time, the IUD, headed by Walter Reuther, has been deeply involved in organizing public school teachers and in conducting campaigns for teacher collective bargaining. Its interest in organizing public school teachers is easy to understand since it believes teachers could be an important stepping stone to the organization of the growing number of white-collar and professional workers. The changes in the composition of the labor force and the failure of the labor movement to organize white-collar workers has been recognized by many commentators.[11] If the AFT could run a successful nation-wide membership drive, however, the image of unions in the eyes of other white-collar and professional workers would be greatly improved.[12] For this reason the UFT received more aid than any other union local had ever received in a collective bargaining election.[13]

After its overwhelming victory, the UFT immediately began negotiating with the school board. When negotiations broke down in April, 1962, the UFT called a strike and over 20,000 teachers refused to work. The work stoppage lasted only one day, however, and after the mayor of the city and the governor of the state became involved, a salary agreement was reached. By the end of August, the parties had negotiated a 40-page written agreement which has been surpassed in its detailed provisions only by the later 1963 and 1965 agreements reached between the same parties.

Changes in NEA Policy

While the UFT was negotiating its written agreement in the summer of 1962, the NEA was holding its annual convention in Denver. Dr. William Carr, Executive Secretary of the NEA entitled

11 Benjamin Soloman and Robert K. Burns, "Utilization of White Collar Employees: Extent, Potential and Implication," *The Journal of Business of the University of Chicago*, XXXVI (April, 1963), 142.
12 *The Wall Street Journal*, April 5, 1962, p. 1.
13 American Federation of Teachers, *AFT in Action* (Chicago: The Federation, January, 1962), p. 8.

his address "The Turning Point" which aptly describes the dramatic changes that took place in the NEA's policy toward collective negotiations at this convention.

In earlier years, the NEA had on occasion spoken about the necessity for group action by teachers, but they had no organized program and issued no guidelines or directives for implementation. At the 1962 convention the NEA's official policy on negotiations was formulated. Objecting to the term "collective bargaining," the NEA passed a resolution emphasizing the need for "professional negotiation." This was the first time the NEA used the term "negotiation" and it ended the search for a suitable substitute to "collective bargaining." In earlier years, other terms were suggested such as "cooperative determination," "collective determination," and even "democratic persuasion."

Another 1962 convention resolution of particular significance is Resolution 19 entitled "Professional Sanctions":

The National Education Association believes that, as a means of preventing unethical or arbitrary policies or practices that have a deleterious effect on the welfare of the schools, professional sanctions should be invoked. These sanctions would provide for appropriate disciplinary action by the organized profession.

The National Education Association calls upon its affiliated state associations to cooperate in developing guidelines which would define, organize, and definitely specify procedureal steps for invoking sanctions by the teaching profession.[14]

This resolution, which was introduced from the floor of the convention instead of by the resolution committee, marks the beginning of the official adoption of a pressure tactic by the NEA.

The main significance of Carr's speech to the 1962 convention was that it set the stage for the battle between the AFT and the NEA. Carr identified unionization as one of the two crises in education, and he outlined the policy the NEA would follow to meet the challenge from the labor movement. "This . . . is the first time in which forces of significant scope and power are considering measures which could destroy the Association." [15]

At the February 18, 1962 meeting of the NEA Board of Directors, less than two months after the UFT victory in New York City, a motion was passed urging each state affiliate to hold regional con-

[14] National Education Association, *Address and Proceedings, 1962* (Washington, D.C.: The Association, 1962), p. 181.
[15] *Ibid.*, pp. 24, 28.

ferences to ". . . explain *why* professional organizations should exist on an independent basis, with professional responsibility and autonomy." More extensive conferences dealing with the same topic were urged in cities with populations over 100,000 persons. In addition, state affiliates were urged to secure passage of state legislation implementing NEA policy on professional negotiations.[16]

At the convention itself, Carr explained that the Urban Project would be formed to meet the needs of large city teachers and to direct the NEA fight against unionization of teachers. The Urban Project budget was $203,900 for the 1962–1963 fiscal year. In the 1964–1965 fiscal year the Urban Project spent a total of $884,663 including $437,990 which had been ". . . spent from the Reserve for Future Emergencies as authorized by the Board of Directors.[17] By 1968, the Urban Project had been elevated to the divisional level in the NEA with a budget of over $1 million out of a total NEA budget of almost $10 million.

In reality "professional negotiations" is a generic term which the NEA uses to refer to a wide variety of different relationships between school boards and local teacher associations. For example, a local affiliate is considered to have a Level I professional negotiations agreement if the school board has made a written statement (which may be in the minutes of the board meeting) that it recognizes the association as the representative of all teachers in the district or even merely as the representative of its own members. Level II agreements consist of recognition and establishment of a negotiations procedure. If a means for settling impasses is added, the agreement is then considered Level III. Level IV agreements include terms and conditions of employment. When an impasse arises, it provides for various forms of third-party intervention most of which consist of modified forms of mediation and fact-finding. At no time, however, do Level IV agreements provide for the utilization of state labor relations agencies or state mediation agencies since, in the NEA's opinion, disputes should always be settled through "educational channels." In extreme cases or when agreement cannot be reached, the Association will resort to sanctions which may range from publicizing unfavorable teaching conditions in a particular school district to a mass refusal to sign contracts by

16 *Ibid.*, pp. 245–46. Emphasis added.
17 National Education Association, *Financial Report* (Washington, D.C.: The Association, 1965), p. 11.

all teachers employed in the district. At its 1967 convention, the NEA took an even more militant stand by voting to support local affiliates who had gone on strike.

In the past five years, the NEA's policy on professional negotiations has gradually become firmly established. The Association favors exclusive recognition whereby one organization represents all staff members in the district, and negotiating units which include both teachers and administrators although decisions on negotiating units should be a matter for local option. The NEA now favors written agreements which include terms and conditions of employment, a grievance procedure with binding arbitration as the terminal point, and a termination date.

The NEA and its affiliates have clearly changed drastically. State-wide and local sanctions and strikes have been used on numerous occasions. Local associations have called strikes or "professional holidays" when agreement on employment conditions has not been reached. In other cases, they have refused to lead extracurricular activities or publicized "unprofessional" conditions in a district as a means of enforcing their demands. In brief, the NEA and its state and local affiliates are now considered militant and determined organizations.

AFT Policy on Collective Bargaining

The AFT makes no effort to distinguish its approach to teacher-board relations from the collective bargaining process carried on in private industry. Delegates to the 1963 National Convention passed a resolution which recognized the right of locals to strike under certain circumstances and urged ". . . the AFL-CIO and affiliated international unions to support such strikes when they occur." [18] This resolution constituted a change in AFT policy since in prior years it had no official strike policy, even though locals had been supported when they had gone on strike.

The AFT has advocated collective bargaining for teachers since 1935; before that time the union had encouraged teacher councils (representatives from each school) and more participation in policy making by teachers. There is strong evidence, however, to indicate that it was not until the UFT victory in 1961 that the AFT actively began to encourage its locals to strive for collective bargaining

[18] *Proceedings,* 1963 American Federation of Teachers National Convention, Resolution No. 79.

rights. For example, a survey conducted in 1947 showed that none of the 41 locals in the AFT which had the majority of teachers in their district as members, had ever engaged in collective bargaining. In answer to a question in the same survey which asked "What further part does the local feel it should play in administration and policy?", only 7 of 141 respondants responded "bargaining agents." [19]

Until recently, the AFT has displayed no clear understanding of exactly what collective bargaining for teachers would entail. In fact the confusion over the AFT's definition of collective bargaining is quite similar to that exhibited by the NEA on professional negotiations. For example, although the AFT claimed to have approximately 12 written agreements between school boards and teachers' unions in 1964, only four of them included terms and conditions of employment, while the others were merely recognition agreements. In addition, several agreements did not provide for exclusive recognition, and in two cases the school boards signed written agreements with both the NEA local and the AFT local.

The agreement negotiated by the United Federation of Teachers, in New York, however, rapidly became the model for agreements later negotiated in other cities. By 1967, AFT locals had won representation rights for teachers in many of the large city school systems in the United States such as Baltimore, Boston, Chicago, Cleveland, Philadelphia, and Washington, D.C. They had negotiated collective bargaining agreements covering over 20 per cent of the teachers in the United States even though they enrolled less than ten per cent of the teaching staff as members.

CAUSAL FACTORS IN THE EMERGENCE OF COLLECTIVE BARGAINING IN PUBLIC EDUCATION

The number of American public school teachers covered by substantive collective agreements grew from virtually none in 1962 to about 210,000 or 13 per cent of all teachers in the spring of 1968. And the movement has by no means reached a plateau. Teachers in those states with newly enacted collective bargaining statutes have barely begun to take advantage of their rights under these new laws. In other states, legislatures have been considering public em-

[19] Philip Kochman, "The Developing Role of Teachers Unions" (Ph.D. diss., Teachers College, Columbia University, 1939).

ployee bills which, when enacted, would surely serve as a spur to teacher organizing and bargaining activity.

Why did this movement begin in the past few years, roughly 25 years after the big organizing drives in private employment, and beyond that, what caused the movement to grow so rapidly once it had begun? Certainly the evidence is not all in at this stage, but there is enough to allow us to hazard a few observations. One thing does seem to be clear: The two essential ingredients for social change, pressure for change and the opportunity for change, were noticeably present in public school employment arrangements in the 1960's.[20]

The pressures stemmed from an apparently increasing dissatisfaction with employment conditions in public education, the changing ratio between male and female teachers, and the intense, sometimes bitter, rivalry between the two teacher organizations. We have said that teacher dissatisfaction is *apparently* on the increase only because there is no hard evidence to support this contention. We conclude merely that the increasing number of strikes, strike threats, sanctions, and slowdowns is a reasonably good barometer of how a great many teachers feel about their working conditions. On the other hand, it should be pointed out that teachers were better off, at least superficially, in the 1960's than ever before in their history. Salaries had increased by over 100 per cent between 1950 and 1965, as compared to a 90 per cent increase for industrial production workers;[21] class size was not so great a problem; teachers were performing fewer clerical and subprofessional chores; and autocratic rule and administrative favoritism were probably less pronounced than they had been in earlier years.

Teachers *were* troubled by the decline in "psychic income," which had set in in many school districts, particularly in urban areas. Many teachers were complaining about meaningless bureaucratic intransigence. There was less opportunity to exercise one's initiative in the classroom. They also complained about the grow-

20 For a more detailed explanation of these causal factors see Robert E. Doherty and Walter E. Oberer, *Teachers, School Boards and Collective Bargaining* (Ithaca, New York: New York State School of Industrial and Labor Relations, 1967) and Myron Lieberman and Michael H. Moskow, *Collective Negotiations for Teachers* (Chicago: Rand McNally and Co., 1966).

21 National Education Association, *Economic Status of Teachers in 1963–64* (Washington, D.C.: The Association, 1964), Research Report 1964-R7, p. 10; *NEA Research Bulletin*, vol. 44, no. 2, p. 36; U.S. Bureau of Labor Statistics, *Employment and Earnings and Monthly Report on the Labor Force* (Washington, D.C.: GPO, May, 1966), vol. 12, no. 11, p. 67.

ing problem of unruly and academically disinterested students. The cities were being abandoned by the upwardly mobile, self-disciplined middle-class students, and many of the new and remaining students were hostile to the schools and to the teachers and were unwilling to conform to normal classroom routines. School administrations, it is alleged, have been reluctant to make adjustments either in the curriculum or in discipline procedures to accommodate to this change. In a relatively short period of time, according to some teachers, a professional calling had been reduced to a job which was often boring, always difficult, and sometimes perilous. It is not surprising that under these circumstances the trade union approach should begin to have a great deal of appeal to teachers.

At the same time that disenchantment was setting in among public school teachers, men were joining the teaching ranks in significant numbers. Although male teachers had accounted for only 17 per cent of all classroom teachers in the middle 1920's, their numbers by 1965 had increased to over 30 per cent.[22] More dramatically, the percentage increase of male teachers from 1954 to 1964 was 93 per cent, as against a mere 38 per cent for females over the same period.[23]

Steadily improving teachers' salaries had evidently served as an important inducement to young men who, looking at career alternatives through the rather innocent eyes of a college undergraduate, saw teaching as an attractive way of earning a living, financially as well as professionally. These young men may have soon become disillusioned about teaching ever providing sufficient financial rewards (80 per cent are married and 66 per cent have children to support),[24] but the disillusionment did not come quickly enough to allow for tooling up for another career, nor was it strong enough to make them willing to abandon their pension rights or their job security.

It is a curious irony that while men teachers appear to be far less certain than women that they have made the correct occupational choice (34.4 per cent would definitely choose teaching again as against 60 per cent for women, according to a recent NEA survey),[25] they seem at the same time to have a much stronger commit-

22 *NEA Research Bulletin*, vol. 43, no. 3, p. 68.

23 *Ibid.*, vol. 43, no. 1, p. 8.

24 "Profile of the American Public School Teacher, 1966," *NEA Journal*, vol. 56, no. 5 (May, 1967), p. 12.

25 *The American Public School Teacher*, 1960–61 (Washington, D.C.: National Education Association, 1962), p. 68.

ment to teaching as a career. Eighty per cent of men teachers questioned in a New York City survey by Rabinowitz and Crawford saw
teaching as a lifetime career, while only 40 per cent of women
teachers planned to continue teaching indefinitely.[26]

If these surveys indeed represent a mood of a substantial number
of male teachers, the picture they portray is that of a great number
of men, resentful over their occupational choice but helpless to
escape it. Collective bargaining may not erase this sense of bitter-
ness and frustration, but it does present an opportunity to act upon
it. It is not difficult, therefore, to understand why men have
assumed leadership roles in so many local teacher organizations, or
why most of the agitation for bargaining has come from junior and
senior high schools where men almost always form the majority of
the teaching staff.

Yet these two developments, the evident decline in job satisfaction and the emergence of a substantial percentage of men teachers,
do not in themselves constitute sufficient pressure to launch a
teacher bargaining drive on a scale such as the one that has developed. Teacher organizations must also be motivated to enroll new
members, to try strenuously to achieve bargaining rights, and to
press hard for their demands at the bargaining table.

If one were to attempt to locate the single event that stimulated
teacher organizations around the country to greater activity, it
would have to be the collective bargaining agreement negotiated by
the United Federation of Teachers and the New York City Board of
Education in 1962. Since the agreement provided for substantial
improvements in working conditions for New York City teachers
(at least it was generally agreed that there would have been fewer
improvements in the absence of bargaining), AFT affiliates in other
school systems began to push for bargaining rights. NEA affiliates,
most of which had heretofore been reluctant to become involved in
collective bargaining, were pressed to do likewise or stand to lose a
considerable portion of their membership. Thus in many school
systems the initiative began to come from NEA affiliates, many of
them evidently feeling that if they did not represent the teachers at
the bargaining table the AFT surely would. This rivalry has been
almost as important a reason for bargaining activity as dissatisfaction with teaching conditions.

As shown later in this chapter, the pressure for bilateral determi-

26 William Rabinowitz and Kay E. Crawford, "A Study of Teachers' Careers,"
The School Review, vol. 68, no. 4 (Winter, 1960), pp. 385, 387.

nation of employment conditions has in several states been happily coupled with opportunity. Indeed, the statutes providing teachers with collective bargaining rights, most of which were enacted initially in response to public employee demands for such legislation, had in several states become a very important *cause* for bargaining activity. Once these laws were passed, a great many teacher organizations which had not sought a change in the informal method of dealing with boards of education began to bargain vigorously with their employers. It is probably fair to say that in some instances legislation *created* dissatisfaction. For example, there had been no pervasive or profound feeling of teacher discontent in Connecticut prior to June of 1965, when the Connecticut teacher bargaining statute went into effect. General teaching conditions in that state were, in fact, considered to be among the best in the nation. Yet within six months after the Governor had signed the bill into law 50 per cent of the state's 30,000 teachers were covered by collective agreements.[27] Truly, opportunity had stimulated a need which a great many teachers barely knew existed.

By 1968, however, neither opportunity nor pressure were serving as the essential stimulants. The question most teachers sitting on the sidelines had been asking—does it work, does collective bargaining really bring about significant improvements in employment conditions?—had been answered in the affirmative. It had become clear even to the most cautious of NEA affiliates, that school boards were, under bargaining conditions, granting teachers concessions which were often far in excess of what they would have granted on their own. Nor could these teachers have helped but notice that demands backed by a strike threat or an actual strike usually resulted in even more concessions. It is not very likely, for example, that the Detroit School Board would have increased its teachers' starting salary from $5,800 to $7,500 yearly, reduced class size, and shortened the school year,[28] had it not been faced with a strike and a determined group of teacher representatives sitting across the bargaining table. Even without a strike threat the bargaining process itself can often change school board members' minds about how much money they can justifiably request from the budgeting authorities for school operations. Early in 1968 teachers in Buffalo

[27] Robbins Barstow, "Connecticut's Teacher Negotiation Law: An Early Analysis" *Phi Delta Kappan,* vol. 47 (March, 1966), p. 345.
[28] *Government Employee Relations Report,* No. 210, September 18, 1967.

won a salary increase variously interpreted as averaging from $1,000 to $1,200 per teacher, plus a number of other important benefits, without even the hint of a work stoppage.[29]

The essential lesson then, and one that probably many public school teachers have learned, is that collective bargaining works. Working conditions do improve, life does get a little bit better. We shall probably see thousands more teachers acting on this lesson, even in districts where there is relatively little job dissatisfaction and where legislation has not yet provided a legal "opportunity."

LEGISLATION AFFECTING TEACHER BARGAINING

The patchwork quilt of statutes governing the employment arrangement in American public education is a dramatic reflection of the American federal system. Under the National Labor Relations Act, which accords collective bargaining rights to private employees, the jurisdiction of the federal government is restricted to the handling of employer-employee relations in those industries engaged in a "significant" amount of interstate commerce. President Kennedy's Executive Order 10988 of January, 1962, granted similar rights to employees in the federal service. The regulation of labor relations in school districts, as well as for state, county, and municipal employees, is left to the states. In the absence of state legislation this burden is occasionally assumed by municipalities, county governments, or school districts themselves.

At least 50 possible varieties of statutes affect employment relations in public schools, and if one were to consider the number of school boards which have dealt with this matter in one way or the other through the adoption of local resolutions, the varieties become almost limitless. Our concern here, however, is not with local executive orders, ordinances, or resolutions (although this type of legislation is still important in the governance of employee relations in the public sector), but with state legislation. For it is in the state legislatures where the most significant and far-reaching developments have taken place in recent years, and it will be these bodies, not local school boards, which will eventually determine to what extent and in what manner teachers shall participate in determining their conditions of employment.

It should be emphasized that not all, or even a majority, of the

29 Rochester *Times Union,* January 11, 1968.

state legislatures have been persuaded that a teacher bargaining statute is necessary. In some cases they have yet to be persuaded that teacher bargaining itself is in the public good. In fact, as of March, 1968, school boards in Alabama, Georgia, North Carolina, and South Carolina—to name but a few states—were forbidden either by statute, court ruling, or attorney general opinion to enter into collective bargaining arrangement with their employees. In a handful of states it was illegal for public employees even to join labor organizations.[30]

In still other states, such as New Jersey, Pennsylvania, Ohio, Indiana, Illinois, the legislatures have been silent on the matter of collective negotiations in public education. But while governments in these states do not grant to teachers the right to bargain collectively, neither do they disallow that right. Thousands of public school teachers are covered by comprehensive collective agreements in such cities as Newark, Philadelphia, Cleveland, South Bend, and Chicago, all of which are located in states without negotiations legislation.

Situated somewhere between the above category and the grouping of states with statutes mandating some form of bargaining are those states having what has come to be called "permissive" legislation—Alaska (1959), New Hampshire (1955), Florida (1965), Nebraska (1967).[31] In essence, these statutes permit, but do not require, school boards and/or public employers generally to negotiate collectively with their employees. The Alaska statute, for example, states that while a school district "may enter into a contract with a labor organization. . . ." nothing in the act "requires" the board to enter into such an agreement. Similarly, the Nebraska statute provides that "no board of education . . . shall be required to meet or confer with representatives of an organization of certificated school employees unless a majority of members of such board determines to recognize such organization." As of March, 1968,

[30] For an excellent though somewhat dated summary of legal opinion on the status of teacher bargaining, see National Education Association, *Professional Negotiations with School Boards: A Legal Analysis and Review*, Research Report 1965-R3 (Washington, D.C.: The Association, 1965), *passim*.
[31] The full text of the statutes discussed in this chapter, with the exception of Nebraska, can be found in National Education Association, Office of Professional Development and Welfare, *Summary of Professional Negotiation Legislation* (Washington, D.C.: The Association, 1967). The text of the Nebraska statute is published in *Government Employee Relations Report*, August 14, 1967, pp. D–1, D–2.

relatively few school districts in the so-called "permissive" states were involved in collective bargaining nor were there many teachers in these states covered by collective agreements.

Comprehensive Statutes

Most bargaining activity is concentrated in the following ten states where school boards are required to engage in some form of negotiation, consultation, or discussion with their employees: Massachusetts, Rhode Island, Connecticut, New York, Michigan, Wisconsin, Minnesota, Oregon, Washington, California.

Here again the principle of local option is illustrated by the great variety of practices and procedures that prevail. If forced to categorize these statutes, one could perhaps develop two rough, though reasonably logical, groupings—those that hue rather closely to the National Labor Relations Act and state labor relations legislation model in form and content, and those that are more or less experimental.

The statutes in Wisconsin (1961), Michigan (1965), and Massachusetts (1965) are illustrative of the first category. In all three states, teachers are lumped together with other public employees. The state labor relations board administers the law as well as the act covering private employees; exclusive representation by one organization for all teachers is provided; the bargaining agent is determined by a secret ballot election if there is a contest between competing employee organizations; specific unfair labor practices are spelled out; and negotiable issues are limited to wages, hours, and other conditions of employment. Unlike the NLRA and state labor relations statutes, these statutes do prohibit the strike; they also provide for fact-finding or advisory arbitration as a means of breaking negotiating impasses.

The above statutes were not at first popular with state affiliates of the National Education Association. Many of these associations promoted bills which were less "labor-oriented"—bills that would have singled out teachers for special treatment and put the administration of the law in the hands of state education departments. Nevertheless, local associations seem not to have suffered under these public sector "Wagner Acts." A year after the passage of the Michigan statute, for example, NEA affiliates in that state had won 48 of 68 representation elections and represented 51,900 teachers. American Federation of Teacher affiliates had won the right to represent 15,770 teachers, 10,500 of whom were in the Detroit school system. In Wisconsin, NEA affiliates fared even better, winning 18 of 23 elections, including one in the state's largest city, Milwaukee. Local associations gained representation rights through stipulation in 100 additional school districts.[32] Indeed they had done so well under the Wisconsin statute that when school board members and administrators proposed that the law be amended to exclude teachers from its coverage, the Wisconsin Education Association resolved at its 1966 convention that the "Association opposes action which seeks to nullify or amend . . . [the Statute] in such ways as to exclude teachers from enjoying the benefits, rights and prerogatives listed therein." [33] Ironically, the WEA had opposed the Wisconsin statute when it was first introduced. As happens in so many other human endeavors, ideology capitulated to success.

Experimental Statutes

The statutes in Rhode Island, Connecticut, New York, Minnesota, Oregon, Washington, and California differ mainly from those discussed above in that, with one exception—New York—they deal only with certificated public school personnel. There are also, however, some rather striking differences *among* these statutes. If one were to construct a continuum of this legislation, the Rhode Island statute would appear most similar to the National Labor Relations Act and, therefore, least experimental. Like the statutes in Michigan, Massachusetts, and Wisconsin, the Rhode Island law uses the state labor board as the administrative agency, excludes supervisory personnel from its coverage, and limits the subject matter of collective bargaining to hours, wages, and working conditions. It differs from these statutes primarily in that it deals with teachers only and provides for binding arbitration of all disputes not involving the expenditure of money.

The Connecticut statute (1965) relies heavily on *ad hoc* administration and differs from all other statutes by providing a mechanism whereby local school district employees can decide whether teachers and administrators should be in the same bargaining unit or should have separate units.

The Washington law (1965) appears to grant teachers the right

[32] *Government Employee Relations Report*, No. 140, May 19, 1966, p. B–5.
[33] Quoted in an address by George E. Watson to the Joint School Board-Administrator Convention, Milwaukee, January 21, 1966.

only to ". . . communicate the considered professional judgment of the certificated staff. . . ." The statute also provides that any and all certificated employees may appear on their own behalf to discuss conditions of employment, and that the committee selected to make recommendations on breaking negotiating impasses must be "educators," appointed by the State Superintendent of Public Instruction. It lists a wide variety of appropriate matters for discussion at the bargaining table: including curriculum, textbook selection, in-service training, student teacher programs, hiring and assignment practices, leaves of absence, salaries and salary schedules, and non-instructional duties. Since the act does not explicitly require good faith bargaining, however, it is questionable how seriously school boards will listen to teacher demands in these areas.

While the Washington statute allows for virtually all school policy issues to be placed on the table (whether these issues are actually bargained is another matter), the Oregon law limits discussions to salaries and related *economic* policies. Also, there is a question as to just how much influence Oregon teachers have under the law since they are only given the right to confer, consult, and discuss these policies with local school boards.

Perhaps the most unique or experimental feature of the Oregon law is that, alone among all the statutes, it does not provide for organizational representation, but for representation by an employee council, elected at large by all eligible voters. A negotiating council could consist of a mixture of AFT members, NEA members, and those without organizational affiliation, whose election is possibly more of a consequence of individual popularity than any identification with educational programs or bargaining objectives.

Even more experimental are the statutes in California (1965) and Minnesota (1967). In both states the legislatures decided against exclusive employee representation and have instead adopted a system whereby representation is accorded on a proportional basis. The number of members each teacher organization is entitled to place on a school district negotiating council (councils have five members in Minnesota, from five to nine members in California) is in proportion to its membership strength in the district. Since there has at this writing been very little experience under the Minnesota law, and most AFT locals have boycotted the councils in California, there is not much evidence as to how this interesting experiment in employee representation is working out. Also, since the statutes do not mandate good faith bargaining on the part of employer (they are required only to meet and confer in both instances), it would be difficult to show that either statute has added much bargaining strength to teacher organizations or has allowed them to intrude very far into the unilateral authority of school boards.

The New York State Public Employee's Fair Employment Act (the Taylor Act) passed in 1967, provides collective bargaining rights for all public employees including teachers. The Taylor Act, according to both its drafters and administrators, is avowedly experimental. In passing the bill the state legislature seemed to be saying that not enough was yet known about public sector bargaining to prescribe rigid rules and procedures. Instead, the statute allows for considerable flexibility, making it possible to reflect the diversity existing in public employment arrangements. Presumably, the parties would over time discover which kinds of arrangements worked best in different circumstances.

The statute provides for considerable local discretion in the method of determining the bargaining agent or agents and whether representation should be on an exclusive or nonexclusive basis. While several of the statutes discussed earlier restrict the bargaining unit to nonsupervisory personnel, the Taylor Act excludes only the chief executive officer. Moreover, local school districts have taken advantage of this flexibility. In the spring of 1968 several bargaining units consisted of classroom teachers *plus* building principals and central office supervisors. In several other school districts all supervisory personnel were excluded, sometimes causing supervisors to form their own bargaining units.

There is also a wide range of options available in ascertaining the employee choice of bargaining agent. Recognition may be extended on the basis of dues deduction authorization, petitions, authorization cards, or a secret ballot election. Because of the relatively small amount of organizational rivalry outside the large cities, most teacher organizations in New York State have won recognition without an election.

Moreover, the act, in keeping with the legislature's experimentalist philosophy, does not mandate just how public employees are to be represented. Exclusivity, members only, and conceivably some form of multiple representation are all available options. Neither school boards nor teacher organizations seem anxious to take advantage of the last two options since virtually all school districts operating under the law have opted for exclusivity.

The Taylor Act is unique in still another way. Feeling, evidently, that the problems of public employment are sufficiently different to warrant special consideration, the legislature created within the act a separate administrative agency, the Public Employee Relations Board.

Like most other statutes, the Taylor Act also outlaws the strike but it goes further in that it spells out the penalties. These penalties, moreover—loss of checkoff of dues for up to 18 months, up to $10,000 per day fine levied against the employee organization for each day of the strike, fines and imprisonment for strike leaders—are directed not at individual strikers but at the employee organization. The reason, presumably, is that such penalties are more easily enforced than those directed at strikers and will, therefore, serve as a greater deterrent to public employee strikes. Provision is made for a hearing to determine whether the employer engaged in acts of extreme provocation before the penalties are invoked.

Future Legislation

Certainly in the next decade several more state legislatures will have enacted legislation granting bargaining rights to teachers and/or public employees generally. At this writing New Jersey, Pennsylvania, Ohio, Indiana, and Illinois seem destined to be in the next legislative wave. In some states, where the educational establishment is particularly influential, one can anticipate that teachers will be singled out for special legislation. In those states where trade unions are strong politically, we shall probably see public employee "Wagner Acts." Several states will probably pass statutes similar to the Taylor Law in New York State since it provides a compromise to the different types of legislation favored by the NEA and AFT.

We can also expect that over time several of the ambiguities contained in the present laws will be cleared up by rulings of administrative bodies and, behind them, the courts. Certainly guidance is needed as to what constitutes the "appropriate" subject matter of collective bargaining. Teachers have argued that since virtually everything a school board decides can have some influence as to whether their working lives will be more or less pleasant, they should share in these decisions. School boards, on the other hand, maintain that bargaining over any and all policy matters denies the board its legal authority and makes administration of the school system much too cumbersome. It seems unlikely that, left alone, the parties will arrive at any reconciliation of these two points of view. We shall probably see, as has happened under the National Labor Relations Act, a series of court and administrative decisions defining the scope of bargaining.

The question of binding arbitration of grievances will probably also be clarified. At this writing most boards of education maintain that arbitrators' decisions should be advisory only since boards cannot, or at least should not, delegate any of their sovereign powers to a third party. Teacher organizations, understandably, disagree with this position, arguing that bilateralism implies equality, and to leave to one of the parties the right to decide whether a bilaterally arrived-at agreement has been interpreted incorrectly or has been unfairly applied makes a mockery of the collective bargaining process.

The area that will probably receive the most attention, however, both in the modification of existing statutes and in the framing of new ones, is that of how best to deal with negotiating impasses. Public employee strikes are illegal in all of the 50 states, either by statute or at common law. Yet legislatures have thus far been unable to provide a satisfactory formula for impasse resolution or for penalties against the strike. When strike penalties are too severe they cannot be enforced, as under New York's old Condon-Wadlin law when public employee strikers could be sent to jail. When penalties are too limited, they will be ignored and accepted by pubilc employees as part of the price they must pay for a good settlement. The penalties under New York's new Taylor Act apparently provided little deterrent to teachers and other public employees who have gone on strike in that state. The act was amended to provide for even stiffer penalties in 1969 and it remains to be seen whether these will serve as an effective deterrent.

As far as negotiation impasses are concerned then, legislatures seem to be faced with two choices: they must either develop impasse-breaking devices that work and are equitable, i.e. are responsive to the bargaining muscle that teachers now enjoy, or they must face up to the issue squarely by legalizing the strike under certain circumstances. The latter alternative minimizes the possibility that teach-

ers, who occupy a very sensitive moral position in our society, will
be regarded as lawbreakers by their students. As a result it may
eventually prove to be the method most consistent with the public
welfare.

DECISION-MAKING IN PUBLIC EDUCATION

Until recently, classroom teachers in elementary and secondary
schools and their organizations have not played an important role
in decision-making in public education. The movement to collective bargaining, however, appears to be giving teachers a greater
voice in many decisions which were previously in the exclusive
province of boards of education or school administrators. This section will describe those subjects that have been negotiated as well as
those still decided by state agencies or local boards of education.

State Level Decision-Making

The decentralized education system in the United States places
ultimate responsibility for public education on the 50 states who
have almost always delegated this power to local boards of education. Nevertheless, state legislation, state education department rulings, and state constitutions establish requirements which must be
adhered to by local districts.

Teacher certification requirements are almost always legislated or
set by state certification boards. These boards consist almost entirely
of lay persons as opposed to certified teachers. In many cases, certified teachers are specifically prohibited from serving on certification
boards, which prevents teachers from controlling entrance to the
teaching profession.

Certification requirements are usually stated in terms of a required number of courses in specified subject fields or pedagogy.
Each local school district within the state is permitted to hire only
those teachers who have been certified by the state board. Provisional certification is usually permitted where sufficient certified
teachers are not available.

Examples of state legislation which has affected salaries and working conditions of teachers are numerous. Thirty-one states have
minimum-salary laws for teachers, and in most cases these laws also
establish a minimum salary for teachers at the top of the salary

schedule. For example, if the minimum for a starting teacher at a bachelor's degree level is $4,500, school districts also will be required to pay teachers who have ten years of experience a minimum salary of $6,500. All states currently have legislated pension and retirement programs for public school teachers.[34]

In some states, legislation has been passed providing each teacher with a duty-free lunch period. These laws often have been called "right to eat" laws. Where such legislation does not exist, teachers often must supervise students during their lunch hours. Another subject of bargaining occasionally affected by legislation is the grievance procedure. For example, in Pennsylvania and New York a law requires each school district to establish a grievance procedure according to certain standards enunciated in the statutes.

Each state has a law requiring schools to be open a certain number of hours each day in order for the district to receive state funds for the operation of the schools. In addition, laws sometimes regulate the maximum size of classes in both secondary and elementary schools.

Thirty-seven states have passed laws giving tenure of employment to teachers after they serve a probationary period of usually three years. Once tenure is received a teacher can be dismissed only for causes which are usually stated in the tenure law. Although the grounds justifying termination of employment vary widely among states, the most usual causes written into the laws, in order of frequency of appearance, are immorality or immoral conduct, incompetency, insubordination, inefficiency, persistent violation or refusal to obey school board rules, and neglect of duty. In addition, most tenure laws provide for dismissal due to contingencies such as reduced pupil enrollment, abolition of position, or reduction of teaching staff. Some laws outline a seniority procedure under which reductions in force and reemployment will take place.[35]

At times state departments of education issue rulings which affect the working conditions of teachers. For example, in some states the law states that school districts must offer specific courses in both secondary and elementary schools—for example, a course in the history of that particular state. Some state laws mandate that teach-

[34] National Education Association, Research Division, *State Minimum Salary Laws and Goal Schedules for Teachers, 1964–65* (Washington, D.C.: The Association, 1965), p. 5.
[35] National Education Association, Research Division, *Research Bulletin*, vol. 38, no. 3 (October, 1960), p. 81.

ers use certain textbooks in specific courses, but courses and textbooks are more usually determined by rulings issued by the state
department of education.

Provisions in state constitutions frequently affect the working
conditions of teachers. Minimum school terms are provided in the
state constitutions of Arizona, California, Colorado, Kansas, Michigan, Mississippi, Montana, Nevada, New Mexico, North Carolina,
and Virginia. In California, the state constitution specifies a minimum salary for public school teachers.

Constitutional amendments also affect the curriculum and the
adoption of textbooks in some states. The Louisiana constitution
provides for control of the entire elementary school curriculum; the
North Dakota constitution provides for "teaching truth, temper-
ance, purity, public spirit, and respect for honest labor"; the Utah
constitution provides for instruction in the metric system; the Oklahoma constitution provides for courses in agriculture; and instruction in the English language is provided in the Arizona, Michigan,
Nebraska, New Mexico, and Oklahoma constitutions. State constitutions specifically prohibit the adoption of textbooks by the legislature or the state board of education in Colorado and Utah; adop-
tions by the state superintendent or legislature are prohibited in
Wyoming. On the other hand, constitutions in California, New
Mexico, and North Carolina provide for uniform state textbook
adoption.[36]

The above description of subjects decided by state legislatures or
state education departments is not intended to give the impression
that local school districts have little decision-making power. Actually, they have considerable autonomy within the overall requirements set at the state level. The state level decisions, however,
have significant implications for teachers and their organizations.
For this reason, traditionally, state teacher organizations have concentrated their efforts for improvements in working conditions in
lobbying activities at the state level. Lobbying has been successful
in some cases, but it is highly unpredictable and subject to vagaries
of the legislative process. As a result, teachers are starting to use
state-wide strikes and sanctions in order to enforce their demands.
Teachers are now also increasing their efforts at the local level
where they can become more intimately involved in decision-
making. Ultimate responsibility at the local level lies with the local

[36] Foshay, pp. 21–31.

board of education which is a much smaller legislative body than the state legislature. Even more important, the board of education and its administrative staff is the employer of the teachers. This enables the parties to agree on specific working conditions for the teachers in a given community instead of general state-wide regulations which must apply to a large number of highly diverse school districts within an entire state.

Scope of Bargaining and Written Agreements

Clearly, statutory provisions are of major importance in determining the nature of education in a state, and teacher organizations consequently try to have a voice in what these provisions should be. But even beyond that, teacher organizations are increasingly adopting collective bargaining as a method of obtaining a share in decision-making in public education. The type of collective bargaining taking place is modified somewhat to account for the unique environment of public education, but in great part it closely parallels collective bargaining in private employment. An increasing number of boards of education and local teacher organizations are signing formal collective bargaining agreements which detail specifically the salaries and working conditions of the teachers employed in the district. In 1967, 1,531 or 25 per cent of all school districts in the United States enrolling over 1,000 students had some type of written negotiations agreement with its teachers. Over 41 per cent of the teaching staff in the United States was employed in these districts. These data contrast sharply with the situation in 1965 and 1963 when only about one per cent of the teaching staff and less than one-tenth of one per cent of all school districts had written negotiations procedures.[37]

The written agreements which include terms and conditions of employment tend to be highly legalistic documents frequently totaling more than 50 pages in length. The agreements usually include clauses governing salaries, length of school year, length of school day, number of class periods, preparation periods, class size, assignment and transfer policies, grievance procedures, and other working conditions.

Agreements signed in different school districts are frequently very

[37] National Education Association, Research Division, *Negotiations Research Digest,* vol. 1, no. 1 (Washington, D.C.: The Association, September, 1967), p. B–4.

similar. Several state associations have formulated model agreements which are distributed to local affiliates and adopted with little change by the local boards of education. Agreements negotiated by both AFT and NEA affiliates are printed and distributed to other affiliates for organizational purposes. In addition, the Urban Services Division of the NEA employs a highly experienced labor law firm to assist its affiliates in negotiations. The firm tends to use the same format for its agreements, making changes to accommodate to local conditions.

Most collective bargaining agreements in public education follow a standard format patterned after agreements in private employment. The first provision is usually a recognition clause stating that the board of education recognizes the teacher organization as the exclusive bargaining representative of all teachers in the school district.

The Board hereby recognizes the LSEA as the exclusive bargaining representative, as defined in Section II of Act 379, Public Acts of 1965, for professional personnel, including personnel on tenure, probation and per diem appointments, classroom teachers, guidance counselors, librarians, school psychologists and social workers, speech and hearing therapists, school social workers, remedial reading teachers, advanced instruction teachers, helping teachers, teachers of the homebound or hospitalized, attendance or truant officers, school nurses, tenure teachers holding a letter of assignment to federal or state programs administered by the Board, employed by the Board, but excluding supervisory and executive personnel.

The significance of this type of exclusive recognition clause is that no other teacher organization is permitted to negotiate for teachers in the district. Other organizations may make statements or recommendations and sometimes even represent individual teachers in grievances, but the organization designated as the exclusive representative has the right and obligation to represent all teachers in collective negotiations regardless of whether they are members of the organization. It cannot discriminate against nonmembers in negotiations or in administering the agreement. This obligation of the organization raises some questions about the responsibility of the teacher to the organization. Should he be required to join the organization or pay a service fee to the organization? Or should he be permitted to refuse to support the organization financially? In 1967 two state teacher organizations officially favored "agency shop" clauses whereby as a condition of employment teachers would be required to pay a service fee to the organization. Only a few collective agreements included agency shop clauses, but the problem concerning such clauses promises to be increasingly important in future years because of their apparent conflict with tenure laws.

Another clause found in most collective agreements in public education reaffirms the authority vested in the board of education by statute.

There is reserved exclusively to the Board all responsibilities, powers, rights, and authority expressly or inherently vested in it by the laws and Constitutions of Michigan and the United States, excepting where expressly and in specific terms limited by the provisions of this Agreement. It is agreed that the Board retains the right to establish and enforce in accordance with this Agreement and its authority under law reasonable rules and personnel policies relating to the duties and responsibilities of teachers and their working conditions including, but without limiting the generality of the foregoing to: the management and control of school properties, facilities, grades and courses of instruction, athletic and recreational programs, methods of instruction, materials used for instruction, and the selection, direction, transfer, promotion or demotion, discipline or dismissal of all personnel.

Private employment collective bargaining agreements frequently include this type of "retained rights" clause emphasizing that the employer retains all rights and powers not specifically modified in the agreement.

A clause or series of clauses is usually included listing and explaining the rights of the teacher organization. The teacher negotiators almost always attempt to obtain released time without loss of pay for contract negotiations and organization activities. Boards of education almost always give the organization the right to hold meetings in school buildings and agree to deduct organizational dues from the teachers' salaries for a small service charge. Payroll deduction of dues is extremely important because it guarantees a steady income to the organization. Without payroll deduction of dues, the organization leaders must contact each member periodically in order to collect dues.

Typical collective negotiation agreements consist mainly of clauses detailing working conditions for the teachers in the district. Salary schedules are either included as appendices or clauses in the agreement. Working conditions usually covered include length of the school day, length and frequency of faculty meetings, relief from nonteaching duties, alleviation of overcrowded conditions, teacher lounges, parking spaces for teachers, severance pay, health and medical insurance, summer school pay and tuition reimbursement for teachers taking courses. Clauses are also usually included covering teacher promotion, reassignment, and transfer. Teachers frequently are guaranteed the right to see their personnel file.

Most agreements have a duration of one or two years, after which they are extended or renegotiated. During the term of the agreement, questions frequently arise relating to the interpretation of a clause in the agreement. The grievance procedure, found in most collective negotiation agreements, details a procedure for interpreting the agreement.

Grievance procedures have four or five steps for resolving complaints submitted by teachers concerning the interpretation of the agreement. The complaint first goes to the principal or immediate supervisor of the teachers. If the complaint is not resolved, the teacher has the right to appeal the decision to the next step of the grievance procedure which is usually an associate superintendent or the superintendent of schools. Next, the teacher may appeal an adverse decision to the next step of the procedure which is usually the board of education.

Prior to 1965, the final step in the grievance procedure was almost always the board of education. Since that time, an increasing number of collective negotiation agreements use binding arbitration as the terminal point of the grievance procedure. Under grievance arbitration, the parties agree in advance to accept as binding the decision of a neutral person they select to serve as arbitrator. The arbitrator rules on the grievance using the collective agreement which the parties negotiated as his criterion.

Educational Policy and Working Conditions

Many provisions in collective bargaining agreements in education such as class size clauses, involve matters of educational policy as well as working conditions. Large classes clearly make a teacher's job more difficult because of the added papers to grade and students to supervise. Yet class size also affects the quality of education which is a matter of educational policy as well as the costs of education. Strict limitations on class size affect the design of school buildings and methods of instruction.

Another provision of teacher collective bargaining agreements which involves both working conditions and educational policy relates to teacher transfer. Many school districts have recently attempted to integrate their faculty and students as a result of court decisions and government agency orders. Citizens and civil rights groups have applied pressure to boards of education to integrate more rapidly. In attempting to integrate school faculties, boards of education have met opposition from teacher organizations which want teacher assignment and transfer to be based on length of service. Teacher organizations claim that teacher transfer policies are important working conditions because the distance a teacher must travel to his job affects his job satisfaction. On the other hand, using length of service as the criterion for teacher transfer leads to a concentration of experienced teachers in upper-middle-class neighborhoods since many of them do not prefer the hardships of teaching in the slums. As a result, inexperienced teachers gravitate to schools in slum areas which, other things being equal, presumably results in poorer educational opportunities in those areas.

Voluntary teacher transfer policies may also result in segregated school faculties thus affecting public policy. Teachers may prefer to teach students of their own race, or segregated faculties may result from the fact that housing is segregated and that teachers prefer to teach in schools close to their homes. In any case, teacher transfer provisions clearly affect both working conditions and matters of public policy.

Handling the discipline of children has recently become a topic of great concern to citizens in large cities. Any policy on removing certain children from a classroom is clearly a matter of educational policy, public policy, and teacher working conditions. School administrators almost always have the power to isolate disruptive children into separate classes or schools, and they sometimes believe it educationally desirable to do so. Teachers claim that their productivity increases when they do not have to spend time handling disciplinary cases. Teaching also becomes easier and more pleasant. Teachers sometimes claim that principals are reluctant to remove disruptive children from their classes because principals are afraid that it will reflect on their own ability to run their schools. In addition, some citizen groups are increasingly concerned about what happens to the students who are isolated into separate classes or schools. It may be educationally sound to isolate disruptive children, but this very act often makes it even more difficult for such students to become productive members of society.

The essential point of this discussion of the interrelationship of educational policy, public policy, and teacher working conditions is to show that bargaining on certain working conditions may decide policy matters. As the scope of bargaining increases to these interrelated topics, teachers assume a voice in policy matters which has implications far beyond problems associated with the scope of bargaining in private employment. Teachers may claim that increasing the scope of bargaining to policy areas is another step toward becoming "true professionals," but valid objections can be raised to giving such power to tenured employees instead of to a legislative body.

FUTURE ISSUES

It is probably much too early now to give anything approaching a definitive assessment of the implications teacher bargaining has had for American public education. Yet there is enough information available to make it possible for us to make a few reasoned observations on some matters and to put forth something better than mere speculation on others.

Although studies of the economic impact of bargaining in public education have not yet been completed, it appears certain that bargaining has led to higher school budgets and, in most cases, higher tax rates than would have prevailed otherwise. Understandably, a significant proportion of these additional funds has been used to increase salaries and to provide other economic benefits for teachers. In some cases bargaining may have caused a shift in the allocation of resources, away from educational programs and student services toward teacher benefits.[38] Since school budgets (and school taxes) would be increasing anyway because of inflation, increased enrollments, curriculum enrichment, and "normal" salary increases, one cannot easily determine to what degree bargaining has been responsible. Neither can we evaluate the educational consequences of dropping certain school programs at the expense of higher salaries if, as is so frequently alleged, these higher salaries make it easier for school districts to recruit and retain superior

[38] See, for example, the consequences of the 1966 settlement in Rochester as detailed by Paul Reason in "Concerns of School Administrators about the Manifestations of Teacher Aspirations when They Result in Some Form of Collective Negotiations," Robert E. Doherty, ed., *Employer-Employee Relations in the Public Schools* (Ithaca: School of Industrial and Labor Relations, 1967), pp. 19–25).

teachers. Be that as it may, there seems to be little doubt that bargaining has often resulted in significant increases in school budgets and some important modifications in educational programming.

Some persons believe that teacher bargaining has caused a rather important lessening of community influence over how local schools are run and a concomitant decline in the degree of accountability local school authorities render to their constituents. To many citizens this is but another regretable step toward total insulation of public institutions from any meaningful public influence. Local control over the conduct of local school affairs has been gradually slipping away for years as state education departments began to mandate basic curricula and personnel matters. Over the years state legislatures have been paying an increasing proportion of the pipers fee and have therefore felt they had every right to call more of the tunes. Many of the course offerings in any given school district are mandated by state education departments, and so are a great many personnel policies, including minimum salaries and increments, tenure regulations, certification, and retirement benefits. While still smarting under this kind of "outside," relatively unaccountable type of control, many local citizens, some of whom are quite sincere in their efforts to influence and therefore hopefully upgrade the community's schools, are faced with a new set of circumstances which tends to push them even further away from the decision-making center.

There would probably be less concern, opponents of teacher bargaining argue, if the parties stuck to purely economic issues, e.g. salaries and fringe benefits, or even to those subjects about which the parties were clearly more expert than the lay public such as textbook selection. As mentioned earlier, the scope of teacher bargaining does not stop there. As a result, the way in which teachers would deal with seniority rights, teacher transfers, student discipline, or techniques for handling educational problems in ghetto schools are not always consistent with the way members of the community believe these problems should be handled. Yet school officials, protected by the secrecy of the bargaining room and sometimes threatened by a strike, sanctions, or mass resignations, will frequently make substantial concessions on these issues. Having lost unilateral authority, they can no longer listen to "public advice" with quite the same attention. Thus, there is no doubt that in some communities, teacher bargaining has frustrated public decision-

making on important social and educational issues. It has, moreover, forced a reconsideration of the problem of how much "direct"
influence citizens should have in operating public institutions, and
whether this influence should be restricted to electing public officials and voting on referenda, thereby leaving the running of the
schools to those who at least claim to have the authority and the
competence to do so. Teacher bargaining also forces society to cast
around for new ways to measure the degree to which public employees should be allowed to "democratize" the workplace.

What the accountability standard does not quite come to grips
with is the difficulty of separating constructive criticism from public
whim or mere meddling. It also does not help solve the problem of
determining whether public officials actually reflect the public good
when they are acutely sensitive to public suggestions and criticisms.
How, for example, does the accountability standard deal with a
situation in which a community group demands that the selection
of textbooks and the appointment of teachers be done by a committee of parents, or that principals be elected by popular referenda?

Another problem with this standard is that it sometimes confuses
the public will with the public good. It overlooks the niggardliness
and short-sightedness of taxpayers. It allows for almost criminally
low teachers' salaries and primitive teaching conditions in many
communities. Assuming poor teaching conditions are almost synonymous with poor learning conditions, the accountability argument
does not recognize the relative social cost of inferior education in
terms of underemployment, unemployment, welfare costs, crime
and delinquency. The question then becomes one of choosing between the larger societal values: the social good that springs from
sound education, on the one hand, and the wishes, however they
might be measured, of local citizens on the other. There are a great
many instances in which the two do not coincide. Thus when teachers in a given community say to the local school board: "We will not
work under present conditions, and will do our best to see that other
teachers do not enter the system," they *may*, if this threat is successful in persuading the employers to improve conditions of teaching
and learning, do more toward promoting the public good by this
pursuit of self-interest than all the pleas and exhortations of school
officials combined.

Yet improvements in education do not "automatically" follow
when teachers negotiate a successful collective bargaining agreement. Teachers and/or their organizations do have interests which

sometimes diverge from good educational practices. If teachers have sufficient bargaining muscle, they can force an allocation of resources which results in personal benefit at the expense of educational improvement. It is possible for salary increases to cause sacrifices in educational programs. Also, since teacher organizations are highly political, negotiated salary schedules generally favor the majority of the organization's constituency, i.e. those teachers with several years of service. This often inhibits the school board's ability to recruit beginning teachers, who almost always come in at the bottom of the scale. For example, a school board may, in an effort to recruit recent college graduates into the system, propose a salary schedule which starts at $7,000 with $250 increments, while the teacher organization holds out for a $6,800 starting salary and $300 increments. In the latter case a teacher would be $50 ahead as he began his fifth year of teaching. This reflects the fact that those teachers with five or more years of experience usually are the most active in teacher organizations and carry the most political weight.

Although the parties might disagree as to the makeup of the salary schedule, both agree that the "concept" of salary schedule should not be disturbed. Teachers are persuaded that any system of compensation which does not rely on experience and accumulated graduate credits as the sole standards for determining individual salaries would open the door to favoritism and administrative tyranny. Administrators, knowing how strongly teachers feel about differential salary schemes such as merit pay, have concluded that it had best let this sleeping dog lie. Given the wide range of teaching competence, and, as a corollary, significant differences in labor markets that exist among subject matter fields, one might easily conclude that the uniform salary schedule is not a very judicious method of allocating scarce resources. Although there have been some rather interesting experiments with differential pay scales in recent years, most administrators have continued using the single salary schedule. In addition, the thrust of collective bargaining is to bring about even greater uniformity. It would be politically dangerous for the leadership of teacher organizations to accept the principle that the excellent teacher and the incompetent teacher should be rewarded in accordance with their contribution. The principle of trade unionism, "Equal pay for equal work," has become as captivating a slogan for teachers as it has always been for industrial workers.

The same psychology that has elevated the system of uniform

salary payments to a matter of principle has also caused seniority provisions to be included in a great many teacher-school board agreements. The majority of comprehensive collective agreements we have studied provide that, if all other matters are equal, i.e., if the same type of training and experience prevails, seniority shall be the determining factor in such areas as making voluntary and involuntary transfers, promotions, and assignments to special classes and extracurricular duties. There has not yet been enough experience under these provisions to allow for any judgment as to the consequences they are having for school administrations. Certainly they protect teachers from capricious or arbitrary behavior of supervisors. What is not known, since those "other matters" of equal training and experience are never really equal, is whether these provisions have served to hamstring or intimidate supervisors to the degree that they are reluctant to make decisions or appointments they sincerely believe are in the best interest of the school system. Critics of teacher bargaining and many administrators are convinced that this is the case. But even if the critics are largely correct, this still does not answer the question as to whether freedom from favoritism does not more than compensate for a possible decline in administrative flexibility.

Indeed, we do not yet know what implications any collective bargaining provisions may have on the quality of the educational enterprise. This is due only in part to the newness of teacher bargaining. Our ignorance stems from the fact that no adequate yardstick exists by which one can measure educational quality. Measurement becomes doubly difficult when one tries to assess the impact bargaining has had in urban school districts. Our strong impression is that urban schools have deteriorated in recent years, but it would be foolish to attempt to show a cause and effect relationship between bargaining and the decline in quality. The decline has probably much more to do with the exodus of middle-class children from urban schools than it has with the language of collective agreements. In fact it might be easier to show that it was the decline in educational quality that precipitated bargaining, and that without some form of collective activity the erosion would have been much more rapid.

For much the same reason neither can we show that the rather dramatic increase in teachers' salaries negotiated by teacher organizations in recent years has actually made the recruitment and retention of teachers any easier. Indeed, the two years in which there was the most critical teacher shortage in recent history coincided with the period in which there was the most intense bargaining activity in public education.[39] But again, would turnover and leakage be even heavier had there been no bargaining? Moreover, we cannot show that the widespread use of teacher aides to handle nonprofessional chores, a development which is largely a product of collective bargaining, has resulted in better teaching or in more of the teachers' time actually being devoted to work with students. Much has been made of the improvements in teacher morale brought about by the "equal voice" teachers have gained through bargaining, but nonetheless the turnover rate, while declining somewhat, remains high, almost scandalously high, for a professional occupation.

What, however, can be shown is that teacher bargaining has forced the community to provide more of the wherewithal needed to operate the schools than would have otherwise been obtained. It has also brought the community to the brink of realizing that other resources will have to be tapped if our educational system is not to stagnate. Bargaining has also made it clear that teachers, acting collectively, have an enormous amount of unsuspected power. But since teacher organizations operate in an area devoid of traditional market restraints, and at the same time represent those who perform a vital social service, society will expect them to exercise a greater degree of responsibility than it expects of many other employee organizations.

Bargaining also creates a new set of responsibilities for school officials. It will tax their ingenuity as they attempt to strike a balance between the aspirations of their employees and the wishes of their constituents, however difficult the latter is to discern. Most school boards by the spring of 1968 had not yet learned how to take advantage of the bargaining mechanism; they had yet to learn how to develop and propose sophisticated counter proposals and "trade-offs." In private employment employers have learned that it is possible to grant sizeable benefits yet at the same time secure concessions which lead to higher productivity. Perhaps one cannot translate the concept of industrial productivity into the educational setting. Yet there are educational problems which could be dealt with at the bargaining table and so far boards of education have rarely taken the initiative in trying to deal with them.

[39] *The New York Times,* September 4, 1966; September 4, 1967.

International Teachers' Organizations and Their Activities   10

Edward Thompson

A cursory glance at the international trade union movement as a whole reveals divisions based essentially on ideological or religious differences. The panorama of international teachers' organizations shows similar ideological and religious differences, compounded with other causes of disagreement, arising in particular from conflicting views as to the very nature and purpose of teachers' organizations.

As the studies of national teachers' organizations in this volume have made clear, they have always been keenly aware of the special status occupied by the teaching profession in modern societies. The resolution adopted by the XVI Assembly of Delegates of the World Confederation of Organizations of the Teaching Profession in 1967 summarizes this attitude: "Man's ability to enjoy the products of modern scientific and technological discovery and to live a full and satisfying life at peace with his fellows depends upon education. Teachers therefore have a particularly important role to play in modern society. They can only play this role in all its aspects if they

EDWARD THOMPSON is Chief, Non-Manual Workers' Section, International Labour Office. The views expressed in this chapter are those of the author and do not represent those of the ILO.

can act collectively through their organizations. Teachers' organizations therefore carry great responsibilities. . . ."

It is safe to say that this statement would be endorsed by all teachers' organizations irrespective of ideological complexion. The differences arise in connection with the way these organizations play their
role in practice and act collectively on behalf of their members. One
of the fundamental differences, which is at the root of interorgani-
zation conflict at both the national and international level, relates
to whether a teachers' organization is to be mainly considered as a
professional association devoted to serving the interests of education
and the status of the teaching profession, or as a trade union defending the interests of teachers against those who employ them. In
fact, of course, teachers' organizations almost invariably perform
both functions at the same time. It is where the emphasis lies with
regard to these questions in the philosophy and day-to-day activities
of a national teachers' organization that characterizes its general
outlook and has often determined its international affiliation.

This problem has accompanied the development of international
teachers' organizations since they first began to be envisaged in the
closing years of the nineteenth century. Ideological—or, rather,
religious—differences also commenced early, a World Federation of
Catholic Teachers being formed even before World War I. However, it was in the interwar years that the various divisions became
manifest. On the one hand, there was an organization inspired by
the National Education Association of the United States—the
World Federation of Education Associations—which included in its
membership not only teachers but also officials engaged in administration of education and individuals concerned with educational
problems. Separate from this, there were two international federations representing primary and secondary school teachers, mostly
from European countries, which mainly stressed educational questions, though the material interests of teachers also received attention. These two federations maintained contact with the World
Federation of Education Associations, but relations were never very
close.

On the other hand, the teachers' organizations which openly proclaimed themselves to be trade unions in their structure and activities began to develop their own international movement in the
1920's. In its turn, this movement was divided on ideological
grounds into one organization favoring socialist or social-

democratic principles—the International Trade Secretariat of Teachers, affiliated to the International Federation of Trade Unions —and another which was communist in character—the Educational Workers International linked with the Red Trade Union International (Profintern).

The same threads run through the development of the international teachers' movement since the end of World War II. At first, the ideals that had inspired the military effort against the Axis powers and the Resistance movements led many teachers to believe in the possibility of a united international movement. These hopes faded very rapidly. The old federations were revived or new ones were created which were to all intents and purposes direct successors of the prewar organizations. However, in spite of the split in the world trade union movement and the pressures of the "Cold War," cooperation among many of these organizations continued for many years.

The main reasons for this are not difficult to find. The first is that all the international teachers' organizations deal with the same problems; leaving aside political or ideological considerations, their practical approach to these problems is very similar. All of them are in constant contact with the intergovernmental organizations dealing with teachers' problems, in particular the International Labour Organization, UNESCO, and the International Bureau of Education. Their representatives attend the same meetings; they know one another well; some of them are personal friends. Almost inevitably, there is a considerable measure of common action to achieve common objectives. This trend seems to be becoming more evident as the controversies that characterized the cold war period have become less violent. There is also no doubt that it has been encouraged by the fact that the constitutions of many international teachers' organizations expressly exclude discussion of political matters.

Another factor that seems to be of increasing importance is the tendency for the distinction between "professional association" and "trade union" to become more blurred. Rightly or wrongly, the idea that teachers' organizations should concentrate on professional questions and not on trade union action was associated for many years with the U.S. National Education Association and the international organizations in which it had an influence. The NEA's approach to this question has changed as the chapter on the United

States in this volume indicates. Furthermore, except for the special case of the teachers' organizations in the Communist countries, the proponents of teacher unions closely linked with the national labor movement and promoting socialist principles do not seem to have recovered their prewar strength and influence. This may be noted in Europe where such important organizations as the National Union of Teachers in England and the Fédération de l'Education Nationale in France are autonomous; it is also clear that if these organizations were to become more closely linked with the national labor movements, it would be for strictly practical rather than for political or ideological reasons.

Thus, at the present time, there exist seven international teachers' organizations, varying considerably in strength and importance. The reasons that led to their establishment, the principles that have governed their growth and in some cases divided them from one another are sometimes still alive, sometimes dormant. Their activities have often achieved quite important results. The history and present situation of each of these organizations will be described in turn before examining what they do and what they have accomplished.

PRIMARY AND SECONDARY EDUCATION

The first moves toward the creation of an international teachers' organization came from the primary school teachers in Europe. As long ago as 1874, teachers in French-speaking Switzerland called for the establishment of an international association of educators. No concrete results occurred until 1905 when the International Committee of Primary Schoolteachers was founded on the initiative of the Belgian primary school teachers' associations. World War I put an end to these first tentative movements toward international cooperation.

After World War I, there were two separate tendencies. In 1923 the National Education Association of the United States took the lead in setting up the World Federation of Education Associations at a meeting in San Francisco. However, the great majority of European teachers' organizations did not join this federation. Instead, in a movement based on the desire for reconciliation and removal of the nationalistic feelings that had led to the immense slaughter of 1914–18, the French *instituteurs* (primary school teachers) made a solemn appeal to their German colleagues to join together in action for the safeguard of peace. In June, 1926, representatives of the French and German organizations took the lead in founding the International Federation of Teachers' Associations (IFTA) "for pedagogical collaboration and the preparation of peace through the co-operation of free peoples"; this was subsequently joined by most of the European primary school teacher's associations. With Hitler's ascent to power in 1933, the German organization lost its independence and left the IFTA. However, at the outbreak of World War II, the Federation had 35 national associations in membership, seven of them from outside Europe.

In the interwar years the leading role in the IFTA was played by the French association of *instituteurs;* Louis Dumas, who directed the activities of the IFTA from its foundation until after the end of World War II, was an outstanding figure in the French teachers' movement. The IFTA devoted special attention to the role of education and the teaching profession in the maintenance of peace. A campaign was launched to revise school textbooks—particularly history textbooks—by removing warlike, nationalistic ideas. This led to international conferences on history teaching in the early 1930's and to a short-lived agreement on history textbooks between France and Germany.

After remaining inactive during 1939–45, the IFTA was revived immediately after the war and rapidly regained its position as the most representative organization of primary school teachers. In 1966, it announced a membership of 31 national associations in 27 countries. The IFTA holds an annual conference, and is administered by an Executive Council. The Secretary-General is Robert Michel of the Swiss teachers' association; headquarters are in Lausanne, Switzerland.

Efforts to establish an international federation for secondary school teachers closely paralleled those for primary school teachers. The idea of founding such an international federation dates back to the beginning of the century. A provisional committee was set up in 1910 and prepared the constitution of the International Committee of National Federations of Teachers in Public Secondary Schools, which came into being in May, 1912. This grouped the organizations in Belgium, France, and the Netherlands. The Belgian secondary school teachers' association played a leading part in this international effort. However, after one congress held in Ghent in August, 1913, World War I brought this movement to a standstill.

In 1919, the international organization was revived on the initiative of the French teachers' association and rapidly gained strength and prestige. In 1935 it adopted the title of International Federation of Secondary Teachers (FIPESO).[1] The main emphasis in its activities in the interwar years was on academic and pedagogical questions, and its publications were highly regarded in educational circles.

Like the IFTA, FIPESO was inactive during World War II but renewed its activities immediately afterwards. In 1948 it took the initiative for the creation of the Joint Committee of International Teachers' Federations, whose activities are described below.

In the postwar years, the leading role in FIPESO has been played by the British and French associations. In 1967, the Federation reported member associations in 22 countries, the overwhelming majority of them in Western Europe.

The structure of FIPESO is similar to that of the IFTA: an annual congress, a Council and an Executive Committee. The President of FIPESO is A. W. S. Hutchings (England) and the Secretary-General is E. Hombourger (France).

The annual congresses of the IFTA and FIPESO are held in the same place and at the same time, with a joint opening session.

CATHOLICS, SOCIAL DEMOCRATS AND COMMUNISTS

As already mentioned, one of the earliest international teachers' organizations to be formed had a denominational basis. This organization united Catholic teachers in 1912 in the World Federation of Catholic Teachers. This federation was subsequently dissolved, but after World War II a congress held in Rome in 1951 set up the World Union of Catholic Teachers. This is a relatively small organization, with membership mostly in European countries. Its influence scarcely extends beyond the schools maintained by the Catholic church.

Mention should also be made of the international teachers' council which groups the relatively small number of teachers' unions affiliated to the International Federation of Christian Trade

[1] The initials FIPESO are derived from the French title of the organization: *Fédération internationale des professeurs de l'Enseignement secondaire officiel.*

Unions of Employees in Public Service. This organization is also of comparatively minor importance.

It was in the traditional socialist-oriented labor movement, represented between the wars by the International Federation of Trade Unions, that most of the teachers' organizations of a trade union character found their place at the international level. The organization concerned was the International Trade Secretariat of Teachers (ITST) which was set up in 1926 and was closely linked with the IFTU like the international trade secretariats for other categories of workers such as miners, transport workers, and so on. Its stated aim was "to improve the material and social position of the teaching profession and to protect its civic rights, to encourage the progress of teaching and education in the widest sense of the term, and to raise the level of culture of the working classes."

This organization was very active until the outbreak of World War II, and its influence, particularly in Europe, was at least as great as that of the two federations of primary and secondary school teachers. Although the trade union approach was stressed, it devoted considerable attention to educational problems and aimed at working out "an international programme of education and teaching in the service of the working classes." One method used to achieve this was the holding of annual "Summer Schools" in different countries, at which leaders of affiliated national unions discussed a particular subject in the educational field such as "The School and Peace," "Educational Neutrality," "International Youth Camps" and similar questions. The ITST organized a large number of study tours for teachers to foreign countries—again mostly in Europe. It also contributed to the spread of the Youth Hostel movement. Like the other international teachers' organizations, the ITST became inactive in 1939.

The interwar split between the IFTU and the Communist Profintern was also reflected in the teachers' international movement. The Communist rival to the ITST was the Educational Workers' International (EWI), founded in Paris in 1922. The bulk of its membership consisted of the USSR teachers' union, and apart from this, it never succeeded in attracting any other major national organizations, its affiliates being small, politically-oriented groups, most of them in European countries. Although its publications and congresses discussed problems of general educational interest, this organization's activities seem to have been almost entirely subordinated to ideological considerations. During the Popular Front period, from about 1935 onward, it made attempts to form a common front with the ITST, but without success. On the outbreak of war in 1939, the EWI's secretariat was transferred to Mexico, and contributed to uniting a number of Latin American teachers' associations in a regional body which also had pro-Communist tendencies—the Confederación Americana de los Maestros.

In the immediate postwar years, the World Federation of Trade Unions (WFTU) briefly united most of the major national trade union centers, both Communist and non-Communist alike (except for the American Federation of Labor). The same was true of the teachers' unions. In July, 1946, the revived ITST, EWI and the Confederación Americana de los Maestros held a joint meeting in Paris, under the auspices of the WFTU, to create a unified organization which was intended to be a "trade department" of the WFTU. However, these trade departments did not come into existence at that time, because of the refusal of the international trade secretariats representing industrial workers to subordinate their identity and autonomy within the WFTU. The new international teachers' organization therefore became the World Federation of Teachers' Unions, at a congress held in Budapest in 1948.

In the following year, the non-Communist organizations left the WFTU and at the end of 1949 joined with the American Federation of Labor in founding the International Confederation of Free Trade Unions. Similarly, the non-Communist teachers' unions also disaffiliated from their organization and in 1951 set up, with the support of the ICFTU, the International Federation of Free Teachers' Unions, with headquarters in Brussels.

This organization does not seem to have gained the same influence as that enjoyed by its predecessor between the wars—the ITST. Its leadership, like that of the ITST, has come from the Belgian socialist movement, and it has succeeded in attracting the affiliation of certain important national teachers' unions such as those in the Federal Republic of Germany (belonging to the DGB), Israel, and Tunisia, in addition to its traditional supporters. It also has the affiliation of the American Federation of Teachers. However, its role in the international discussion of teachers' problems has not yet come to equal that of the World Confederation of Organizations of the Teaching Profession (see below).

Meanwhile, the Communist-led World Federation of Teachers'

Unions has continued its activities. It now groups teachers' organizations in the Communist countries and those under pro-Communist influence elsewhere.

It is interesting to note that even after the 1949 split in the world labor movement, cooperation continued between the World Federation of Teachers' Unions and the two international federations of primary and secondary school teachers.

JOINT COMMITTEE OF INTERNATIONAL TEACHERS' FEDERATIONS

This cooperation took place in a body known as the Joint Committee of International Teachers' Federations. This was set up in 1948—before the split in the WFTU—on the initiative of the secondary school teachers' federation, FIPESO. It functioned solely as a liaison committee, on the basis of unanimous decisions, and its constituent federations were the IFTA, FIPESO and the World Federation of Teachers' Unions.

The aim of the Joint Committee was to coordinate the activities of the independent international federations. Its activities were restricted to questions relating to education and the teaching profession, to the exclusion of all ideological or political questions. One of its main functions was the coordination of relations with official intergovernmental institutions such as UNESCO, with which it had consultative status, the United Nations, the International Labour Organization and the International Bureau of Education.

Perhaps the most lasting result of the Joint Committee's activities was the so-called "Teachers' Charter." This was an attempt to define the essential principles that should govern the role of teachers in education and in the defence of their own professional interests. It formed the basis for subsequent official action at the international level by the ILO and UNESCO, culminating in the adoption of the International Recommendation on the Status of Teachers by a special intergovernmental conference in Paris in September-October 1966.[2]

Attempts were made to associate the World Organization of the Teaching Profession, founded in 1946 on the initiative of the U.S.

---

2 The Activities of the Joint Committee of International Teachers' Federations are described in a pamphlet published in Paris in 1959, with the title: *Joint Committee of International Teachers' Federations.*

National Education Association (see below), with the work of the Joint Committee, and observers from the WOTP attended a number of its meetings. The Joint Committee continued to function for some time even after the two federations of primary and secondary school teachers had joined with the WOTP in founding the World Confederation of Organizations of the Teaching Profession in 1952. However, with the increasing involvement of the IFTA and FIPESO in the WCOTP, and in the general political atmosphere prevailing in the world in the 1950's, the Joint Committee finally ceased to function in May 1960. Its continued survival for so long, in spite of political differences, was undoubtedly due to its concentration on matters of interest to all teachers, irrespective of ideology, and to the close and friendly relationship that had developed among leaders of the international federations involved in the Joint Committee's work.

WORLD CONFEDERATION OF ORGANIZATIONS OF THE TEACHING PROFESSION

The World Confederation of Organizations of the Teaching Profession (WCOTP) was founded in 1952 as the result of the fusion of three existing international teachers' organizations, after negotiations lasting many years which were often very difficult and sometimes near to breakdown.

The three founder organizations were: the World Organization of the Teaching Profession (WOTP), the International Federation of Teachers' Associations, and the International Federation of Secondary Teachers. The two last-named federations have already been described.

The WOTP was set up in 1946 at a meeting held in Endicott, New York, sponsored and financed by the National Education Association of the United States. As already mentioned, in the interwar years, the NEA had played an important role in the establishment and activities of the World Federation of Education Associations, which held eight biennial meetings: San Francisco 1923; Edinburgh 1925; Toronto 1927; Geneva 1929; Denver 1931; Dublin 1933; Oxford 1935; Tokyo 1937. This federation suspended its operations with the coming of World War II. At the Endicott meeting in 1946, it was decided not to try to revive the World Federation of Education Associations, but to set up a new organization—the WOTP.[3]

[3] William G. Carr, "World Teachers' Organization," *World Affairs,* Fall, 1960.

However, the WOTP was generally considered by teachers' organizations as the direct successor of the World Federation of Education Associations, and was also considered as being under the influence of the NEA.[4] By the end of the 1940's, the WOTP had members in 17 countries, the most important outside the United States being the British National Union of Teachers.

The main issues at stake in the negotiations that led to the foundation of the WCOTP in 1952 are reflected in the confederations' constitution and bylaws. In effect, the WCOTP is the successor of the WOTP, with which the IFTA and FIPESO amalgamated while retaining considerable autonomy. Thus the WCOTP constitution states:

Within the framework of the World Confederation there shall be from the outset two international federations representing the particular interests of primary and secondary education, these federations being called the International Federation of Teachers' Associations (IFTA) and the International Federation of Secondary Teachers' Associations (FIPESO) . . .

The World Confederation shall be competent to establish and define policies affecting education and the teaching profession generally and to represent the member associations collectively in the international aspects of such matters.

Each international federation shall have complete control of the internal organization and shall have full power to study and deal with problems within its special sphere and maintain its own external relations within that sphere, provided that its constitution, its bylaws and its activities are brought into harmony with the general policy of the World Confederation. . . .

The influence of the two constituent federations may also be seen in the WCOTP constitutional provision which now states that "the Confederation shall exclude from its debate all questions involving political, party-political or religious controversy and shall make no racial discrimination." According to E. Hombourger, Secretary-General of the International Federation of Secondary Teachers, the WCOTP constitution "is the result of a compromise between the idea that European countries and that which other countries (and, in particular, Anglo-Saxon countries) have of a confederation. . . . If in 1952 the Federations consented to merge

4 From its foundation, the WOTP was attacked by organizations affiliated to the World Federation of Trade Unions. See, for example, the resolutions adopted by the Confederación Americana de los Maestros at its Conference in Mexico in November 1946, which accused the WOTP of seeking to divide the international teachers' movement, and of being reactionary and anti-democratic in ideology. These resolutions are reproduced in: Fédération Internationale Syndicale de l'Enseignement: *1946–1966 Vingt Années de Luttes au service des éducateurs et de l'éducation,* Prague, 1966.

their national associations in the Confederation, it was, above all, due to the fact that guarantees of autonomy were definitely stated in the Statutes." [5] Observations of this kind are indicative of the atmosphere which existed at the time the WCOTP was established, which was also the time when the Joint Committee of International Teachers' Federations, in which Communist organizations participated along with the IFTA and FIPESO, was active. Since then, with the disappearance of the Joint Committee and the relaxation of the "Cold War," these reservations have diminished and become dormant, though they may be reawakened from time to time, particularly within certain European teachers' organizations.[6]

Membership of national teachers' associations in the WCOTP takes place as follows:

(a) Associations which represent exclusively primary or secondary, or another specific stage of education will affiliate to the Confederation through their respective international federations (IFTA, FIPESO, etc.) where these exist.

(b) Associations which represent more than one stage of education will have the choice of two methods of affiliation: They will allocate their members to the above-named federations and affiliate to the Confederation in the manner described under (a), *or* they will affiliate directly to the Confederation, and may, if they so desire, allocate their members to the appropriate international federations.

(c) Associations other than those described under (a) and (b) and, in particular, those for which an international federation corresponding to their stage of education does not yet exist, will affiliate directly to the Confederation.

Provision is also made for associate membership of regional or local associations of the teaching profession, universities and similar institutions, and societies for the scientific study of educational problems and the improvement of the teaching profession.

In 1967, the WCOTP had 154 member associations from over 60 countries, representing about five million teachers. By virtue of its size, its deliberately non-ideological approach to professional problems of the teaching profession, and its flexible constitution which permits the constituent federations a large measure of autonomy, the WCOTP has now become the most important and most repre-

[5] Office of the Joint Committee of International Teachers' Federations, *Joint Committee of International Teachers' Federations* (Paris, 1959).
[6] For example, in 1967, in connection with allegations that the Vernon Foundation, from which the WCOTP had received substantial grants, was a channel for funds from the U.S. Central Intelligence Agency.

sentative international organization representing teachers in the non-Communist countries.

The WCOTP has as its highest authority the Assembly of Delegates which under the constitution must meet at least every two years and in fact in recent years has met annually. Each national association is entitled to at least one delegate with the right to vote, with additional delegates in proportion to membership, up to a maximum of 50. It is the practice for each Assembly to discuss a particular theme of major interest to the teaching profession; for example, the 1967 Assembly held in Vancouver, Canada, had as its main theme "The Professional Responsibilities of Teachers' Organizations." Previous meetings of the WCOTP Assembly of Delegates had been held in Oxford, Oslo, Istanbul, Manila, Frankfurt, Rome, Washington, Amsterdam, New Delhi, Stockholm, Rio de Janeiro, Paris, Addis Ababa, and Seoul.

An Executive Committee is elected by the Assembly of Delegates. The Secretary-General is appointed by the Executive Committee and is responsible for directing WCOTP activities in accordance with the decisions of the Assembly and the Executive Committee. Since the WCOTP's foundation, the Secretary-General has been Dr. William G. Carr, who was Executive Secretary of the U.S. National Education Association for many years until his retirement in 1967. WCOTP headquarters are located in Washington D.C.

RANGE OF INTERNATIONAL ACTIVITIES

Reference has already been made in passing to the kind of activities in which all international teachers' organizations engage. Irrespective of political differences or of the emphasis placed on "professional" or "trade union" aspects, these are essentially the same.

All the major international teachers' federations discuss questions relating to education and the status of the teaching profession at their meetings and seminars; all of them issue publications in which these problems are ventilated; all of them—to the extent their resources permit—engage in educational and training activities. For example, the WCOTP has devoted particular attention to training of teachers and development of teachers' organizations in the developing countries, and the International Federation of Free Teachers' Unions has concerned itself with vocational training. All the organizations have attempted to provide assistance and material support, where possible, to teachers' organizations faced with difficulties. There is no doubt that these activities have benefited the teaching profession, both directly and indirectly, and that these international exchanges have widened the horizons of national teachers' associations and their members.

However, it is primarily in the field of relations with official international institutions that these teachers' federations have proved their worth. They act as "pressure groups" with those bodies. In some cases, they undertake specific activities on behalf of the international agencies and receive financial support—this is particularly true with regard to UNESCO.

Perhaps the most important result of these contacts with intergovernmental agencies—in the long run, at least—was the International Recommendation on the Status of Teachers adopted in 1966. All the international teachers' organizations contributed, in varying degrees, to ensuring that this international instrument would lay down the principles that should govern educational objectives and policies; preparation for the teaching profession; further education for teachers; employment and career; rights and responsibilities of teachers; conditions for effective teaching and learning; teachers' salaries; social security; and the teacher shortage. This Recommendation is intended to provide guidelines for national legislation and practice with regard to the determination of teachers' conditions of employment. The way this Recommendation came into existence is illustrative of the activities of international teachers' organizations as pressure groups operating on behalf of teachers in relation with the intergovernmental agencies.

As already mentioned, the Joint Committee of International Teachers' Federations adopted the so-called "Teachers' Charter" in 1954. When the ILO's Advisory Committee on Salaried Employees and Professional Workers came to discuss teacher's conditions of employment later in the same year, many of the members of the Joint Committee were among the delegates, and the conclusions of the ILO meeting were clearly based on the provisions of the "Teachers' Charter." Subsequently, pressure by the international teachers' organizations on the ILO and UNESCO was steadily maintained: international standards should be laid down to establish the principles governing the status of the teaching profession. At successive international meetings convened by the ILO and UNESCO, at first separately, then jointly, the representatives of the teachers' organizations were always present, and it was to a large extent due to their efforts that the draft of an international recommendation was finally prepared at a joint ILO-UNESCO Meeting of Experts on the Status of Teachers held in Geneva in January 1966.

In September-October of the same year, a special intergovernmental conference was convened in Paris by UNESCO, with the participation of the ILO. This was attended by representatives of 75 countries, who considered this draft and finally unanimously adopted the International Recommendation on the Status of Teachers. The Conference also adopted a resolution calling on the ILO and UNESCO to take measures for the implementation of the Recommendation. Here again, the international organizations played their part; thus, Dr. William G. Carr, Secretary-General of the WCOTP, was a member of the United States delegation and Rapporteur-general of the Conference, while representatives of all the other organizations were also active.

Adoption of this Recommendation was greeted with acclaim by the teachers' organizations. For example, at the joint opening meeting of the 1967 Congresses of the IFTA and FIPESO in Copenhagen, the President of the IFTA said that the Recommendation "constituted a veritable teachers' charter which, if implemented, would enhance the prestige of teachers and of the profession of teaching everywhere. Its implementation would not come to pass without a long and hard campaign undertaken by teachers to coax, cajole or even to coerce their governments. . . ."

Steps are now being taken to set up the procedures to ensure implementation of the Recommendation. These will no doubt include reports by governments on the effect given in the various countries to the provisions of the Recommendation, and examination and analysis of these reports by an independent body set up jointly by the ILO and UNESCO. With the adoption of the International Recommendation, teachers now have a set of standards they can use "to coax, cajole or even to coerce their governments" to give practical recognition to the role of teachers' organizations in the educational system and in defence of teachers' interests. It can be taken for granted that the international teachers' organizations —and their national associations—will try to ensure that governments live up to the commitments they accepted when they agreed to the Recommendation.

Index

origin, 55; strike, 68; structure, 55-56

Khuru Sapha (Thailand), 280; activities, 281-283; drawbacks, 283-284; functions, 281; origin, 280-281; social welfare, 282-283

Keimeikai (Japan): origin, 154

Labor legislation: Canada, 5, 11; Japan, 157, 176-177, 194; U.S.A., 310-318

Laws of Reforms (Mexico), 201

Legal Statute of Civil Servants (Mexico), 212

Madras Teachers' Guild, 124

Manchester City Education Committee, 79

Manitoba Teachers' Society, 16

Mexican Confederation of Teachers: anti-Cristero activities, 210; composition, 210-211

Mexican Regional Labor Conference, 204-206

Morgan Commission (Nigeria), 248

National Association of Head Teachers (England), 45; aims, 57; membership, 57; origin, 57; structure, 57

National Association of Schoolmasters (England), 45; activities, 67; demands, 58; membership, 58; origin, 58; policy, 57-58; structure, 59

National Confederation of Workers in Teaching (Mexico), 218

National Education Association (U.S.A.): lobbying, 300; militancy, 305; policy, 302-304; professional negotiation, 305; strategy, 303-304; structure, 299-301; urban project, 304

National Union of Elementary Teachers (England): demands, 48; origin, 47

National Union of Teachers (England), 45; activities, 51-54; demands, 49; membership, 49; origin, 47; politics, 67-68; rank and file, 79; strikes, 67; structure, 49-51; Teachers' Provident Society, 53

National Union of Workers in Education (Mexico): activities, 227-231; aims, 227-228; and Communists, 225; composition, 222; economic activities, 223; organization, 227-229; origin, 222; Section IX, 224-225

Nigeria Union of Teachers: aims, 254; business unionism, 236; and colonial government, 249; elitist union, 263-264; membership, 255; origins, 240; philosophy, 247; political bargaining, 248-249; structure, 257

Nikkōkyō, 169

Nikkyōso: bargaining power, 186-187; consumer cooperative, 168-169; control of school boards, 177-180; demands, 172-177, 180-186; economic gains of 1948, 175; and government, 61, 67, 178-180, 195-196; international trade union politics, 173-174; intra-union politics, 172-173, 178-180; and labor movement, 170-171; membership, 142, 165-166; origin, 164; and politics, 63, 166-168, 183-186; problems, 166-167; research conferences, 168; and Sōhyō, 172-174; structure, 164-166

Nikkyōren, 169

Pelham Committee (England), 64

Philologenverband, 104, 105-106

Pre-School Education Association of Thailand, 289

Private Schools Association (Thailand), 288

Private School Teachers Association (Thailand), 287-288

Prussian Land Code, 88